Responsibility and Distributive

Responsibility and Distributive Justice

EDITED BY

Carl Knight and
Zofia Stemplowska

OXFORD
UNIVERSITY PRESS

OXFORD

UNIVERSITY PRESS

Great Clarendon Street, Oxford, OX2 6DP

Oxford University Press is a department of the University of Oxford.
It furthers the University's objective of excellence in research, scholarship,
and education by publishing worldwide. Oxford is a registered trade mark of
Oxford University Press in the UK and in certain other countries

Published in the United States of America by Oxford University Press
198 Madison Avenue, New York, NY 10016, United States of America

British Library Cataloguing in Publication Data

Data available

Library of Congress Control Number: 2010940322

ISBN 978-0-19-956580-1 (Hbk)
ISBN 978-0-19-870795-0 (Pbk)

Contents

Notes on Contributors   vii

Acknowledgements   viii

Responsibility and Distributive Justice: An Introduction   1
Carl Knight and Zofia Stemplowska

1. Luck Egalitarianism—A Primer   24
   Richard J. Arneson

2. Justice, Equality, Fairness, Desert, Rights, Free Will, Responsibility, and Luck   51
   Larry Temkin

3. Four Approaches to Equal Opportunity   77
   Marc Fleurbaey

4. Luck Egalitarianism and Group Responsibility   98
   Kasper Lippert-Rasmussen

5. Responsibility and Respect: Reconciling Two Egalitarian Visions   115
   Zofia Stemplowska

6. Mad, Bad, or Faulty? Desert in Distributive and Retributive Justice   136
   Matt Matravers

7. Responsibility, Desert, and Justice   152
   Carl Knight

8. Responsibility and False Beliefs   174
   Peter Vallentyne

9. The Public Ecology of Responsibility   187
   Susan Hurley

10. The Apparent Asymmetry of Responsibility   216
    Avner de-Shalit and Jonathan Wolff

11. Taking Up the Slack? Responsibility and Justice in Situations of Partial Compliance   230
    David Miller

12. Luck Prioritarian Justice in Health 246
    Shlomi Segall

13. Individual and Social Responsibility for Health 266
    Norman Daniels

Bibliography 287
Index 303

Notes on Contributors

RICHARD J. ARNESON is Distinguished Professor in the Department of Philosophy at the University of California, San Diego and Co-Director of the Institute for Law and Philosophy at the University of San Diego.

NORMAN DANIELS is Mary B. Saltonstall Professor and Professor of Ethics and Population Health in the Department of Global Health and Population at Harvard University.

MARC FLEURBAEY is Robert E. Kuenne Professor of Economics and Humanistic Studies at the Woodrow Wilson School and the Center for Human Values, at Princeton University.

SUSAN HURLEY was Professor in the Department of Philosophy at the University of Bristol and Fellow of All Souls College, Oxford. She died in 2007.

CARL KNIGHT is British Academy Postdoctoral Fellow at the University of Glasgow.

KASPER LIPPERT-RASMUSSEN is Professor in the Department of Political Science at Aarhus University.

MATT MATRAVERS is Director of the Morrell Centre for Toleration at the University of York.

DAVID MILLER is Official Fellow at Nuffield College, Oxford and Professor of Political Theory at the University of Oxford.

SHLOMI SEGALL is Associate Professor at the Program in Politics, Philosophy, & Economics (PPE), The Hebrew University of Jerusalem.

AVNER DE-SHALIT is Max Kampelman Professor of Democracy and Human Rights in the Department of Political Science at the Hebrew University of Jerusalem.

ZOFIA STEMPLOWSKA is Associate Professor of Political Theory and Asa Briggs Fellow of Worcester College, University of Oxford.

LARRY TEMKIN is Professor of Philosophy at Rutgers, the State University of New Jersey.

PETER VALLENTYNE is Kline Professor of Philosophy at the University of Missouri, Columbia.

JONATHAN WOLFF is Professor in the Department of Philosophy at University College London.

Acknowledgements

In addition to all those we thank in the notes to the 'Introduction' and our chapters, we would both like to express our gratitude to the British Academy for the Small Research Grant that helped advance work on this book. We would also like to thank the Manchester Centre for Political Theory (MANCEPT), University of Manchester, for hosting the initial conference on 'Responsibility in the Nonideal World' that gave rise to the idea for the volume, as well as the Adam Smith Research Foundation (ASRF), University of Glasgow, for holding a subsequent workshop that brought together the contributors to the collection. We are also extremely grateful to two anonymous Oxford University Press readers for invaluable comments, to Adrian Stenton for his expert copy-editing, and to the Senior Commissioning Editor of Philosophy at Oxford, Peter Momtchiloff, for his help and guidance. Above all we would like to thank all of the authors for contributing such engaging chapters and for being such a pleasure to work with. We split the rest of the acknowledgements between us.

CK and ZS

I was primarily based at the ASRF and the Department of Politics, University of Glasgow while we were preparing the collection. I greatly benefited from discussions there with Chris Berry, Kevin Francis, Paul Graham, Andrew Lockyer, Cian O'Driscoll, Chris Thornhill, and Kerri Woods, who all have my gratitude. I would also like to thank Hillel Steiner, who was my PhD supervisor at MANCEPT and gave impetus to the collection early in its life, in spite of the fact that I had a thesis to finish. I moved to the Department of Politics, University of Johannesburg as the final touches were being put to the volume, and am grateful to Lawrence Hamilton and everyone else who has made the transition an easy one.

CK

The bulk of my work on this collection was completed while I was at MANCEPT. I am extremely grateful to Kimberley Brownlee, Alan Hamlin, Martin O'Neill, Jonathan Quong, Hillel Steiner, and Steve de Wijze for discussions, advice, and support. I am also grateful to the Center for Ethics in Society, Stanford University, for funding my year-long research leave from teaching at Manchester and providing the perfect environment for completing my work on the collection. Finally, I thank Ben Jackson for his essential help with every aspect of this project.

ZS

Responsibility and Distributive Justice: An Introduction[1]

Carl Knight and Zofia Stemplowska

Distributive justice is perhaps the central topic in contemporary Anglo-American political philosophy, and the place of responsibility in theories of distributive justice is among the most hotly debated aspects of that topic. This collection aims to advance this debate by examining problems such as: Under what conditions should we see people as responsible for their choices and the outcomes of those choices? How could such conditions be fostered by liberal societies? Should justice be sensitive to responsibility, that is, should what people are due as a matter of justice depend on what they are responsible for? If so, how should one depend on the other? For example, how far should health assistance and benefits depend on the past choices made by the sick and injured—say, a choice to smoke or a choice to engage in dangerous sports? What values would be realized and which hampered by making justice sensitive to responsibility? For instance, would it advance or hamper fairness or equality?

The relationship between responsibility and equality has been especially prominent in the philosophical debates. This is partly on account of the fact that the relationship raises difficult philosophical problems. But the explosion of philosophical interest in the relationship has also undeniably been fuelled by the wider political debate and, specifically, the growing political hegemony of right-libertarian views of responsibility and the rise of so-called 'conditionality' in welfare regimes in the US and Europe that appealed to the personal responsibility of welfare recipients.[2] Egalitarians responded to such developments by attempting to recapture responsibility—'the most powerful idea

[1] We are grateful to participants at the Historical, International, Normative Theory meeting at the University of Glasgow in January 2009, where a draft of this introduction was presented. Special thanks go to Jonathan Quong, Peter Vallentyne, and anonymous Oxford University Press readers for their written comments.

[2] D. King, *In the Name of Liberalism: Illiberal Social Policy in Britain and the United States* (Oxford: Oxford University Press, 1999), 219–286; S. White, *The Civic Minimum* (Oxford: Oxford University Press, 2003), 129–152; D. Gallie, *Resisting Marginalization: Unemployment Experience and Social Policy in the European Union* (Oxford: Oxford University Press, 2004), 197–200, 220–222.

in the arsenal of the anti-egalitarian right'—for their own cause.[3] This collection both reflects the recent interest in the relationship between responsibility and equality, and contributes further to our understanding of the relationship. It re-examines the so-called 'luck egalitarian' (responsibility-sensitive egalitarian) stance on the relationship between responsibility and egalitarian justice by investigating arguments that are supportive as well as those that are opposed to the luck egalitarian view.

In this 'Introduction' to the volume we provide an overview of the current state of the debate about the problem of responsibility and locate the contributions of the chapters of the volume in the context of this debate. But we will begin by mapping the rise to prominence of the subject over the last few decades.

1. A brief history of the recent debate

The key events in the rise of the debate about distributive justice are of course John Rawls's publications of the mid twentieth century, culminating in 1971 with *A Theory of Justice*. Rawls's great work made talk of the death of normative political theory seem thoroughly outdated.[4] It sought to defend two principles of justice, which are initially described thus: first, that 'each person is to have an equal right to the most extensive scheme of equal basic liberties compatible with a similar scheme of liberties for others'; and second, that 'social and economic inequalities are to be arranged so that they are both (a) reasonably expected to be to everyone's advantage and (b) attached to positions and offices open to all'.[5] Two lines of argument offered by Rawls as support for and illumination of his principles are especially relevant in tracking the history of the recent debate over the place of responsibility in theories of distributive justice, as the debate developed partly in response to the ambiguous status of the concept of responsibility in Rawls's work.

The first of the arguments relevant to the status of responsibility in theories of justice offered by Rawls concerns the second of the two principles he put forward. Recognizing that 'everyone's advantage' and 'open to all' can each be taken in two ways, Rawls considers three interpretations of equality of opportunity.[6] The first, 'the system of natural liberty', requires only that there are no legal barriers to persons gaining positions; there is formal equality of opportunity, but no attempt to control the

---

[3]   G. A. Cohen, 'On the Currency of Egalitarian Justice', *Ethics*, 99 (1989), 906–944: 933. This is an oft-quoted phrase, and has become almost the political theory equivalent of a sound bite. Similar points about the importance of egalitarians capturing responsibility have also been well expressed by, among others, C. M. Macleod in his *Liberalism, Justice and Markets: A Critique of Liberal Equality* (Oxford University Press, 1998), 10.

[4]   The best-known such statement was qualified in a way that proved quite fitting: 'For the moment, anyway, political philosophy is dead' (P. Laslett, 'Introduction' in P. Laslett (ed.), *Philosophy, Politics and Society* (Oxford: Blackwell, 1956), vii–xv, at vii).

[5]   J. Rawls, *A Theory of Justice*, revised edition (Oxford: Oxford University Press, 1999), 53.

[6]   A fourth interpretation, 'natural aristocracy', is mentioned after the main discussion of the relevant section of *A Theory of Justice*. This interpretation can be set aside for present purposes.

economic inequalities that result from variations in natural talent, social circumstance, and sheer luck. As Rawls notes, '[i]ntuitively, the most obvious injustice of the system of natural liberty is that it permits distributive shares to be improperly influenced by these factors so arbitrary from a moral point of view'.[7] The second interpretation, 'the liberal interpretation', adds to formal equality of opportunity the requirement that each individual has a 'fair chance' of attaining positions, and thus advocates what Rawls has called fair equality of opportunity. Fair equality of opportunity requires that social background does not affect individuals' chances of attaining positions. While observing that this system removes the arbitrary influence of social class that is prevalent in the system of natural liberty, Rawls criticizes the liberal interpretation on similar grounds: '[w]ithin the limits allowed by the background arrangements [those required to maintain equal basic liberties and fair equality of opportunity], distributive shares are decided by the outcome of the natural lottery; and this outcome is arbitrary from a moral perspective'.[8] In other words, Rawls worries about the influence people's native talents and abilities, which are arbitrary from the moral point of view, can have on their positions: those whose abilities are, or can be made, marketable would have an advantage over those without such abilities. He settles, therefore, on the final 'democratic interpretation' of equality of opportunity, which curtails the influence of differential distribution of natural talent on people's life chances. The democratic interpretation combines the more demanding fair conception of equality of opportunity with the 'difference principle', which only allows inequalities where they are to the benefit of the worst-off members of society. Hence Rawls's final statement of the second principle requires social and economic inequalities to be (a) 'to the greatest benefit of the least advantaged' and (b) 'attached to positions and offices open to all under conditions of fair equality of opportunity'.[9]

Before explaining the relevance of the above argument for the debate over responsibility and distributive justice, let us introduce the second argument found in Rawls that has implications for the debate. Rawls thinks that distributive justice should be concerned with the distribution of primary social goods (that is, among other things, rights, liberties, income, and wealth). In taking primary social goods, rather than (say) welfare or resources in general (including natural ones such as, for example, intelligence or health), as the appropriate object of, or grounds for, (re)distribution, Rawls faces the objection that some convert goods such as income and wealth into welfare at very different rates to others and thus big differences in welfare can arise. This happens, for example, when some people have so-called cheap tastes and thus can reach relatively high welfare levels with the help of relatively cheap goods. In reply, Rawls draws attention to our 'capacity to assume responsibility for our ends', and notes that, since

---

[7] Rawls, *A Theory of Justice*, 63.

[8] Rawls, *A Theory of Justice*, 64. Rawls also makes the separate point that 'the principle of fair opportunity can only be imperfectly carried out, at least as long as some form of the family exists'.

[9] Rawls, *A Theory of Justice*, 266. Part (a) of the second principle includes consistency with the just savings principle, which makes allowance for obligations to future generations.

persons with cheap tastes have acquired those in response to their reasonably expected income and wealth, 'it is regarded as unfair that they should now have less in order to spare others from the consequences of their lack of foresight or self-discipline'.[10]

What is the relationship between Rawls's discussions of 'moral arbitrariness' and 'assuming responsibility for ends', and debates more explicitly concerned with justice and responsibility? Will Kymlicka has interpreted Rawls's theory as a precursor of those later accounts that give individual choice and responsibility a central role. In Kymlicka's view, Rawls is motivated by the 'choices—circumstances distinction' and 'the "ambition-sensitive" and "endowment-insensitive" goal', even if the democratic interpretation of equality of opportunity and the difference principle do not quite deliver the goal in question.[11] Roughly speaking, distributions are 'ambition-sensitive' (or 'choice-sensitive', or 'responsibility-sensitive') when they depend on choices made by individuals (in ways that may reflect option luck[12]) and are 'endowment-insensitive' when they do not depend on differential brute luck. Brute luck is fortune over which individuals have no control (or which they have no responsibility for) while option luck is the upshot of risks that were in some sense deliberately taken on.[13]

According to Kymlicka, Rawls aims at endowment-insensitivity since he holds that '[n]atural talents and social circumstances are both matters of brute luck, and people's moral claims should not depend on brute luck'.[14] To achieve ambition-sensitivity Rawls should have recognized, as Ronald Dworkin later has, that differential option luck can justify inequality; implementing the difference principle, however, would likely obliterate at least some inequalities arising out of differential option luck. This is because the difference principle is concerned with improving the position of the worst-off members of society, as measured by primary social goods, and people with bad option luck can fall into this same category. In addition, Rawls fails to deliver endowment-insensitivity since his use of primary social goods as the metric of equality makes some brute luck inequalities invisible (most notably, those in health). According to Kymlicka, then, 'while Rawls appeals to [the] choices—circumstances distinction, his difference principle violates it in two important ways'.[15]

This interpretation is, however, disputed.[16] Samuel Scheffler reads Rawls as denying any fundamental distinction between choices and circumstances, and so sees no

---

[10] J. Rawls, 'Social Unity and Primary Goods' in A. K. Sen and B. Williams (eds), *Utilitarianism and Beyond* (Cambridge: Cambridge University Press, 1982), 159–185, at 168–169.

[11] W. Kymlicka, *Contemporary Political Philosophy*, second edition (Oxford: Oxford University Press, 2002), 75. The terminology is borrowed from Ronald Dworkin.

[12] Cf. P. Vallentyne, 'Brute Luck, Option Luck, and Equality of Initial Opportunities', *Ethics*, 112 (2002), 529–557; K. Lippert-Rasmussen, 'Egalitarianism, Option Luck, and Responsibility', *Ethics*, 111 (2001), 549–579; Larry Temkin's contribution to this volume, especially the final section.

[13] R. Dworkin, *Sovereign Virtue* (Cambridge, MA: Harvard University Press, 2000), 73.

[14] Kymlicka, *Contemporary Political Philosophy*, 58.

[15] Kymlicka, *Contemporary Political Philosophy*, 74.

[16] See S. Scheffler, 'What is Egalitarianism?', *Philosophy and Public Affairs*, 31 (2003), 5–39; 'Choice, Circumstance and the Value of Equality', *Politics, Philosophy and Economics*, 4 (2005), 5–28; S. Freeman, *Justice*

contradiction in his position. Scheffler points out that Rawls discusses 'the principle of redress', which holds 'that undeserved inequalities call for redress; and since inequalities of birth and natural endowment are undeserved, these inequalities are to be somehow compensated for'. This principle could well be motivated by the goal of endowment-insensitivity and the centrality of the choice/circumstance distinction. But Scheffler draws attention to Rawls's assessment of the principle as having appeal 'only as a prima facie principle, one that is to be weighed in the balance with others'.[17] That is, while the principle is taken into account by Rawls, it is only one consideration among several. Rawls's overall goal is to establish which conception of justice is the most reasonable for the purpose of regulating the basic structure of a heterogeneous democratic society. The claims of 'moral arbitrariness' are then put forward as a rebuke to the rival goal of rewarding talent or hard work, through the largely unregulated free market of the system of natural liberty. Moral arbitrariness matters in so far as 'it helps to clarify the distributive implications of taking equal citizenship seriously', but it is equal citizenship rather than the absence of brute luck inequality that Rawls sees as fundamental.[18] Similarly, people are expected to assume responsibility for their ends because this is part of the division of responsibilities between the individual and society. This division is appropriate simply because people can be expected to cope with the fair shares allocated to them. The fairness of the shares is not a matter of choice-sensitivity, but is rather grounded in the fact that choices 'are part of a distributive scheme that makes it possible for free and equal citizens to pursue their diverse conceptions of the good within a framework that embodies an ideal of reciprocity and mutual respect'.[19]

Two things seem to emerge clearly from this dispute: first, that Rawls does not take the choice/circumstance (or option luck/brute luck) distinction to be fundamental, and second, that some have nevertheless taken his occasional invocation of similar ideas, especially references to the moral arbitrariness of factors such as social class and natural talent, to be suggestive of a concern with the distinction.[20] At any rate, responsibility only came to the fore in debates about distributive justice with the publication of Dworkin's 'What is Equality?' articles.[21] Like Rawls's 'justice as fairness', Dworkin's 'equality of resources' is a complex account of justice and equality, only some parts of which need concern us here. In Dworkin's case, however, these parts are at the core of his theory.

---

and the Social Contract (Oxford: Oxford University Press, 2006), ch. 4; M. Matravers, Responsibility and Justice (Cambridge: Polity, 2007), ch. 3.

[17] Rawls, A Theory of Justice, 86.

[18] Scheffler, 'What is Egalitarianism?', 26.

[19] Scheffler, 'What is Egalitarianism?', 28.

[20] See the essays by Richard J. Arneson, Norman Daniels, and Shlomi Segall in this volume for further discussion of the contrast between Rawlsian and responsibility-sensitive views.

[21] R. Dworkin, 'What is Equality? Part 1: Equality of Welfare', Philosophy and Public Affairs, 10 (1981), 185–246; 'What is Equality? Part 2: Equality of Resources', Philosophy and Public Affairs, 10 (1981), 283–345. Reprinted as chapters 1 and 2 of Dworkin, Sovereign Virtue.

Dworkin asks us to imagine that all the resources in a society are to be distributed on the basis of an auction. Each individual has the same level of control over the composition of the lots, and each has the same amount of currency. Dworkin holds that the outcome of the auction will be equal if it satisfies the 'envy test'—that is, if each individual is satisfied with the bundle they end up with, in that they would not trade it for anybody else's. Over time, however, as people make different choices, their bundles will change. According to Dworkin, it is unproblematic for some to come to hold more than others where that is the result of free and informed exercises of preference from equal starting positions. Those who play it safe and consequently hold less than successful gamblers can have no complaint as 'the price of a safer life . . . is precisely forgoing any chance of the gains whose prospect induces others to gamble'.[22] The difference between successful and unsuccessful gamblers is justified similarly: the risk of losing was the price paid for the chance of winning. Ex post redistribution from winners to losers cannot be prescribed as this would be to deny both groups their preference for risk taking, and so would amount to a denial of their equal role in creating the auction lots.

Variations in option luck are then a legitimate basis for departures from an initial equality of resources. Brute luck is a different matter. If an individual is unforeseeably struck by a meteor, or is the victim of sudden blindness, the disadvantage he suffers as a result is not explicable in terms of the risks the individual has taken. Dworkin acknowledges that the availability of insurance can transform what would otherwise be brute luck into option luck, but also that insurance against some types of brute luck is not and cannot be available in the real world. He therefore argues that elaborate *hypothetical* insurance markets are required to set the right level of compensation for natural disabilities and talent deficits, the most prevalent forms of uninsurable brute bad luck in the real world that cannot be eliminated through social reform, as class could be. The compensation is paid for through taxation of those without natural disabilities and talent deficiencies.

One of the key considerations Dworkin presents in support of adopting equality of resources as the egalitarian ideal concerns persons with 'expensive tastes'—those that require above average resources to secure average levels of welfare. Equality of resources' major egalitarian rival, *equality of welfare*, would require that those with 'champagne tastes' are maintained at the general welfare level, at societal expense. As Dworkin notes, 'most people would resist the conclusion that those who have expensive tastes are, for that reason, entitled to a larger share than others'.[23] But his position, unlike Rawls's, does not require that persons assume responsibility for their tastes, with compensation for expensive tastes ruled out altogether. 'Cravings'—those expensive tastes with which the holder does not identify—may give rise to compensation on Dworkin's scheme.[24] Thus, in distinguishing between tastes that do and that do

---

[22] Dworkin, *Sovereign Virtue*, 74.
[23] Dworkin, *Sovereign Virtue*, 15; see also 48–59.
[24] Dworkin, *Sovereign Virtue*, 82.

not give rise to compensation, Dworkin appeals to the distinction between 'the person', which defines what success in life would be like, and 'circumstances', which facilitate or impede that success. Compensation can be claimed for disadvantageous circumstances, but compensation cannot be claimed for that which is part of the person, as this sets the terms for a successful life rather than merely impede or facilitate such success. In this way equality of resources can recognize unfavourable obsessions for what they are without creating incentives for the cultivation of expensive tastes.

Dworkin's theory can, on account of its use of the brute luck/option luck distinction, be seen as the first major account of egalitarian distributive justice to place considerations of responsibility and choice at its centre. Subsequent egalitarian theories have sought to accommodate the distinction in even more explicit fashion. Two significant such theories are Richard Arneson's equal opportunity for welfare and G. A. Cohen's equal access to advantage.[25] The principal difference between the two is the favoured measure of (equal) distributive shares: while Arneson preferred welfare, as measured by informed preference satisfaction, Cohen favoured a measure that included both welfare and resources. Both views endorse a deep equal opportunity (or equal access) conception of equality which objects to all disadvantages that do not result from the holder's genuine choice (construed in some way).[26] Arneson offers this more detailed specification: 'Equal opportunity for welfare obtains among persons when all of them face equivalent decision trees [of possible complete life-histories]— the expected value of each person's best (= most prudent) choice of options, second-best, ... nth-best is the same.'[27] Arneson and Cohen both require that the opportunities are (to use Arneson's term) 'effectively equivalent', in that the persons have sufficient information, ability, and character to actually pursue the opportunities equally.

Such equal opportunity views might be thought to provide a better account of egalitarian justice than equality of resources.[28] The defensive aspect of this is that they provide a ready response to Dworkin's expensive tastes objection to equality of

---

[25] R. J. Arneson, 'Equality and Equal Opportunity for Welfare', *Philosophical Studies*, 56 (1989), 77–93; G. A. Cohen, 'On the Currency of Egalitarian Justice', 906–944. For a noteworthy early attempt at practical application of this sort of theory see J. E. Roemer, 'A Pragmatic Theory of Responsibility for the Egalitarian Planner', *Philosophy and Public Affairs*, 22 (1993), 146–166.

[26] Two sample statements: 'Other things equal, it is bad if some people are worse off than others through no voluntary choice or fault of their own' (Arneson, 'Equality and Equal Opportunity for Welfare', 85); '...what currently strikes me as the right reading of egalitarianism [is] that its purpose is to eliminate involuntary disadvantage, by which I (stipulatively) mean disadvantage for which the sufferer cannot be held responsible, since it does not appropriately reflect choices that he has made or is making or would make' (Cohen, 'On the Currency of Egalitarian Justice', 916). Compare with Larry Temkin's equally canonical statement: 'what is objectionable is some being worse off than others *through no fault of their own*' (*Inequality* (Oxford: Oxford University Press, 1993), 17, original emphasis).

[27] Arneson, 'Equality and Equal Opportunity for Welfare', 85–86.

[28] Note that there is a sense in which both equality of resources and equality of opportunity for welfare (or advantage) are equality of opportunity views; namely both views can be distinguished, at least conceptually, from equality of outcome, in giving some fundamental distributive significance to individual choice and/or responsibility. For the remainder of this section, however, whenever we refer to equal opportunity or equality of opportunity views, we mean equality of opportunity for welfare or advantage.

welfare. The equal opportunity view differs from equality of welfare by only advocating compensation for expensive tastes in the less objectionable—or perhaps, wholly non-objectionable—cases where the holder is not responsible for bringing about their taste (or more precisely, the expense of their taste). The more positive, and more contentious, aspect is that these views identify welfare deficits as a source of disadvantage, and so can provide compensation in some compelling circumstances when equality of resources sees no disadvantage. Dworkin is probably right to say, contrary to Cohen,[29] that painful but non-disabling medical conditions do not fall into this category, as equality of resources would advocate compensation in such cases as well, specifically when the sufferers do not identify with their conditions.[30] Troubling cases arise, however, where (i) a welfare deficiency, (ii) identification with taste, (iii) disidentification with the taste's expense, and (iv) lack of genuine choice regarding that expense all coincide.[31] Consider, for instance, women who strongly identify with their preference (taste) for looking after their own babies personally.[32] Relative to parents whose identification with that preference is weak, these mothers would often be disadvantaged whether they look after their babies or not, absent special redistributive action by the state. Such women can rarely if ever be said to have genuinely chosen their preference, and would usually disidentify with the welfare expense of it (resulting either directly from lack of contact with their child or indirectly from a radically reduced income should they devote themselves to childcare). By focusing on whether or not disadvantages are chosen, equal opportunity can explain why assistance from the state in such a case might be appropriate. Even where there is identification with preferences themselves, compensation may be due on account of *bad price luck*, 'which is bad luck in the high cost of the preferences'.[33]

Equal opportunity might, then, be thought to provide a more plausible cut between compensable and non-compensable expensive tastes. Cohen points out that in Dworkin's paradigmatic case of a holder of expensive tastes, the holder—Louis, who has a taste for plovers' eggs and pre-phylloxera claret—both endorses his tastes (grounds for denial of compensation according to equality of resources) and came to have them voluntarily (an irrelevance on Dworkin's scheme, but grounds for non-compensation on Arneson's and Cohen's schemes). It is, according to Cohen, the second feature of the case that injects Dworkin's treatment of it with some appeal. Where the two features come apart—where, for instance, a photographer identifies with their

---

[29] Cohen, 'On the Currency of Egalitarian Justice', 917–921.

[30] Dworkin, *Sovereign Virtue*, 297.

[31] See Arneson, 'Equality and Equal Opportunity for Welfare', 81; Cohen, 'On the Currency of Egalitarian Justice', 926–927.

[32] For related discussion of 'career-sacrificing mothers' see A. Mason, *Levelling the Playing Field: The Idea of Equal Opportunity and Its Place in Egalitarian Thought* (Oxford: Oxford University Press, 2006), 182–188.

[33] Dworkin, 'Replies' in J. Burley (ed.), *Dworkin and His Critics* (Oxford: Blackwell, 2004), 339–396, at 344. Dworkin himself rejects compensation for bad price luck.

expensive taste in pastime, but the taste came about involuntarily—it is the (in)voluntariness that seems relevant to distribution.[34]

The general view of distributive equality defended by Arneson, Cohen, and (in a less pure form) Dworkin continues to generate internal disputes over these and other matters.[35] It has also come in for considerable criticism from other egalitarians. One prominent critic, Elizabeth Anderson, has named the view 'luck egalitarianism', and joined others in objecting to it on two distinct grounds.[36] The first claim is that luck egalitarianism *insults* individuals both through intrusive investigations aimed at finding out what in their lives is due to luck and what they brought about themselves, and by expressing pity, envy, and paternalism. An early and particularly careful statement of this sort of argument is provided by Jonathan Wolff.[37] He observes that a person's respect-standing might be undercut through a failure of common courtesy, through a failure of trust, or through 'shameful revelation'. Though Wolff grants that luck egalitarianism need not undercut respect-standing in the first two ways, he avers that the sort of detailed information it requires necessitates shameful revelation. For instance, an unemployment benefits claimant would have to try to convince the relevant authorities that she has made a serious effort to secure a job, in the process acknowledging her own powerlessness and eliminating any remaining self-respect.[38] According to Anderson, luck egalitarianism not only insults its citizens: it *abandons* them as well. The most common kind of abandonment concerns 'negligent victims'. Marc Fleurbaey's iconic example features 'Bert', an uninsured motorcycle rider who likes to feel the wind in his hair, in spite of his knowledge of the risks.[39] When Bert crashes, suffering severe but treatable injuries, luck egalitarianism will, according to Fleurbaey, note the free and deliberate character of his actions, and conclude that he has no egalitarian claim against being left to die. But such harsh treatment may seem contrary to our moral judgement. Fleurbaey urges that individual responsibility is not all that matters here—the scale of the disadvantage being suffered also counts.

Anderson takes these two objections as sufficient to undermine luck egalitarianism's egalitarianism, and holds that it cannot be said to treat persons with 'equal concern and respect', as Dworkin himself requires of an egalitarian theory.[40] The objections might also be thought to pose independent problems for any attempt to place responsibility at the heart of distributive justice, as it may appear that any resulting account of justice will be both demanding in information terms (and hence potentially disrespectful) and

---

[34] Cohen, 'On the Currency of Egalitarian Justice', 923. Dworkin addresses the problem of involuntariness in acquisition of expensive tastes in *Sovereign Virtue*, especially ch. 7.

[35] See especially Dworkin, *Sovereign Virtue*, ch. 7, and Burley (ed.), *Dworkin and His Critics*.

[36] E. S. Anderson, 'What is the Point of Equality?', *Ethics*, 109 (1999), 287–337.

[37] J. Wolff, 'Fairness, Respect, and the Egalitarian Ethos', *Philosophy and Public Affairs*, 27 (1998), 97–122.

[38] Wolff, 'Fairness, Respect and the Egalitarian Ethos', 114.

[39] M. Fleurbaey, 'Equal Opportunity or Equal Social Outcome?', *Economics and Philosophy*, 11 (1995), 25–55, at 40-41; see also Anderson, 'What is the Point of Equality', 295–297; Scheffler, 'What is Egalitarianism', 33.

[40] R. Dworkin, *Taking Rights Seriously* (London: Duckworth, 1977), 272–273.

exacting in its distributive judgements (and hence potentially harsh). These problems would arise even in non-egalitarian accounts of justice.

Some writers, moreover, have found problems with luck egalitarianism's use of the concept of responsibility itself. Susan Hurley has pointed out that luck egalitarians have refused to open the 'black box of responsibility', have sometimes conflated more than one notion of responsibility, and cannot in any case specify or justify their egalitarianism by reference to responsibility-based goals such as luck neutralization.[41] Other critics have suggested that luck egalitarianism assumes the truth of metaphysical libertarianism (that human free will exists and causal determinism is false), which is very much in doubt, and/or cannot be applied in practice in the absence of some such metaphysical certainty.[42]

Those identified as 'luck egalitarians' have responded to this wide variety of critiques in an equally wide variety of ways.[43] Dworkin, despite often being considered the first luck egalitarian, has been at pains to repudiate the label, and has sought to explain how equality of resources is not susceptible to the criticisms targeted at luck egalitarianism.[44] Arneson and Cohen are happier to accept the label, but have also sought to defend their positions, both emphasizing that the contrast between their abstract principles and their policy implications may be greater than critics have allowed.[45] It may, for instance, not be good luck egalitarian policy to conduct investigations into individual benefit claims, on account of the costs this imposes on some unfairly disadvantaged persons, and less precise policy tools may be utilized instead. Arneson has also been happy to accept Hurley's suggestion that equality must be postulated separately from luck neutralization, and has emphasized that luck egalitarianism might be practically indistinguishable from outcome egalitarianism if hard determinism is true (that is, free will is an illusion).[46] Both writers ended up endorsing significantly revised positions, Arneson combining responsibility considerations with considerations of the total amount of welfare and the amount held by the worse-off in a pluralistic position he calls 'responsibility-catering prioritarianism', and Cohen providing compensation for

---

[41] S. Hurley, *Justice, Luck, and Knowledge* (Cambridge, MA: Harvard University Press, 2003).

[42] See Scheffler, 'What is Egalitarianism'; 'Choice, Circumstance and the Value of Equality'; M. Fleurbaey, 'Egalitarian Opportunities', *Law and Philosophy*, 20 (2001), 499–530; 'Equal Opportunity or Equal Social Outcome?'.

[43] See C. Knight, *Luck Egalitarianism: Equality, Responsibility, and Justice* (Edinburgh: Edinburgh University Press, 2009).

[44] See R. Dworkin, '*Sovereign Virtue* Revisited', *Ethics*, 113 (2002), 106–143; 'Equality, Luck and Hierarchy', *Philosophy and Public Affairs*, 31 (2003), 190–198.

[45] See R. J. Arneson, 'Luck Egalitarianism and Prioritarianism', *Ethics*, 110 (2000), 339–349; 'Egalitarian Justice versus the Right to Privacy', *Social Philosophy and Policy*, 17 (2000), 91–119; G. A. Cohen, 'Facts and Principles', *Philosophy & Public Affairs*, 31 (2003), 211–245.

[46] See R. J. Arneson, 'Luck and Equality', *Proceedings of the Aristotelian Society*, Supplementary Volume, 75 (2001), 73–90; 'Luck Egalitarianism Interpreted and Defended', *Philosophical Topics*, 32 (2004), 1–20; see also Arneson, 'Equality and Equal Opportunity for Welfare', 86; G. A. Cohen, 'Equality of What? On Welfare, Goods and Capabilities' in M. Nussbaum and A. K. Sen (eds), *The Quality of Life* (Oxford: Oxford University Press, 1993), 9–29, at 28. See also Larry Temkin's chapter in this volume.

judgmental tastes—those that are 'informed by valuational judgment'[47]—where they are disadvantaging, even when they are chosen. Although both positions are something of a departure from the earlier, stricter views, in that they allow for some cases of bad option luck to be compensable, they both appear to retain a significant role for considerations of responsibility.

2. Responsibility and distributive justice

We set out below some of the key themes in recent debates about distributive justice and responsibility, all of which are developed further in this volume.

2.1 The concept of responsibility

As H. L. A. Hart once illustrated with the example of a drunken sea captain,[48] there is not one but many different concepts of responsibility. The three probably most familiar are those of *causal responsibility* (A is causally responsible for X when A has caused X), *moral responsibility* (A is morally responsible for X when she is blameworthy or praiseworthy for X), and *responsibility as obligation* (A is responsible for X in the sense that A has some obligations with regard to X), including legal obligation. Which concepts of responsibility are most relevant to debates about distributive justice? Before answering this question, we want to emphasize that we think this is the right question to ask. While political philosophers have by now developed sophisticated accounts of the various organizing principles of distributive justice such as equality, priority, and sufficiency, the discussion about the place of responsibility in relation to distributive justice remains relatively underdeveloped, partly because not enough attention has been paid to what it is that theorists enquire about when asking about the place of responsibility in theories of distributive justice. Following a distinction commonly made in discussions of responsibility in moral philosophy, we want to suggest that there are two distinct concepts of responsibility that are most relevant to distributive justice: agent responsibility and consequential responsibility.[49]

First, to be responsible for something can mean that one has brought this something about. This is *agent responsibility*. To say that Ann is agent responsible for breaking a

---

[47] G. A. Cohen, 'Expensive Taste Rides Again' in Burley (ed.), *Dworkin and His Critics*, 3–29, at 7.

[48] H. L. A. Hart, 'Postscript: Responsibility and Retribution' in H. L. A. Hart, *Punishment and Responsibility* (Oxford: Oxford University Press, 1968), 211.

[49] Different moral philosophers use different terms for very similar (though not always identical) versions of this distinction. T. M. Scanlon distinguishes between attributive responsibility (which can be interpreted as agent or moral responsibility) and substantive responsibility (which is a version of consequential responsibility). (Norman Daniels adopts Scanlon's usage in this volume). Michael Zimmerman prefers a distinction between 'appraisability' and 'liability', while Gary Watson differentiatates 'attributability' and 'accountability'. See T. M. Scanlon, *What We Owe to Each Other* (Cambridge, MA: Harvard University Press, 1998), ch. 6; M. J. Zimmerman, *An Essay on Moral Responsibility* (Totowa, NJ: Rowman & Littlefield, 1988); G. Watson, 'Two Faces of Responsibility' in *Agency and Answerability* (Oxford: Oxford University Press, 2004), 260–288. For different ways of cutting the concept of responsibility presented in this volume see especially Peter Vallentyne's and Susan Hurley's chapters.

window means that she has brought it about, qua free agent, that the window is broken. So understood, attributions of responsibility for attitudes, outcomes, or actions to an agent are attributions of authorship. It might be helpful to locate the concept of agent responsibility with regard to the more familiar concepts of causal and moral responsibility. To attribute agent responsibility for X we need to find both a causal link between the person and X (i.e. attribute causal responsibility) as well as establish, in addition, that X stems appropriately from that person's agency. Thus a person who breaks a window because she is thrown against it by a sudden gust of wind may be casually responsible for breaking the window but would not normally be seen as agent responsible for it if we believe that the force of the wind simply overrode her agency. On the other hand, to attribute moral responsibility we need to go one step beyond attributions of agent responsibility and decide whether the agents should be blamed or praised for what they brought about. Attributions of agent responsibility do not require us to make this call: we can say that a person is agent responsible for tying his shoelaces, or agent responsible for giving money to a bank robber at gunpoint, without the need to see such actions as blameworthy or praiseworthy.

We thus distinguish between (1) attributions of authorship, and (2) attributions of moral blame/praise, reserving 'moral responsibility' only for the latter. The idea here is to distinguish between seeing people as responsible for X in the sense that X (appropriately) flows from their agency, and seeing them as morally blameworthy or praiseworthy. We know that sometimes in the literature a single term (be it agent or moral or attributive responsibility) is used to denote both attributions of authorship, and that it would now be appropriate to morally blame or praise the agent if moral blame or praise were appropriate (given some further facts). But we think in the context of debates about distributive justice, it is helpful (at least sometimes) to disambiguate the issue of whether the agent is morally blameworthy/praiseworthy or whether only the first condition for moral blame/praise—i.e. that s/he is the author of X—has been (established to have been) met. One of the reasons why we think it is helpful is that it allows us to flag up in a relatively straightforward way that luck egalitarian judgements of who is owed what as a matter of egalitarian justice need not track attributions of moral blame and praise.

More often than not what is at stake in debates about distributive justice and responsibility is precisely how people's entitlements to resources (including opportunities) are affected by what they bring about—i.e. by their agent responsibility. This problem is frequently expressed as one of two questions: 'When, if at all, does the fact that one has brought about one's disadvantage annul one's entitlement to assistance?'; or, with 'choice' serving as proxy for agent responsibility: 'Are those whose choices led to their disadvantage less entitled to assistance than those whose disadvantage is not a matter of choice?'

Agent responsibility, then, is the first concept at the heart of debates about distributive justice and responsibility. But since the idea of authorship is simultaneously complex and elusive, the concept itself can be developed in different ways. For one, authorship may be variously seen as a matter of what people choose as freely willing agents, or what they control, or deliberately choose, or choose when well-informed, or choose in the sense of responding to reasons, or choose in the absence of some autonomy-undermining conditions, or bring about absent-mindedly when they should have paid attention, or bring about through forgetfulness, or some combination of those and similar proposals.

In addition, fixing on a specific conception of agent responsibility requires establishing which outcomes, if any, can be linked to the conduct that is seen as itself appropriately reflective of the agency of the person whose responsibility is at stake. Are persons to be seen as authors only of outcomes that were certain to follow from their choices, or also outcomes that were merely likely to follow, or outcomes that were reasonably foreseeable, or what?[50] Peter Vallentyne, in his contribution to this volume, offers a systematic proposal for how to deal with an aspect of this problem, namely the problem of how false beliefs affect which outcomes could be attributed to an agent who has them. To make the problem more concrete, imagine, with Vallentyne, a person who intentionally undergoes a painful medical procedure because she falsely—and through no fault of her own—believes that it will cure a disease she has. Is she responsible for the reduction in her well-being brought through the pain, or not? In his chapter, Vallentyne develops an account of how false or incomplete beliefs affect agent responsibility, and thus entitlements, on a luck egalitarian account of justice.

The second concept of responsibility that is key to debates about responsibility and distributive justice is that of *consequential responsibility*.[51] To say that a person is consequentially responsible for X is to say that the burdens and benefits that come with or constitute X are justly his or hers to bear (or to enjoy). Moral or legal responsibility can hence be understood as versions of consequential responsibility with the relevant burdens and benefits being, respectively, blame/praise and legal sanctions/opportunities. But the type of consequential responsibility that is at the core of debates about distributive justice may be seen as distinct in three senses. First, it is focused on burdens and benefits whose distribution is the concern of distributive justice such as, in the most general terms, advantage and disadvantage.[52] Second, attributions of consequential responsibility normally presuppose the presence of agent responsibility. In this sense consequential responsibility is similar to moral responsibility, as attributions of blame and praise normally presuppose the presence of agent responsibility, but may be distinct

---

[50] Tony Honoré's work on outcome responsibility can be seen as an early attempt to map out the problem. We should also emphasize that the similar but wider question of which outcomes can be attributed to people in the sense that they will need to bear them without entitlement to assistance has been examined in some detail in the recent literature. And so has the related question under what conditions, if any, can leaving an individual to bear a disadvantage be justified by appealing to her earlier opportunity to avoid that disadvantage. T. Honoré, 'Responsibility and Luck: The Moral Basis of Strict Liability' in *Responsibility and Fault* (Oxford: Hart, 1999), 14–40.

[51] Dworkin, *Sovereign Virtue*, 287.

[52] For a further discussion of the concept of justice see Larry Temkin's chapter in this volume.

from legal responsibility, which can take the form of strict liability.[53] Finally, and connectedly, consequential responsibility in the distributive sphere is seen by some as 'holistic', in the sense that whether any particular attribution (and thus any economic (dis)advantage) is correct (i.e. just) is dependent upon whether the many other attributions of consequential responsibility (and thus allocations of economic (dis)advantage) in society are correct. Retributive justice, by contrast, is often said to be 'individualistic', in that the justice or injustice of any particular attribution of consequential responsibility turns on facts about the subject—usually whether they are agent responsible for some thing that society finds intolerable—rather than on any general assessment of societal benefits and burdens.[54] That noted, in his chapter in this volume, Matt Matravers maintains that arguments put forward in support of distributive justice's holism also support holism in the retributive sphere. In both cases there are no morally relevant differences between persons prior to or independent of principles of justice. Even if there were such differences, it would be too complex to establish the appropriate rewards and penalties.

If we put both agent and consequential responsibility together we can phrase the problem at the core of current debates about distributive justice as follows: Under what conditions, if any, could being agent responsible for finding oneself in a situation in which one suffers a disadvantage (or enjoys an advantage) make one consequentially responsible for the (dis)advantage as far as distributive justice is concerned? Notice that it is possible to pose this question without direct reference to the concepts of responsibility, and in this sense, as with other concepts, responsibility can be understood as a mere epiphenomenon—a handy short cut for talking about what really matters, that is agency and (dis)advantage. This is most clearly seen in Susan Hurley's contribution to this volume, which challenges the traditional liberal view that assigns priority to individual responsibility. The cognitive sciences show that rational agency, which is presupposed by individual responsibility, is in fact formed by the public realm, and so individual responsibility cannot independently set the bounds of that realm. Hurley argues that those concerned with individual responsibility should focus on the conditions in which agency is exercised; they should endorse a progressive social liberalism that aims to combat manipulation and promote the social and political prerequisites for rational agency.

---

[53] It may, however, be observed that, though by definition crimes of strict liability have no requirement of proving mens rea as regards one or more elements of the crime, they do typically require mens rea for *some* (one or more) elements of the crime. Usually, some form of agent responsibility is required 'further back', and where such responsibility is absent—for example, where automatism (externally caused unconscious involuntary conduct) obtains—there can be no strict liability. As Steven Sverdlik notes, strict liability offences 'typically concern specialized activities (like bottling milk or using explosives) where practitioners have been put on notice in advance beforehand that penalties attach to even unintentional violations. . . . So while it may be true that lack of intention does not excuse in such cases, it still seems possible to hold that violators have been given a fair opportunity to conform their behavior to the law' ('Punishment', *Law and Philosophy*, 7 (1988), 179–201, at 195–196). A retributivist who construes strict liability in this way may resist the second distinction between distributive consequential responsibility and legal responsibility that we make in the text.

[54] S. Scheffler, *Boundaries and Allegiances* (Oxford: Oxford University Press, 2001), ch. 10.

As mentioned earlier, there are other concepts of responsibility. For example, *vicarious responsibility* and *role responsibility* figure prominently in legal and social philosophy. We will introduce the concept of *collective responsibility* below (see section 2.4), but first we want to explain how the concepts of responsibility introduced above fit in relation to concepts that, for want of a better word, can be said to frame them.

2.2 Responsibility and other concepts

Much controversy and interest in the debate about responsibility and distributive justice comes from attempts to explain the relationship between responsibility and crucial related concepts such as luck and desert. With regard to the relationship between luck and responsibility, one major conceptual question is whether people can be agent responsible for what is a matter of luck for them or whether identifying something as a matter of luck for someone means accepting that the person is not agent responsible for it. It is possible, of course, to simply reserve the concept of luck to delineate the inverse correlate of agent responsibility. We are all in favour of conceptual clarity but it is also worth briefly noting the relationship between agent responsibility and the concept of luck that is not in this sense derivative of the concept of agent responsibility. Following Hurley, we will use the term 'thin luck' to denote luck that is the inverse correlate of (agent) responsibility and 'thick luck' to denote luck that is not derivative of the concept of responsibility in this way.[55]

Thick luck can be understood—on one conception—as the absence of control: it is whatever happens to the agent that the agent did not control. So understood, the concept of thick luck differs from that of thin luck in two ways. First, control is not necessarily needed for agent responsibility,[56] so while the form of thick luck at hand requires an absence of control, thin luck need not—whether it does depends on which account of agent responsibility turns out to be correct. Second, regardless of whether control is thought necessary for agent responsibility, there may be additional conditions for agent responsibility (for example, concerning reason-responsiveness), so while the presence of control ensures that thick luck is absent, thin luck may persist merely because further conditions have not been met. In sum, then, the absence of control is necessary and sufficient for thick luck, but the absence of control is neither necessary

---

[55] Hurley, *Justice, Luck, and Knowledge*, ch. 4.

[56] For instance, one well-known conception of control is what J. M. Fischer and M. Ravizza (*Responsibility and Control: A Theory of Moral Responsibility* (Cambridge: Cambridge University Press, 1998)) call 'regulatory control'—the power to do other than one actually does. Suppose that Black is secretly prepared to manipulate Jones's 'brain and nervous system . . . so that causal forces running in and out of his synapses and along the poor man's nerves determine that he chooses to act and that he does act in the one way and not in the other', but that Black 'never has to show his hand' because his victim, 'for reasons of his own, decides to perform and does perform the very action Black wants him to perform' (H. Frankfurt, 'Alternate Possibilities and Moral Responsibility', *Journal of Philosophy*, 66 (1969), 829–839, at 835–836). Jones has had no regulatory control over how he acts, but the concept of agent responsibility is at least open to the idea that he nevertheless has agent responsibility for it.

nor sufficient for thin luck (except, indirectly, if control is necessary and sufficient for agent responsibility).

We will not attempt to specify fully the various concepts of luck and the relationships between them, but let us briefly note the relationships in which thick and thin luck stand to brute and option luck. Option luck, as mentioned above, is a mixture of what the agent controlled or had agent responsibility for (e.g. she pursued a given risky option) *and* what she did not control or did not have agent responsibility for (e.g. the odds came out one way rather than another), while brute luck is the inverse of option luck. As these formulations suggest, option luck and brute luck can refer either to control or to agent responsibility. Thick luck can take the form of either brute luck or option luck. Thin luck stands in a complex conceptual relationship to option luck. On the one hand, option luck requires the presence of control or agent responsibility *for choices*, and where agent responsibility is present thin luck is by definition absent. On the other hand, option luck requires that agents lack full control over or full agent responsibility *for the causal mechanisms which shape the consequences of their choices*, and where agent responsibility is absent thin luck is by definition present. After all, there would be no question of luck if a fully agent responsible and controlling hustler not only tossed a coin, but also manipulated it in advance to ensure that it landed heads up. The relationship between brute luck and thin luck is simpler. Brute luck is either identical to thin luck (being the inverse of agent responsibility), or it is identical to the first form of thick luck canvassed above (being the inverse of control).

Given all these conceptual possibilities, it is worth emphasizing that many examples in the literature are vague about the exact sense in which the fictional persons described are or are not subject to luck. For instance, an aspect of a person's situation may be neither a matter of thick luck nor thin luck—that is, they may both have controlled events and have agent responsibility for them—and writers who want to press on with examining the appropriate consequential responsibility in such cases may legitimately bracket off the question of whether it is the absence of thin or thick luck that matters. It is nevertheless useful to notice that terms like thin luck and agent responsibility, thick luck and control, and brute luck and option luck can each have a specific meaning that potentially marks a difference in the assignment of consequential responsibility—in what people are due.[57]

Another concept that frames that of responsibility is the concept of desert. The two most straightforward ways in which the concepts of 'responsibility' and 'desert' relate is that agent responsibility can be thought to be one of the conditions for attributions of desert and/or desert can be thought to ground attributions of consequential responsibility. Regarding the first possibility, the thought here is that agent responsibility is a precondition for attributions of desert. On this conception of desert, a person can be

---

[57] Note also that moral and political philosophers do not usually base their distinctions on empirical claims. It may be an open question whether any particular conception of responsibility or luck can be attributed to anyone in the real world.

said to be deserving of say, a prize for rescuing someone only if she is agent responsible for rescuing him. Regarding the second, and related, possibility, some have argued that the burdens and benefits that people should be made to bear or enjoy are those that they deserve to bear or enjoy on a plausible theory of desert. In post-Rawlsian scholarship the idea that desert should dictate people's entitlements is not fashionable, but it persists and perhaps nowhere more visibly than in the debates over responsibility and distributive justice.[58] Two contributions to this volume provide qualified defences of that idea.

Carl Knight defends the view that desert can be thought to ground consequential responsibility more effectively than can agent (or, as Knight refers to it, basal) responsibility. He holds that desert can plausibly be construed as responding to both agent responsibility and certain weighty 'responsibility-independent considerations'—especially those concerning basic needs—and it therefore provides a better approximation of the demands of justice than do purely responsibility-sensitive accounts of justice.

Larry Temkin's chapter also addresses, among other things, the relationship between responsibility and desert. He presents a position he calls 'equality as comparative fairness', which focuses on how persons fare relative to one another, largely (but not entirely) in terms of comparative desert. Temkin suggests that focusing on comparative fairness appears to reveal several misunderstandings and ambiguities in the positions taken by egalitarians. For instance, comparative fairness rejects the alleged implication of luck egalitarianism that persons who become worse off than others through their own responsible choice, or through option luck, are always legitimately disadvantaged. Such inequalities are objectionable where they make equally deserving persons unequally well off, or unequally deserving persons well off disproportionately to their deserts—for instance, where a meritorious act of saving a drowning child leaves one relatively disadvantaged.[59]

The relationships between responsibility and ideas that, unlike luck and desert, are *not* closely connected to its various senses (but which are nevertheless crucial in debates about distributive justice), are also relevant here. For instance, understanding the specific roles of responsibility and welfare promotion in a writer's account of justice may be necessary for one to understand just what work responsibility is supposed to be doing. It would be unfair to complain that a particular responsibility-sensitive view showed no concern for efficiency, for example, were it the case that the view included a utilitarian principle as well as a responsibility-sensitive principle. Thus, although purely responsibility-sensitive views may appear uncompromising, in that they are typically construed as being solely backwards-looking, pluralistic views can include

---

[58] For recent discussion of desert and distributive justice see S. Olsaretti (ed.), *Desert and Justice* (Oxford: Oxford University Press, 2003).

[59] For further discussions of desert in this volume, see Richard J. Arneson's, Kasper Lippert-Rasmussen's, and Matt Matraver's chapters.

both backwards-looking and forwards-looking elements that together affect the role responsibility plays in such an account.

Leading luck egalitarians have argued for pluralistic accounts of distributive justice. On Temkin's view, a wide range of normative considerations—including humanitarian concerns with reducing pain and suffering, and prioritarian concerns with promoting the condition of the worse- or worst-off—should be taken into account in addition to concern with comparative fairness. In his chapter, Richard Arneson treats principles of sufficiency and priority as alternatives to standard (comparative) equality when it comes to selecting the egalitarian's 'maximizing function'. The maximizing function, taken together with the thing to be maximized (typically welfare, resources, or capabilities), constitutes the egalitarian component of luck egalitarianism. This is then combined with the 'luckism' component, which may be construed in terms of choice or desert. Arneson's typology demonstrates the wide range of normative concepts that can be accommodated by responsibility-sensitive *egalitarianism*, which in any case does not itself exhaust the possibilities for responsibility-sensitive *justice*.

2.3 Responsibility sensitivity and equality of opportunity

As has already been made apparent in section 1, arguments over responsibility sensitivity intersect with and can even take the form of arguments over the proper meaning of or the requirements of equality of opportunity. We want to flag up two important ways in which responsibility sensitivity relates to equality of opportunity.

The first issue is the extent to which equality of opportunity is a precondition for egalitarian responsibility sensitivity. The egalitarian credentials of responsibility-sensitive egalitarianism might be easiest to defend if it is assumed that equality of opportunity is a precondition for making people's entitlements responsibility-sensitive.[60] This would, however, as Avner de-Shalit and Jonathan Wolff observe in this volume, make responsibility sensitivity inapplicable in our world, in which equality of opportunity of the type envisaged by egalitarians is nowhere on the horizon. De-Shalit and Wolff go on to argue that limited responsibility sensitivity can be introduced even in the absence of equality of opportunity. This is clearly a normative problem, but it also poses difficulties for responsibility sensitivity as a viable policy and we return to this in section 2.5 of this 'Introduction'.

Second, there is the conceptual issue of when, if at all, requirements of responsibility sensitivity depart from the requirements of equality of opportunity. We want to mention three possibilities, but our list is not meant to be exhaustive.

The first possibility is that specifying what responsibility sensitivity requires is simply specifying what genuine equality of opportunity requires: nothing more and nothing less. This view is explicit or implied in the early luck egalitarianism of Arneson

---

[60]   Z. Stemplowska, 'Making Justice Sensitive to Responsibility', *Political Studies*, 57 (2009), 237–259.

and Cohen.[61] It would follow that theorists could appeal to the value of equal opportunity to justify responsibility sensitivity.

The second possibility is that egalitarian responsibility sensitivity is a specific version/subset of equality of opportunity. Advocating responsibility sensitivity therefore requires appealing to both the value of equality of opportunity and some other value(s). Both possibilities are explored in this volume by Zofia Stemplowska, who opts for this second understanding of the relationship between equality of opportunity and responsibility sensitivity. She then uses the argument to claim that there is much less of a conflict between luck egalitarians and democratic egalitarians (such as Anderson and Scheffler) over the virtues of responsibility sensitivity than the proponents of the debate seem to acknowledge.

The third possibility is that responsibility sensitivity conflicts with equality of opportunity. There are two possibilities here. First, equality of opportunity may be thought to require elimination of initial brute luck inequalities but not those that occur after the starting point, while responsibility sensitivity may be sensitive to such later brute luck. Second, responsibility sensitivity may not require equality of opportunity since unequal initial opportunities can be compensated for later. For instance, some may argue that there is no equality of opportunity unless people have an identical propensity to exert effort, but also hold that people are agent responsible for what they do on the basis of their differential propensity to exert effort and that entitlements ought to be (agent) responsibility-sensitive. Such a combination of views, or similar views, is perhaps most familiar from debates about punishment, when it is simultaneously asserted that, under certain conditions, people are responsible for and should be punished for the crimes they commit even though they did not have an equal opportunity to avoid committing such crimes because, say, they were raised in a hate-inspiring environment.

Fleurbaey, in his chapter, shows that it has been largely unacknowledged in the literature that there are four incompatible ways of structuring equal opportunities in order to achieve responsibility sensitivity. Proponents of responsibility sensitivity first need to decide if they want to conceive of it as a middle way between egalitarianism and libertarianism or as a middle way between egalitarianism and utilitarianism. In essence, they have to choose whether they want to neutralize inequalities due to factors for which people are not responsible, or make sure that there is a stable relationship between one's exercise of responsibility—for example through high effort—and one's outcome. Whichever of the two models they adopt, they will then face a further choice between privileging, to use Fleurbaey's vocabulary, compensation or reward. Fleurbaey goes on to show how such choices would translate into very different wage policies, thus illustrating the need to disambiguate and provide more specific defences of proposals aimed at responsibility sensitivity and/or equality of opportunity.

---

[61] Arneson, 'Equality and Equal Opportunity for Welfare'; Cohen, 'On the Currency of Egalitarian Justice'.

2.4 Collective responsibility

Discussions of responsibility and distributive justice have mostly proceeded by focusing on individual responsibility (in the way described above). As Kasper Lippert-Rasmussen observes in this volume, however, there can be collective as well as individual readings of the key proposals for how to make justice sensitive to responsibility. Specifically, he shows that once we look not only at individual but also collective responsibility we will notice that there are more versions of responsibility-sensitive egalitarianism than have been examined in the literature, and new normative questions emerge regarding the power of differential choices to justify disadvantages.

In general, debates about collective responsibility centre around three sets of questions. First, what does it mean to attribute responsibility (moral, legal, consequential, etc.) to groups? Do we ever attribute responsibility to groups or do we talk of collective responsibility as a convenient short cut for saying that we attribute responsibility to the individuals who make up the group? Second, what type of groups can be held collectively responsible? For example, must such groups be capable of agency or rationality? If so, which groups are capable of that? Can we, for example, attribute responsibility to groups that are not seen as persons in the light of the law or that do not even have formal decision structures? And third, what does it mean for individuals who are part of such groups that their group is seen as collectively responsible in some sense? This third question is the least explored in the literature on distributive justice and responsibility as well as in the literature on collective responsibility in its own right. It is taken up by Lippert-Rasmussen and by David Miller in this volume.

Focusing on collective responsibility, argues Lippert-Rasmussen, exposes hidden ambiguities in the standard formulations of luck egalitarianism. More importantly, it shows that individual responsibility has a less prominent role in egalitarian justice than is normally acknowledged: there are cases when it is not inegalitarian that an individual is worse off than others through no choice of her own and cases where it is inegalitarian that an individual is worse off than others through her own choices.

Miller's chapter does not take egalitarian justice as its starting point. His focus is on situations in which individuals share a collective responsibility for averting some anticipated harm, but some members of the group fail to do their fair share. Miller asks if this means that the remaining members of the group must now pick up the slack. His general answer is that they may have a humanitarian obligation to do so in certain cases. However, they do not have a duty of justice to do it. To deny this, according to Miller, would mean not being able to make sense of a fundamental distinction between 'primary' and 'secondary' responsibility for harm and the moral judgements that rest on it. But the argument also has wider significance for policy because, according to Miller, only duties of justice are more or less straightforwardly enforceable while the use of compulsion with regard to humanitarian obligations is problematic. It is to issues of policy that we turn next.

2.5 Implementing responsibility sensitivity

We stressed earlier that the philosophical debate over responsibility and distributive justice developed against the backdrop of political controversy in welfare state democracies over responsibility-sensitive policies, that is policies advocating conditionality (or so-called 'activation to work') in the provision of unemployment insurance and other welfare/social security benefits. And yet the implications for policy of the philosophical debate over making distributive justice sensitive to responsibility are not straightforward. Worries over adopting responsibility-sensitive policies point to the conceptual difficulties in settling on a robust concept of responsibility; the potential of conditionality to undermine the self-respect of those who are helped and those who are left behind as well as to undermine the more abstract ideals of equal moral worth and equal social status of every person; informational difficulties in gathering the type of information that would be needed to determine who is responsible for their (dis)advantage or to test whether a given system allows people to self-select into the right categories; and, to mention one more, the costliness of setting up the necessary administrative system. These worries are, of course, juxtaposed against the potential advantages of adopting responsibility-sensitive policies such as, for example, showing respect for those who made good use of their opportunities; making distributions track desert; and efficiency gains due to incentive effects of conditionality (assuming conditionality is not designed to be merely or predominantly punitive).

Of course, that the implications for policy design of the philosophical debate are not straightforward, even among those who agree on the fundamental normative principles in play, is in one sense unsurprising: philosophical debates are not policy debates. But the egalitarian debate over responsibility sensitivity faces a special difficulty; the persistent, if not always explicit, criticism is that it has next to no relevance at the level of policy. Deciding which choices should be seen as genuine, for example, may be philosophically interesting, the criticism goes, but the ever more sophisticated answers philosophers give cannot be taken on board with the crude policy tools and constraints on political feasibility that we face. After all, even the best brain scans will not tell us how truly free our choices are and, in any case, there are good reasons not to request visits to the hospital neurology wing from welfare claimants. Indeed, the key protagonists of responsibility sensitivity are themselves only too willing to acknowledge that the normative principles they recommend should not be seen as calls for conditionality in our very imperfect world.[62]

Nonetheless, there are two ways in which the recent debate over responsibility sensitivity seems especially relevant at the policy level, beyond the obvious fact that the debate can alert policy makers to the advantages and disadvantages of adopting responsibility-sensitive policies.

---

[62] R. J. Arneson, 'Egalitarianism and the Undeserving Poor', *Journal of Political Philosophy*, 5 (1997), 327–350; Cohen, 'Equality of What?'. For discussion over the degree of 'idealness' of the conditions that can be profitably assumed in debates over responsibility sensitivity see also Richard J. Arneson's, Norman Daniels's, Shlomi Segall's, and Avner de-Shalit and Jonathan Wolff's chapters in this volume.

First, perhaps ironically, the recent debate over responsibility sensitivity can be used to undermine a number of (at least nominally) responsibility-sensitive policies. This may seem surprising. Advocates of responsibility sensitivity such as welfare condition-ality and activation policies used to come from the conservative or libertarian camps. With prominent egalitarians attempting to show that responsibility sensitivity may be required by equality, such policies seem to gain inescapable momentum. Indeed, one of the claims often raised at conferences, if not in print, is that egalitarians are shooting themselves in the foot by placing such an emphasis on responsibility. For even if their calls for responsibility sensitivity are carefully worded and come only as part of a package of wider egalitarian reforms and preconditions, they seem to add momentum to responsibility-sensitive policies, if only because they can be taken out of context and used to justify welfare conditionality of the most brutal kind.[63] Nonetheless, making responsibility the focus of egalitarian thought has resulted in far greater awareness than before of the many assumptions and countless difficulties involved in attributing responsibility to people in a way that could justify withholding assistance from those in need. Having accepted responsibility sensitivity at the level of principle, luck egalitarians and their critics have shifted the debate over conditionality away from simple ideological disagreements towards debates that expose the controversial nature of the assumptions needed to justify attributions of responsibility. As a result, those who oppose responsibility sensitivity can no longer be dismissed with mere assertions that hard work, not laziness, should be rewarded. We now have a clearer sense than ever before of the many pitfalls involved in adopting responsibility sensitivity even if it is seen as desirable at some level. Some policies advertised as responsibility-sensitive can even be rejected because they in fact decrease the extent to which benefits are linked to responsibility properly construed.

Second, as a number of contributors to this volume emphasize, even if ideal responsibility-sensitive policies are beyond our reach due to informational and other difficulties, it might still be the case that some degree of responsibility sensitivity is necessary as a second-best policy within certain domains. De-Shalit and Wolff in their chapter explicitly ask what type of responsibility sensitivity, if any, would be feasible and acceptable in the non-ideal circumstances of the real world. They argue for what they call the 'weak asymmetry thesis'. According to this thesis people should be allowed to benefit from their choices that turn out well to a greater extent than they should have to bear the costs of those that turn out badly. They defend the thesis with reference to the overall positive effects of adopting such asymmetry and by rejecting arguments that such limited sensitivity to responsibility would be unfair to those who have to share some of the costs of choices that turn out badly.

One area of policy for which questions of responsibility seem especially pressing is health care. The health-care schemes of different nations and different US states can be

---

[63] See Wolff, 'Fairness, Respect and the Egalitarian Ethos', 112.

construed as drawing the line between those matters of health which are the responsi-bility of the individual, and those matters of health which are the responsibility of society, in different places—sometimes in *very* different places. While political phil-osophers can agree that some ways of assigning consequential responsibility in health are more likely to reflect agent responsibility than others, there is disagreement about whether agent responsibility should play a significant role in determining health-care access in the first place. Often this is played out as a dispute between luck egalitarianism and the account of distributive justice from which it draws much of its inspiration, Rawls's justice as fairness.

Shlomi Segall argues in this volume that Rawlsian 'fair equality of opportunity for health' is subject to two objections: first, it does not mandate treatment for genetically caused medical conditions; and second, it does mandate an equalization of health-care opportunities, even when unequal opportunities would be of benefit to everyone's health. Noting that standard luck egalitarianism is just as vulnerable to this second 'levelling down' objection, Segall proposes to (in the terms used earlier) replace its maximizing function of equality with a maximizing function of priority, creating a position that is concerned to promote the health of those who are not responsible for their low level of health and, among those, to give higher priority to those whose health is (even) worse.

Over many years Norman Daniels has developed a highly refined Rawlsian ap-proach to health and health care. In his chapter here he argues that society's responsi-bility to promote health is normatively primary. This primacy derives from the role health has in protecting opportunities of free and equal citizens, the protection of these (fair) opportunities being a key feature of Rawls's justice as fairness. A form of agent responsibility matters on Daniels's view, since it helps direct certain health promotion efforts (for example, 'safe sex' campaigns), but such responsibility is not the basis of society's obligations, as it would be under a luck egalitarian model. Daniels argues that that model harshly refuses treatment for those who are responsible for worsening their health, and also has no rationale for promoting health.

3. Outline of the volume

The volume opens with chapters by Arneson and Temkin that map the conceptual terrain of responsibility-sensitive justice. The following chapters by Fleurbaey, Lippert-Rasmussen, and Stemplowska focus in particular on competing interpretations of responsibility-sensitive egalitarianism while those by Matravers and Knight zoom in on the relationship between responsibility, justice, and desert. Vallentyne's chapter explores how the presence of false beliefs bears on the type of responsibility that is relevant to responsibility-sensitive egalitarianism. Hurley, and De-Shalit and Wolff, as well as Miller, focus on responsibility—understood in various ways—in non-ideal contexts. The volume concludes with two chapters, by Segall and Daniels, that examine the principle and policy of responsibility sensitivity as applied to health care.

1

Luck Egalitarianism—A Primer[1]

Richard J. Arneson

Karl Marx was a fierce critic of early capitalist market relations.[2] His characterization of these relations, as they were forming in the nineteenth century when he observed them or as they have matured in subsequent centuries, strikes many people as inaccurate. But few doubt that an economy that resembled his description of early capitalism would be unjust.[3] In that economy, some people are born into extreme poverty and never have a chance to experience a life of decent quality. These proletarians through no fault or choice of their own have no lucrative marketable skills and in order to stay alive must work long hours at brutally hard and unrewarding jobs for bare subsistence pay throughout their lives. Moreover, alterations of these conditions that would give everybody reasonably good life prospects are feasible.

Imagine that Marx's critique had been different. Imaginary Marx holds that capitalism is unjust because under this regime a group of persons, the proletarians★, though they begin life with inherited wealth and fortunate inheritance of genes for traits and immensely nurturing childhood experiences, somehow in their early adulthood years manage to squander all of these initial advantages through dissolute living and from then on are forced to work at rote boring jobs for subsistence pay in order to stay alive.

The imaginary Marxian critique I just sketched might make some sense. Maybe there is some unfairness in the plight of the proletarians★. Granted, they had initial opportunities, and second and third chances, but maybe everyone always deserves another chance for a better life. But the charm and simple intuitive moral appeal of

[1] I wrote this chapter while enjoying the hospitality of the Centre for Applied Philosophy and Public Ethics, Charles Sturt University (Australian National University location), as Visiting Professor, January–February 2007. I thank the Centre for a congenial working environment and UCSD, my home university, for sabbatical support. Thanks especially to Andrew Cohen and Andrew Star for excellent discussions. I discussed the chapter at Harvard Law School, the Murphy Institute at Tulane University, and workshops at the University of Melbourne, Australia, and at the University of Glasgow, Scotland. I thank the audiences and participants, especially Carl Knight and Steven Wall, for helpful comments.
[2] See K. Marx and F. Engels, 'Manifesto of the Communist Party' in Robert Tucker (ed.), *The Marx–Engels Reader*, second edition, (New York: W. W. Norton and Co., 1978), 469–500. Marx's full view on the topic appears in K. Marx, *Capital*, vol. 1.
[3] Allen Wood vigorously argues for (what is in effect) this claim in 'The Marxian Critique of Justice', *Philosophy and Public Affairs*, 1 (1972), 244–282.

Marx's critique of the condition of the proletarians disappear entirely when we imagine a parallel critique of the condition of their imaginary counterparts.[4]

In recent years several political philosophers have begun to articulate principles of social justice that combine egalitarianism and a personal responsibility ethic that holds that more favourable treatment is owed to proletarians than to proletarians*. Ronald Dworkin, G. A. Cohen, and John Roemer are prominent members of this group.[5] This family of views has come to be called 'luck egalitarianism'. This broad doctrine has attracted some estimable critics, who doubt that the luck egalitarian project is worth pursuing. The critics have tended to fasten on the 'luckism' component of the doctrine, but of course its egalitarianism is also controversial and stands in need of defence.[6]

---

[4] I do not mean to claim that Karl Marx was a luck egalitarian. He criticizes capitalism on the ground that its normal functioning requires exploitation, but one does not exploit another if one merely lets her alone, does nothing to her or for her. So perhaps Marx is best interpreted as what I call later in this chapter a 'social interactionist'. Also, Marx at least flirts with the idea that each person is the full rightful owner of herself and therefore ought to receive the 'full fruits of her labor'. The luck egalitarian opposes the self-ownership doctrine. On the exegesis of Marx regarding these issues, see G. A. Cohen, chs 5 and 6 of his *Self-Ownership, Freedom, and Equality* (Cambridge: Cambridge University Press, 1995). On the question what we should think on the issues, as distinguished from the question how we should interpret Marx, Cohen's entire book is also apt.

[5] R. Dworkin, *Sovereign Virtue: The Theory and Practice of Equality* (Cambridge, MA: Harvard University Press, 2000). This book includes versions of two seminal essays, 'What Is Equality? Part 1: Equality of Welfare', *Philosophy and Public Affairs*, 10 (1981), 185–246; and 'What Is Equality? Part 2: Equality of Resources', *Philosophy and Public Affairs*, 10 (1981), 283–345. See also G. A. Cohen, 'On the Currency of Egalitarian Justice', *Ethics*, 99 (1989), 906–944; also Cohen, *If You're an Egalitarian, How Come You're So Rich?* (Cambridge, MA: Harvard University Press, 2000). For Roemer's contributions, see J. E. Roemer, 'Equality of Talent', *Economics and Philosophy*, 1 (1985), 151–188; *Theories of Distributive Justice* (Cambridge, MA: Harvard University Press, 1996); *Equality of Opportunity* (Cambridge, MA: Harvard University Press, 1998). In this group I would also include Larry Temkin, author of *Equality* (Oxford: Oxford University Press, 1993) and the stage of Thomas Nagel that wrote *Equality and Partiality* (Oxford and New York: Oxford University Press, 1991). Other contributors include Richard Arneson, Eric Rakowski, Philippe van Parijs, Andrew Williams, Peter Vallentyne, Michael Otsuka, Kasper-Lippert Rasmussen, and Paula Casal. For Arneson's views, see his 'Equality and Equal Opportunity for Welfare', *Philosophical Studies*, 56 (1989), 77–93; 'Egalitarianism and the Undeserving Poor', *Journal of Political Philosophy*, 5 (1997), 327–350; 'Egalitarianism and Responsibility', *Journal of Ethics*, 3 (1999), 225–247; 'Perfectionism and Politics', *Ethics*, 111 (2000), 37–63; 'Why Justice Demands Transfers to Offset Income and Wealth Inequalities', *Social Philosophy and Policy*, 19 (2002), 172–200; 'Desert and Equality' in K. Lippert-Rasmussen and N. Holtug (eds), *Egalitarianism: New Essays on the Nature and Value of Equality* (Oxford: Oxford University Press, 2007), 262–293. See E. Rakowski, *Equal Justice* (Oxford: Oxford University Press, 1991); P. Van Parijs, *Real Freedom for All* (Oxford: Oxford University Press, 1995); M. Otsuka, *Libertarianism without Inequality* (New York and Oxford: Oxford University Press, 2006); A. Williams, 'Equality for the Ambitious', *Philosophical Quarterly*, 52 (2002), 377–389; A. Williams and P. Casal, 'Equality of Resources and Distributive Justice' in J. Burley (ed.), *Ronald Dworkin and His Critics* (Oxford: Basil Blackwell, 2004), 150–169; P. Vallentyne, 'Brute Luck, Option Luck, and Equality of Initial Opportunities', *Ethics*, 112 (2002), 529–557; and K. Lippert-Rasmussen, 'Equality, Option Luck, and Responsibility', *Ethics*, 111 (2001), 548–579.

[6] Critics include M. Fleurbaey, 'Equal Opportunity or Equal Social Outcome?', *Economics and Philosophy*, 11 (1995), 22–55; J. Wolff, 'Fairness, Respect, and the Egalitarian Ethos', *Philosophy and Public Affairs*, 27 (1998), 97–122; E. S. Anderson, 'What Is the Point of Equality?', *Ethics*, 109 (1999), 287–337; S. Scheffler, 'What Is Egalitarianism?', *Philosophy and Public Affairs*, 31 (2003), 5–39; 'Choice, Circumstance, and the Value of Equality', *Philosophy, Politics, and Economics*, 4 (2005), 5–28; S. Hurley, *Justice, Luck, and Knowledge* (Cambridge, MA: Harvard University Press, 2003).

This chapter surveys varieties of the luck egalitarian project in an exploratory spirit, seeking to identify lines of thought that are worth developing further and that might ultimately prove morally acceptable. I do not attend directly to the critics and assess their concerns; I have done that in other essays.[7] I do seek to identify some large fault lines, divisions in ways of approaching the task of constructing a theory of justice or of conceiving its substance. These are controversial in the sense that in the present state of discussion it is unclear how best to view them or to which side it is better to scramble.

1.1 Preliminaries

First, a preliminary clarification. The reader might be forgiven for wondering what could be controversial about allowing room for responsibility within the theory of social justice. Who would disagree? To see that there is room for controversy, distinguish treating personal responsibility as intrinsically or as instrumentally significant. Tomorrow, all of us might decide that responsibility is not intrinsically significant, perhaps because we all become convinced that what we call human actions are caused events, that occur according to probabilistic or deterministic physical laws, and that thinking through what this signifies, we conclude that if actions are events, they can't be actions as we ordinarily conceive them—choices for which one can be responsible. We might reasonably take this line, roughly the line of hard determinism. Adopting this view would not in the least threaten to subvert the vast mass of our responsibility practices. In myriad institutional contexts we hold people responsible for the good or bad outcomes of their choices by attaching negative and positive sanctions, punishments and rewards, to them. An instrumental justification of this host of practices is available. Holding people responsible in these ways improves the future, contributes to the promotion of goals we want to achieve, and, if the goals are morally sound, contributes to the cause of morality. Negotiation, criticism, and reform at the margins of these practices may be salutary, but no one proposes scrapping the lot.[8]

In contrast, holding that the fulfilment of some norm of responsibility is intrinsically morally valuable is controversial. Look back to the counterpart proletarian. We might

[7] R. J. Arneson, 'Luck Egalitarianism Interpreted and Defended', *Philosophical Topics* (Spring and Fall, 2004) [actually published in Fall, 2006], 1–20; 'Luck and Equality', *Proceedings of the Aristotelian Society*, Supplementary Volume, 75 (2001), 73–90; 'Luck Egalitarianism and Prioritarianism', *Ethics*, 110 (2000), 339–349; 'Equal Opportunity for Welfare Defended and Recanted', *Journal of Political Philosophy*, 7 (1999), 488–497.

[8] For a statement of the difficulty involved in conceiving human actions as caused events, and the unavoidability of conceiving them in just that way, see T. Nagel, 'Moral Luck', reprinted in his collection, *Mortal Questions* (Cambridge: Cambridge University Press, 1979) 24–48. On viewing responsibility as instrumental, see J. J. C. Smart, 'Free-will, Praise, and Blame', *Mind*, 70 (1960), 291–306; also M. Vargas, 'The Revisionist's Guide to Responsibility', *Philosophical Studies*, 125 (2005), 399–429; also Vargas's contribution to J. Fischer, J. Kane, D. Pereboom, and M. Vargas, *Four Views on Free Will* (Oxford: Basil Blackwell, 2007), 126–165; and R. J. Arneson, 'The Smart Theory of Responsibility and Desert' in S. Olsaretti (ed.), *Desert and Justice* (Oxford: Oxford University Press, 2003), 233–258.

justify high taxes on hard liquor and other commodities useful for dissolute living, vagrancy laws, subsidies for adult education and drug rehabilitation programmes, on the grounds that by some appropriate measure, the benefits to be gained exceed the costs. We improve the future by seeking to 'reward' the responsible and 'punish' the irresponsible in these ways. Alternatively, we might dispense with the scare quotes in these phrases and hold it is intrinsically more valuable to improve the lives of the saints and heroes by a certain amount than it would be to bring about an identical gain for the sinners and scoundrels. Those who behave responsibly intrinsically merit policies that provide them better lives than those who behave irresponsibly. This moralism is controversial.

The term 'responsibility' is used in different ways to express different ideas. When someone is appalled by the inclusion of responsibility norms into the theory of justice and someone else is horrified by the possibility of their exclusion, they might be talking past each other. Some explanation of terms is needed.

In one sense, responsibilities are obligations or duties. As a parent, one has responsibilities to care for one's own child. Saying someone is a responsible person sometimes conveys that the person reliably fulfils her obligations and duties. Saying someone is a responsible person can also convey something quite different: that the person has the normal human capacities for choice and agency, so that she is, apart from special excuses or justifications that may apply, apt for assessment in the light of the good or bad quality of her choices and actions.[9] In this sense a dog and a human infant are not responsible; a normal adult human is. Saying someone is responsible for some outcome may just mean she caused it but may also be used to convey the further thought that since she, a responsible agent, did this thing, leading to this outcome, she is apt for assessment depending on its quality. Saying someone is responsible for the outcomes of her choices and actions may also be used to convey the different thought that it is appropriate (given her choices and the social environment in which choice occurs) that she bear the costs of these actions whether they fall on herself or on others. In a like vein, saying one is responsible for taking care of one's own needs may convey the thought, not that one is obligated to take care of one's own needs, but that no one else has obligations to make good any shortfall in need fulfilment that results from one's self-affecting actions. The different usages of the term are somewhat ordered, not just a random heap, but still, amidst the plethora of meanings of the term, talk of 'responsibility' can breed confusion.[10]

---

[9] See the distinction between 'attributive responsibility' and 'substantive responsibility' in T. M. Scanlon, *What We Owe to Each Other* (Cambridge, MA: Harvard University Press, 1998).

[10] Susan Hurley argues that luck egalitarianism founders on its advocates' confusions about the concept of responsibility in her *Justice, Luck, and Knowledge*. For replies, see Arneson, 'Luck and Equality'; also K. Lippert-Rasmussen, 'Hurley on Egalitarianism and the Luck-Neutralizing Aim', *Politics, Philosophy, and Economics*, 4 (2005), 219–265.

1.2 Two faces of personal responsibility

The personal responsibility issue as framed by luck egalitarians faces in two directions. Looking one way, the doctrine is a response to conservative critics of the welfare state and egalitarian redistributive policies who assert that they erode personal responsibility, reward the undeserving, and punish the deserving.[11] The luck egalitarian response in brief is that the question of what it is fair to hold an individual responsible for admits of coarse-grained answers which assess behaviour as meeting or failing to meet a standard of conduct. Such coarse-grained standards may in some contexts be appropriate components of sensible, administrable social policies. But at a fundamental moral level, a more fine-grained approach to the questions of personal responsibility is far more compelling. On the fine-grained approach, one looks not just at whether or not the individual met a given standard of behaviour but at the degree to which the individual's talents and capacities and the myriad background factors operating on the pertinent choice of conduct substantially modify the coarse-grained assessment whether by hardening or softening it. Most often, the fine-grained approach leads to softening judgements at least for the types of undesirable behaviours that are the concern of political conservatives.

Oriented toward academic political philosophy debates, the luck egalitarian line on personal responsibility is first and foremost a reaction against the desert-eschewing core of John Rawls's influential and powerful theory of justice.[12] In particular, attention has focused on Rawls's formulation of the difference principle, which affirms that inequalities in the distribution of social and economic benefits other than basic liberties are just only if they work to maximize the benefit level of the least advantaged members of society. (Inequalities to be just must also satisfy a stringent equality of opportunity principle stronger than the traditional liberal principle of careers open to talents.) Rawls was somewhat undecided about how to define the worst-off group in society for the purposes of applying the difference principle, but one formulation he suggests is that the worst-off are those whose yearly income is less than one half of the median. The suggestion appeared to be that in the just economy institutions and practices are set to maximize the income of those whose income is well below the median regardless of the characteristics of this group such as their labour force attachment.[13] On the face

---

[11] See C. Murray, *Losing Ground: American Social Policy 1950–1980* (New York: Basic Books, 1984). In *Rethinking Social Policy: Race, Poverty, and the Underclass* (Cambridge, MA: Harvard University Press, 1992), C. Jencks concedes considerable ground to Murray on the failure of state intervention in the US in the 1960s and 1970s to hold recipients of state aid to standards of behaviour viewed as morally right to impose coercively. For a recent sophisticated development of Murray's theme, see David Schmidtz's contribution to R. E. Goodin and D. Schmidtz (eds), *Social Welfare and Individual Responsibility* (Cambridge: Cambridge University Press, 1998), 1–96.

[12] J. Rawls, *A Theory of Justice*, revised edition (Cambridge, MA: Harvard University Press, 1999) [originally published 1971].

[13] For an interpretation of Rawls on this topic that opposes the suggestion in the text, see P. Van Parijs, 'Difference Principles' in S. Freeman (ed.), *The Cambridge Companion to Rawls* (Cambridge: Cambridge University Press, 2003), 200–240. In 'The Priority of Right and Ideas of the Good', *Philosophy and Public*

of it, the Rawlsian worst-off group looks to be morally heterogeneous. It includes some people whose plight intuitively merits a great deal of consideration and other people whose plight should elicit less than that. When I first read *A Theory of Justice*, it struck me as odd that the basic distributive justice norm called for maximizing the income and other basic resources of a group of people that includes the Alfred Doolittles of the world—Doolittle being a working-class sage and self-declared representative of the undeserving poor, a scrounger who tries to sell the sexual services of his daughter to Henry Higgins upon noticing that this gentleman is showing some interest in her. He is a character in G. B. Shaw's play *Pygmalion*.[14] Something is wrong, was my initial response. Luck egalitarianism tries to elaborate this thinking.

The two faces of luck egalitarian personal responsibility are not necessarily inconsistent but they are definitely in tension with one another. Picture the luck egalitarian saying to the social conservative that denying the provision of welfare state benefits to the likes of Alfred Doolittle is probably unjust all things considered, because (1) it is hard and maybe too costly in practice to identify the truly undeserving and deserving poor and accord different treatment to each, (2) any negative assessment attaching to an Alfred Doolittle type may be significantly mitigated and even entirely compromised by further investigation that reveals any of a number of background causal factors that make it difficult, painful, and costly for that particular individual to conform to social duties and norms of prudence, and (3) even if the Doolittle character can be shown to be genuinely responsible for bad conduct that dampens his claim to aid from the rest of us, offering him a helping hand may still be morally required all things considered, taking into account the great well-being gains that further provision of aid to him can bring about and his low lifetime well-being prospects, which trigger egalitarian/prioritarian priority for the project of bringing about improvement in his lifetime well-being.

Then the luck egalitarian turns around and says to a follower of John Rawls that the difference principle and other justice principles you embrace imply that the economy of a just society should be set so that the long-run income (and other social benefits) accruing to the least advantaged class should be maximized. But this class includes undeserving types like Alfred Doolittle along with prudent virtuous people in need. Your theory is unresponsive to this factor and denies that it is morally better as a matter of justice to benefit the deserving in preference to the undeserving. In the same vein, when it comes to paying for policies that benefit the worst-off, your favoured theory of justice does not register any difference between a taxpayer's financial holdings earned

---

Affairs, 17 (1988), 251–276, John Rawls suggests that one might hold that voluntarily unemployed persons have extra leisure, compared with the employed, that should result in their being considered to have more of primary social goods overall than the employed who work at lowest-paying jobs.

[14] G. B. Shaw, *Pygmalion*. Doolittle actually thinks he notices that Henry Higgins and his daughter Eliza are romantically involved or on the verge of that, assumes Higgins is sensitive to the peer pressure of respectable bourgeois opinion, and tries to extort money from him. The implicit threat is that unless Higgins pays, Doolittle will publicize the fact that Higgins and Eliza are involved.

by hard work and entrepreneurial energy, on the one hand, and holdings that just fall on people by sheer good luck on the other.[15] In both directions your theory gives short shrift to considerations of desert and is deeply defective for this reason.

Again, I don't say the objections against the social conservative advanced by the luck egalitarian must undermine her objections against Rawls's neglect of desert in his theory of justice. The discussion with the social conservative is conducted at the level of policy and the discussion with Rawls is conducted at the level of fundamental principle, and these levels of discourse are different, though connected.[16]

But at the very least the luck egalitarian's theoretical quarrel with Rawls on the topic of desert turns out not to issue in obvious large differences in the social policy recommendations the luck egalitarian as opposed to the Rawlsian is committed to endorsing. On this subject the dispute has the other-worldly quality of a tempest in a teapot.[17]

The luck egalitarian has two strategies available in response to the 'tempest in a teapot' difficulty. She might adopt what I am calling a coarse-grained account of responsibility and desert or something close to it and insist that the view has clear policy implications, so the theoretical quarrel with Rawls is not purely academic. This response involves conceding ground to the social conservative. (Critics of luck egalitarianism tend to presuppose that the doctrine must go in this direction and that following this path is morally and politically misguided.)

Alternatively the luck egalitarian might insist on affirming fine-grained conceptions of responsibility and desert. The rough idea here is that given that one has failed to conform one's behaviour to a social standard, and that the extent of this failure to conform partly determines one's social justice duties and entitlements, what matters ultimately is not just that one's behaviour misses the mark but the degree to which it is reasonable to hold one fully responsible for this behaviour in the light of the full set of mitigating and aggravating circumstances. Here it is not reasonable to hold a person responsible for what lies beyond her power to control and a further companion principle also conditions responsibility assessments: given all the past and present causal

---

[15] It might be possible to tax the one type of income but not the other without altering incentives in undesirable ways (very much), and so the difference would then register in a Rawlsian office of tax planning. But the advocate of desert-catering principles of justice holds the difference should matter even if it does not influence the proper calculation of Rawlsian tax planners.

[16] The dispute may also come to centre on the question, what level of abstraction is the appropriate one for formulating a theory of justice. Some may hold that a theory of justice consists of public rules. The rules must be public in that they are understandable by all members of society and learnable by anyone who applies herself to the task, feasibly administrable or implementable, and such that members of society can check that others are complying or not complying with the rules. Others may hold that some fundamental moral principles are not suited to be public rules in one or more of these three senses, but are fundamental moral principles nonetheless, and should serve as the standard against which feasible implementable conceptions of justice should be assessed.

[17] The statement in the text relies on a tired cliché to make its point. An even more stylistically atrocious formulation is available: the luck egalitarian finds no chocolate cake waiting for her at the end of her dispute with Rawls on desert.

factors that press on one's choice in question and render it more or less difficult or easy, painful or pleasant, costly or advantageous to do what is right as one sees it at the time of decision, one thereby becomes more or less blameworthy if one does wrong and more or less praiseworthy if one does right. On the fine-grained view, two serial axe murderers who committed identical murders might vary greatly in the degree to which each is truly responsible for his bad deed, and in principle my slightly faulty conduct might be amplified in its blameworthiness by serious aggravating factors, so that my blameworthiness for kicking the dog might exceed the blameworthiness that attaches to the axe murderer for a heinous crime.

But this line of thought is exactly the line of thought that leads Rawls to say that since true merit, desert, and the like, even if we could agree on the right standard to employ, are in practice beyond our capacity to measure accurately for purposes of public policy, we must eschew the attempt and drop notions of moral worth and true deservingness from fundamental principles of justice.[18]

The luck egalitarian can deny that the formulation of fundamental principles of morality should be conditioned on such facts as what we can implement in public policy with current administrative technologies. Moral principles are universal truths valid in all possible worlds. Hence in our quest for true principles, a single compelling description of a logically possible counterexample defeats the proposed theory. At the level of policy, things are different. Policies are devices for fulfilling correct moral principles to the maximum feasible extent. One defeats a proposed policy not with a counterexample but by proposing an alternative policy that better advances the ensemble of our moral goals properly weighted. Taking Rawls to be in the business of propounding a fundamental moral theory, the Alfred Doolittle counterexample stands. One should not deny the intellectual interest and integrity of pure moral theory, whether or not one can here and now draw practical recommendations for conduct and policy from the pure principle one has the strongest theoretical reasons to accept.

At this point the debate becomes at least in part a debate about the proper level of abstraction on which to conduct the theory of social justice. There is also a danger that the antagonists will in part be talking past one another—one objecting on policy grounds to what another is advancing as pure theory, another objecting on pure theory grounds to what another is proposing only as good public policy.[19]

The luck egalitarian might also deny that her line on responsibility and desert, incorporating a fine-grained account of responsibility, has no policy implications that conflict with Rawls's approach. In my opinion this denial would be correct. However, the issue is tricky. Suppose one says that in the absence of people's differential responsibility for viciously imprudent conduct—failure to seek and hold gainful employment, for example—social policy should bring it about that among able-bodied persons, those with strong labour force attachment do better than those with weak

---

[18] Rawls, *A Theory of Justice*, revised edition, 64 and 274.
[19] Cf. Avner de-Shalit and Jonathan Wolff's chapter in this volume, section 10.3.

labour force attachment. However, degree of labour force attachment might not be a good statistical proxy for true desert. If we roughly identify desert with conscientious-ness, trying to orient one's will towards what is right and good, we must straightaway acknowledge the existence of subtle handicaps, so that even if one person registers as more conscientious than another, we should allow the possibility that with a proper adjustment for differential inner obstacles to becoming conscientious, the person who is overtly more conscientious would earn a lower properly adjusted score than the person who is overtly less conscientious.

The trick would be to find situations in which one is able confidently to hold that the fine-grained considerations (that threaten to render all personal deservingness assessments moot and undecidable) either cancel one another out, weigh decisively in one direction, or do not rise to the level of significance at which they begin to unseat coarse-grained judgements. Below I describe some toy examples (not intended even as a preliminary sketch of serious policy proposals) to illustrate how this might go.

1.2.1 Overuse of antibiotics by well-off people[20]

Consider the current threat that virulent forms of bacterial infectious disease resistant to antibiotic therapies might develop and pose large-scale health threats. The problem has many facets, but one significant one is that affluent consumers in wealthy countries overuse antibiotics. They pressure their doctors to prescribe antibiotics when they are inappropriate (e.g. for what is probably viral infection), or when their use is dubious (e.g. for bacterial infections overwhelmingly likely to clear up without the administra-tion of antibiotics). They also fail to follow through with complete antibiotic doses prescribed, and save a few pills to self-medicate when what strikes them as the same problem recurs. Affluent consumers in advanced countries also arguably passively tolerate, when they could effectively oppose, current pricing policies that make antibiotics in poor countries so expensive for poor people that underutilization there also seriously risks the development of resistant bacteria. The empirical facts here are not entirely clear, but just suppose the behaviours described pose serious threats by way of increasing the likelihood that antibiotic-resistant forms of disease will develop. A public health campaign can make affluent consumers aware of the problem if they are responsibly attentive. In that setting an array of public policies might mitigate the problem—for example, including changing the law to insulate doctors from legal liability when they decline to prescribe demanded antibiotics to their patients, even when the prescription might do some good for the patient, but at too great an expected cost to others. The justification for such policies includes the consideration that on the whole and on the average, the health costs to affluent consumers who would lose out as a predictable effect of these measures should be discounted to some extent because in

---

[20] I borrow this example and the analysis of it from M. J. Selgelid, 'Ethics and Drug Resistance', *Bioethics*, 21 (2007), 1–12; see also Selgelid, 'Ethics and Infectious Disease', *Bioethics*, 19 (2005), 272–289.

the situation the affluent consumers are behaving badly and in this respect morally undeserving.[21]

1.2.2 Excessive health care resources showered on affluent consumers in the last six months of their lives

Suppose that one could devise a programme that reduces the health-care costs incurred by aged affluent consumers during the last six months of their lives, captures some of the savings, and divert it to health care and elementary education for the poor in poor countries. One might devise tax policies that apply higher tax rates to the estates of people who, having already lived to a ripe old age, insist on expensive medical interventions with very slight prospect of significant benefit at what reasonable observers would perceive to be the end of their lives. Again, a part of the justification of such policies, perhaps tipping the scale towards adopting them if other considerations are finely balanced or uncertain, is that the aged affluent medical consumers who behave this way at the end of their lives are, again on the whole and on the average, behaving in a selfish and feckless fashion and hence their interests should be correspondingly discounted in public policy formation owing to their negative deservingness.

1.2.3 Drunk driving

Inebriated drivers cause a disproportionate percentage of serious car accidents and car accident fatalities. Any number of subtle factors can influence the decision to drive drunk, and render it more or less blameworthy. But the extent to which an excuse lessens blame depends on what is at stake. (The difficulty I have controlling my reaction to my wife's clever sarcastic quips at my expense may sometimes excuse a counterquip but not a murderous attack against her.) We might hold that the relevant facts about drunk driving are so well known and embedded in the culture that the act is for ordinary problem drinkers virtually never excusable. A public policy that works to lessen the inconvenience for stranded drunks in need of transportation, effectively bans from the roadway those so deeply in the grip of alcoholism that their responsibility in this matter is impaired, and imposes serious informal and formal penalties on all other drunk drivers might be justified, in part, by the fact that this behaviour is almost always significantly morally blameworthy. In balancing opposed interests of drunken drivers and everybody else, the state is not impartially neutral, but tilts against the undeserving in its calculations.[22]

---

[21] There is an issue as to whether deservingness should be assessed situation by situation or over the person's life as a whole. Perhaps administrable policies will be responsive only to situational, local deservingness, but from the standpoint of fundamental theory what should matter is each person's lifetime deservingness.

[22] For a discussion that complements and supports the line of thought in the text, see B. Steinbock, 'Drunk Driving', *Philosophy and Public Affairs*, 14 (1985), 278–295. For a contrary view, see D. Husak, 'Is Drunk Driving a Serious Offense?', *Philosophy and Public Affairs*, 23 (1994), 52–73.

1.3 Desert and choice

To this point I have described the luck egalitarian position as though it consisted of some form of egalitarianism modified by responsiveness to desert. Justice should favour the deserving. This is not how the doctrine is standardly portrayed. A more common summary formulation is that distributive justice according to the luck egalitarian requires that unchosen or uncourted inequalities be undone and that chosen or courted equalities should be let alone. Ronald Dworkin distinguishes between option luck and brute luck: 'Option luck is a matter of how deliberate and calculated gambles turn out—whether someone gains or loses through accepting an isolated risk he or she should have anticipated and might have declined. Brute luck is a matter of how risks fall out that are not in that sense deliberate gambles.'[23] Dworkin's slogan is that his equality of resources doctrine requires initial equal division of resources, one's initial endowment of resources being viewed as having the quality of brute luck, and from then on no social tinkering with the results of option luck but full compensation for brute luck misfortune (and full expropriation of brute luck resource windfalls).[24] He presupposes here a fair (equal) initial distribution of resources among the members of a society, and a setting in which people are free to interact as they choose provided they abstain from imposing certain costs of their behaviour onto non-consenting others (as when my careless driving causes my car to bump yours in traffic or my factory smokestack emits pollution that befouls your lungs).

In this view, the luck egalitarian distinguishes brute and option luck. You own the effects of your option luck, in familiar ways. If you decide to take an umbrella to the picnic and it rains, you enjoy the good fortune of being able to keep yourself dry. In contrast, the brute luck good and bad fortune that falls on you, does not belong to you—there is no moral presumption that the fortune should stick to the person on whom it has fallen. The line between brute and option luck does not neatly coincide with the line between what results from a person's substantially voluntary choices and substantially non-voluntary choices. Negligence and carelessness can render unanticipated bad effects yours as though you had voluntarily chosen them or chosen to risk them. I don't intentionally fail to notice the slippery spot on the pavement while running pell-mell down the street, but if the risk is one I should have anticipated and might have declined, it falls on the side of option luck as Dworkin characterizes it.

---

[23] Dworkin, *Sovereign Virtue*, 73.

[24] The text discusses Dworkin's 1981 views. His later writings move towards a view that identifies just distribution with policies that mimic the results of what people of average preferences and ambitions would choose in hypothetical insurance markets proceeding from fair (equal) initial conditions. See especially chapters 8 and 9 of *Sovereign Virtue*. For criticism of the hypothetical market approach as Dworkin develops it, see M. Otsuka, 'Liberty, Equality, Envy, and Abstraction' in Justine Burley (ed.), *Ronald Dworkin and His Critics* (Oxford: Basil Blackwell, 2004), 70–79; 'Luck, Insurance, and Equality', *Ethics*, 113 (2002), 40–54; J. E. Roemer, 'Egalitarianism Against the Veil of Ignorance', *Journal of Philosophy*, 99 (2002), 167–184; and M. Fleurbaey, 'Equality of Resources Revisited', *Ethics*, 113 (2002), 82–105; *Fairness, Responsibility, and Welfare* (Oxford: Oxford University Press), 2008.

Along the same line, I suppose a misinformed choice can count as giving rise to option luck, if I am culpable for being misinformed, perhaps also if the misinformation comes to me as the predictable result of a fully voluntary considered choice of mine—I am really in a hurry so reasonably forego reading today's newspaper. Choices can be more or less voluntary along several different dimensions of voluntariness, and negligence also varies by degree. Simplifying by supposing we know how to combine the scores on these various dimensions into an overall judgement, we might think of choices that an individual makes and behaviours undertaken ranging from zero to one in the degree to which they manifest option luck.

Call the view of personal responsibility for the theory of just distribution described in the previous paragraph the 'Choice' view. Choice can be contrasted with Desert.

Suppose that so far as the egalitarian component of luck egalitarianism is concerned (more on this in the next section), there is a justice reason to bestow benefits on needy Smith or take away benefits from Jones in order to use them to provide benefits for needy Smith. The luckism component of luck egalitarianism asserts that this justice reason is dampened (weakened), depending on the degree to which either:

1. *Choice*. One or both of Smith and Jones have arrived at their present condition via option luck not brute luck processes.

or

2. *Desert*. Smith has behaved in ways that qualify her as undeserving and/or Jones has behaved in ways that qualify her as deserving. (If Smith has behaved in ways that qualify her as deserving, or if Jones has behaved in ways that qualify her as undeserving, the case for transfer would be correspondingly strengthened.)

A test case for deciding between Choice and Desert is voluntary do-goodism. Suppose Sally and Harry up to this point have been fairly treated according to distributive justice norms. Say their resource holdings are fair. Then they both have an opportunity to do some great good deed that let us assume is clearly not morally required but is clearly very virtuous and admirable. Suppose that in the manner of Mother Teresa[25] Sally devotes her life and fortune to the poor of Calcutta. There is no great fulfilment or personal pay-off for her; she is just licking stamps for a good cause. (If doing this were morally required, we might then view her choice as forced and not fully voluntary and so not clearly giving rise to option luck.) Harry has the same opportunity to do good but declines it and behaves with impeccable bourgeois prudence. Sally ends up badly off and Harry ends up well off. According to Desert, there is now a justice reason to bring it about that Sally becomes better off, in view of her high level of deservingness (I assume that the deservingness standard yields this

---

[25] The assumption being made here is that the conventional assessment of Mother Teresa's character is correct. For a dissenting view, see C. Hitchens, *The Missionary Position: Mother Teresa in Theory and Practice* (London and New York: Verso, 1995).

result[26]). Putting it another way, if one's egalitarianism says there is reason to aid Sally, her desert strengthens the case for coming to her aid. According to Choice, no such strengthening reason exists. From initial fair equality Sally and Harry have moved via pure option luck processes to a new distribution. If your preferred version of egalitarianism says there is an egalitarian reason to boost Sally's current condition, Choice says this reason is weakened or dampened by the fact that the inequality here has arisen in impeccable option luck fashion.

1.4 Varieties of egalitarianism

In luck egalitarianism the personal responsibility or luckism component combines with some form of egalitarian commitment. What version of egalitarianism is most reasonable?[27]

We can separate the egalitarian ideal into two elements: a view about how to measure or assess people's condition for the purposes of applying the egalitarianism principle, and a view about the nature of the maximizing function to which our egalitarianism commits us. The two elements clearly interact, so in deciding which to choose we have to consider the whole package of elements and its overall appeal. (The same is true for luckism and egalitarianism; to give the theory a run for its money we need to find the total package of elements that is overall most appealing.)

A simple example of interaction effects: one objection to opting for equality of welfare or equal opportunity for welfare as our egalitarian ideal is that taken by itself the demand to equalize welfare predictably will result in extreme redistribution policies in plausible circumstances. Suppose there are severely disadvantaged or disabled people who will be unavoidably far below the average level of welfare whatever we do, but whose welfare increases continuously ever so slightly as greater and greater sums of resources are applied to them. The disabled so conceived happen to be poor transformers of resources into welfare. Predictably then on any plausible interpersonal standard for measuring welfare, this norm recommends that justice requires ever more resource transfers that lower the average and aggregate welfare levels in society to exceedingly low levels. If we find this counter-intuitive, these views must be rejected, but it does not follow that welfare should not be the measure of people's condition for the theory of justice. Perhaps the problem lies in opting for *equality* of welfare.

1.4.1 What maximizing function?

I simply list three principles that might give content to egalitarianism's maximizing function.

---

[26] I discuss how a luck egalitarian should conceive desert in 'Desert and Equality'.

[27] See D. McKerlie, 'Equality and Time', *Ethics*, 99 (1989), 475–491; 'Justice Between the Young and the Old', *Philosophy and Public Affairs*, 30 (2002), 152–177.

1. *Sufficiency.* Maximize the extent to which all persons attain a decent or good enough quality of life.
2. *Equality.* Maximize the extent to which the quality of life enjoyed by every person is the same (or stays within a certain allowable range).
3. *Priority.* Maximize the aggregate of benefit (good quality of life) of all persons with extra weight given to achieving gains and avoiding losses for the worse-off, as follows. The moral value of gaining a benefit for a person is greater, the greater the size of the benefit, and greater, the worse off in benefit level in absolute terms she would be over the course of her life absent this benefit.

Regarding sufficiency, one problem is to determine how non-arbitrarily one might fix the good enough or decent quality of life, the threshold that justice strives above all to bring it about that as many as possible reach.[28] Dworkin expresses scepticism that this problem admits of solution. He remarks that once we identify justice with enabling everyone to attain some decent minimum standard of living, 'then too much is allowed to turn on the essentially subjective question of how minimum a standard is decent'.[29] That seems unfair. As I have characterized the luck egalitarian doctrine, at many points in order to arrive at a determinate principle, we would have to assign determinate weights to factors the rough preliminary theory tells us must be integrated but without specifying exactly how. So the type of exercise about which Dworkin is sceptical is going to be needed in any event, even just to fill out and complete Dworkin's own view (for example, by weighting the components of voluntariness to give a determinate conception of option luck).

A related doubt troubles me, however. For practical policy purposes we might decide on a good enough level, a poverty level of resources, for example. Such contingencies as the present level of wealth and the need for saving for future generations may help fix the reasonable poverty line for a time. Policies need clear cut-offs and thresholds, rigid lines. But the underlying considerations we care about seem ineluctably scalar, so one would think fundamental moral principle should reflect this underlying moral fact. There are just different levels of welfare, higher being better.

Regarding equality, the pros and cons are well known. Some doubt that it is per se morally important that everyone have the same in any respect, or indeed that how one person's condition compares with another's per se matters from the moral perspective.[30] This doubt is for some strengthened when one asks, among whom should equality obtain? There does not seem to be a principled reason for scope limitation, so equality then should obtain across all people, all rational agents past, present, and future

---

[28] One might wonder why sufficiency is being considered as an interpretation of egalitarianism. See A. K. Sen, 'Equality of What?', which suggests that one might construe the ideal of distributive equality as basic capability equality. This is a sufficientarian view. Sen's essay, originally published in 1980, is reprinted in Sen, *Choice, Welfare, and Measurement* (Cambridge, MA: MIT Press, 1982), 353–369.

[29] Dworkin, *Sovereign Virtue*, 3.

[30] Harry Frankfurt gives forceful expression to this view in 'Equality as a Moral Ideal', *Ethics*, 98 (1987), 21–43.

anywhere in the universe. If we suspect equality appeals because equality (or better, limited inequality) in a small group tends perhaps to foster solidarity and community and other goods enjoyed by group members, then thinking about the imperative of equality unlimited in scope makes plain its lack of intrinsic appeal. But others disagree.

Regarding priority, one should note that it contains an apparent appeal that one quickly realizes is illusory or at best promissory. Priority conveys the idea of a single principle that combines two fundamentally important moral values—the value of maximizing the total amount of good in people's lives and a concern for fair distribution of the sum of good, here understood as a tilt toward boosting the welfare of those with less. But of course the bare statement of prioritarian principles does not achieve that feat or even attempt it. To get a determinate principle we must actually carry out the task of assigning relative weight to the two goals of maximizing and tilting to the worse-off. In an aggressive spirit, one might say prioritarianism names a problem and does not contribute to its solution. But that also would be unfair. Priority says boldly that nothing matters except two things. Even if one qualifies priority by luckism, one still is saying there are just three values to which a just society needs to be properly responsive. If the framework is correct, its articulation is a great achievement.

But is the framework correct? This chapter does not pursue this question. Notice there are two issues to face: one issue is what form of egalitarianism is most appealing and renders luck egalitarianism as plausible as it can be made. Another issue is whether any form of egalitarianism makes sense and is normatively acceptable.

1.4.2 What should we maximize?

The next question is, what to maximize (in the sufficiency, equality, or priority way). In the luck egalitarian literature, debate has swirled around two alternatives—resources and welfare. A resourcist view says we should assess people's condition in terms of their holdings of all-purpose resources they will need to develop and pursue valuable plans of life. Given there are surely several distinct such resources, the question arises how to provide an index, a measure of how much by way of resources all in all a given individual has.

Welfare is usually understood as preference satisfaction or informed preference satisfaction. A variant identifies welfare with achievement of objectively valuable goods, items on a specified Objective List.[31]

A confusing feature of debate on this issue is that personal responsibility considerations, which I have so far tried to cabin under the issue of whether to interpret the luckism component of luck egalitarianism in terms of Choice or Desert, surface again in the welfare-versus-resources discussions.

The literature is large, but admits of brief summary.

---

[31] On Objective List accounts of well-being or personal good, see D. Parfit, *Reasons and Persons* (Oxford: Oxford University Press, 1984), appendix. See also R. J. Arneson, 'Human Flourishing versus Desire Satisfaction', *Social Philosophy and Policy*, 16 (1999), 113–142, along with the references cited in that essay.

John Rawls supports a version of resourcism by appealing to personal responsibility.[32] According to Rawls justice does not look behind the distribution of resources to determine, much less to maximize, the quality of lives people obtain by use of their resources. What quality of life you get, given a fair distribution of resources and the maintenance of a fair framework for interaction, is up to you. The just society as it were provides each person access to a car, supplies of gas, and a system of maintained roads and maps of off-road territory. How each person lives, what trips she takes to what places in what order at what speed, is up to her, a non-delegable responsibility for the conduct of her own life.

This view is subject to the objection that a division of external resources that might seem fair in the abstract will inevitably mean that individuals with a poor endowment of personal traits relevant to achieving success in valuable goals will have very little real freedom to achieve a good life, compared to the prospects of individuals who are fortunate to have a more capacious endowment. To decide what allocation of resources is fair, one needs to consider how a given allotment of external resources will interact with the recipient's internal traits to yield what combination of real freedom. One has the real freedom to do X if there is a course of action one can choose that will bring it about that one does or gets X. So the currency of justice, the measure of people's condition for justice purposes, should be real freedom or capability to achieve what we have good reason to value.[33]

Notice that the real freedom approach retains the responsibility conception. Given a fair share of real freedom, it is up to each individual to form values and make plans and live her life as best she can. Justice does not survey or presume to assess an individual's achieved quality of life. That is a private not a public matter.

There is a simple but I think serious objection against the capability or real freedom approach. If capability were what we ultimately cared about, then it should be just as morally important to improve people's capabilities whether or not this will actually bring about anything good for themselves or others. Suppose one knows the capability will be wasted. One can save Smith from a beating at the hands of thugs but Smith will then immediately inflict a comparably bad beating on himself for some misguided reason. If society arranges to build huge opera houses and staff them with great performers and musicians so that every person in society has the real freedom to experience great opera, it should be a don't care from the standpoint of social justice

---

[32] Rawls, *A Theory of Justice*; also Rawls, 'Social Unity and Primary Goods', reprinted in John Rawls, *Collected Essays*, S. Freeman (ed.) (Cambridge, MA: Harvard University Press, 1999), 359–387.

[33] See A. K. Sen, 'Justice: Means versus Freedoms', *Philosophy and Public Affairs*, 19 (1990), 111–121; Inequality Reexamined (Cambridge, MA: Harvard University Press, 1992), chs. 1–3 and 5; also M. Nussbaum, 'Aristotelian Social Democracy' in R. B. Douglas, G. Mara, and H. Richardson (eds), *Liberalism and the Good* (New York: Routledge, 1990), 203–252; M. Nussbaum, 'Human Functioning and Social Justice: In Defense of Aristotelian Essentialism', *Political Theory*, 20 (1992), 202–246. For Nussbaum's current views, see her *Frontiers of Justice: Disability, Nationality, and Species Membership* (Cambridge, MA: Harvard University Press, 2006).

if nobody actually avails himself of that option. Nobody actually attends the operas. But still, marvellous capabilities are had by all.

Reflection on these types of example persuades me that justice must look behind the distribution of resources, opportunities, capabilities and the like, to see to what extent these freedom enhancements actually succeed in enhancing the quality of anyone's life, the goods that people actually enjoy. We care about freedom and capability because many important goods are such that their attainment requires or is partly constituted by a complementary freedom. For example, we value freely chosen personal attachments more than relationships one must sustain no matter what one's will in the matter. But at the fundamental moral level, the currency of justice that registers in principles of justice must be individual well-being, excellent quality of life.

That an individual has a non-delegable responsibility to decide how to live her life does not preclude other people and institutions having back-up responsibilities to help her live well if she stumbles or otherwise fails to discharge the responsibility to a satisfactory degree. So the primary responsibility each of us has for her own life does not require that social justice principles must assess people's condition in terms of capabilities not life outcomes.

Objections to welfare as the measure of people's condition for justice purposes sometimes take the form of appealing to our sense that some particular conception of welfare under review is an inadequate tool for this purpose. If informed preference satisfaction is the candidate conception of welfare, one might doubt that the fully informed anorexic who prefers to conform to her thin body ideal even if doing so will bring about her swift demise is improving her life by satisfying this informed preference. But if such appeals succeed, they implicitly or explicitly call to mind a superior interpretation of the idea of welfare or personal good. Such an argument may persuade us to reject one or another proposed conception of welfare but not to cease regarding welfare rightly conceived as the proper measure of people's condition.

This quick sketch of a line of thought on the issue, what should be the currency of justice, obviously introduces the topic and is not intended to be definitive.

I conclude this section by noting that if we take the maximand in the theory of justice to be human well-being, we are protected against a criticism frequently levelled against the luck egalitarian project—namely that it goes astray at the start by conceiving of the problem of justice as fundamentally a problem of distributing or allocating some stuff or other among some group of passive recipients. The objection is that justice is not fundamentally concerned, or at least not centrally concerned, with distribution at all. But if what is being distributed is what we really on reflection believe matters, this criticism falls flat. Moreover, to think in terms of distribution here is in many respects misleading. The fundamental justice imperative is to take efficient steps to improve the quality of people's lives giving fair attention to its distribution. But improving people's lives is not a matter of treating them as passive recipients. People are agents, who gain good by doing and achieving valuable things for self and others. Welfarist justice is a matter of facilitating agency.

1.5 Consequentialist and non-consequentialist frameworks

Luck egalitarianism can be housed in either a consequentialist or a non-consequentialist moral theory. On the face of it, the choice immediately has far-reaching consequences. According to the consequentialist luck egalitarian, what matters is what the actions and policies one might choose would do to advance luck egalitarian goals, the extent to which luck egalitarian principles are realized.

Also, the consequentialist will assess a society's institutional arrangements by their overall impact on the quality of people's lives. No special significance is assigned to official state action or the policies of major institutions as opposed to the ensemble of actions by individuals living under the rules and arrangements. Consider a stylized example. Suppose the egalitarian planner can choose either (1) to raise the tax rate on the incomes of high earners and use the proceeds to fund redistributive transfer programmes that improve the lives of the truly disadvantaged or (2) to maintain the status quo tax system. She might worry that raising the tax rate will induce high earners to shift their behaviour from economically more productive to less productive uses; just suppose for the sake of the argument that she finds no appreciable effect of this sort to worry about. But it might be the case that the regime with the lower tax rates on high earners contributes to an ethos of philanthropy among very high earners and the effect of the extra philanthropic giving that the lower tax rate induces outweighs by prioritarian accounting the effect of the extra state transfers that higher taxes would generate. If this is so, the egalitarian planner prefers to keep tax rates low, since her concern is not what people do for the poor through the agency of the state but what is done for the poor by whatever means and agencies.[34]

However, this way of putting the point may exaggerate the significance of this division.[35] There could be a consequentialist theory that attaches special value to the improvement of people's lives by state agency, and this consequentialism will not

[34] The example in the text raises the broad issue of whether a lightly regulated free market economy would be reasonably expected over the long run to do better or worse than heavily regulated alternatives at advancing egalitarian justice goals. Richard Epstein is not a luck egalitarian, nor is David Schmidtz, but were they to adopt this type of morality, their empirical beliefs about the superiority of lightly regulated free enterprise systems to feasible alternatives according to the standard of being productive of good consequences in the long run would make them right-wing luck egalitarians. See R. Epstein, *Simple Rules for a Complex World* (Cambridge, MA: Harvard University Press, 1995); also D. Schmidtz, *The Elements of Justice* (Cambridge: Cambridge University Press, 2006).

[35] A standard non-consequentialist morality would attach great significance to the distinction between doing or causing harm oneself and allowing others to cause harm and to the distinction between causing harm and merely allowing some harmful causal process not of one's making to unfold. The consequentialist holds that one morally ought always to do an act that brings about an outcome no worse than what would have occurred if one had done anything else instead. Consequentialist ethics is revisionary with respect to ordinary common-sense morality (the pretheoretical moral opinions of well brought up people in modern societies). Inheriting this disagreement, the luck egalitarian consequentialist and non-consequentialist would have lots to argue about. The text here simply notes how one's standards for assessing consequences may dampen (or for that matter amplify) the practical importance of this theoretical ethical disagreement.

count improvements in people's lives achieved by the Bill and Melinda Gates Foundation as counting for as much as improvements in people's lives brought about by state action.

Consequentialism versus non-consequentialism should be distinguished from a further significant divide within luck egalitarianism. One might affirm luck egalitarianism as one's comprehensive fundamental morality or as merely a component of that. Luck egalitarianism might be one principle affecting distributive justice, but not the whole of it. Or luck egalitarianism might be all of distributive justice, which itself is one among several elements of social justice. Or luck egalitarianism might be affirmed as the whole story about social justice, which is one among several components of fundamental morality. Or finally one might affirm luck egalitarianism as comprehending all of fundamental morality.

The comprehensive versus non-comprehensive issue affects the possible responses available to the advocate of luck egalitarianism in the face of criticisms. For example, if the critic affirms that it is unfair to let people in peril languish unaided when luck egalitarianism dictates no provision of help, the non-comprehensive luck egalitarian can respond that the neediness of the person in peril is a social justice reason for offering aid that sits along with luck egalitarianism in the panoply of social justice reasons.[36] The comprehensive luck egalitarian cannot follow this line.

Comprehensive luck egalitarianism is a bolder, more ambitious view. Being bolder, it is more exposed to criticism.[37] Although one might concoct a non-consequentialist comprehensive luck egalitarianism, I suspect that a plausible comprehensive version of the view will also be consequentialist. Priority views profess to amalgamate the values of maximizing aggregate well-being and achieving fair distribution of it. The desert-catering priority view I myself favour is both comprehensive and consequentialist.

1.6 An asocial theory of justice

In its pure form luck egalitarianism is an asocial theory of social justice. This is so in two ways. First, the particular social relationships that obtain in a given setting do not fundamentally affect what we morally owe to one another according to this doctrine. Such facts as that we are fellow members of the same community, that we are fellow citizens of a single nation state, that we are engaged in ongoing significant cooperative schemes regulated by non-optional rules, that we trade regularly or are together

---

[36] Kok-Chor Tan emphasizes what he takes to be the non-comprehensive character of luck egalitarianism to defuse some criticisms of it in his 'A Defense of Luck Egalitarianism', *Journal of Philosophy*, 105 (2008), 665–690.

[37] The view in the text is only roughly true. In principle, one might affirm a comprehensive consequentialist position that attempts to handle objections not by rebuffing them but by adding more and more values to the set of values that is to be maximized, with correct weights attached to each value. This strategy might look like death by a thousand qualifications or a gradual approach to the complicated, messy truth, depending on your point of view.

involved in a single wide encompassing trading network, do not have intrinsic normative significance so far as luck egalitarianism is concerned. These facts might well be among the various circumstances that fix what policy in these circumstances would best fulfil luck egalitarian goals, but of course any facts could conceivably play this role. Call a theorist of justice who thinks egalitarian justice principles apply only on the condition that some form of social interaction is in play a 'social interactionist'.

Luck egalitarianism is asocial in a second way. The luck egalitarian is concerned to alleviate bad brute luck of any kind. Or if she is a desertarian, she is concerned about all misfortunes that fall on people, modulating her response by the size of the misfortune, the badness of the person's life on whom this extra misfortune falls, and the person's virtue or vice level. In contrast, some believe firmly that justice regulates advantages that come to people through society not nature. The mere natural fact that someone is born with natural disadvantages and therefore has bad life prospects is insufficient in itself to trigger justice concerns. (If society treats the poorly endowed person in ways that count as unfair, magnifying the negative consequences of natural misfortune, then justice concerns are triggered.) Sometimes the luck egalitarian responsiveness to natural misfortune is viewed as per se a liability, a sign the theory has gone off the tracks. Here is an allegedly absurd implication of the luck egalitarian Don Quixote quest to right natural wrongs: if there is a distribution of physical attractiveness, then this is potentially a social justice problem for the luck egalitarian. The just health care system provides cosmetic surgery—but this is clearly absurd. So the theory that implies this result is wrong-headed.

I fail to see the absurdity. It would be nice to alter human culture so that people pay less attention to physical attractiveness than they do and reflect that beauty's only skin deep, yea, yea, yea.[38] But that aspiration may be utopian. Short of that, we should note that physical attractiveness, crucially useful not only for attracting sexual partners but for attracting partners for social interaction generally, is an important factor affecting human well-being prospects. If we consider for simplicity a single scale of attractiveness from beautiful to ugly, we should note that in the middle ranges of the scale, physical attractiveness levels may not be a crucial determinant of life prospects, but at the extremes, degree of attractiveness matters massively. To be ugly as sin is a curse, and not only during adolescence. There are serious questions about what policies would be sensible for a just society to adopt in this domain, and one can easily conjure up silly and counterproductive policies. But it strikes me as narrow-minded to fail to see the issue as a serious one for social justice. For example, a health care system might offer effective cosmetic surgery and other attractiveness-enhancing medical therapies, along with counselling, to people who are located at the negative tail end of the physical attractiveness spectrum. The service is available to those who seek it and provided in discreet locations and in privacy-protecting ways. Such a policy would be desirable,

---

[38] Quoting a song recorded by The Temptations.

I suppose. (I assume compressing the distribution of physical attractiveness would eliminate stigma for those who have less of it than others; observers of an individual are responsive to absolute as well as relative levels of his attractiveness.)

The asocial character of luck egalitarianism emerges from examination of an example introduced by Robert Nozick and also by David Gauthier.[39] They imagine people as living independently and self-sufficiently on separate islands, one individual on each island. Each person is the first appropriator of whatever land and natural resources she finds on the island on which she happens to find herself living. The separated islanders engage in no trade and nobody's activities have any impact on anyone living on any other island. The islanders we suppose differ in strength, intelligence, and other personal traits that affect their ability to prosper in their circumstances. The islands are variously hospitable to human habitation. Some have rocky soil and scant rainfall; others have fertile soil and plentiful rainfall.

Nozick made two claims regarding the isolated islanders:

1. So long as the islanders live autarchically, none has any moral right to any of the possessions or property of any of the others. Each has moral rights not to be harmed by the others (in certain ways that would qualify as violation of someone's Lockean natural rights). But none has any moral right, and certainly not an enforceable justice right, to receive aid from any of the others. Everyone has her own life to live and is morally free to pursue it. (In this setting it is supposed to be clear that first appropriation of land and resources yields full valid property rights to them.)

2. If absent trade and interaction no islander is under any moral obligation (corresponding to potential recipients' moral rights) to supply any aid to any other islander, merely engaging voluntarily in mutually beneficial trade and other forms of cooperative social interaction does not give rise to positive duties to aid and rights to be aided.

The luck egalitarian agrees with Nozick on claim 2 but disagrees on claim 1. The social interactionist might or might not agree with Nozick on claim 1 but is committed to denying claim 2.[40]

From a luck egalitarian standpoint, what generates distributive justice obligations is the sheer fact that some people are leading avoidably bad lives, or anyway lives whose quality is not high as measured by an appropriate standard, and other people are better off and able to help.[41] One further condition is that help can be carried out in such a

---

[39] R. Nozick, *Anarchy, State, and Utopia* (New York: Basic Books, 1974), 185. D. Gauthier, *Morals by Agreement* (Oxford: Oxford University Press, 1986), 218–219.

[40] Or something in the neighbourhood of claim 2. For example, the social interactionist might deny that trade alone generates strong egalitarian duties, but hold that some form of social interaction thicker than trade does this.

[41] The statement in the text is not quite right. In principle, prioritarian ethics might require that badly off people should transfer their resources to assist the projects and improve the lives of already better off people.

way that it is reasonably cost-effective. This condition admits of various construals, but the general idea is that it is not the case that for a prosperous islander to get one unit of happiness to his less fortunate counterpart he does not have to give up an excessive amount—say, ten units of happiness—for himself or gouge ten units from others. The more favourable the ratio of the gain-to-recipient-if-aid-is-forthcoming to the loss-to benefactor-if-she-supplies-aid, other things being equal, the stronger the moral case for providing aid.

No social context or community relationship needs to be introduced in order to generate justice-based duties to aid on the luck egalitarian account. If it somehow came about that by pressing a button resources would magically disappear from the island of Prosperous and magically reappear on the island of Needy, there would be moral reason for Prosperous to press the button.

So far in this section I have been concerned to describe the asocial character of the broadly egalitarian component of luck egalitarian thinking. Egalitarianism, at least when it takes the form of priority, is asocial. It does not matter per se that the people are living on separate islands rather than together as a band of brothers. Only the facts that some are on the way to leading lives of lower quality than others, and that there are available courses of action that will improve the aggregate sum of priority-weighted well-being, are per se morally important for deciding what policy to choose.

The other component of luck egalitarianism is luckism. Luckism is asocial just as egalitarianism is. In broad terms, for one who accepts luckism, there is a standard of behaviour, and conforming to a greater or lesser degree to the standard of behaviour brings it about that the moral value of improving one's condition (or the moral disvalue of worsening one's condition) is correspondingly amplified or dampened. It does not matter per se that the people who are possible recipients of aid, or possible people to be tapped on the shoulder and asked to aid the needy, are engaged in a dense network of cooperative activity, are fellow members of a nation state, share solidarity in their common membership in a tribe or other social group, and so on.

It should be noted that the asocial character of luck egalitarianism's luckism component is controversial. Absent social relations or any social context, the so-called egalitarian planner might be challenged: 'Who gave you the authority to impose this standard of conduct on us and assess our conduct by it and declare that the outcome of this assessment exercise conditions the moral value of improving our lives?' Standards of desert and deserving conduct might seem to presuppose a social arrangement that gives some people authorized standing to carry out this type of evaluation.[42]

Upward transfers might be justified, says the prioritarian. What one should do depends on what action of those available would do most to boost the priority-weighted aggregate sum of well-being. The luck egalitarian prioritarian adds a further modification, so one is to maximize priority-weighted and desert-weighted well-being. (This position is a family of views not a definite proposal pending determination of the proper weight to assign to its three elements.)

[42] Stephen Darwall presses this line of thought in his recent work on the second-person standpoint. The consequentialist will hold that whenever challenged from the second-person standpoint, one can always

Being an asocial account of social justice, luck egalitarianism contains nothing inside itself that provides a rationale for confining its scope. In responding to the Nozick—Gauthier separated islanders example, nothing hinges on the islands being in close proximity to one another. Move the islands farther and farther apart, and nothing in our judgement should change, unless the greater distances have an effect in altering the costs of transferring resources or the damage that resources being transferred will suffer by decay or spoilage. Moreover, not only is it the case that the physical distance separating people is not per se a determinant of what they morally owe one another. It is also the case that national borders and political jurisdictions do not matter per se for luck egalitarian assessment as characterized to this point. Luck egalitarianism in its core, unless encumbered with added moral commitments that do not arise from the internal development of its rationale but are instead just slapped on from outside, is a global cosmopolitan account of social justice.[43]

Whereas the responsibility component of luck egalitarianism has rather ambiguous or uncertain practical implications, the practical implications of the asocial character of luck egalitarian doctrine are simple and substantial.

The global (or for that matter, universal) scope of luck egalitarian justice turns our usual ways of thinking about egalitarianism on their head. For example, the Scandinavian social democracies are usually thought to be among the most egalitarian societies in the world. If any societies in the modern world conform or roughly conform to egalitarian justice norms, one might think, these societies do. However, a global perspective on social justice unseats these preliminary verdicts. For example, suppose that virtually all of Norway's citizens are prosperous and lead lives of high quality. Egalitarian transfer programmes and universal provision of an array of services and (once upon a time) solidaristic wage policies all work to compress the distribution of after-tax income and (or so one might hold) the distribution of after-tax lifetime well-being prospects as well. However, viewed from a global perspective, the impact of Norway's policies on Norwegians (who are all very likely to be above-average on the world scale virtually regardless of the state policies enforced) might be negligible in ameliorating the condition of the global poor. In contrast, we might imagine that a highly inegalitarian society that lacks Norway's generous social infrastructure might nonetheless allow illegal immigrants precariously to gain and hold jobs at the very bottom of its occupational hierarchy, but the net result is that these hard-working immigrants use their bottom-of-the-barrel labour market opportunities to amass sums

---

simply affirm the impartial, third-person justification of what one is doing. Darwall demurs, and presents interesting arguments. See his *The Second-Person Standpoint: Morality, Respect, and Accountability* (Cambridge, MA: Harvard University Press, 2006).

[43] This claim in the text needs to be modified by consideration of Ronald Dworkin's view. Dworkin holds that the duty to treat everyone with equal consideration and respect (the duty from which equality of resources is derived) applies to governments, and applies because they claim to act in the name of all members and subject all members to a heavy dose of coercion. The duty does not apply to an individual acting in a private capacity. In my terms, Dworkin is a social interactionist.

of money that they regularly disburse to even poorer relatives living back in their countries of origin. Judged by luck egalitarian standards applied on a global scale, the impact of the ungenerous bare tolerance of illegal immigrants by the inegalitarian rich country might swamp the highly democratic and egalitarian policies implemented in Scandinavian social democracy. The former might do more for the global poor, and hence score higher according to a luck egalitarian global justice norm, than the latter.

1.7 Against social interactionism

In this section I try indirectly to support the first aspect of the asocial character of luck egalitarianism by raising doubts about the social interactionist rival.[44] There are various versions of this view on offer. I shall suppose that the central idea is that while some duties of humanity may hold across all persons, significant egalitarian social justice obligations such as those imposed by the Rawlsian difference principle hold only among fellow members of a community who are bound together by significant social interaction of the sort that takes place among the members of a single unified nation state.

One source of doubt is that if social justice obligations are triggered only by some form of significant interaction, one can evade the obligations of social justice by avoiding that form of interaction with people. The rich can decide to refrain from interacting with the poor, and more generally, well-off people can eschew whatever threshold level of interaction would trigger strong justice obligations when dealing with disadvantaged, badly off people.

This social interactionist stance denies the core luck egalitarian premise. Some may be cheerfully prepared to bite that bullet. Is there anything that can be said against this cheerful social interactionist? What can be said here depends on what the social interactionist asserts. The discussion must become piecemeal, and challenge the various possible rationales for taking egalitarian social justice obligations to hold only within the borders of each single nation state.

One suggested rationale is that a state massively coerces its own members but not those residing outside the borders of that nation state, and this massive coercion is a

---

[44] Many authors belong to the broad family of views I am calling social interactionist. See T. Nagel, 'Justice and Nature', *Oxford Journal of Legal Studies*, 17 (1997), 303–321; A. Buchanan, D. W. Brock, N. Daniels, and D. Wikler, 'Genes, Justice and Human Nature' in their *From Chance to Choice: Genetics and Justice* (Cambridge and New York: Cambridge University Press, 2000); C. Beitz, *Political Theory and International Relations* (Princeton: Princeton University Press, 1979); M. Blake, 'Distributive Justice, State Coercion, and Autonomy', *Philosophy and Public Affairs*, 30 (2001), 257–296; M. Blake and M. Risse, 'Two Models of Equality and Responsibility', *Canadian Journal of Philosophy*, 38 (2008), 165–199; T. Nagel, 'The Problem of Global Justice', *Philosophy and Public Affairs*, 33 (2005), 113–147; R. Miller, 'Cosmopolitan Respect and Patriotic Concern', *Philosophy and Public Affairs*, 27 (1998), 202–224; A. J. Julius, 'Basic Structure and the Value of Equality', *Philosophy and Public Affairs*, 31 (2003), 321–355; A. J. Julius, 'Nagel's Atlas', *Philosophy and Public Affairs*, 34 (2006), 176–192; J. Cohen and C. Sabel, 'Extra Rempublicam Nulla Justitia?', *Philosophy and Public Affairs*, 34 (2006), 147–175; and A. James, 'Constructing Justice for Existing Practice: Rawls and the Status Quo', *Philosophy and Public Affairs*, 33 (2005), 281–316.

presumptive violation of the individual autonomy of the coerced, which can be allayed only if social arrangements satisfy egalitarian justice principles.[45] However, if one is coerced not to do what would anyway be morally wrong to do, no violation of autonomy is thereby threatened, and if on the other hand one is coerced not to do what one morally has a right to do, the remedy is just to stop the coercion directed against that activity. In neither case do special justice obligations magically arise. In principle there might be an intermediate case, in which one is permitted to coerce, but only if special moral conditions are fulfilled. Conceivably these conditions might consist of egalitarian justice requirements. However, for any case in which one might suppose sustaining state coercion is only acceptable if done via arrangements that specially favour the local worse-off, one can counter with an alternative arrangement which specially favours to that same extent the globally worse-off, whoever they may be, rather than the locally coerced worse-off. One then says to the local worse-off that the coercive arrangements are morally acceptable, given the benefits they bring for people who are worse off than they would be without any special local favouritism.

Another suggested rationale is that the state not only massively coerces its members but also claims to do so in their name.[46] The state claims, or at least any legitimate state will claim, to be authorized by those coerced to maintain the coercive scheme. Moreover, this claim to authorization involves the will of those coerced in a way that triggers strong egalitarian justice requirements.

In reply: the claim that one acts with authorization is not unique to coercive imposition but is latent whenever one person chooses to act in a way that affects or could affect another person. The latent claim is that what one is doing (or omitting) can be justified to those who are affected or might have been affected by what one is doing (or omitting). The claim is that one is acting in accordance with principles that every person qua rational can accept. This so far says nothing about what the content of those principles must be. So the fact that one implicitly must appeal to the agreement of those who might be affected by what one does is not by itself the basis for any inference to any contentful moral requirement and a fortiori not to any egalitarian social justice requirements.

Another suggested rationale appeals to the extended friendship relationship that obtains among members of a well-functioning national community. Just as friends morally ought to be partial to their friends, the members of a well-functioning national community ought to be partial to one another.[47]

In reply: even if we grant that friends ought specially to favour their friends, nothing like these intimate special ties hold or should hold among all those who happen to

---

[45] Blake takes this line.

[46] Versions of this idea appear in Nagel and also in Dworkin, *Sovereign Virtue*.

[47] See T. Hurka, 'The Justification of National Partiality' in R. McKim and J. McMahan (eds), *The Morality of Nationalism* (New York: Oxford University Press, 1997), 139–157.

inhabit the same nation state. So the starting premise of any argument that runs from special tie partiality to egalitarian justice requirements among the members of each national community is not well supported.

These quick sketches of arguments and rebuttals are not meant to be decisive but just to indicate how a sound defence of luck egalitarianism would have to proceed.

1.8 Conclusion

Luck egalitarianism combines two ideas, 'luckism' and 'egalitarianism'. The best version of the doctrine interprets the two ideas so that they together are as plausible and sensible as they can be made.

The luckism idea is that personal responsibility matters intrinsically for social justice. One possible construal is that being more deserving enhances whatever egalitarian reasons there are to improve one's condition if one is badly off and dampens whatever egalitarian reasons there are to worsen one's condition to benefit the needy if one is well off. Another possible construal takes the relevant factor to be voluntary choice or the distinction between option luck and brute luck.

The egalitarian idea might be interpreted in sufficientarian, straight egalitarian, or prioritarian terms. Whichever of these principles is selected, some measure of people's condition is needed to fill in its content. This measure could be resourcist or welfarist. If welfarist, it could incorporate an objective or a subjective conception of welfare (individual well-being). Whether resourcist or welfarist, the egalitarian component in luck egalitarianism might be interpreted as opportunity-oriented (as in capability accounts) or as outcome-oriented.

A luck egalitarian doctrine might be embedded in either a consequentialist or a non-consequentialist ethic. Luck egalitarianism might be affirmed as a comprehensive doctrine or alternatively as one component in a pluralistic ethic containing other fundamental principles. The comprehensive versions have more bite.

Unadorned and unmodified, luck egalitarianism is naturally an asocial view in at least two different senses. First, the luck egalitarian imperative is to improve people's lives, giving special emphasis on improvements for the worse-off and allowing for personal responsibility. The doctrine tells us to respond to people's disadvantages regardless of whether they are socially or naturally caused (or indeed regardless of whether this distinction can be made coherent and serviceable). Disadvantage due to social arrangements has the same fundamental moral status as disadvantage due to natural causes like bad weather. Second, the luck egalitarian imperative sets duties for each and every person that are fundamentally and unconditionally owed to each and every person, rather than triggered by social relations. Luck egalitarianism is thus a radically cosmopolitan doctrine that disagrees with all manner of social interactionist social justice theories that affirm that egalitarian justice requirements apply only among people who interact or are socially related in significant ways such as being members of a single political society. Though controversial, the asocial character of luck egalitarianism in its pure form has the quality of plausible simplicity, or so I would argue.

Luck egalitarianism has attracted significant criticism, but a definitive verdict on the doctrine must wait for a systematic, sympathetic elaboration of the core ideas. For now, a correct assessment of the prospects of luck egalitarian theory is simply 'it's too soon to tell'.

2

Justice, Equality, Fairness, Desert, Rights, Free Will, Responsibility, and Luck[1]

Larry Temkin

John Rawls defended a view he famously called 'justice as fairness'.[2] I have defended a position I called 'equality as comparative fairness'.[3] The notions of justice, equality, and fairness are all intimately related to each other, and to a host of other notions, such as desert, rights, free will, responsibility, and luck. This chapter aims to illuminate some connections between these deeply important overlapping notions.

Each of these notions is exceedingly complex. Hence, a full treatment of them is not possible here. Still, by focusing on a few key aspects of these notions some progress can be made in understanding the relations between them.

The chapter is divided into two main sections. In section 2.1, I discuss justice. I begin by distinguishing between different conceptions of justice, including a conception of justice as involving the respecting of rights, two different versions of proportional justice, and the Rawlsian conception of justice as fairness. I then note the importance of distinguishing between *acting justly*, where one is acting for *agent-relative* justice-based

[1] Section 2.1 draws on my 'Thinking about the Needy, Justice, and International Organizations', *The Journal of Ethics*, 8 (2004), 349–395. Section 2.2 draws on 'Illuminating Egalitarianism' in Thomas Christiano and John Christman (eds), *Contemporary Debates in Philosophy* (Oxford: Blackwell, 2009), 155–178. I am grateful to Ruth Chang, Shelly Kagan, Frances Kamm, Jeff McMahan, Derek Parfit, and the editors, Carl Knight and Zofia Stemplowska, for their helpful comments; also to many others who have influenced my thinking about this topic, including John Broome, G. A. Cohen, Roger Crisp, Nils Holtug, Susan Hurley, Thomas Nagel, Jan Narveson, Ingmar Persson, Thomas Pogge, Peter Unger, and Andrew Williams.

[2] See J. Rawls, 'Justice as Fairness', *Philosophical Review*, 67 (1958), 164–194; *A Theory of Justice* (Cambridge, MA: Harvard University Press, 1971); 'Justice as Fairness: Political not Metaphysical', *Philosophy and Public Affairs*, 14 (1985), 223–252; and *Justice as Fairness: A Restatement*, E. Kerry (ed.) (Cambridge, MA: Harvard University Press, 2001).

[3] The intimate connection between equality and fairness is indicated in my book *Inequality* (Oxford: Oxford University Press, 1993), though, partly out of deference to Rawls, I didn't use the expression 'equality as comparative fairness' or refer to my position by that name until fairly recently; see, for example, 'Egalitarianism Defended', *Ethics*, 113 (2003), 764–782 and 'Larry S. Temkin' in Morten Ebbe Juul Nielsen (ed.), *Political Questions: 5 Questions on Political Theory* (Automatic Press/VIP, 2006), 147–167.

reasons, and acting for *reasons of justice*, where one is acting for *agent-neutral* justice-based reasons.

In section 2.2, I discuss equality. Arguing that there is an intimate connection between a central concern for equality and a concern about comparative fairness, I focus on a view I call *equality as comparative fairness*. I discuss luck egalitarianism, the option/brute luck distinction, the role of responsibility and desert, and the difference between comparative fairness and comparative justice. I also argue that egalitarians should be concerned about both equality of opportunity and equality of welfare broadly construed, about both ex ante and ex post equality, and about both procedural and substantive fairness.

The chapter reveals that different plausible conceptions of justice and equality have different and important connections with fairness, desert, rights, free will, responsibility, and luck. The chapter also explores some implications of these different conceptions.

2.1 Justice

2.1.1 Recognizing some different conceptions of justice

The notion of justice is extremely rich and complex. Correspondingly, there are many powerfully attractive and deeply important conceptions of justice. I shall discuss several of these here.

One general conception of justice is that justice requires giving each person her 'due'. This conception, dating back at least to Plato, is widely accepted.[4] But this conception gives rise to many distinct alternative views about what justice requires, tracking different substantive views about what people are 'due'.

One particular view about what people are 'due' is the respecting of their rights. On this view, the notion of justice is tied to the notions of rights and rights violations. Specifically, on this conception an individual or society acts unjustly when, and only when, it violates someone's rights. If, for example, you have a right to life or property, and I violate that right by killing you or taking your property, I act unjustly in so treating you. A view of this sort, combined with a narrow, parsimonious, conception of rights, is advocated by Robert Nozick and Jan Narveson.[5]

Clearly, on this conception of justice it is crucially important to determine the nature and scope of rights. Are there any natural rights, or are all rights social in basis? Are there any positive rights—rights to assistance, for example, to adequate food, shelter, or medical care—or only negative rights—rights not to be harmed, or interfered with in certain ways, for example, to not be killed, tortured, or have one's property taken

---

[4] See *The Republic*, Book I, and also Aristotle's *Nicomachean Ethics*, Part V.

[5] See R. Nozick, *Anarchy, State, and Utopia* (New York: Basic Books, 1974) and J. Narveson, 'Welfare and Wealth, Poverty and Justice in Today's World', and 'Is World Poverty a Moral Problem for the Wealthy', *The Journal of Ethics*, 8 (2004), 305–348 and 397–408.

away. Are there any inalienable rights, and if so what are they? Are some rights alienable, and if so, under what conditions?

Most people believe that most rights are alienable by word or deed. I can, for example, voluntarily renounce my right to property or not to be harmed, in which case you may take my property or harm me for certain desirable goals without acting unjustly. Similarly, many believe that certain of my rights are conditional upon my respecting similar rights in others. Thus, on this view, justice, rights, and responsibility are intimately entwined. My responsible actions can limit or alter the scope of my rights, and thereby affect what may be justly done to me. So, for example, if I steal from another or harm an innocent person, then the state may perhaps fine or incarcerate me without violating my rights or acting unjustly. Likewise, there is no rights violation, and hence no injustice, if the state duns the wages of a parent who abandoned his children.

What about the role of luck? Well, I may not be able to *lose* a right because of bad luck, but the rights one has may be *conditional* on certain states whose obtaining may be a matter of luck. For example, I have a right not to have my property taken from me, *provided* I meet my fiscal responsibilities towards others. If, however, I default on my car payments, my car may be taken from me without violating my rights, and hence not unjustly *in the sense under discussion*, even if the only reason I defaulted on the payments is due to bad luck. Perhaps I have innocently come down with a rare disease and cannot work, or my employer has moved overseas, or my spouse has run off with my life's savings! Similarly, there is an old saying that 'your rights end where the next person's nose begins'. In accordance with this, many believe that even such fundamental rights as the rights to life and liberty are circumscribed by the conditions in which I find myself, including circumstances beyond my control. Thus, many believe that if I posed a sufficiently serious threat to enough others—say, if I developed a highly infectious fatal disease—it would be neither unjust, nor a rights violation, if I were quarantined against my will, or perhaps, if necessary, even killed.

So, on one important view there is a connection between justice and rights, and the connection is such that both individual responsibility and luck may play a significant role in how one may be justly treated.

Two other important conceptions of justice are alternative versions of *proportional justice*. The principle of proportional justice might be roughly framed as follows: there ought to be a proportion between *living* well and *faring* well. This notion is intimately connected to the notion of desert. Intuitively, the thought is that in so far as one lives well, one *deserves* to fare well, and in a fully just world one *would* fare well. Unfortunately, the notion of 'living well' is ambiguous. It may mean that one is *doing* well— that is, *acting* rightly or *doing* good deeds. Alternatively, it may mean that one is *being* well—that is, possessing good *character* or high moral *virtue*. I don't think these positions have been sufficiently distinguished, since they tend to agree about most actual cases. Nevertheless, they are distinct positions with different implications, and though there is something to be said for each, I favour a version of the latter.

Suppose that Alan and Randi are both equally virtuous. Each would do everything possible to help someone in need. But Alan lives in a neighbourhood where he can effectively help someone three times a week, while Randi lives in a neighbourhood where she can only effectively help someone once a week. If, in fact, Randi would do everything Alan actually does, if she were in his position, and vice versa, then on the view of proportional justice I favour Alan and Randi ought to fare equally well, from the standpoint of justice, even if in fact, given their different circumstances, Alan actually *acts* rightly, and *does* good, more often than Randi. Though not conclusive, such considerations lead me to think that the most plausible versions of proportional justice should focus on *character* more than *actions*. Accordingly, it is such versions of proportional justice, properly qualified, that I shall focus on here.

There are two main versions of proportional justice. The first corresponds to a conception of *absolute* justice or desert. This reflects the general conception, noted above, that justice involves each person receiving her *due*, but the thought is that people *should* fare well precisely to the extent that they are *morally deserving*, where this is a function of their virtue or moral character.[6] On this view, it is unjust when one fares either better or worse than one morally deserves to, where this is understood in *absolute* terms. So, for example, saints (understood as extremely virtuous people) deserve to fare extremely well, sinners (understood as extremely vicious people) extremely poorly, and the rest of us somewhere in between. Thus, on this view, it would be unjust for a saint to fare extremely poorly, and likewise for a sinner to fare extremely well.

The second main version of proportional justice corresponds to a conception of *comparative* justice or desert.[7] On this view, to the extent that someone is more virtuous than another she deserves to live a proportionally better life. Here, justice determines the *relative* standing of the two lives, but not their absolute standing. John Broome defends such a conception of proportional justice.[8] For Broome, it would be unjust for sinners to fare better than saints, but it wouldn't be unjust for both to fare well, or poorly, as long as the saints fared better than the sinners in proportion to how much more virtuous they were. Thus, for Broome, 'Sinners should be worse off than saints, but...justice does not determine how well off each group should be absolutely.' To Broome, a world containing only saints who fare poorly due to natural conditions may

---

[6] This view has historical antecedents in Plato and Aristotle (see footnote 4), and was accepted by Kant and W. D. Ross. See Kant's *Critique of Practical Reason*, Part I, and *The Philosophy of Law*, Part II, and W. D. Ross, *The Right and the Good* (Oxford: Oxford University Press, 1930).

[7] This view also has historical antecedents in Aristotle, who claimed that there should be equal treatment for equals, so that likes should be treated alike, and unalikes should be treated unalike. See the *Politics*, 1282b lines 16–21, and the *Nicomachean Ethics*, Part V, especially 1131a lines 10–29.

[8] Other defenders of comparative desert are Louis Pojman and Shelly Kagan. See Pojman's 'Does Equality Trump Desert?' and Kagan's 'Equality and Desert' in O. McLeod and L. P. Pojman (eds), *What Do We Deserve?: A Reader on Justice and Desert* (Oxford: Oxford University Press, 1998), 298–314, 283–297.

not be 'a very good one' but it is not unjust. 'Similarly,' Broome writes, 'in a world containing only sinners, I see no injustice if the sinners fare well.'[9]

Some people believe that all that proportional justice requires is that there *be* the relevant connection between living well and faring well, no (or few) questions asked, as it were. On this view, it doesn't matter *why* one is, or is not, virtuous or vicious, what matters is simply *whether* one is virtuous or vicious, and to what extent. My own view is that this makes a mockery of the notion of justice. If the only reason I am virtuous and you vicious is that we have each been brainwashed or drugged to be the way we are, then I believe that neither of us is responsible for our character, and neither of us is morally deserving of faring well or faring poorly. In such a case, I believe that absolute justice would not require that I fare well, and you poorly, and comparative justice would not require that I fare better than you; similarly, if our characters are simply the result of genetic endowment or manipulation for which we are not responsible. So, for example, if God created Adam to be perfectly virtuous, and Eve to be perfectly vicious, and then sent Adam to a wonderful afterlife and Eve to a terrible one, he could not, in my view, defend his actions or their afterlives as *just*. More particularly, he could not claim to have acted in accordance with either absolute or comparative justice, since Adam doesn't *deserve* a wonderful afterlife, Eve doesn't *deserve* a terrible afterlife, and neither *deserves* to be better off than the other.

Thus, on my view, the conception of proportional justice understood in terms of absolute justice sees a tight connection between justice, moral desert, and responsibility. People must, in a robust sense, be responsible for their characters for them to be morally deserving of being well or poorly off in virtue of their characters, and hence for it to be a matter of absolute justice that they be well off in direct proportion to the degree to which they are virtuous. On this view, good or bad luck that results in our getting either more or less than we deserve should be rectified, though good or bad luck that results in our getting what we actually deserve should not. On the other hand, luck can have no fundamental role to play in the formation of our characters. In so far as it is a matter of luck whether we are virtuous or vicious, we are not morally deserving of faring well or poorly, and the notion of absolute justice loses its traction.

My own view is that the robust conception of responsibility required to make sense of our deepest convictions regarding absolute justice is inextricably tied to the mare's nest of free will. More specifically, I believe that the most compelling conception of absolute justice requires the kind of free will that is incompatible with both determinism and indeterminism, and that is notoriously difficult to square with our scientific

---

[9] *Weighing Goods* (Oxford: Basil Blackwell, 1991), 169. Broome's discussion is in response to an early draft of my saints and sinners example which later appeared in 'Harmful Goods, Harmless Bads' in R. G. Frey and C. W. Morris (eds), *Value, Welfare, and Morality* (Cambridge: Cambridge University Press, 1993), 290–324, and in *Inequality*, ch. 9. I responded to Broome in 'Weighing Goods: Some Questions and Comments,' *Philosophy and Public Affairs*, 23 (1994), 350–380, and also in 'Equality, Priority, and the Levelling Down Objection' in M. Clayton and A. Williams (eds), *The Ideal of Equality* (Basingstoke: MacMillan, 2000), 126–161.

world view and the obvious way in which both nature and nurture influence our characters. I think we must face this fact head on, and not try to deny it or run from it. I am aware, of course, that many will regard my claims here as tantamount to a *reductio* of the notion of absolute justice. But I don't share this sentiment. Though I don't have the foggiest idea how to solve the mare's nest of (meaningful!) free will, I believe that there is reason to believe, or at least hope, that many rational beings *are* sufficiently free, in the relevant sense, as to make attributions of responsibility for their characters appropriate. Correspondingly, I suspect that the notion of absolute justice is not incoherent—even if we don't understand how it could be coherent—and believe that it should be given significant weight in our moral deliberations. Though I hasten to add that there may be many cases where people are not (fully) responsible for their characters, in which cases the notion of absolute justice will not be (fully or straight-forwardly) applicable.

Let us next consider the view of proportional justice that involves a commitment to *comparative* justice or desert. Although most advocates of comparative justice probably assume that most people are responsible for their choices and character, the notion of comparative justice does not require that there be meaningful free will for it to retain its intuitive plausibility and force. According to comparative justice, if two people are responsible for the extent to which they are virtuous, then one person should fare better than another in proportion to the extent to which she is more virtuous; which is to say, only to the extent that she is morally more deserving than the other of faring well. But this suggests that if one person is not morally more deserving than another, then it is unjust if they do not fare equally well. Thus, as I understand this view, in a world where there is no meaningful free will, everyone is *equally* deserving—as well as equally *un*deserving!—since no one morally *deserves* anything at all. Since, according to comparative justice, at least as I understand it, it is unjust for one person to be worse off than another who is no more deserving than she, in such a world *all* inequalities in terms of overall quality of life would be comparatively unjust.

Let me sum up the preceding discussion. On my view, in a world lacking meaning-ful free will—for example, a purely deterministic or indeterministic world—no one would be morally *deserving* of anything. A fortiori, no one would morally *deserve* to fare well or poorly or at *any* particular level, and the conception of absolute justice would lose its traction. But a meaningful conception of comparative justice would remain. In such a world, all substantive inequalities would involve some being worse off than others no more deserving than they, and this would be comparatively unjust. Corres-pondingly, in such a world comparative justice would amount to a version of egalitar-ianism. All inequalities would be solely due to luck, and comparative justice would seek to rectify the impact of such luck by removing all inequalities of normative significance.[10]

---

[10] Roughly, inequalities are normatively significant when they account for some people being better off than others. Not all inequalities are normatively significant, and an inequality that is normatively significant in some contexts may be insignificant in others.

So, in a world with meaningful free will, where people are responsible for their choices and characters, both absolute and comparative justice will be plausible, and proportional justice will be compatible with, and almost certainly require, inequality. But in a world lacking meaningful free will—which some people believe is ours—only comparative justice will be plausible, and proportional justice will require equality.

Finally, let me mention Rawls's well-known conception of *justice as fairness*. On Rawls's view, 'Justice is the first virtue of social institutions',[11] and there are two principles of justice by which a society's basic structure, or principles and institutions, are to be judged: 'First: each person is to have an equal right to the most extensive basic liberty compatible with a similar liberty for others. Second: social and economic inequalities are to be arranged so that they are both (a) reasonably expected to be to everyone's advantage, and (b) attached to positions and offices open to all.'[12] Clause (a) of the second principle is fleshed out into Rawls's famous difference principle: society's principles and institutions are to be arranged so as to maximize the expect-ations of the representative member of society's worst-off group.[13] Importantly, in *A Theory of Justice*, Rawls restricts the scope of his claims to 'sufficiently developed' societies, and contends that his two principles may not govern the relations between sovereign nations. Later, he further suggests that his two principles may only apply to modern Western-style democracies.

Rawls's theory of justice as fairness gives expression to a conception that we have of ourselves as free and equal rational beings.[14] But as Rawls later emphasizes, his conception of justice as fairness is political, not metaphysical, so he is not committed to free will in any deep, metaphysical, sense.[15] His concern is with a conception of *social* justice, and for Rawls questions about individual responsibility have little, if any, bearing on whether or not we should regard society's basic structures as just.

In a key paragraph illuminating the aim, scope, and motivation of his position, Rawls writes the following:

The intuitive idea is that since everyone's well-being depends on a scheme of cooperation without which no one could have a satisfactory life, the division of advantages should be such as to draw forth the willing cooperation of everyone taking part in it, including those less well situated. Yet this can be expected only if reasonable terms are proposed. The two principles [of justice] mentioned seem to be a fair agreement on the basis of which those better endowed, or more fortunate in their social position, neither of which we can be said to deserve, could expect the willing cooperation of others when some workable scheme is a necessary condition of the welfare of all.[16] Once we decide to look for a conception of justice that nullifies the accidents of

---

[11] Rawls, *A Theory of Justice*, 6.

[12] Rawls, *A Theory of Justice*, 60.

[13] See Rawls, *A Theory of Justice*, 75–83.

[14] Rawls, *A Theory of Justice*, 11.

[15] In 'Justice as Fairness: Political not Metaphysical'. Revealingly, *A Theory of Justice's* careful index has no entry for 'free will'.

[16] Here Rawls acknowledged Allan Gibbard for originally formulating this intuitive idea.

natural endowment and the contingencies of social circumstance as counters in quest for political and economic advantage, we are led to these principles. They express the result of leaving aside those aspects of the social world that seem arbitrary from a moral point of view.[17]

So, for Rawls, social justice amongst free and equal rational beings reflects recognition of the fact that no one *deserves* the 'accidents of natural endowment' or the 'contingencies of social circumstances'. Recognizing that such factors are 'arbitrary from a moral point of view', Rawls believes that it will only be 'reasonable' and 'fair' for the disadvantaged to agree to a set of principles and institutions comprising society's basic structure that, in essence, treats natural endowments and social circumstances as common assets to be used for everyone's benefit. In particular, Rawls believes that the correct principles of justice will tolerate inequalities in natural endowments and social circumstances only to the extent that they can be harnessed for the maximal benefit of those most disadvantaged by such morally arbitrary inequalities. Since, arguably, it is a matter of luck whether one is advantaged in one's natural and social circumstances, Rawls's principles of justice can be seen as attempting, among other things, to mitigate the role that society allows luck to play in its citizens' lives.

It is important to emphasize that in *A Theory of Justice*, Rawls offered his theory of justice as fairness strictly as a theory of *social* justice, and in particular as a theory for assessing the justness of a society's principles and institutions with respect to how it treats its *own* citizens, when the society is a sufficiently advanced Western-style democracy. As Rawls acknowledged, his theory does not capture the *whole* of our notion of justice. Thus, in *A Theory of Justice*, Rawls says little about what justice requires of societies that are not sufficiently advanced Western-style democracies, of individuals in their treatment of others, or of societies in their treatment of other societies or non-citizens.[18]

I have canvassed four specific conceptions of justice. Each is plausible and important. Though much more needs to be said about these issues, it is apparent that the different conceptions of justice are connected, in different ways and to varying degrees, with the related notions of fairness, equality, desert, rights, responsibility, and luck. Thus, a full understanding of the dictates of justice requires a much better understanding of the nature and significance of these other, related, notions.

2.1.2 *Acting justly versus acting for reasons of justice*

Having recognized several plausible and important conceptions of justice, let me next introduce an important, but often overlooked, distinction between *acting justly* and acting for *reasons of justice*. Let us say that one *acts justly* when one acts for *agent-relative* justice-based reasons, whereas one acts for *reasons of justice* when one acts for *agent-neutral* justice-based reasons. These categories are not exclusionary. One might act for

---

[17] Rawls, *A Theory of Justice*, 15.
[18] Rawls addresses justice between different societies in *The Law of Peoples* (Cambridge, MA: Harvard University Press, 1999).

both agent-relative and agent-neutral justice-based reasons. The distinction I have in mind can be illustrated with the aid of the following examples.

Suppose that John has promised to pay Mary $100 for a day's work. If Mary does the work, then John acts justly if he pays her, and unjustly if he doesn't. Suppose now that John decides to cheat Mary, and not pay her. I can try to talk John into paying Mary, but he's my boss, and I'm afraid he'll fire me if I do. It would be good of me to talk with John, perhaps I even act wrongly if I don't. Still, if I fail to confront John, *he's* the one who is *acting* unjustly, not me. I'm (just!) being a coward. Still, there are *reasons of justice* for me to talk with John. If I do, I may promote a just situation. He may heed my words and act justly. Suppose I do talk to John, and it has the desired effect. In that case, I'd say I've acted courageously, perhaps even rightly, but not justly. *John* is the one who has acted justly, I've merely acted for reasons of justice.

Analogously, suppose John is going to pay Mary what he owes her, but I want him to lend me the $100 instead. Suppose I know that if I ask John to lend me the $100 he will do so, and not pay Mary. I then have reasons of justice not to ask John for the money. But if I ask John to lend me the money and he does, I may be acting selfishly, and perhaps even wrongly, but *I'm* not the one *acting unjustly*, John is. John is the one who owes Mary the money, not me.

So, accordingly, we can distinguish between *agent-relative* justice-based reasons, which are those an individual must comply with to avoid acting unjustly, and *agent-neutral* justice-based reasons, which are those anyone might have to help promote a more just situation. Agent-neutral reasons are distinct from agent-relative reasons, but both are important.

Notice, nothing I have said bears on the relative weight of agent-relative or agent-neutral justice-based reasons. Although we often think of agent-relative justice-based reasons as having overwhelmingly compelling force ('I *cannot* act unjustly'), in fact, there are stronger and weaker agent-relative justice-based reasons. For example, while I have a strong agent-relative reason not to enslave another, I only have a weak agent-relative reason not to take my brother's candy. Likewise, there might be stronger and weaker agent-neutral justice-based reasons. For example, while I might have a strong agent-neutral reason to help end child exploitation, if I can, I might only have a weak agent-neutral reason to ensure that my colleague carefully reads the admissions folders.

Though permitting or tolerating injustice may not be the *same* moral shortcoming as *acting* unjustly, it is important to bear in mind that agent-neutral justice-based reasons are still reasons of *justice*. And strong reasons of justice, whether agent-relative or agent-neutral, are not to be sniffed at lightly. Or so I contend, though I cannot argue for this here.

Suppose, then, that A would be a more just outcome than B. On the view sketched above, everyone will have justice-based reasons to promote A rather than B, if they can. If failing to promote A rather than B would be acting unjustly, then at least some of the justice-based reasons for promoting A would be agent-relative. If not, then the justice-based reasons would be agent-neutral. But, as emphasized above, they would still be reasons of *justice*, and they may still carry significant moral weight.

The distinction between different kinds of justice-based reasons helps illuminate the nature and scope of the different conceptions of justice. In so far as justice is seen as involving the respecting of rights, agent-relative reasons are primary, and it makes most sense to talk of particular individuals as acting justly or unjustly when they respect or violate other people's rights. In so far as justice is seen as involving proportional justice, whether absolute or comparative, agent-neutral reasons are primary. We don't normally think that each individual is responsible for seeing that people 'get what they deserve' in the senses required by proportional justice; hence, we won't accuse someone of acting unjustly just because they haven't acted so as to make good people fare well, bad people fare poorly, or good people fare well relative to bad people. Still, we can recognize that the state of affairs where good people fare well, or better than bad people, would be proportionally just, and hence that there are agent-neutral reasons of justice to promote such a state of affairs if we can.

To see the importance of the distinction between agent-relative and agent-neutral justice-based reasons, imagine that someone in another society who has responsibly developed a saintly character has been the victim of great natural misfortune. Suppose, in fact, that despite the best possible personal and social responses to her situation, her life is one of unremitting pain and misery, though this doesn't stop her from maintaining her saintly character and continually aiding others. If one believes in the absolute conception of proportional justice, one will believe that it is naturally unjust that this saint's life has gone so badly. Since she has lived well she deserves to fare well, and it is a bad thing—naturally unjust—if she doesn't.

Suppose now that it becomes possible to easily improve the saint's life. Do we have reason to do so? On the view in question we have a justice-based reason to improve her life—but it is an agent-neutral justice-based reason, not an agent-relative one. If we don't help the saint we may not be *acting unjustly*—since we did not cause her plight, promise to help her, and so on—but even so we have a reason of justice to help the saint. Helping the saint would promote justice by promoting a better proportion between living well and faring well.

Notice, it may be impossible for us to help the saint. On my view, this would be a case of irremediable natural injustice. It wouldn't merely be that her life was tragic, though it would be that too, rather she would be a victim of cosmic or natural injustice. What is the point of calling such a situation unjust? It tells us something important about the situation. It tells us that if, contrary to fact, we *could* do something about it, then, *ceteris paribus*, we *should* do something about it, and one of the *reasons* to do so would be to bring about a proportion between the saint's level of well-being and her moral desert or character. In aiding the saint we would not necessarily be *acting justly*, but we would be *promoting* absolute justice. We would be acting for *reasons of justice*.

Similar remarks would apply, mutatis mutandis, if one accepted the comparative conception of proportional justice.

Some people, like Robert Nozick and Jan Narveson, would acknowledge that the saint's misfortune is regrettable, and that it would be nice, good, and perhaps even desirable for us to act on her behalf; but they vehemently deny that we act unjustly if we fail to do so.[19] On their view, justice only requires us to rectify those misfortunes for which we are, in some relatively narrow and straightforward sense, directly and socially responsible.[20] Correspondingly, they think that victims of natural misfortune may warrant our sympathy, and that there may be various reasons to aid them, but that they have no claim on us regarding *justice*.

Many people feel some force to Nozick's and Narveson's claim that I don't *act unjustly* simply by failing to rectify a situation for which I am not responsible. This claim seemingly tracks the widespread view that there is a big difference between the culpability of someone who exploits another, and someone who 'merely' fails to aid a victim of natural misfortune. By the same token, however, many of these same people feel the force of proportional justice, believing that it is unjust for the saint to suffer, or to be worse off than the sinner, even if this results from natural misfortune. The distinction between agent-relative and agent-neutral justice-based reasons helps reconcile these beliefs. Perhaps Nozick and Narveson are right that there is an important source of justice-based reasons, agent-relative reasons, that don't apply to me in situations for which I'm not responsible. Correspondingly, Nozick and Narveson may be able to plausibly claim that I'm not *acting unjustly*, if I fail to remedy a situation I'm not responsible for producing. Even so, there may be powerful agent-neutral justice-based reasons to do something about the situation. If we believe it would be more just for the saint to fare well, and for the saint to fare better than the sinner, we may also believe that we have *reasons of justice* to promote such outcomes if we can, even if we are not *acting unjustly* if we fail to do so. We see, then, that there is room for capturing what seems plausible about Nozick's and Narveson's position, without having to deny that there may be reasons of justice to help those whose plight we are not responsible for producing.

2.2 Equality

Just as there are many different conceptions of justice, there are many different conceptions of equality. In this part, I explore some connections between one central conception of equality, and the notions of fairness, luck, and responsibility. I believe that many of the points made here are directly relevant to, and help illuminate, certain central conceptions of justice, but I shall not pursue this here.

---

[19] See footnote 5.

[20] It is not easy to spell out the criteria for which misfortunes we are, in the relevant sense, responsible. But I take it the issue is not merely one of unavoidability or some social role in the causal nexus. That is, on the view in question, I take it there might be cases where we are not required to ameliorate the effects of some 'natural' misfortune, even if that misfortune was socially preventable. For example, even if society could develop and distribute a vaccine which would prevent natural blindness, on this view there might be no *requirement* regarding *justice* that it either do so or improve the lot of those born blind.

2.2.1 Fairness, luck, and responsibility

If I give one piece of candy to Andrea, and two to Rebecca, Andrea will immediately assert 'unfair!' This natural reaction suggests an intimate connection between equality and fairness. I believe that there is one central conception of equality—I do not claim it is the only one—that focuses on how people fare *relative to each other*, where the concern for equality is not separable from our concern for a certain aspect of fairness; they are part and parcel of a single concern. On this conception we say that certain inequalities are bad, or objectionable, when, and because, they are *comparatively unfair*; but by the same token, we say that there is a certain kind of comparative unfairness in certain kinds of undeserved inequalities. As indicated above, I now call this conception of equality *equality as comparative fairness*,[21] and it is this conception that I shall be addressing throughout this chapter. So, egalitarians of my sort are not motivated by *envy*, as is frequently charged, but by a particular conception of *fairness*.

Many contemporary egalitarians, including Gerald Cohen, Ronald Dworkin, and Richard Arneson, have been identified as so-called *luck egalitarians*.[22] Acknowledging the importance of autonomy and personal responsibility, *luck egalitarianism* supposedly aims to rectify the influence of luck in people's lives. Correspondingly, a canonical formulation of luck egalitarianism, invoked by both Cohen and myself, is that it is bad when one person is worse off than another through no fault or choice of her own.[23] So, luck egalitarians object when equally deserving people are unequally well off, but not when one person is worse off than another due to her own responsible choices, say to pursue a life of leisure or crime.

In fact, I think luck egalitarianism has been misunderstood by both its proponents and its opponents. The egalitarian's *fundamental* concern isn't with luck *per se*, or even with whether or not someone is worse off than another through no fault or choice of her own, it is, as noted above, with *comparative fairness*. But people have been confused about this because, as it happens, in most paradigmatic cases where inequality involves comparative unfairness it *also* involves luck, or someone being worse off than another through no fault or choice of her own.[24]

---

[21] See footnote 3.

[22] See R. J. Arneson, 'Equality and Equal Opportunity for Welfare', *Philosophical Studies*, 56 (1989), 77–93; R. Dworkin, 'What is Equality? Part 1: Equality of Welfare' and 'Part 2: Equality of Resources', *Philosophy and Public Affairs*, 10 (1981), 185–246 and 283–345; and G. A. Cohen, 'On the Currency of Egalitarian Justice', *Ethics*, 99 (1989), 906–944.

[23] See Cohen's 'On the Currency of Egalitarian Justice' and my *Inequality*.

[24] One anonymous reader remarks that 'it is not clear that it is helpful to describe the position in question as a luck egalitarian one (or to say that 'luck egalitarianism has been misunderstood by both its proponents and its opponents'), rather than as an alternative to luck egalitarianism'. I find this remark slightly puzzling. I *agree* that it is not helpful to describe the position in question as *luck egalitarianism*; my *point* is to show that the egalitarian's fundamental concern is *not* with luck *per se*, but with *comparative fairness*. Thus, my preferred name for the kind of view I think egalitarians are concerned with is *equality as comparative fairness*, or *comparative fairness egalitarianism*.

Indeed, as I understand the view in question, one could not only drop the reference to *luck*, but also the reference to *egalitarianism*, and say that the wider view on which the concern for equality arises in (important

On close examination, the intimate connection between equality and fairness illuminates the ultimate role that luck plays in egalitarian thinking, as well as the relevance and limitations of the 'through no fault or choice of their own' clause. Among *equally* deserving people, it *is* bad, because *unfair*, for some to be worse off than others through no fault or choice of their own. But among *unequally* deserving people it isn't bad, because not unfair, for someone less deserving to be worse off than someone more deserving, even if the former is worse off through no fault or choice of his own. For example, egalitarians needn't object if a fully responsible criminal is worse off than a law-abiding citizen, even if the criminal craftily avoided capture, and so is only worse off because, through no fault or choice of his own, a falling tree branch injured him.

Additionally, in some cases inequality is bad, because unfair, even though the worse-off *are* responsible for their plight; as when the worse-off are so because they chose to do their duty, or perhaps acted supererogatorily, in adverse circumstances not of their making. So, for example, if I'm unlucky enough to walk by a drowning child, and I injure myself saving her, the egalitarian might think it *unfair* that I end up worse off than others, even though I am so as a result of my own responsible free choice to do my duty to help someone in need.[25]

Correspondingly, on reflection, luck *itself* is neither good nor bad from the egalitarian standpoint. Egalitarians object to luck that leaves equally deserving people un-equally well off, not to luck that makes equally deserving people equally well off, or renders unequally deserving people proportionally well off. Thus, luck will be opposed *only to the extent* that it undermines comparative fairness.

Some luck egalitarians distinguish between *option luck*, to which we responsibly open ourselves, and *brute luck*, which simply 'befalls' us, unbidden.[26] This distinction's

---

and widespread, but still) special cases, just is a view about comparative fairness. Still, I believe that the view I favour really lays at the *foundation* of the views of many who *thought* that they were fundamentally concerned with the way in which luck produces inequality, and so regarded themselves as luck egalitarians. I came to realize that this was true of me, and in discussions with Jerry Cohen I came to realize that it was true of him as well. It isn't really that Jerry and I *abandoned* our previous views; rather, we developed a better understanding of what we have actually been committed to all along, and so our articulation of our views evolved in important ways. This is why I say that 'luck egalitarianism has been misunderstood by its proponents'. And, of course, if it has been misunderstood by its proponents, it isn't surprising if it has also been misunderstood by its opponents! So, opponents have been able to raise serious objections to luck egalitarianism *as it was originally described*, without really successfully undermining the substantive view to which so-called (and poorly named) 'luck egalitarians' were fundamentally committed.

[25] Here I'm assuming that one might have a duty to save the drowning child. But one might feel the same way about the case if we thought aiding the child was supererogatory. However, as I discuss below, perhaps not all instances of someone's ending up worse off than others as a result of supererogatory action would involve comparative unfairness and hence warrant egalitarian rectification.

[26] Ronald Dworkin distinguished between option luck and brute luck in 'What is Equality?' See also R. Dworkin, *Sovereign Virtue* (Cambridge, MA: Harvard University Press, 2000), chs 1 and 2. For an important critique of the distinction, see K. Lippert-Rasmussen, 'Egalitarianism, Option Luck, and Responsibility', *Ethics*, 111 (2001), 548–579.

advocates believe that any option luck inequalities—e.g. those resulting from people autonomously choosing to gamble or invest in the stock market—are unobjectionable, while brute luck inequalities—e.g. those resulting from genetic variations or unavoidable accidents—are objectionable.

I reject the way the option/brute luck distinction is typically invoked. In part, this is because drawing the line between them is difficult. But, more importantly, I believe it *is* objectionable if Mary takes a prudent risk, and John an imprudent one, yet Mary fares much worse than John, because she is the victim of bad, and he the beneficiary of good, option luck. Likewise, I believe there *is* an egalitarian objection if Mary and John are equally deserving, and choose similar options, but John ends up much better off than Mary because he enjoys vastly greater option luck. As with paradigmatic cases involving brute luck, in such a case Mary ends up much worse off than John, though she is in no way less deserving. This seems patently unfair. It is a case of *comparative* unfairness to which my kind of egalitarian should object.

This discussion is relevant to many public policy issues. *If* it is true that people can have personal responsibility for their actions in a way compatible with a meaningful conception of desert—a big 'if', but one that many accept, and that I shall assume for this discussion—then not *all* substantive inequalities will involve comparative unfairness, and hence be objectionable from an egalitarian standpoint. This position has deep and important implications for the nature and extent of our obligations towards the less fortunate whose predicaments resulted from their own fully responsible choices. This might include conditions resulting from individually responsible choices involving job selection, lifestyle, risky behaviour, and so on.

Clearly, this issue is too large to deal adequately with here, but let me just make five relevant points. First, this discussion's starting point is that the mere fact that some are worse off than others, does *not* mean that there is an *egalitarian* reason to aid them. There is an egalitarian reason to aid someone if her situation is *unfair* relative to others, and whether this is so depends on pertinent facts of individual responsibility.

Second, even if there is no *egalitarian* reason to aid someone needy, many powerful normative considerations may dictate our doing so. These may include maximin or prioritarian considerations that give special weight to the claims of the worse-off, humanitarian considerations to ease pain and suffering, utilitarian reasons to promote the general welfare, virtue-related reasons of compassion, mercy, beneficence, and forgiveness, and so on. As I have argued elsewhere, egalitarians are rightly committed to pluralism, and we have to be sensitive to the *full range* of reasons for aiding the needy besides those of comparative fairness.

But third, where other morally relevant factors are sufficiently close, egalitarian reasons of comparative fairness may help determine who has the strongest moral claim on scarce resources. For example, if one *has* to choose between who gets the last available bed in the intensive care unit, perhaps it should go to the innocent pedestrian, rather than the drunk driver who ran into him. (Though this point raises many complicated questions, some of which I shall return to shortly.[27])

Fourth, regarding comparative fairness, it is crucial that one determine appropriate comparison classes, so that one is comparing all relevant types of behaviour in the same way. For example, it would be objectionable to downgrade the medical claims of AIDS patients who engaged in unprotected sex, if one wasn't similarly prepared to downgrade the medical claims of pregnant women who engaged in unprotected sex, or perhaps obese stroke victims who did nothing to curb their appetite.

Fifth, in accordance with my point about option luck, it is important for comparative fairness that one not merely compare the 'losers' of those making poor choices with the 'winners' of those making good choices, but that, in addition, one compare the winners and losers of *both* categories with each other. Most people who overeat don't have a stroke, and most helmetless motorcyclists don't end up in the emergency room. Thus, regarding comparative fairness, one must remember that full responsibility for one's choices doesn't entail full responsibility for one's predicament. Indeed, as Kant rightly saw, the two are only loosely, and coincidentally, connected. Correspondingly, consideration of equality as comparative fairness requires that we pay attention not only to *actual* outcomes, but to the extent to which different people end up better and worse off than the expected value of their choices. Unfortunately, I cannot pursue these issues here.

Let us return to the case of the drunk driver who was fully responsible for getting drunk and then hit a pedestrian. By hypothesis, the drunk driver is responsible in a way the pedestrian is not for both being in need of urgent care.[28] And I suggested that this may provide some reason for giving the ICU's last available bed to the pedestrian rather than the driver, as it might be unfair if the 'guilty' person *responsible* for the accident were saved rather than the 'innocent' victim of his behaviour. But, as I said, the situation is complicated. We might say there is an important *local* reason of comparative fairness to favour the pedestrian over the drunk driver in this case, attributable to their different degrees of responsibility for the specific situation they each now face; but there are also *global* reasons of comparative fairness to consider, at least *ideally*, from an egalitarian perspective in determining who should get the last hospital bed.

---

[27] An important question I shall not address is whether we should be concerned about inequalities between people over the course of their whole lives, or between corresponding segments of their lives (say, teenagers of today with teenagers from previous years), or between simultaneous segments of their lives (say, the elderly of today with the youth of today). See *Inequality*, ch. 8, and D. McKerlie's pioneering article 'Equality and Time', *Ethics*, 99 (1989), 475–491. This question is especially relevant regarding issues of responsibility; since, for example, it is questionable whether a sixty-year-old should be much worse off than his contemporaries, or previous or later sixty-year-olds, just because of some responsible action performed by his twenty-year-old self.

[28] I am aware, but here put aside, the important questions raised by Coase's theorem, according to which both the drunk driver and the pedestrian can be seen as responsible for the situation and imposing costs on each other. I'm willing to go out on a limb and assign the greater moral responsibility for the predicament to the drunk driver in most such cases! See R. Coase, 'The Problem of Social Cost', *Journal of Law and Economics*, 3 (1960), 1–44.

Suppose that the drunk driver was a saint who had never been drunk before and had no reason to believe that his getting drunk would produce such a tragic outcome. Suppose, further, that despite the vast good he had done for others, his own life had been filled with suffering and tragedy. Next, suppose that the pedestrian was an evil man who had harmed countless innocents, but whose own life had overflowed with good fortune. Here, egalitarianism might favour giving the last bed to the driver, rather than the pedestrian, notwithstanding the driver's responsibility for their current dire predicament.

I submit, then, that individual responsibility *is* important from the egalitarian perspective, but it clearly isn't *all* that matters. Moreover, in so far as it does matter, *global* responsibility for one's overall character and predicament matters, not merely local responsibility for any specific predicament one confronts.

An interesting question is whether egalitarians should treat both 'local' and 'non-local' components of one's global responsibility for a given predicament similarly, or whether they should give special weight to someone's 'local' responsibility.[29] The latter view might be akin to the view that in promoting self-interest it can be rational to give special weight to one's *present* desires in contrast with one's past or future desires. I'm inclined to think that egalitarians should treat local responsibility similarly to the other components of global responsibility, but I'm not certain of this. As long as 'local' responsibility is given the same weight for everyone in similar contexts, it may be both consistent and desirable for egalitarians to give it special weight in assessing comparative fairness. This is an important issue requiring further thought.

The issue of responsibility has an important bearing on the relationship between comparative fairness and comparative justice.[30] I used to think that 'comparative

---

[29]   Carl Knight raised this question.

[30]   An anonymous reader raised a concern which I have also heard from many others over the years: 'If the intervention of luck is undesirable only when it disrupts the situation of equally deserving individuals, and if responsibility does not always recommend departures from equality but only when it is manifested in people's deserving actions, then it might be argued that desert, not equality, is doing all the moral work.' The following paragraphs in the text are intended to explicate the manner in which, assuming there is a meaningful conception of free will, moral desert *is* central, but *not* all that matters from the standpoint of equality as comparative fairness. But let me make several additional points here.

Most people assume that the normative significance of desert presupposes a meaningful conception of free will. On this view, if there is no free will, then the notion of desert has no moral traction, and it has nothing to tell us about what people should get or how we should act. But, as I showed in section 2.1, the notions of *comparative* justice and fairness *do* have traction in a world without free will. We can say, if we like, that in a world without free will people are 'equality deserving' in the sense that *no one deserves anything*; but it is clear that it is our concern about *comparative fairness* that would oppose inequalities in such a world, not a concern that people haven't got what they deserve. This is enough to show that desert *isn't* doing all the work in our thinking about equality as comparative fairness.

Also, many assume that if we only object to inequalities among equally deserving people, this suggests that our *fundamental* concern is simply with each person getting what they deserve absolutely. But this isn't right. If there were two equally deserving people, one of whom got what he deserved, and one of whom got *more* than he deserved, there would be two *distinct* objections to the situation. One objection would be that the one person got more than he deserved in absolute terms. But the other objection would be an objection of comparative unfairness. If one lowered the better off person to the level he deserved, this would make the

fairness' and 'comparative justice' were merely terminological variants of the same substantive position, with some people favouring one expression, and some the other, because of slightly different linguistic intuitions about the notions of 'fairness' and 'justice'. For example, some people who have the linguistic intuition that there can only be an *injustice* where there is an agent responsible for perpetrating the injustice, might prefer to describe inequalities resulting from natural events as involving comparative *unfairness* rather than comparative *injustice*. Hence, some who balk at the claim that it is *unjust* that some people are born blind, and others not, nevertheless agree that such inequalities are *bad*, and that the comparative *unfairness* of the situation constitutes a reason to alleviate such inequalities if we can. Still, I now think that comparative fairness and comparative justice represent two substantively distinct positions related to the role that responsibility plays in the two positions. Let me explain why.

As indicated previously, I believe that comparative justice involves comparative desert, where the desert is *moral* desert. So, as seen, the idea is that saints morally *deserve* to fare better than sinners, on the supposition that there is a meaningful notion of free will, and that the saints and sinners are responsible for their moral characters. So, as discussed previously, on my view the responsibility that is relevant to comparative *justice* is the responsibility for one's character as a moral agent.

Advocates of comparative fairness *also* care about moral desert, because they, too, believe that it is, in a sense, unfair if a less morally deserving person fares better in proportion to her character than a more morally deserving person does. So, like advocates of comparative justice, advocates of comparative fairness will think it is fundamentally important if people are responsible for their characters, and they need not, for example, object to inequalities between saints and sinners where those inequalities are morally deserved. However, I believe the notion of comparative fairness allows greater scope to the importance of responsibility than the notion of comparative justice. For we can be responsible for our choices, and their consequences, as well as our characters, and this is relevant to what we regard as comparatively fair in a way that extends beyond the narrower notions of moral desert and comparative justice.

---

outcome better in terms of both absolute desert and comparative fairness. On the other hand, if one raised the worse off person to the level of the better off person, this would be *just as good* from the standpoint of comparative fairness, though it would *worsen* the outcome regarding absolute desert. Many people who claim to care about equality would, in fact, opt for the latter outcome over the former one. This is enough to show that the concern for comparative fairness is distinct from the concern that everyone get what they deserve, if this is understood in absolute terms.

But the question remains what the connection is between comparative desert and comparative fairness in a world with significant free will. I address this question in the following pages. But note, even if one were convinced that on the assumption of free will the two views had the same implications, this wouldn't be enough to show they *were* equivalent. And if they were equivalent, this would undermine any claims that one should dispense with one in favour of the other. Thus, the view I have articulated may lead us to see that there is an intimate connection between desert and fairness, but this wouldn't show that we should care about desert *rather than* fairness, any more than it would show that we should care about fairness *rather than* desert.

Suppose John and Mary are both fundamentally decent people, but that they choose different, morally permissible, life paths. Consistent with meeting all his duties and obligations to others, John freely and responsibly chooses a path that will predictably benefit himself more than other paths available to him. Mary freely and responsibly chooses a path involving many selfless actions. She is constantly choosing to put others before herself, with the predictable result that she will end up worse off than she would have had she followed John's path. Naturally, John ends up better off than Mary.

From the standpoint of comparative *justice*, the situation is unjust. Mary is worse off than John, who is no more morally deserving than she. Indeed, it is arguable that Mary is *more* morally deserving than John, so that in a perfectly *just* world, she would fare even better than John. The advocates of comparative fairness may agree that in an important sense it *is* unfair that Mary fares worse than John, but in another important sense it is *not* unfair. Mary *could* have chosen to be as well off as John, without in any way shirking her duties or responsibilities. She freely and responsibly chose a path that she *knew* would leave her worse off than John. Given this, it is arguable that her situation relative to John's is *not* comparatively unfair overall. Accordingly, perhaps the egalitarian need not object to the inequality between them, notwithstanding the fact that she had laudable reasons for choosing her path. In any event, the objection to the relative conditions of John and Mary seems weaker on grounds of comparative fairness than on grounds of comparative justice, and this is because the notion of fairness may give weight to considerations of responsibility beyond responsibility for one's moral character.

Similarly, suppose I can choose between two morally neutral lifestyles. One will be harder in the short run, but ultimately benefit me more over the course of my life. Being fully apprised of the differences between the two lifestyles, I freely and responsibly choose the easier path; while Mary, confronting the same choice, freely and responsibly chooses the harder one. By hypothesis, Mary and I may be equally *morally* deserving. So, from the standpoint of comparative *justice*, it may be bad, because unjust, if I end up worse off than Mary. But egalitarians may not object to the inequality between Mary and me. Though in one sense it may be unjust, and unfair, for Mary to fare better than me, in another important sense it is *not* comparatively unfair for me to be worse off than her. I *could* have been as well off as her, but freely and responsibly chose another path knowing its ramifications. Having made my bed, as it were, I now have to lie in it. Under such circumstances, one might reasonably think that, overall, the inequality between Mary and me is not (especially) unfair, and hence not (especially) objectionable.

Finally, consider the case of someone with a high moral character, overall, who responsibly commits a crime to promote some desirable end. Compare that to someone with a decent, but not especially high, moral character, overall, who responsibly follows the law, perhaps simply for the self-interested reason that he fears jail. In the ideal world, the first person should fare better than the second from the standpoint of comparative justice, assuming that both are responsible for their characters. But is it comparatively *unfair* if the first person fares less well than the second, because she spends time in jail? Well, in one important respect—one where the notion of fairness tracks the notion of justice—it *is* comparatively unfair. But in another important respect, one that gives significant weight to individual responsibility for our choices and their consequences, it is not comparatively unfair. One person responsibly chose to break the law, another to abide by it; whatever their moral motivations and characters, it would be unfair if we simply ignored the role that their responsible decisions played in their predicaments.

In sum, I now think that though they are related, the notions of comparative justice and comparative fairness differ. On the assumption that there is a meaningful conception of free will, both attach important weight to the role that individual responsibility plays in the formation of our moral characters. So both pay attention to the extent to which we are morally deserving of faring well relative to others. But comparative fairness *also* attaches weight to the role that individual responsibility plays in our choices and their consequences. Moral desert is central, but not all that matters from the standpoint of equality as comparative fairness. By the same token, as important as individual responsibility is, it is circumscribed, from the standpoint of comparative fairness, by the kinds of considerations presented in the fourth and fifth points noted above. Finally, as indicated, the discussion here assumes that there is a meaningful conception of free will and individual responsibility. If there is not, then I believe that comparative justice and comparative fairness will amount to the same, egalitarian, view. In that case, all inequalities will be both morally undeserved, and ones for which no one is responsible; hence, all normatively significant inequalities will be both comparatively unjust and comparatively unfair.

2.2.2 Equality of what?

Many egalitarians have debated the following question: In so far as we are egalitarians, what *kind* of equality should we seek? A host of candidates have been championed, including: income, resources, primary goods, wealth, power, welfare, opportunity, needs satisfaction, capabilities, functionings, rights, and liberties. It is difficult to exaggerate this topic's importance, since equality of one kind often *requires* inequality of another. For example, equality of income may correlate with *inequality* of need satisfaction between the handicapped and the healthy, and vice versa.

I shall not offer a particular substantive answer to the 'equality of what?' question. But I shall address a number of related topics, such as whether egalitarians should care about equality of welfare or opportunity, ex ante or ex post equality, and procedural or substantive fairness. Considering these topics will further illuminate the conditions of, and connections between, desert, fairness, responsibility, and equality.

I begin with a methodological remark. Philosophers favouring different conceptions of what kind of equality matters have gone to great lengths illustrating cases where rival conceptions have implausible implications. These philosophers seem to assume that such considerations provide good reason for rejecting the rival conceptions. Moreover, many seem to implicitly assume that concern for one kind of equality rules out concern for others. Unfortunately, on a pluralistic view of morality, to which *all* reasonable egalitarians are committed, such assumptions are dubious.

Elsewhere,[31] I have pointed out that the fact that ideals like equality, utility, or freedom sometimes have implausible, or even terrible, implications, does *not* show that those ideals do not matter. It merely shows that each ideal, alone, is not *all* that matters. Likewise, the fact that different conceptions of what kind of equality matters some-times have implausible implications does not necessarily show that those conceptions do not matter. Equality, like morality itself, is complex. And more than one conception may be relevant to our 'all things considered' egalitarian judgements. Perhaps different kinds of equality matter in different contexts. Or perhaps even in the same context there are strong reasons for promoting different kinds of equality. Thus, the 'equality of what?' question may have several plausible answers.

My own view is that for comparative fairness egalitarians, a large component of their concern should be with *welfare*—specifically, with whether the distribution of welfare is comparatively fair; but as I use it, 'welfare' is a technical term that needs to be interpreted broadly, and with great care. It must appropriately include, among other things, most of the elements that Amartya Sen carefully distinguishes in his sophisticated account of functionings, capability sets, freedom, agency, and well-being.[32] However, I also think that for comparative fairness egalitarians, a large component of their concern should be with *opportunity*—specifically, with whether the distribution of opportunities is comparatively fair. Thus, the comparative fairness egalitarian will want both equality of welfare and equality of opportunity in those cases where people have made similarly responsible choices and where no one is more deserving than anyone else.

Suppose, for example, that we lived in a world not too unlike the actual one, in which a relatively small percentage of people were very well off, while the vast majority were much worse off. Concern for equality of welfare would impel us to raise everyone to the level of the best-off. But suppose, given limited resources, this were not possible. Concern for equality of welfare might then impel us to redistribute from the better- to the worse-off. But if the percentage of the better-off were small, this might do little to improve the worse-off; its main effect might be to reduce the better-off to the worse-off's level. Even if we think this *would* be an improvement regarding equality of welfare and even, perhaps, regarding total welfare, we *might* think it would *not* be an improvement all things considered,[33] and in any event it might not

---

[31] See *Inequality*; 'Equality, Priority, and the Levelling Down Objection' and 'Egalitarianism: A Complex, Individualistic, and Comparative Notion' in E. Sosa and E. Villanueva (eds), *Philosophical Issues* 11 (Oxford: Blackwell Publishers, 2001), 327–352.

[32] See *Inequality Reexamined* (Cambridge, MA: Harvard University Press, 1992), and also 'Well-being, Agency, and Freedom: The Dewey Lectures 1984', *Journal of Philosophy*, 82 (1985), 169–220.

[33] For considerations supporting this, see my 'A 'New' Principle of Aggregation' in Ernest Sosa and Enrique Villanueva (eds), *Philosophical Issues* 15, *Normativity*, (Oxford: Wiley-Blackwell, 2005), 218–234.

be politically feasible. Thus, we might conclude that in such a case we must accept, even if not happily, a significantly unequal situation regarding welfare.

Still, we might distinguish two versions of this scenario. In one, the better-off are members of a hereditary aristocracy. They, and their descendants, are guaranteed a place in the better-off group, while the worse-off and their descendants are destined to remain in the worse-off group regardless of their abilities or efforts. In a second version, there is genuine equality of opportunity. At birth, each person, and his or her descendants, has an equal chance of ending up in the better-off group.

By hypothesis, the two versions of the scenario are equivalent regarding equality of welfare. Yet, most would agree that the second is better than the first all things considered, since it is better regarding equality of opportunity. I think, then, that qua egalitarian, one should care about equality of opportunity. But this concern should be *in addition to*, rather than *in place of*, a concern for equality of welfare. The second situation may be *perfect* regarding equality of opportunity—but it still involves many who are worse off than others through no fault or choice of their own, in a way that involves comparative unfairness. The egalitarian, qua egalitarian, will regard this as objectionable. It would be better, regarding equality, if, in addition to everyone having equal *opportunities*, those equally deserving actually fared equally well.[34]

The preceding considerations are relevant to several related topics, such as whether we should be concerned about ex ante equality—equality in people's *prospects* concerning the lives they might lead—or ex post equality—equality in *outcomes* concerning the actual lives that people end up leading; and similarly, whether the egalitarian's concern should be mainly with *procedural* fairness, or with some more robust outcome-related conception of *substantive* fairness, according to which an outcome that resulted from a perfectly fair procedure might nonetheless be substantively unfair and require amelioration. So, just as one should care about both equality of opportunity and equality of welfare (broadly construed), for similar reasons I think one should care about both ex ante and ex post equality, and also about both procedural fairness and a more robust outcome-related conception of substantive fairness. Moreover, while in some cases, perhaps, ex ante equality, or procedural fairness, will be all that is realizable, and in others our main concern might be with ex post equality, or substantive fairness, at times the different positions will be intimately related. So, for example, it is arguable that under certain circumstances, whatever outcome results from a situation that meets sufficiently demanding criteria for ex ante equality, or procedural fairness,

---

[34] Recall that I am elucidating a version of egalitarianism that expresses a concern for comparative fairness. I have tried to illuminate the relation between this conception and luck egalitarianism, desert, responsibility, and so forth. This view will only advocate equality of welfare or opportunity when this is warranted by considerations of comparative fairness. Hence, the comparative fairness egalitarian will regard it as bad, because comparatively unfair, if some are worse off than others in terms of welfare or opportunities through no fault or choice of their own, but not otherwise (subject to the qualifications discussed earlier). So understood, it is a mistake to contrast the concern for equality of welfare or equality of opportunity with luck egalitarianism. The views are intimately related, as the most plausible versions of each ultimately reflect a concern about comparative fairness.

will, in fact, also be guaranteed to meet the most plausible conception of ex post equality, or substantive fairness. Moreover, it is also arguable that under certain circumstances, no coherent account can be given of what ex post equality, or substantive fairness demands, independently of certain favourable conditions initially obtaining that would at least partially satisfy the criteria for ex ante equality or procedural fairness.

I cannot fully defend these claims here, but let me offer some observations to illuminate them.

Egalitarians recognize that in the game of life, each of us, to some extent, must play the cards we are dealt. But they also recognize that sometimes our cards are both dealt to us, and played for us. On this analogy, the concern for ex ante equality, and procedural fairness, reflects the concern that the deck should not be stacked against certain players, and that there should be no cheating in the play of the hand. So, minimally, the egalitarian wants each person's hand to be determined by a fair deal and fairly played. If, for example, the deck is stacked in favour of whites or men, so that they are always dealt aces and kings, while blacks or women are always dealt deuces and treys, that situation will be patently unfair, and it can be rightly criticized from the standpoint of ex ante equality or procedural fairness. Likewise, it will be unfair if the cards are dealt fairly, but unfairly played; if, for example, whites or males are allowed to look at the hands of blacks or women before deciding what cards to play.

Ensuring that each person's hand will be determined by a fair deal and played fairly insures that, in advance of the deal, the *expected value* of each hand is the same, and we can say that that meets an important criterion for ex ante equality or procedural fairness. But the egalitarian wants more than just a fair deal and a fair play, since, by itself, this would do nothing to preclude some people being dealt aces and kings, while others, no less deserving, are dealt deuces and treys. That is, in the game of life, the cards don't have to be *stacked* against particular groups or individuals for it to still *turn out* that some are born with extraordinary life prospects relative to others. For egalitarians this is deeply unfair, even if, in an important sense, it is not *as* unfair as it would have been had it resulted from a 'stacked' deck, say, of bias or discrimination.

So the egalitarian not only wants the *deal* to be fair, he wants, as it were, each *hand* to be fair. That is, he does not merely want the expected value of each hand to be the same in *advance* of each deal, he wants the expected value of each hand to be the same *after* the deal. Thus, it should not only be that *in advance* of bringing a child into the world, one can reasonably expect the expected value of its life to be as good as anyone else's, but rather that any child that is actually brought into the world should face a constellation of natural and social circumstances that give its life prospects an expected value as good as anyone else's. Notice, this view reflects a concern that in one way resembles an ex post view—since it seeks equality in people's life prospects after the deal, as it were. But in another way it resembles an ex ante view—since it focuses on the expected value of people's life *prospects*, rather than the outcome that will result when the hand is actually played, which is to say the value of the lives that the people actually end up *leading*. For my purposes, I shall count such a view as setting further requirements on the criteria that must be met for ex ante equality or procedural fairness to be fully satisfied.

But these criteria need strengthening. To see this, let us further develop our card analogy. Suppose that each person is to be dealt four cards, each of which represents a life prospect. Suppose further that one of these cards will be selected at random. If an ace is selected, someone will lead a very high quality life with a value of 20,000, if an eight is selected someone will lead a moderately high quality life of value 10,000, and if a deuce is selected someone will lead a very poor quality life of value 0. Now suppose that in outcome A each member of a large population has been dealt four cards. And suppose that as a result of a completely fair deal, involving many decks, half the population has been dealt two aces and two deuces, while the other half has been dealt four eights. Here, we meet the initial criteria that prior to the deal the expected value of each life is the same, and we further meet the additional criteria that after the deal the expected value of each life is the same, namely 10,000. Still, although the *expected values* of their lives are the same, it is clear that some people in A face significantly different life prospects. Those who have been dealt four eights face the certainty of a life of value 10,000, and the statistically near certain outcome of ending up in their society's middle-off group. Those who have been dealt aces and twos, face the equal probability that they will end up with a life of value 20,000 or a life of value 0, and it is certain that they will either end up in their society's best-off group or its worst-off group. Hence, whatever happens, it is *certain* that those who were dealt different kinds of cards will lead lives of significantly different value.

Contrast outcome A with outcome B, where, *everyone* is dealt four eights, and hence faces the certain prospect of living a life of value 10,000, or outcome C, where, *everyone* is dealt two aces and two deuces, and hence faces an equal probability of living a life of value 20,000 or a life of value 0. Clearly, there is a respect in which each person's overall life prospects are the same in B, and similarly in C, but not in A. I believe that the respect in which this is so reflects an important element of what one should care about in so far as one cares about ex ante equality or procedural fairness. Arguably, from the standpoint of ex ante equality or procedural fairness, B and C are both perfect. One should be indifferent between them, and each should be preferred to A.

If right, the preceding suggests that in so far as one cares about ex ante equality, or procedural fairness, one should not merely be concerned with the *expected value* of different lives, either in advance of their coming to be, or even at birth. Rather, for each kind of life, L, with value V, that someone faces at birth with probability p, it will be desirable if everyone else, at birth, also faces a kind of life, L´, with probability p, that also has value V. Note, this position does *not* commit one to the kind of radical egalitarian position that Kurt Vonnegut Jr. skewered in his notoriously anti-egalitarian diatribe 'Harrison Bergeron', which would require that everyone be exactly the same in all respects.[35] On the view in question, L and L´ may differ substantially in all sorts of respects, as long as their *overall* value is the same.

Suppose we fully achieved ex ante equality, or procedural fairness, along the lines suggested above. So, for every two people there would be a one-to-one correspondence of equivalent alternatives involving the different life prospects they faced, and the probabilities and values of those prospects. In this case, we would have met the egalitarian goal that no one should be disadvantaged relative to another merely by the circumstances surrounding their birth. Still, the egalitarian wants more than this, as such ex ante equality or procedural fairness would be compatible with undeserved *ex post* inequalities of any size. And egalitarians will object to such inequalities precisely when, and because, they involve the substantive comparative unfairness of some being worse off than others, though they are no less deserving and not responsible for their plight.

Consider an outcome like C above. Suppose, at birth, everyone faces one of two prospects with equal probability, either a very high quality life of value 20,000, or a very low quality life of value 0. Assume this reflects a fair situation, equivalent to each being fairly dealt a fair hand, and that pure chance will determine which kind of life they end up leading, so that no charge of bias or unfairness can be made regarding the 'play of the hand'. Even so, given that no one is less deserving than anyone else or responsible for their situations, egalitarians will regard it as comparatively unfair if half the people end up with lives of value 20,000 and half with lives of value 0. Ex ante equality and procedural fairness may be desirable, but in such circumstances they are no substitute for ex post equality or substantive fairness. In such a case, at least, egalitarians would much prefer the fairer substantive outcome where each person lived a life of value 10,000.

Next, suppose that the game of life was 'stacked' so that at birth certain groups had a much greater chance of ending up well off than others. Using our card analogy, imagine that some people have been unfairly dealt three aces and a deuce, while others have been unfairly dealt three deuces and an ace, but that, as before, a random selection of the cards will determine what life each person actually leads. Clearly, this situation would be objectionable from the standpoint of ex ante equality and procedural fairness, and presumably there would be egalitarian reason to try to prevent such unfairness in people's initial starting points if one could. Still, *assuming that no one was less deserving than the others*, if, in fact, everyone had aces drawn, so that everyone ended up living equally high quality lives, egalitarians would see no reason to change the outcome;

---

[35] 'Harrison Bergeron' appeared in *Welcome to the Monkey House* (New York: Dell Publishing, 1998), 7–14; it is reprinted in L. P. Pojman and R. Westmoreland (eds), *Equality* (Oxford: Oxford University Press, 1997), 315–318. Bernard Williams raised a worry similar to Vonnegut's in 'The Idea of Equality' in P. Laslett and W. G. Runciman (eds), *Philosophy, Politics, and Society*, Second Series (Oxford: Basil Blackwell, 1962), 110–131. Hugo Bedau dubbed the ludicrous view that everyone should be exactly the same 'radical egalitarianism' in 'Radical Egalitarianism' in R. Pennock and J. Chapman (eds), *Nomos IX: Equality* (New York: Atherton Press, 1967), 3–27.

similarly, if everyone had deuces drawn. On the other hand, if half had an ace drawn, and half a deuce, egalitarians would favour redistribution from the better- to the worse-off no matter *who* was better off. Here, the concern for ex post equality and substantive fairness would dictate the egalitarian's response to the actual lives led, and any concerns she might have about ex ante equality or procedural justice would play no role in *that* response.

Might the egalitarian simply focus on achieving ex post equality, and not worry about ex ante equality or procedural fairness? I think not. Let me make several points regarding this.

First, the concern for ex ante equality and procedural fairness reflects the view that it not only matters how people *end up*, it matters how they have been *treated*; for example, that they are treated *as equals* so that no one is discriminated against or otherwise dealt an unfair hand to play. Importantly, it also matters that each person be given a fair start from which to autonomously plan their life, so that each person is significantly responsible for their own lot in life. Moreover, such factors are relevant to telic considerations regarding the goodness of outcomes, and not merely deontic consider-ations of how people ought to act. Thus, for example, it is not only true that people *ought* to treat people as equals, it is true that treating people as equals is *itself* a good-making feature of outcomes. That is, other things equal, an outcome where people have been treated as equals is better than one where they have not.

Second, as noted in discussing equality of opportunity, there may be some cases where ex post equality is unobtainable, or undesirable all things considered, where it would be better, precisely because fairer, if the outcome resulted from an initial situation of ex ante equality or procedural fairness than if it didn't.

Third, ex post equality is desirable only when it reflects comparative fairness. So, as indicated earlier, other things equal, egalitarians should not want fully responsible criminals to end up equally well off as law-abiding citizens. Likewise, suppose that John's initial starting point enables him to live a life ranging in value from 10,000 to 20,000, while Mary's only enables her to live a life of value from 0 to 10,000. Even if John and Mary end up equally well off, with lives of value 10,000, egalitarians would have good reason to worry that the outcome was comparatively unfair. Perhaps Mary, having done her best to take full advantage of her opportunities, ought to end up much better off than John, who may have responsibly squandered his abundant oppor-tunities. So, comparative fairness egalitarians can't just ignore questions of ex ante equality and procedural fairness, and focus on bringing about outcomes of ex post equality.

But this raises a fourth important issue. One can't simply assume that Mary deserves to be better off than John, based on the extent to which they differed in maximizing their potential. Perhaps if John had been given Mary's initial starting point, he would have acted as Mary did, and vice versa. In that case, perhaps Mary and John deserve to be equally well off after all, despite their completely different, and seemingly unfair, initial starting points. This shows that it may be important to promote ex ante equality and procedural fairness, to ensure that people have sufficiently comparable starting points, in order to make meaningful judgements of comparative fairness.[36] Furthermore, if, contrary to fact, one could ensure that people's initial starting points fully met the robust criteria for ex ante equality and procedural fairness—so, in particular, people had been dealt similar hands in terms of talents, temperament, and life prospects—and if, in addition, one could later remove or rectify the influence of luck on people's choices—so, ultimately, each person was responsible for how they ended up relative to others; then, of course, the comparative fairness egalitarian *would* be fully satisfied with the outcome regardless of whether it involved ex post equality.

2.3 Conclusion

This has been a long chapter. Let me give it a brief conclusion. In section 2.1, I discussed various conceptions of justice, including justice as the respecting of rights, proportional justice as absolute justice, proportional justice as comparative justice, and Rawls's conception of justice as fairness. I also discussed the distinction between *acting justly* and acting for *reasons of justice*, where the former involves *agent-relative* justice-based reasons, and the latter *agent-neutral* justice based reasons.

In section 2.2, I discussed a view I call *equality as comparative fairness*, and explored its connection with luck egalitarianism, desert, free will, and the importance of choice and responsibility. I noted an important, but often overlooked, difference between comparative fairness and comparative justice, with responsibility playing a larger role for the former than the latter given a robust conception of free will. I also argued that egalitarians should not only be pluralists regarding competing moral ideals, they should be pluralists regarding equality itself. In particular, I argued that egalitarians should care about equality of both welfare (broadly construed) and opportunity, about both *ex ante* and *ex post* equality, and about both procedural and substantive comparative fairness.

I believe that each of the conceptions of justice and equality discussed are plausible and significant, and that they have different connections to, and commitments regarding, each other, and the notions of desert, rights, free will, responsibility, and luck. I have tried to illuminate many of these connections and commitments, and to explore some of their implications. But I am well aware that I have barely scratched the surface regarding these complex, interrelated, and fundamentally important notions. Much more work remains to be done.

---

[36] Susan Hurley stressed this important point in 'Luck and Equality', *Proceedings of The Aristotelian Society*, Supplementary Volume, 75 (2001), 51–72, and in *Justice, Luck and Knowledge* (Cambridge, MA: Harvard University Press, 2003).

3

Four Approaches to Equal Opportunity[1]

Marc Fleurbaey

The philosophical literature on responsibility-sensitive egalitarianism contains a richness of proposals and controversies. Among the main issues addressed, one may list the following: (1) Should individuals be held responsible for their preferences or for their genuine choices?[2] (2) Should we focus on opportunities for subjective welfare or for a more objective metric of well-being?[3] (3) Does responsibility-sensitive egalitarianism ignore the true value of social equality and misplace the focus of the egalitarian project?[4] (4) Should we supplement responsibility-sensitive egalitarianism with guarantees that the exercise of responsibility by individuals will not lead to excessive inequalities or to extreme poverty?[5]

In this chapter, I'd like to draw attention to two other topics which have been highlighted by the economics literature on fair opportunities and may have some philosophical relevance. They may even enhance our understanding of the multifaceted notion of responsibility itself. Philosophers are often disdainful of the insights brought by formal economic analysis. I will therefore try to explain these matters in a totally non-formal way.[6]

[1] This chapter has benefited from presentations at Columbia and Oxford, from comments by B. Barry, A. Bilgrami, J. Broome, and J. Elster, and from a discussion with G. Cohen. It was written during a sabbatical stay at Nuffield College, the hospitality of which is gratefully acknowledged.
[2] E.g. G. A. Cohen, 'On the Currency of Egalitarian Justice', *Ethics*, 99 (1989), 906–944; R. Dworkin, *Sovereign Virtue: The Theory and Practice of Equality* (Cambridge, MA: Harvard University Press, 2000).
[3] E.g. R. J. Arneson, 'Equality and Equal Opportunity for Welfare', *Philosophical Studies*, 56 (1989), 77–93; 'Liberalism, Distributive Subjectivism, and Equal Opportunity for Welfare', *Philosophy and Public Affairs*, 19 (1990), 158–194; Cohen, 'On the Currency'; 'Equality of What? On Welfare, Goods and Capabilities', *Recherches Economiques de Louvain*, 56 (1990), 357–382; A. K. Sen, 'Capability and Well-Being' in M. Nussbaum and A. K. Sen (eds), *The Quality of Life* (Oxford: Oxford University Press, 1993), 30–53.
[4] E.g. E. S. Anderson, 'What is the Point of Equality?', *Ethics*, 109 (1999), 287–337; S. Scheffler, 'Choice, Circumstance, and the Value of Equality', *Politics, Philosophy and Economics*, 4 (2005), 5–28.
[5] E.g. R. J. Arneson, 'Luck Egalitarianism and Prioritarianism', *Ethics*, 110 (2000), 339–349; M. Fleurbaey, 'Egalitarian Opportunities', *Law and Philosophy*, 20 (2001), 499–530.
[6] A much expanded analysis of the issues discussed in this chapter can be found in M. Fleurbaey, *Fairness, Responsibility, and Welfare* (Oxford: Oxford University Press, 2008).

Here is a brief summary of these two topics. The first one is about two possible interpretations of the distributive implications of personal responsibility. According to one interpretation, in so far as individuals are responsible for their achievements no redistribution between them is needed. According to an alternative interpretation, the social objective can then have a zero aversion to inequality. This is a very different notion since such a social objective may advocate redistributing in order to enhance the total outcome, which is a forbidden operation in the first view. This distinction is often blurred in the literature, even in its economic branch, but, as will be explained in detail here, the two interpretations lead to very different criteria and policies.

The second topic is about the possibility for the social criterion to focus either on the neutralization of inequalities due to characteristics for which individuals are not responsible or on the relation between individuals' exercise of responsibility and their final achievements, which shapes the opportunities or prospects offered ex ante to individuals. Again the distinction is not trivial and its implications are far from negligible.

For each of these two topics, there is an ethical choice to be made between two options. These two choices being quite independent, this makes four possible combinations of choices, justifying the title of this chapter. I will show that for each of these four possible approaches there is a well-defined criterion or set of criteria which embodies it and makes it possible, in application to policy issues, to select specific redistributive policies. This chapter is a call for a comparative evaluation of these approaches in future philosophical debates. In this chapter I express a rather clear preference for one of these four options, but the chapter is meant to widen the scope of current debates, not to narrow it.

3.1 A natural policy

For ease of exposition, it is useful to fix some notions at the outset. Individuals' achievements will be called 'outcomes' and can be any subjective or objective notion of outcome that is deemed relevant. Individuals' achieved level of outcome, whatever the precise meaning of 'outcome', can most generally be described as determined by their personal characteristics and their social environment (in particular social policy and institutions). The personal characteristics for which they are deemed responsible will be simply called here their responsibility characteristics and the others their circumstance characteristics or, simply, their circumstances. We will often use the expression 'responsibility class' (or circumstance class) to refer to a sub-group of individuals having identical responsibility (or circumstance) characteristics.

The general problem of responsibility-sensitive egalitarianism in this context is to nullify the inequalities due to differences in circumstances while holding individuals responsible for their responsibility characteristics. But what does it mean, for a redistributive policy, that individuals are held responsible for some characteristics?

There is one case in which the answer seems simple. Suppose that the inequalities in circumstances can be directly compensated by transfers of resources, so that it is equivalent for any individual, no matter what his responsibility characteristics are, to be endowed with good circumstances or to be compensated with some transfer instead. This simple situation occurs, for instance, when circumstances consist in a bequest of resources (from parents), so that resource transfers can act as surrogate bequests. For further reference let us call it the case of 'transferable circumstances'. This simple case is to be distinguished from more complex cases in which transfers do not perfectly replace a deficit in circumstances, in particular when their ability to compensate differences in circumstances depends also on responsibility characteristics. Such complex cases will be important in relation to the second topic of the chapter and can be ignored for the moment.

In the simple case at hand, then, one obviously appealing redistributive policy is, whenever possible, to equalize the 'extended' circumstances made up by circumstances and transfers. For instance, redistribute bequests so that the disposable bequests, after transfer, be equal across individuals. Let us call this the 'natural' policy, because it comes to mind immediately in this kind of example. Of course, this policy is not always possible in practice when incentive constraints and information limitations prevent the government from implementing it fully. But let us ignore such practical issues for the moment. It is important, in particular, to explain why this policy is intuitively appealing. One apparent reason is that it equalizes exactly what individuals are not responsible for, namely, their extended circumstances which depend on personal circumstances and on the redistributive policy. All the other sources of inequalities belong to the sphere of personal responsibility. In the special case in which circumstances happen to be equal by chance, so that there is no worry about illegitimate inequalities, this policy boils down to laissez-faire, the absence of redistribution.

3.2 An alternative

The above justification of the natural policy is a little short. Indeed, a prominent proposal in the literature, Roemer's definition of an equal opportunity policy, would head in a different direction.[7] Roemer's criterion consists in computing the smallest value of outcome in every responsibility class, then computing the average value of these figures over all responsibility classes, and eventually trying to maximize the result of the computation by choosing an appropriate policy. For further reference, let us call this the 'mean-of-mins' criterion (because it computes the mean value of minimum outcome across responsibility classes), which appears egalitarian (or prioritarian) within responsibility classes and somehow utilitarian across responsibility classes.

---

[7] J. E. Roemer, 'A Pragmatic Theory of Responsibility for the Egalitarian Planner', *Philosophy and Public Affairs*, 22 (1993), 146–166; *Equality of Opportunity* (Cambridge, MA: Harvard University Press, 1998).

In the simple case of transferable circumstances, we can sort out individuals in responsibility classes and look for the worst level of outcome in each class. This is easy, as the worst level of outcome will necessarily be obtained by the individuals with the worst 'extended' circumstances. A good policy for the mean-of-mins then consists in seeking to maximize the average level of outcome of the individuals with worst extended circumstances. But the extended circumstances are determined in part by transfers. In general, transfers have a greater impact on outcome for certain responsibility characteristics than for others. For instance, the individuals who make an effort may be more able to benefit from transfers. For further reference, let us call this the 'help yourself' context, thus denominated because of the synergy between transfers and personal effort. The opposite case is the 'talent spoils' case, in which responsibility characteristics are important when circumstances are unfavourable, but not so much when they are favourable (e.g. the talented don't need to work, whereas effort is all important for the untalented). The 'help yourself' case is typical of production contexts in which the output jointly depends on some endowment and some effort: when transfers increase the endowment, their final impact on output depends on the multiplicative effect of effort. The 'talent spoils' case can be found in artistic contexts in which the well endowed (in talent or network) succeed independently of their effort whereas the less gifted need a lot of toil in order to obtain similar outcomes. In this context transfers reduce the importance of effort for the beneficiaries.

In the 'help yourself' case, a transfer from an individual with low effort to an individual with high effort increases their total outcome because the outcome gain of the latter is greater, thanks to his effort, than the reduction endured by the former. Therefore, in this case the mean-of-mins criterion advocates concentrating positive transfers on the responsibility class corresponding to high effort, because this is where transfers are the most effective in order to enhance the average outcome of those with worst extended circumstances. In the alternative 'talent spoils' case, symmetrically, resources would be entirely diverted to the responsibility class corresponding to low effort, because this is where it is most effective (providing surrogate talent to the most lazy is most efficient, as talent is a good substitute for effort in this case). Such policies, which concentrate resources on some special responsibility classes, are obviously radically different from the natural policy which is strictly limited to compensating circumstance inequalities, and submits all members of any given circumstance class to the same transfer, irrespectively of their various responsibility characteristics.

This alternative to the natural policy forces us to deepen our understanding of the intuitive appeal of the natural policy. The special (hypothetical) case in which all circumstances are equal may be quite relevant in order to highlight the contrast between the two approaches. In this case, individuals are fully responsible for their outcome inequalities, and the natural policy refrains from tampering with the distribution. In contrast, the mean-of-mins criterion advocates any intervention that maximizes average outcome. As already explained above, the more complex cases in which circumstances are unequal can be analysed in the same way. The natural policy does not redistribute between individuals having identical circumstances, whereas the mean-of-mins policy does redistribute from those for whom transfers are less productive to those for whom they are more productive.

Notice that both approaches may appear to equalize 'opportunities' in the sense that they seek to remove any inequality due to differential circumstances, so that the relation between responsibility characteristics and outcome, after transfer, becomes the same for all individuals. In a different way, therefore, the two policies achieve a state of affairs in which all individuals face the same options, i.e. the same possibilities in terms of combinations of responsibility characteristics and outcome. This shows that equalizing 'opportunities' in this sense, or neutralizing the effect of circumstances, is far from determining the optimal policy in a precise way.[8] Beyond the neutralization of circumstances, one must decide how to reward the exercise of responsibility by individuals, i.e. how to apportion their outcome achievements to their responsibility characteristics. It is on this 'reward' pattern that the natural policy and the mean-of-mins diverge dramatically.

3.3 Two interpretations of responsibility

The contrast between the two policies can be analysed as a difference between two interpretations of the implications of personal responsibility for distributive justice. One interpretation is that personal responsibility nullifies some reasons to interfere with the distribution, so that responsibility-sensitive egalitarianism is understood as *a middle way between egalitarianism and libertarianism*. The alternative interpretation is that personal responsibility removes reasons to adopt an inequality-averse social criterion, so that responsibility-sensitive egalitarianism is understood as *a middle way between egalitarianism and utilitarianism*.

The two interpretations are prima facie coherent and reasonable, but certainly quite incompatible with each other. There seems to be an important philosophical divide here, which has not received much attention in the philosophical and economic literatures.

Let us try to review some of the arguments that can be used in favour of either interpretation. The libertarian interpretation of responsibility is closer to the usual understanding of responsibility. When an individual assumes responsibility for his good or bad fate, it usually implies that others are relieved from any duty to intervene in order to modify his situation. By extension, when two individuals are held responsible for the differences that create unequal achievements between them, this normally

---

[8] This indeterminacy is stressed in B. Barry, *Liberty and Justice: Essays in Political Theory*, volume 2 (Oxford: Oxford University Press, 1991). He argues that a more precise determination of optimal redistribution would 'have to be made on other grounds, presumably security and efficiency...on one side and personal liberty...on the other' (p. 148). The approaches discussed in this chapter, however, suggest some possible ways to squeeze more precise distributive conclusions out of the concept of responsibility.

means that redistribution between them is not needed. Redistribution in such a case would have to be based on differences in responsibility characteristics, and this seems in direct contradiction with the idea that redistribution is targeted on differences in circumstances only.

Performing redistribution depending on responsibility characteristics would also appear to imply a lack of neutrality with respect to such characteristics. Transferring resources to those with particular responsibility characteristics could be described as rewarding them and penalizing the others, displaying an open preference for these particular characteristics and against the others. Now, this preference may be derived from another general goal which does not involve any comparative judgement of responsibility characteristics as such. An example is precisely the utilitarian view which implies transfers from those with low marginal utility toward those with high marginal utility, without necessarily relying on the judgement that a high marginal utility is morally good and a low one is 'evil'. But there is indeed a sense in which the utilitarian view is not neutral because it makes transfers in this systematic way.

It is common to distinguish two senses of the word 'neutrality'. Neutrality of intent (or judgement) is observed when there is no direct intention to punish or reward a particular trait. It is opposed to neutrality of effect, which requires the absence of any influence over the success of those with a particular trait. There seems to be room for a third sense, which lies somewhere in between. 'Neutrality of intervention' can be defined as the absence of reaction when a particular trait is modified in a particular sense. This is the usual diplomatic sense of neutrality and it seems applicable to other social interactions as well, in particular redistributive policy. It presumably implies neutrality of intent in most contexts, since the absence of intervention makes it possible to refrain from any judgement about the particular traits under consideration. It is stronger than neutrality of intent since the latter is compatible, as in the example of utilitarianism, with strong rewards and punishments motivated by other considerations (the social good in the case of utilitarianism). It is, however, a rather immediate extension of it because it would sound paradoxical for a social policy to make pronouncements of neutrality towards a particular characteristic and to severely penalize those and only those who have it. In so far as a social objective implies setting up a conspicuous reward-punishment scheme, it conveys a derivative value judgement about the relevant characteristics. For instance, a utilitarian who says that he is neutral with respect to the value of people's marginal utility sounds quite hypocritical, and would be more consistent admitting that his view of the social good implies a derivative positive assessment of high marginal utility and a negative assessment of low marginal utility.[9]

Viewed as a strengthened but close variant of neutrality of intent, neutrality of intervention can be related to liberalism as much as to libertarianism. I will hereafter call

---

[9] This assertion refers to high or low marginal utility viewed not as a consequence of redistribution but as a fixed characteristic of the individual utility function (some functions have a higher derivative at every level of income and people with such functions deserve more income according to the utilitarian criterion).

the non-interventionist interpretation of responsibility the 'liberal' one, since it can be adopted, apparently, without embracing the libertarian single-minded focus on negative freedom.

The natural policy has this particular feature that two individuals with the same circumstances are submitted to the same transfer, independently of their responsibility characteristics. There is a direct logical link between non-intervention and equality of treatment that goes as follows. If there is no difference between two individuals' responsibility and circumstance characteristics, then a basic impartiality requirement is that they should be treated in the same way. Now, if one individual changes his responsibility characteristics, by the non-intervention principle this does not require any change in the treatment he gets, so that equality of treatment is obtained for individuals with the same circumstance characteristics, independently of whether they also have identical responsibility characteristics or not. This shows the logical link between non-intervention and equality of treatment.

Non-intervention, as is well known, would sometimes let inefficiencies persist. Suppose, for instance, that neutrality is sought regarding consumer preferences. This can be implemented by giving exactly the same consumption bundle to all individuals,[10] which typically produces gross inefficiencies. However, neutrality is still well achieved, or so it seems, by giving individuals incomes that do not depend on their consumer preferences and letting them choose their own consumption bundle in a market. In this way neutrality and efficiency seem to be made compatible. The market device may not be the only way to achieve this kind of situation. More fundamentally, what matters is that nobody envies anybody (in the sense of preferring another's bundle), or that they can choose in the same set of options. In summary, the neutral kind of responsibility-sensitive egalitarianism requires that individuals who differ only in their responsibility characteristics be given the same treatment either in terms of resources, or sets of options, or envy-freeness.[11]

Let us now turn to the utilitarian interpretation of responsibility. It can be defended by the argument that personal responsibility removes a concern for inequalities. When inequalities do not matter, maximizing the sum of outcomes or the average outcome seems a reasonable objective. There is, however, a problem with this reasoning. The fact that inequalities do not matter does not imply that two distributions with the same sum are equivalent, because they may differ in other respects that do matter. This is precisely where neutrality considerations, for instance, may strike. It may be that

---

[10] We are dealing with neutrality of intervention, not neutrality of effect. Of course, giving the same bundle to all, in effect, favours those who like this particular combination of goods. But this is compatible with neutrality of intervention.

[11] P. Vallentyne ('Brute Luck Equality and Desert' in Serena Olsaretti (ed.), *Desert and Justice* (Oxford: Oxford University Press, 2003, 169–185) mentions a principle that, according to him, implies the non-intervention interpretation but relies on the idea of respecting individuals' 'reasonable expectations' instead of neutrality. However, assuming that expectations of a neutral reward scheme are more reasonable than expectations of a utilitarian redistribution towards the more productive seems to beg the question.

a particular distribution is produced by a neutral policy whereas another involves redistributing in a transparently non-neutral way. Then, even though we do not care about inequalities, the two distributions need not be considered equivalent.

The liberal interpretation of responsibility implies an absence of intervention whereas the utilitarian interpretation warrants interventions that increase the average outcome. The contrast between the two views may be particularly clear in the following example. Suppose that individuals are deemed responsible for their utility function, which measures how they transform income into utility. Then the liberal view will push in the direction of equal income, letting differential utility 'production' across individuals remain a private business. In contrast, the utilitarian approach will transfer income from those with low marginal utility to the 'utility machines'. The utilitarian philosophy has been famously criticized[12] for performing such transfers in cases of inherited handicaps that reduce marginal utility. What should we think of cases when individuals are responsible for their low marginal utility? This certainly seems less repugnant, but there is still something strange with the idea that one could say to an individual: 'Since you are responsible for your utility function, you better choose one with a high marginal utility, otherwise you will be penalized.'

3.4 Information requirements

There is, however, a setting in which these objections are not really operative. There might not be any information available except the distribution of outcomes. The way in which it is produced, with more or less intervention in particular, may be hidden for some practical reason. In such a poor informational context, there may be no way to formulate liberal concerns and utilitarianism may be the proximate approach. This pragmatic justification, however, is not very strong since it does not impugn the idea that if the information were available, the liberal approach would be more attractive than the utilitarian.

On the other hand, it is quite interesting to note that the utilitarian approach actually needs more information of another kind, in so far as it seeks to reward the productive agents. To that effect it needs a cardinal measure of outcome and is sensitive to the particular measure that is retained. For instance, if outcome is defined in terms of subjective utility, as in the above example, the optimal policy for mean-of-mins depends on the particular shape of individual utility functions. In contrast, in this example the natural policy equalizes resources independently of utilities, because the fact that individuals are deemed responsible for their utility functions makes it legitimate to disregard this characteristic (and in the particular example at hand this does not entail any inefficiency).

---

[12] A. K. Sen, *On Economic Equality* (Oxford: Oxford University Press, 1973).

Therefore, the two interpretations of responsibility induce policies which depend on different kinds of information. The liberal interpretation needs information about the procedure by which the allocation is obtained, whereas the utilitarian interpretation needs information about the cardinal measurement of outcome.

There is a greater degree of welfarism in the mean-of-mins criterion than in the natural policy, but the former is not purely welfarist.[13] A purely welfarist criterion would look only at the distribution of outcome, without considering the relation between outcome and responsibility characteristics. In contrast, the mean-of-mins criterion looks at this relation, and in particular at the conditional distributions of outcome for every value of responsibility parameter. It may therefore make the comparative evaluation of two distributions depend on how responsibility characteristics are spread among individuals with different levels of outcome.

3.5 The liberal approach at a crossroads

There is some asymmetry in the above discussion of the utilitarian and the liberal approaches to responsibility. The utilitarian view has been illustrated by a precise criterion, the mean-of-mins. In contrast, the liberal approach has been exemplified only in the particular 'transferable circumstances' case when a 'natural' policy presents itself as an obvious option. This approach would be more credible if it provided a fully fledged criterion applicable in all contexts.

A natural policy is not conspicuously available in all contexts. Let us for instance consider a context in which individual characteristics determine a pre-transfer level of outcome, so that transfers between individuals operate only ex-post and directly influence their outcome with the same marginal effect independently of their pre-transfer level. For further reference let us call this the case of 'transferable outcome'. A simple example corresponding to this situation is when outcome is disposable income, with pre-tax income being determined by talent and effort, and disposable income being equal to pre-tax income modified by income transfers. The situation is more complex in this kind of case than in the transferable circumstances case, because transfers are then unable to compensate unequal circumstances independently of how circumstances interfered with responsibility characteristics.

In the income-talent-effort example, the effects of inequalities in talent are exacerbated in the class of high-effort individuals, as compared to the other classes, so that more transfers would be needed in this class in order to neutralize the impact of any given inequality in talent. But if greater transfers are made in high-effort classes than in low-effort classes, neutrality is violated because the transfer to which an individual is submitted depends on her level of effort.

---

[13] As noted in J. E. Roemer, 'Equality of Opportunity: A Progress Report', *Social Choice and Welfare*, 19 (2002), 455–471.

An alternative possibility consists in insisting on neutrality, but this is at the risk of failing to neutralize the inequalities due to circumstances. If the same transfer is given to all individuals of a same circumstance class, it is very likely that inequalities due to circumstances will fail to be neutralized within the high-effort class, while they may be over-compensated in the low-effort class, producing inequalities in the opposite direction.

As this reasoning on a simple example illustrates, there is no way to reconcile the two requirements (compensation and neutrality) and this raises an ethical dilemma. This entails in particular that there is not one but two different kinds of criterion related to the liberal approach. A good criterion that stresses compensation is the 'egalitarian-equivalent' criterion, which has retained a good deal of attention in the economic literature. A general description of this kind of criterion is as follows. For any individual, ask what level of external treatment (e.g. transfers) would maintain her current level of outcome if she had a reference (say, average) level of circumstance characteristics. Then give priority, in the sense of the maximin criterion, to those individuals with the least favourable level of external treatment in this counterfactual computation.

This is a rather intuitive, albeit not trivial, method of evaluation. When equality is obtained over all the individual evaluations, this means that the current distribution of outcome would also be obtained if everyone had the reference level of circumstance characteristics and if equality of treatment (as recommended by the natural policy when circumstance characteristics are equal) were implemented. Of course, it is typically impossible to actually alter individuals' circumstance characteristics, but it is comforting when the distribution of outcomes mimics what would be obtained if that were possible. This is the gist of the egalitarian-equivalent approach, which gets its name from the objective of producing a situation that is equivalent, in terms of outcomes, to a hypothetical perfectly egalitarian situation.

The hypothetical perfectly egalitarian situation is also useful to get an intuitive understanding of the individual measure described above. Instead of asking what level of external treatment would restore the individual's level of outcome if his circumstance characteristics were at the reference level, one may equivalently ask what kind of perfectly egalitarian society, in which everyone's circumstance characteristics would be at the reference level and full equality of treatment would be provided, would make this individual's outcome equal to its current level. The more affluent (in terms of resources) this hypothetical perfectly egalitarian society, the better off the individual in the current distribution.

It may be useful to check that this approach embraces the compensation side of the dilemma. Two individuals with the same responsibility characteristics will have their evaluation always go in the same way as their level of outcome. Indeed, they are both compared to a counterfactual situation with the same responsibility characteristics and the reference circumstance characteristics, so that a greater outcome can be obtained only by a more favourable external treatment, implying therefore a higher evaluation.

In other words, priority is always given to the worst-off (in outcome) within every class of responsibility characteristics.

This of course implies, as can be expected from the above description of the compensation-neutrality dilemma, that full neutrality with respect to responsibility characteristics is not satisfied by this criterion. Nonetheless, some degree of neutrality remains and the egalitarian-equivalent criterion never departs from neutrality in such a striking way as the mean-of-mins criterion. In particular, in the class of individuals whose circumstance characteristics correspond to the reference level, the criterion achieves neutrality since these individuals are evaluated strictly in terms of external treatment. The best policy will then typically give them equal treatment irrespective of their responsibility characteristics.

Let us now introduce a criterion which embraces the neutrality side of the dilemma. This criterion is called 'conditional equality' in the economics literature. It is somewhat simpler than egalitarian-equivalence, and consists in evaluating an individual's situation by computing the level of outcome she would obtain if she adopted a reference (say, average) level of responsibility characteristics. Then the maximin criterion is applied to such hypothetical levels of outcome. Although simpler, this criterion appears less attractive since it fails to fully neutralize the effect of circumstance characteristics, an objective which may look more important than full neutrality. The reason why it partly fails on the compensation front is that it evaluates the consequences of unfavourable circumstance characteristics by considering what happens when they are combined with reference responsibility characteristics instead of the individual's actual responsibility characteristics.

The egalitarian-equivalent and the conditional-equality criteria, consistent with the above analysis, both advocate the natural policy in the transferable circumstances case, when the dilemma between compensation and neutrality does not occur.

3.6 Compensation versus neutrality

Giving priority to compensation over neutrality is not necessarily the obvious choice in all contexts. In the transferable outcome case, compensation can be defended by arguing that inequalities in circumstances produce inequalities in the opportunities of outcome. For instance, in the income-talent-effort example, a greater talent increases not only the level of income at any level of effort, but also the marginal return on effort. A transfer policy which, out of neutrality, would treat individuals only for inequalities in level and not for the differential returns would somehow fail to recognize the interplay between talent and effort.[14] In contrast, a fully compensating

---

[14] This point has been emphasized in particular by A. W. Cappelen and B. Tungodden ('Responsibility and Reward', *FinanzArchiv*, 59 (2002), 120–140; 'Reward and Responsibility: How Should We Be Affected When Others Change Their Effort?', *Politics, Philosophy and Economics*, 2 (2003), 191–211; 'A Liberal Egalitarian Paradox', *Economics and Philosophy*, 22 (2006), 393–408; 'Rewarding Effort', *Economic Theory*,

policy which performs larger transfers among high-effort individuals neutralizes both kinds of illegitimate inequalities. It somehow mimics what would happen if transfers could be made on talent directly, as in the transferable circumstances case. Indeed, in the latter case, giving a transfer to an individual with bad circumstances not only increases his outcome but also the amount of outcome he may obtain with better responsibility characteristics. In summary, in the transferable circumstances case as in the transferable outcome case, compensation is a quite imperative goal, and it appears to take precedence over neutrality.

Let us now consider a third category of cases, in which outcome depends on transfers and responsibility characteristics primarily, while circumstances play only an incremental role on the level of outcome, without interfering with transfers and responsibility characteristics. This kind of situation occurs, for instance, when the government distributes education vouchers to students, who may exert more or less effort in their education, while circumstances take the form of inherited capital that serves to start one's own business, without interfering with the education process. In this context, circumstances influence the level of outcome but do not affect the marginal return on effort, which depends only on the transfers (vouchers in this example). Therefore, it seems quite natural to consider that individuals who are bound to receive the same bequest should receive the same amount of education vouchers, independent of their effort in education. This is precisely what neutrality commands. In contrast, full compensation would require that individuals with the same level of effort should end up with equal outcome. Given that vouchers are more productive with high-effort individuals, this would entail making smaller 'transfers' between high-effort individuals, leading to a violation of neutrality: among those with a low level of bequest, high-effort individuals would receive a smaller quantity of vouchers because their high effort in itself will help compensate for the low bequest. This violation of neutrality is hard to justify. It amounts to telling low-bequest high-effort students: 'You will later receive a low bequest, and therefore we give you more vouchers, but we retain a special tax that takes account of the fact that your effort partly compensates for your low bequest.'

Therefore there are contexts in which neutrality is more strongly defendable. There are even contexts in which it is unavoidable. When redistribution is made before the responsibility characteristics are determined, there is no way to differentiate individuals who have identical circumstances, implying that they must be submitted to the same transfer.

Another context in which neutrality is quite attractive and full compensation is less so is when responsibility characteristics are preference characteristics while circumstance characteristics are non-transferable resources which are hard to evaluate

---

39 (2009), 425–441) and B. Tungodden ('Responsibility and Redistribution: The Case of First Best Taxation', *Social Choice and Welfare*, 24 (2005), 33–44), who have studied the income-talent-effort example in detail.

objectively. Then, full compensation requires the allocation of transfers to be tailored to every particular preference over internal resources and that may not be desirable. Consider, for instance, two individuals who have the idiosyncratic view that less than perfect pitch is such a bad handicap that it requires a massive compensating transfer. If one of them has perfect pitch and not the other, then a strict application of full compensation would imply such a large transfer from the former to the latter, a rather strange perspective. In contrast, neutrality is more sensible in such a context since it may be satisfied by transfers based on some consistent and standard evaluation of internal resources (as with the conditional-equality criterion).

All in all, the proper attitude towards the compensation-neutrality dilemma is probably not a dogmatic rejection of any of these terms but a case-by-case examination of the various contexts of application and the comparative ethical relevance of these two principles.

3.7 A similar dilemma for the utilitarian approach

Even though neutrality is replaced in the utilitarian view by a focus on the sum of outcomes (zero inequality aversion), there is a similar divide in the utilitarian approach. Recall how the mean-of-mins criterion is computed. It is the average smallest outcome obtained in the various responsibility classes. There is an alternative way of combining the maximin criterion across circumstance characteristics and the utilitarian average over responsibility characteristics, and it is actually simpler. For every circumstance class, compute the average outcome in this class, and then focus on the class with the smallest average. This is a quite simple criterion, since it can be described as computing the 'value' of opportunities offered to every individual, and applying the maximin criterion to these figures. This value of opportunities is, in a plausible way, computed as the average outcome of the individuals with the same circumstance characteristics as the individual under consideration. Clearly enough, this alternative criterion, due to Van de gaer, may be called the 'min-of-means' criterion.[15]

The difference between the mean-of-mins and the min-of-means can be connected to a conflict between compensation and reward, where reward is of the utilitarian brand. The mean-of-mins always considers it acceptable to reduce outcome inequalities within a given responsibility class, because this can only raise the lowest level of outcome in this class, thereby raising the average value of the lowest outcome across responsibility classes. In contrast, the min-of-means does not always respect this basic compensation principle, because reducing inequalities within a responsibility class may lower the average outcome of the worst-off circumstance class, in the case when the members of this class are not the worst-off in the responsibility class where redistribution takes place. But the min-of-means always considers it acceptable to increase the

---

[15] D. Van de gaer, 'Equality of Opportunity and Investment in Human Capital', PhD thesis (Katholieke Universiteit Leuven, 1993).

average level of outcome in any given circumstance class—a quite transparent expression of the idea of zero inequality aversion corresponding to the utilitarian conception of reward—because it focuses on such average figures for all circumstance classes, whereas the mean-of-mins may reject such increase in average level in one circumstance class because this may decrease the lowest level of outcome in some responsibility class, and therefore the average value of the lowest levels across responsibility classes.

Just as it is impossible to comply with the requisites of compensation and liberal reward simultaneously, one can check that it is impossible to do so for utilitarian reward as well. The two criteria, mean-of-mins and min-of-means, appear to be the natural options offered by this dilemma. Interestingly, however, the dilemma vanishes, and the two criteria coincide, when the worst-off circumstance class (in terms of average outcome) is uniformly dominated by the other classes, in the sense that its members are always the worst-off in their respective responsibility classes.[16]

3.8 Four approaches

Combining this general tension with the opposition between the liberal and the utilitarian interpretations of responsibility, one obtains four different approaches displayed in Table 3.1.

Table 3.1

	Liberal	Utilitarian
Compensation	Egalitarian-equivalent	Mean-of-mins
Reward	Conditional equality	Min-of-means

Let us summarize the definition of the four criteria in the general case. The *egalitarian-equivalent* criterion gives priority to the worst-off, and the worst-off individuals are those for whom the current value of their outcome would be obtained with an unfavourable external treatment by social policy if their circumstance characteristics were at a reference level (and their responsibility characteristics unchanged). The *conditional-equality* criterion differs in its definition of the worst-off. For this criterion the worst-off are those who would obtain a low outcome with a reference value of responsibility characteristics (and their circumstance characteristics unchanged). The *min-of-means* criterion also gives priority to the worst-off, but defines the worst-off as those belonging to a circumstance class with low average outcome. The *mean-of-mins* criterion maximizes the average outcome obtained by the worst-off in every class of responsibility, where the worst-off are those with the lowest outcome.

---

[16] M. Hild and A. Voorhoeve ('Equality of Opportunity and Opportunity Dominance', *Economics and Philosophy*, 20 (2004), 117–146) have proposed a partial criterion based on the application of the leximin criterion on the distribution of outcomes in every responsibility class. This does not take a stand on the reward problem, and embraces only the compensation ideal.

The literature on responsibility-sensitive egalitarianism has not paid much attention to those distinctions, and it seems an urgent task to sort out the underlying ethical divides. Given the fact that rather precise proposals for criteria are available for the four approaches, the ethical analysis can rely on the study of likely consequences and not only on the abstract evaluation of basic principles. The next sections present an example in which the four criteria of Table 3.1 can be compared and contrasted.

If, as seems reasonable from the above, one adopts the liberal approach and puts priority on compensation rather than neutrality, the egalitarian-equivalent kind of criterion seems to be the most appealing option on the table. It has a drawback that follows from its superiority, though. Because it is sensitive to the way in which outcome is produced out of redistributive policies and personal characteristics, there is no simple and general way to define it. Every context has specific forms of the egalitarian-equivalent criterion. Moreover, in many contexts there are several different egalitarian-equivalent criteria, depending on how the reference value for circumstance characteristics is chosen, in particular. This issue will be illustrated in the example that follows.

3.9 Wages and work

We now examine an example which is closer to real-life issues of redistribution than the previous ones, even though many simplifications will still be introduced in order to make things easier.[17] Let us indeed consider a population of pure wage-earners who live only one period (this period may cover active life and last forty years) and assume that every individual has only two characteristics, her wage rate on the labour market, for which she is not responsible, and her utility function defined over her own labour and net income, for which she is responsible. This assignment of responsibility is obviously rather questionable, but is convenient as a first approximation to see what the various criteria entail in terms of redistribution.

The egalitarian-equivalent approach can be illustrated by the following kind of criterion. Pick a reference value of wage rate and compute, for every individual, the income transfer he would need when working at this wage rate in order to obtain the same satisfaction as in his current situation. Then give priority to individuals for whom this income transfer is the lowest (or the greatest in the negative values). For instance, assume that the reference wage rate is $7 per hour (a rather low value may be warranted for reasons explained below). Now, one asks every individual the following question: 'Suppose you worked at $7 per hour, choosing your labour time freely. What amount of income transfer would you need, or how much could you relinquish, in order to keep your current satisfaction?' Answering this question is not simple, in particular because the choice of labour time in this hypothetical situation is likely to be influenced

[17] What follows extends a short presentation made in M. Fleurbaey, 'Equality of Resources Revisited', *Ethics*, 113 (2002), 82–105.

by the amount of transfer considered. A typical answer would be something like: 'I would need $11,400 per year in transfer, and would work thirty-four hours per week (earning an additional $238 per week).' (Fortunately, in practical applications one never has to ask this kind of question, because one can rely on indirect devices in order to estimate the distribution of the answers.) An individual who answers '$11,400' is then considered worse off than another who answers '$17,150'. The egalitarian-equivalent criterion gives priority to the individuals with the smallest answer.

Note that two individuals with the same utility function will provide answers which match the ranking of their utilities, since with a given utility function a higher utility level can be obtained, in the hypothetical setting of the question, only with a greater income transfer. Therefore this criterion satisfies the compensation principle, as we already know.

On the other hand, it is less good in terms of neutrality. This is related to the issue of the selection of the reference wage rate. It was mentioned above that a low value is preferable. Suppose instead that a high wage rate is picked as the reference. Then, among the agents whose actual wage rate is lower than the reference, those with a greater aversion to work will tend to give higher answers than others about the income transfer. This is due to the following phenomenon. When presented with the possibility of working at a greater wage rate, an individual thinks of working more hours and would accept a lower transfer (or greater tax) than in his current situation. But this reduction of transfer (or increase in tax) is greater for those who are willing to work more. On the contrary, at the limit, an individual who does not work at all, even with the greater wage rate, would not endure any decrease in transfer.

The fact that low-wage 'lazier' individuals give higher answers means that the criterion is biased against 'lazy' preferences among low-wage individuals. This is quite problematic, because even though individuals are considered responsible for their preferences by assumption here, one should be careful about penalizing those who work and earn less. With a high value of the reference wage rate, a 'slavery of the lazy' can even occur, in which the individuals with high aversion to work are worse off than with a subsistence income and zero labour. Such a bias against 'lazy' preferences will be avoided only if the reference wage rate is not greater than the smallest wage rate in the population.

In particular, a value of zero for the reference wage rate is not unreasonable at all. It makes the question to be asked simpler: 'What amount of income would be needed in order to maintain your current satisfaction if you no longer had to earn it by working?' One may think of early retirement as a concrete example of this hypothetical situation. This particular measure is quite appealing because it has a very intuitive interpretation. Current income is not a good measure of outcome because individuals with the same income but different quantities of work or different kinds of jobs need not be on a par. By deducting the amount of income that individuals would relinquish if offered a fixed income, one directly takes account of the cost of labour as evaluated by every individual's own preferences. The 'leisure-equivalent' income that is obtained by this computation is therefore a good measure of the standard of living.

Admittedly, as can be deduced from the above analysis, the leisure-equivalent income is a measure that involves a bias in favour of 'lazy' preferences. Considering a given position with a positive amount of work and a certain level of consumption, the lazier the preferences, the lower the leisure-equivalent income. This criterion therefore gives priority to the poor with preferences that are very averse to work. This is not unreasonable if one wants to be cautious about the implications of personal responsibility for preferences.

3.10 Job quality and aversion to work

One reason why individuals may be particularly averse to work is that they may only have access to unpleasant jobs. This phenomenon can be given a more thorough treatment by enriching the framework of the analysis. Suppose that individuals now have preferences over consumption, work, and job quality, and that they are responsible for their preferences but obviously not responsible for the constraints imposed on their access to different kinds of jobs. Job quality may be a multidimensional notion, involving such dimensions as manual/intellectual, health hazards, responsibilities and autonomy, work atmosphere, contact with customer, etc. An application of the egalitarian-equivalent idea in this richer setting would have individuals answer the following kind of question: 'Suppose you worked at $7 per hour, choosing your labour time freely and the quality of your job in this range [to be made precise in the question]. What amount of income transfer would you need, or how much could you relinquish, in order to keep your current satisfaction?' This is one possibility among many others. One could imagine, for instance, that a more complex set of wage-quality packages is put on the table and that the individual is asked to choose among them in addition to choosing her labour time.

Someone who is averse to work in certain jobs, but less so in other jobs, would give an answer that depends on the possible disparity between his current job and his ideal job. In this way, apparent laziness due to constraints on job quality cannot be misattributed to individual responsibility. This reduces the pressure to pick the reference wage rate at a very low level.

It is not clear, however, that this method is sufficient in order to take account of the constraints bearing on individuals' aversion to work. Differences in competence and skill, for which individuals are not held responsible, are likely to have a direct influence on their preferences about job quality. Those who do not like intellectual jobs may simply be suffering from a sour grapes effect, or even more directly from the phenomenon that expertise in an activity is in itself part of its attraction. It may therefore be quite problematic to disentangle preferences and skills in order to attribute responsibility to preferences only.

As a consequence, in advance of further refinement of the theory, it seems that the leisure-equivalent income is still a safe option. It avoids a harsh attribution of responsibility for apparent 'laziness' to those whose expertise is limited to unpleasant kinds of jobs.

3.11 Other criteria

The conditional-equality criterion works quite differently. Recall that its general principle is to compute the outcome that would be obtained if the individual adopted a reference value for the responsibility characteristics. A simple way to apply this to the present context is to ask what level of utility every individual would achieve if she adopted a reference utility function. There are, however, different possible ways of computing this hypothetical utility. For simplicity, we come back to the simple setting in which job quality is not identified as a separate dimension.

A first option for the application of the conditional-equality idea is to apply the reference utility function to the individual's current bundle. This is, however, rather naive since with a different utility function the individual would make different choices. An alternative method is then to compute the utility that the individual would obtain after adapting his labour time, in his current budget set. This makes more sense. If an individual is very averse to work, this computation would take account of the fact that with standard preferences he would work and earn more, and conversely for a workaholic.

These two methods of computation, however, have a common drawback. They fail to satisfy the Pareto principle. Improving individuals' situations according to the criterion may sometimes worsen their situation in their own eyes. This is not necessarily a drawback, actually. One may consider that, since they are responsible for their preferences, the evaluation of individuals' situations need not respect their idiosyncratic preferences in all respects. On the other hand, it is worthwhile to explore the possibility of applying the idea of conditional equality in a way that respects individual preferences.

This can be done as follows. For every individual, make the same computation as in the egalitarian-equivalent question but with a reference wage rate which is equal to the individual's own market wage rate: 'Suppose you work at your market wage rate, choosing your labour time freely. What amount of income transfer would you need, or how much could you relinquish, in order to keep your current satisfaction?' This identifies a hypothetical budget set which comprises a fixed transfer plus work freely chosen at the individual's own wage rate. This hypothetical budget set refers to the individual's wage rate but is likely to differ from her actual budget because of the various taxes and transfers to which the individual may be submitted in her current situation, as well as various impediments on her choice of labour time. The hypothetical budget set is a faithful representation of individual preferences because a more satisfactory current situation for the individual implies a greater hypothetical budget set.

Now, one can compute the utility that would be achieved on any given budget set by a reference utility function. When this is done on the hypothetical budget sets just defined, this provides an application of the conditional-equality idea that satisfies the Pareto principle, since a better situation for an individual, in terms of his own preferences, means a greater budget set which yields a greater utility for the reference utility function.

This approach is more neutral than the egalitarian-equivalent, since it displays no systematic bias in favour of or against preferences of a particular type. In counterpart, it is less good for compensation, since two individuals with the same preferences and unequally satisfactory situations may be ranked by the criterion in the opposite way. This may happen when they have different wage rates and their hypothetical budget sets are not nested (the budget lines cross). What budget set is considered best then depends on the reference utility function. When the reference function represents preferences which are sufficiently different from the two individuals' preferences, its comparative evaluation of the two budget sets may contradict the individuals' own ranking.

An important common feature of the egalitarian-equivalent and conditional-equality criteria just analysed is that, in this example, they ultimately disregard individual utility functions and only take account of ordinal non-comparable preferences. This is well in line with the liberal interpretation of responsibility. If an individual keeps his preferences but changes his utility function, this is simply ignored and has no impact on the allocation of resources. Preferences are taken into account, however, in order to calibrate compensation and also for efficiency purposes (respect of the Pareto principle).

The mean-of-mins and min-of-means criteria, to which we now turn, are quite different in this respect since they are very sensitive to individual utility functions. The min-of-means criterion focuses on classes of individuals with identical wage rates and computes, for each such class, the average utility obtained within the class. It then gives priority to increasing the lowest of these figures, across all classes of wage rate. In ordinary taxation settings, individuals with lower wage rates typically have a smaller budget set, implying a lower average utility if one assumes that the distribution of utility functions is independent of wage rates (as discussed above, this is questionable, but let us ignore this complication here). Therefore the objective will concretely become that of maximizing the average utility of low-skilled individuals.

The same result will be obtained in this setting with the mean-of-mins criterion under the same assumption of statistical independence between utility function and wage rate. For every class of utility function, the worst-off will be those with the smallest budget and that means those with the smallest wage rate. The two utilitarian criteria coincide when the worst-off in every class of responsibility characteristics all have the same circumstance characteristics. This is what happens here.

3.12 Policy consequences

Let us briefly conclude the discussion of this example with a review of the likely distributive consequences of the four criteria in the familiar context of income taxation. In this context, redistribution is made on the basis of earned income, no distinction being made between individuals obtaining the same income with different wage rates and different amounts of labour time.

It is hard to be precise about the utilitarian criteria. Economic analysis has shown that maximizing average utility generally involves a bias in favour of those with high marginal utility of consumption and against those with low marginal disutility of labour. This may be a sufficient insight for present purposes. A more precise determination of the optimal policy may be quite complex depending on the richness of the set of utility functions observed in the population. Available results in economics deal only with simple cases where the heterogeneity of individuals is limited to one dimension (wage rate, or one parameter of preference), whereas here we have at least two dimensions (wage rate and utility functions).[18]

The egalitarian-equivalent and conditional-equality criteria display an interesting convergence. If the lowest wage rate of the population is retained as the reference for the egalitarian-equivalent criterion, then the best income tax policy is obtained by maximizing the minimum income (allotted to those with zero earnings) under the constraint that the marginal tax rate for earnings between zero and the lowest wage be zero. This constraint means that any additional dollar earned below the lowest wage is neither taxed nor subsidized. There is, actually, an additional constraint about what happens to higher incomes for the conditional-equality criterion. This somehow reduces the degree of redistribution towards low incomes but does not radically change the policy outlook.

If the lowest wage in the population is zero (some individuals having a null productivity), then both criteria simply advocate maximizing the minimum income, an already quite popular slogan.[19] This is also the conclusion obtained with the egalitarian-equivalent criterion formulated in terms of leisure-equivalent income, no matter what the distribution of wage rates is in the population.

---

[18] The special case of linear taxation is, however, easier. See E. Schokkaert, D. Van de gaer, F. Vandenbroucke, and R. Luttens ('Responsibility-Sensitive Egalitarianism and Optimal Linear Income Taxation', *Mathematical Social Sciences*, 48 (2004), 151–182) for an examination of the two criteria in this context and W. Bossert, M. Fleurbaey, and D. Van de gaer ('Responsibility, Talent, and Compensation: A Second-Best Analysis', *Review of Economic Design*, 4 (1999), 35–56) for a comparison of the liberal and utilitarian criteria.

[19] It is defended in particular by P. Van Parijs, *Real Freedom for All* (Oxford: Oxford University Press, 1995).

3.13 Conclusion

Hopefully, the examples used in this chapter have helped the reader to get an intuition of the meaning and implications of the two ethical divides discussed. The first divide separates a liberal and a utilitarian interpretation of responsibility, while the second opposes a focus on compensation and a focus on reward.

The first divide is more important because it goes deeper into the meaning of concepts and basic principles and also because it has stronger implications. The examples, especially that of the labour market, have shown a relative similarity between the practical implications of the compensation-oriented and reward-oriented criteria, but a much greater gap between the consequences of the liberal and the utilitarian views. It therefore seems rather urgent to examine whether one approach is superior to the other, or whether they have different domains of validity or different areas of application.

4

Luck Egalitarianism and Group Responsibility[1]

Kasper Lippert-Rasmussen

4.1 Introduction

Luck egalitarianism is often formulated as the view that 'it is [in itself] bad—unjust and unfair—for some to be worse off than others [through no fault or choice of their own]'.[2] This formulation is ambiguous in three ways: first, it is ambiguous between views that locate the badness in individuals being worse off and views that locate the badness in groups of individuals being worse off (or both); second, it is ambiguous between different views about the relevant subject of fault or choice (individuals, groups of individuals, or both); finally, it is ambiguous between different views about the relevant object of fault or choice (individuals being worse off, groups of individuals being worse off, or both).[3] When these ambiguities are sorted out it can be seen that

[1] A previous version of this chapter was presented at the ALSP conference in Dublin, 1 July 2006; at CollIntV, Helsinki University, 1 September 2006; at the 6th meeting of the Nordic Network for Political Theory (generously supported by Etikkprogrammet at the University of Oslo) in Rome, 31 October 2007; and at the 'Distributive Justice and Responsibility Workshop', the Adam Smith Research Foundation, University of Glasgow, 12 January 2008. I thank Gustaf Arrhenius, Dick Arneson, Daniel Attas, Michael Bratman, Alexander W. Cappelen, Jerry Cohen, Avner de-Shalit, Nir Eyal, Marc Fleurbaey, Nils Holtug, Magnus Jedenheim-Edling, Carl Knight, Sune Lægaard, David Miller, Mike Otsuka, Thomas Søbirk Petersen, Björn Petersson, Zofia Stemplowska, Peter Vallentyne, Andrew Williams, and Jonathan Wolff for helpful discussions and comments.

[2] L. Temkin, *Inequality* (Oxford: Oxford University Press, 1993), 13; D. Parfit, 'Equality and Priority?' in A. Mason (ed.) *Ideals of Equality* (Oxford: Blackwell, 1998), 1–20, at 3.

[3] Examples of relevantly similar formulations of the basic egalitarian principle are: (i) Roemer's formulation of 'the general form of the egalitarian ethic' found in Dworkin, Arneson, and Cohen, i.e. 'society should indemnify people against poor outcomes that are the consequences of causes that are beyond their control, but not against outcomes that are the consequences of causes that are within their control' (J. Roemer, 'A Pragmatic Theory of Responsibility for the Egalitarian Planner', *Philosophy and Public Affairs*, 22 (1993), 146–166, at 147); (ii) Cohen's claim that 'the fundamental distinction for an egalitarian is between choice and luck in the shaping of people's fate' (G. A. Cohen, 'On the Currency of Egalitarian Justice', *Ethics*, 99 (1989), 906–944, at 907); and (iii) Arneson's egalitarian norm that 'distributive justice does not recommend any intervention by society to correct inequalities that arise through the voluntary choice or fault of those who end up with less, so long as it is proper to hold the individuals responsible for the voluntary choice or faulty behaviour that give rise to the inequalities' (R. Arneson, 'Liberalism, Distributive Subjectivism, and Equal

choice and responsibility play a different and less prominent role in egalitarian justice than it is normally assumed. Specifically, there are cases of individual unavoidability and collective avoidability where each member of a group is worse off through no choice or fault of his own and yet this is not bad from a luck egalitarian point of view because the group is worse off through the choices or faults of its members. Moreover, there are cases of individual avoidability and collective unavoidability where each member of a group is worse off through his own choice or fault and yet this is bad because the group is worse off regardless of the choices or faults of its members. These are the core critical points of this chapter.[4] In section 4.2, I present and exemplify the differences between the various readings of the standard egalitarian formula. The aim of this section is simply to provide a conceptual map, not to evaluate the different principles located on that map. This task is taken up in section 4.3, where I suggest a revised version of the standard egalitarian formula that accommodates cases involving the above-mentioned asymmetries between choice or fault at the individual level and at the group level. Finally, I consider and reject an alternative response involving a multilevel account of the badness of inequality, according to which inequalities between groups may be bad even if there are no regrettable inequalities between individuals, and vice versa.

4.2 Ambiguities in the luck egalitarian formula

Here is a non-exhaustive list of different readings of the standard luck egalitarian formula, 'it is [in itself] bad—unjust and unfair—for some to be worse off than others [through no fault or choice of their own]', applied to situations involving two worse-off persons:[5]

(1) For all individuals, x, y, and z, it is bad if x is worse off than z and it is bad if y is worse off than z if, and only if, (i) it is not the case that x is worse off than z through his own fault or choice and (ii) it is not the case that y is worse off than z through his own fault or choice.

(2) For all individuals, x, y, and z, it is bad that the group consisting of x and y is worse off than z if, and only if, it is not the case that the group consisting of x and y is worse off than z through the choices or faults of x and y.

Opportunity for Welfare', *Philosophy and Public Affairs*, 19 (1990), 158–194, at 176). These formulations, too, are ambiguous in the way I expound below.

[4] Since the ambiguity I address arises partly due to the 'through no choice or fault of their own bit', a similar ambiguity arises in the case of non-egalitarian views, e.g. prioritarianism, that accommodates the concern for responsibility through a similar qualification, e.g. a clause saying that improving people's situation has less value to the extent that they are at a low level of well-being through a choice or fault of their own.

[5] There are many other possible readings of the standard luck egalitarian formula—see the Appendix. To make the core critical and constructive points of this chapter, I need not go through a complete list of possible readings. It is easy to see how the distinctions I draw below apply, mutatis mutandis, to situations involving more than two worse-off persons.

(3) For all individuals, x, y, and z, it is bad if x is worse off than z and it is bad if y is worse off than z if, and only if, it is not the case that the group consisting of x and y is worse off than z through the choices or faults of x and y.

(4) For all individuals, x, y, and z, it is bad that the group consisting of x and y is worse off than z if, and only if, it is neither the case that x is worse off than z through his own fault or choice, nor that y is worse off than z through his own fault or choice.[6]

Note that (2) and (4) are collectivistic views in that they locate the badness of inequality in groups of individuals being worse off, while (1) and (3) are individualistic views in that they locate the badness of inequality in how each worse-off individual fares. The collectivistic readings of the formula, while possible, are not plausible as readings of the standard luck egalitarian formula, at least as championed by the leading luck egalitarians, and I shall be focusing on the two individualistic readings until section 4.4.

To illustrate how these four positions differ, consider a community consisting of three persons, Adam, Betty, and Charles. For some reason or other, whatever Charles does, he will end up with 100 units of the relevant equalisandum, which for present purposes can be left unspecified. Adam and Betty, however, face a prisoner's dilemma-like situation. If they both cooperate in growing crops, they will both end up with 100. If they both tend their own crops failing to assist each other, they will both end up with 95. If they act differently, the one who cooperates will get 90, and the one who only tends his or her own crops will get 110. They have no way of knowing if the other person cooperates prior to harvest.[7] Suppose they both tend their own crops. As a result, Adam and Betty have 95, while Charles has 100. Is this inequality bad?

The answer to this question depends on when people are worse off through their own choice or fault.[8] Choice and fault require separate accounts. In what follows, I assume that a person is worse off through a choice of his own if, and only if, (i) he

---

[6] Strictly speaking, 'it is [in itself] bad—unjust and unfair—for some to be worse off than others [through no fault or choice of their own]' does not entail that it is not bad—neither unjust, nor unfair—for some to be worse off than others through a fault or choice of their own. However, I believe that the luck egalitarian formula is normally meant and understood to entail this. If one thought that it is bad for some to be worse off even when he is worse off through his own fault or choice, then one would bring across one's view much more effectively simply by saying that 'it is [in itself] bad—unjust and unfair—for some to be worse off than others'. Hence, I have formulated (1)–(4) in terms of bi-conditionals.

[7] If both parties somehow knew, or (reasonably) believed, in advance that the other party would not cooperate, and this knowledge, (or these beliefs), explains why neither party cooperates, the case for considering the resulting inequality to be bad is considerably stronger than in the case I consider.

[8] Some egalitarians (P. Vallentyne, 'Brute Luck, Option Luck, and Equality of Initial Opportunities', *Ethics*, 112 (2002), 529–557) would say that the answer to this question depends on what the prospects of Adam, Betty, and Charles were ex ante. Thus, if all had equally good prospects ex ante, then there is nothing bad about the resulting unequal outcome. I disregard this view here, since it clearly does not consider it in itself bad that some people are worse off through no fault or choice of their own as long as people have equally good prospects ex ante. For present purposes, the relevant measure of being worse off is outcome-focused.

would not have been worse off had he chosen to act differently, and (ii) he believed that had he chosen to act differently the likelihood of his ending up worse off would have been sufficiently smaller.[9] A group is worse off through a choice of its own if, and only if, (i) this group would not have been worse off, i.e. on average its members would not have been worse off, had a sufficient number of its members acted differently, and (ii) a sufficient number of its members believed that had a sufficient number of the members of the group acted differently the likelihood of their—they themselves or the group as such—ending up worse off would have been sufficiently smaller.[10] There are cases which suggest that it is too simplistic to assume, as I have done here, that how well off members of a group are on average is what determines whether this group of people is worse off than another group of people. For instance, if 999 out of a group of 1,000 persons have 1 and the last member has 100.000 we might think that the group consisting of these persons is worse off than another group of 1,000 persons all of whom have 50 even if members of the former group are on average better off. However, since nothing in the present argument hinges on this particular point and since the average is a simple measure for how well off a group is, I shall simply stick to this assumption.

'Being worse off through a fault of one's own' is trickier, since there are at least three different interpretations of the relevant notion of 'fault'. On the prudential interpretation, a person is worse off through a fault of his own if, and only if, he is worse off because his conduct is blameworthy from a prudential point of view. On the equality-based interpretation, a person is worse off through a fault of his own if, and only if, he is worse off because his conduct is blameworthy from a prudential point of view provided that the agent did not conduct himself imprudently in order to reduce the badness of inequality. For instance, it is bad from the point of view of equality if

---

[9] First, in the present sentence, I can leave it an open question whether 'worse off' should be read in an intrapersonal or in an interpersonal sense. Second, I shall disregard here and in what follows questions about strength of the will. A person who suffers from genetically induced weakness of the will may end up worse off through his own choice and yet this may not reduce the badness of his ending up worse off. Third, by 'sufficiently' I mean to accommodate cases where an agent believes that he faces a choice between an option which with a tiny possibility will not leave him worse off, but which is also very likely to leave him much worse off, and another option which is certain to leave him worse off, but only slightly worse off. Fourth, one can be worse off through one's own choice even though one is not worse off to the degree to which this is the case through one's own choice, e.g. I go by bike, rather than by car, believing that due to the rain I will be slightly worse off than the others who go by car and end up being hit by a car. For present purposes, I only need to address the issue of when one is worse off through one's own choice.

[10] Admittedly, the notion of group choice employed here is a rather undemanding one. Disregarding the belief requirement, a group choice in my sense simply is the mereological sum of the acts of all members. A more demanding definition of group choice would require, say, that all members of the group coordinate their individual actions, have interlocking intentions, and are all committed to shared aims, etc. (M. Bratman, 'Shared Cooperative Activity' in M. Bratman, *Faces of Intention* (Cambridge: Cambridge University Press, 1999), 93–108, at 93; M. Gilbert, *On Social Facts* (London: Routledge, 1989); J. Searle, 'Collective Intentions and Actions' in P. R. Cohen, J. Morgan, and M. E. Pollack (eds), *Intentions in Communication* (Cambridge, MA: MIT Press, 1990), 401–416. Unlike me, some might think that it is this more demanding notion of group choice—let us call it 'collective group choice' as opposed to my weaker notion of 'mere aggregate group choice'—that matters in the present context. I address this issue below.

someone ends up worse off as a result of his making himself worse off in order to raise all other persons who are presently worse off through no fault or choice of their own to the level of the better-off.[11] Finally, on the morality-based interpretation, a person is worse off through a fault of his own if, and only if, he is worse off because his conduct is blameworthy from a prudential point of view provided that the agent did not conduct himself imprudently in order to do what was morally desirable for him to do (or what he believed was morally desirable for him to do) (possibly for reasons that are not equality-based, but instead, say, autonomy-, perfection-, or welfare-based).[12] On this view, someone who voluntarily sacrifices a significant part of his income (or his own limbs) to save the lives of fifty people who, even if left to die will have lived lives much better than all others, is not worse off through his own fault, since he is worse off because he chose to do what was morally required (or supererogatory) for non-equality-based reasons.[13] To each of these notions of individual fault corresponds a notion of collective fault. So, for instance, on the prudential interpretation, a group is worse off through a fault of its own if, and only if, had some or all of its members acted differently it would have been better off (considered as a group) and it was sufficiently easy for the members to act in this way. Since I do not employ any of the collective notions of fault in what follows, I shall not state the analogous equality- and morality-based notions of fault.

With these clarifications in mind, we can now see that according to (1) it is bad that Adam is worse off than Charles and bad that Betty is worse off than Charles. Neither Adam nor Betty is worse off through a fault or choice of his or her own. Adam is not worse off because he chose not to cooperate. Indeed, had he instead chosen to cooperate, he would have been even worse off. Nor is it the case that Adam is worse off through his own fault. Prudentially speaking, he had reason to believe that cooperating would make him worse off whatever Betty did. So, prudentially speaking, he was not at fault. Consider the equality-based and the morality-based interpretations. Let us assume for a moment that it was a fault on either view not to cooperate. (I return to this issue later.) Even so, Adam did not end up worse off *through* this fault. Had he not been at fault, given Betty's choice not to cooperate, he would have been even worse off, so it is more correct—although still incorrect in a strict sense, since he would have ended up

---

[11] Suppose someone acts in a way that is blameworthy from a prudential point of view thereby raising all presently worse off persons to the level of the better-off, but not in order to do so. Because of the subjective nature of the view proposed here, the agent is at fault, on the equality-based interpretation, nevertheless.

[12] For a discussion of these issues, see N. Eyal, 'Egalitarian Justice and Innocent Choice', *Journal of Ethics and Social Philosophy*, 2 (2007), 1–18.

[13] Exactly because in these cases the reasons why it is morally obligatory (or morally desirable, albeit not morally obligatory) to act in such a way that one becomes worse off need not be equality-based, it may be questioned whether these reasons can be reflected in a formulation of what is bad from the point of view of equality. For present purposes, I can ignore this question, since even if it amounts to a valid objection this would not imply that there is no distinction between (1)–(4).

worse off whatever he did—to say that he is worse off *in spite of*, rather than through, his fault. This brings out a difference between (1) and (3). According to (3) it is neither bad that Adam, nor that Betty, is worse off, since their being worse off is a result of how they chose to act. Had they both acted differently, they would have ended up as well off as Charles.

If we turn to the collectivistic views, on (4) the fact that the group consisting of Adam and Betty is worse off is bad. On this view, what matters is that neither is worse off through his or her own fault or choice. Here (2) differs from (4), for on the former view the fact that the group consisting of Adam and Betty is worse off is not bad. According to (2), what matters is that they are worse off as a result of how they chose to act. Had both of them cooperated, they would have ended up just as well off as Charles. So, unlike each of its members, all the members of the group cannot say together that had they cooperated, they would have been even worse off. What is true of each member of the group is not true of the group as such.

We could also have the opposite situation, that is, one in which it is true of each member of a group that he is worse off through his own choice or fault, but not true of the group that it is worse off through the choice or fault of its members. Suppose again that, for some reason, whatever Doris does, she will end up with 100 units of the relevant equalisandum. Eric and Fred each has the option to appropriate a treasure washed ashore and accordingly end up with 100 as well, leaving the other person stuck with 90. Only one of them can appropriate it, however, but it is true of each of them that if he makes an effort to acquire the benefit he will get it provided the other does not. Suppose that both of them fail to make a minimal effort to acquire the benefit. As a result Eric and Fred end up with 90 and Doris ends up with 100. Is this inequality bad?

According to (1), it is not. It is true of both Eric and Fred that he is worse off through his own choice not to make a minimal effort. However, according to the other individualistic view, i.e. (3), this inequality is bad. For Eric and Fred do not end up worse off as a result of choice or fault of their own. Whatever they had done, they would still, considered as a group, have ended up worse off than Doris. Hence, they are not worse off because of what they chose to do or because of a fault of theirs (although, of course, the extent to which they are worse off is partly a result of what they chose to do).

If we turn to the collectivistic views, on (4) the fact that the group consisting of Eric and Fred is worse off is not bad. On this view, what matters is that each is worse off through his own fault or choice. It is true of each that had he appropriated the treasure, he would not have been worse off. Again, (2) evaluates the situation differently from (4). According to (2), the fact that the group consisting of Eric and Fred is worse off is bad. For on this view, what matters is that they considered as a group are not worse off as a result of how they chose to act. Had either of them appropriated the treasure, they would still have ended up worse off considered as a group. So what is true of the group—that it is worse off though no fault or choice of its own—is untrue of each member of the group.[14]

4.3 The favoured specification of the luck egalitarian formula

So far I have distinguished between four readings of the standard luck egalitarian formula and shown these to have different implications. I believe the differences between the readings are important, because in most cases the costs and benefits of the choices each of us makes depend crucially on choices we make together with others. Hence, quite often when people face disadvantageous options the disadvantageousness of these options comes about partly through how these people act together, but not separately. For instance, it may be true of people who are untalented in the Rawlsian sense, i.e. people whose skills—however talented they may be in any ordinary sense of the word—do not command high levels of reward on the job market, that through their own choices of consumption they contribute to bringing about their being untalented (and others, e.g. Dworkin's movie-star and Nozick's Wilt Chamberlain, being extremely talented), and, accordingly, that they are worse off partly through what they, considered as a group, choose to do.[15] My point in this paragraph is not to argue that justice or, more specifically, luck egalitarian justice does not demand compensation for untalented people. Indeed, for all I have said here I may agree with Samuel Scheffler's suggestion that to invoke considerations about collective choice to deny the justice of compensation generally constitutes a 'familiar form of right-wing moralism' that in an unjustified way neglects 'the often complex reality of people's circumstances'.[16] Moreover, there is also the view to consider that it may be bad that a group is worse off even if each of its members are worse off through his or her own fault or choice. My point here is simply that the distinction between the different readings of the luck egalitarian formula is important, because the differences between what the formula implies on these readings are important. Accordingly, it is important to determine which of the different readings, perhaps in some modified form, is the most plausible one. This is the question to which I now turn.

As already mentioned, many egalitarians will want to reject the collectivistic readings of the egalitarian formula. On their view, the concern for equality is a concern for 'how

---

[14] The distinctions drawn in this section parallel some of those drawn by G. A. Cohen in relation to (un)freedom in *History, Labour, and Freedom* (Oxford: Clarendon Press, 1988), 255–285.

[15] I explore this argument in K. Lippert-Rasmussen, 'Publicity and Egalitarian Justice', *Journal of Moral Philosophy*, 5 (2008), 30–49.

[16] S. Scheffler, 'Choice, Circumstance, and the Value of Equality', *Politics, Philosophy, and Economics*, 4 (2005), 5–28, at 14. Scheffler's right-wing moralist appeals to 'ideas of desert and *individual* [my emphasis] responsibility' (Scheffler, 'Choice, Circumstance, and the Value of Equality', 14), while what I appeal to here might better be seen as ideas of collective choice. Still, this hardly makes a difference which is relevant to the present point.

different individuals fare relative to one another', not a concern for how groups fare relative to one another.[17] A concern for equality between groups will, in their view, often and in implausible ways involve a lack of concern for inequality within groups and inequality across sub-groups from different groups. So, by way of illustration, if we have a non-derivative concern that men and women are equally well off, to witness, a concern that does not derive from our concern that all individuals are equally well off, then we must consider it in one respect good if the worst-off men are made even worse off to benefit the best-off women if this would make men and women equal even if the worst-off men are much worse off than everyone else and the best-off women are few but much better off than everyone else.

While I return to the collectivistic reading in section 4.4, I find it reasonable, in the light of the paragraph above, to concentrate first on the individualistic readings of the egalitarian formula, i.e. (1) and (3). I want to show that, for reasons partly brought out in my examples in section 4.2, the luck egalitarian formula so construed must be revised: (i) an individual may be worse off through no fault or choice of his own and yet it need not be bad, from the point of view of equality, that he is worse off and (ii) an individual may be worse off, belong to a group that, considered as such, is worse off through no fault or choice of its own and yet it need not be bad, from the point of view of equality, that he is worse off. To see how the first claim is true consider my example of Adam, Betty, and Charles. I believe that this example, or perhaps an elaborated version of this example, refutes the view that it is always bad from the point of view of inequality if an individual is worse off through no fault or choice of his own. Suppose that Adam and Betty both know what they should do to end up at 100. Suppose, moreover, that the expected value of choosing to act in a way that might possibly result in an equal outcome is only slightly smaller than the expected value of choosing to act in the way that is best from a prudential point of view, e.g. because the differences in pay-off are much smaller than in my original example, or that both Adam and Betty falsely believe that it is certain that the other person will cooperate. Accordingly, acting in a way that might bring about equality does not involve unacceptable subjective risks. Suppose, finally, that it is in no way difficult to cooperate. It is just that neither of them will cooperate to bring about an equal outcome when doing so does not serve his or her own interest. By both taking this unreasonable stance, they together end up worse off. But it is also true of each of them that had he or she cooperated, she would have been even worse off. Hence, it is true of neither of them, that he or she is worse off through his or her own choice not to cooperate in bringing about an equal outcome.[18]

---

[17] Temkin, *Inequality*, 92.

[18] If Adam's, Betty's, and Charles's choice-making dispositions are identical, Adam and Betty might complain that it is Charles's good luck that he did not have to face the choice situation they faced and, accordingly, that they ended up worse off than Charles not only through their own choice or fault, but also through their bad brute luck with regard to their choice situation. To avoid this complication we could simply assume that Charles would indeed have chosen differently. I thank Andrew Williams for pressing me on this point.

Surely, if they were to argue, in advance of their choice about whether to cooperate, that they should be compensated should they both decide to be uncooperative, those who should, if relevant, compensate them could reasonably reject their demand on the grounds that while it is not up to each of them to bring about that they both cooperate, it is up to them together to bring that about. Moreover, if post factum we can either provide Adam and Betty with a benefit of 5 or provide the same benefit to Al and Beatrice who are also at 95 and who, unlike Adam and Betty, could not affect their own situation, I submit that—setting aside a complication expounded in footnote 18—giving the benefit to Al and Beatrice would be better from the point of view of equality. They would have an (additional) egalitarian complaint if the benefit were given to Adam and Betty. This shows that the badness of the inequality between Adam and Betty, on the one hand, and Charles, on the other, is mitigated at least (if not eliminated) because it is an inequality that arose through their own choices (independently of whether they each made a decision about how to act on their own or they together made a collective decision about how to act). Hence, (1) is false.

One confusing thought that should be set aside here is that Adam and Betty should be compensated, relative to Al and Beatrice, for facing a disadvantageous choice situation. Whether sound or not, this is different from saying that they should be compensated for each ending up worse off through no choice of his or her own. This could be seen if we imagine that neither Adam, nor Betty, is risk-averse. In that case, their choice situation may actually be preferable to Al's and Beatrice's, i.e. if there is some significant probability that at least one of them will cooperate. Yet, if they both end up with 95, it is still true of each of them that he or she ends up worse through no choice of his or her own.

By way of further support for my intuitive judgement about Adam and Betty, note that we do not normally refrain from subscribing responsibility to agents for a certain outcome, simply because the agents who brought about that outcome all had to act differently to avoid bringing about that outcome (or something even worse). So suppose that if Adam and Betty both abstain from closing a switch Charles will suffer a very mild pain. If one closes the switch and the other does not, Charles will be electrocuted. If both close the switch, Charles will suffer extreme and traumatizing pain. Suppose both of them reasonably believe that there is a 0.5 probability that the other will close his or her switch and a 0.5 probability that other will not close it. Surely, if they both close their switch, we will not refrain from attributing responsibility to them for Charles's extreme pain which they brought about together, although each of them correctly can say that had he or she not closed the switch the result would have been even worse. If this is so, it is not clear why luck egalitarians, who appeal to common-sense notions of choice and responsibility, should not similarly attribute responsibility to Adam and Betty in my original version of the example for ending up worse off and deny them compensation on those grounds.[19]

To see how it might be the case that an individual is worse off, belongs to a group that, considered as such, is worse off through no fault or choice of its own, and yet it need not be bad, from the point of view of equality, that he is worse off, consider my example involving Doris, Eric, and Fred. Suppose that Eric and Fred both abstain from appropriating the treasure out of sheer laziness. I submit that from the point of view of egalitarian justice, the resulting inequalities between Eric and Doris and between Fred and Doris are not bad—whatever the truth is about the badness of the inequality between, on the one hand, the group consisting of Eric and Fred and, on the other hand, Doris—on the assumption that if a person is worse off through sheer laziness, then this person is worse off through a choice or fault of his own. Hence, (3) is false.

Since the first counterexample works because the right-hand side of the bi-conditional in (1) does not contain (3)'s condition concerning collective fault or choice, i.e. (ii) 'it is not the case that the group consisting of x and y is worse off than z through the choices or faults of x and y', and the second counterexample works because (3) does not contain (1)'s clauses concerning individual fault or choice, i.e. '(i) it is not the case that x is worse off than z through his own fault or choice' and '(ii) it is not the case that y is worse off than z through his own fault or choice', we might accommodate these two counterexamples, while keeping our egalitarian focus on how each worse-off individual fares, by strengthening (1) and (3):

> (5) For all individuals, x, y, and z, it is bad if x is worse off than z and it is bad if y is worse off than z if, and only if, (i) it is not the case that x is worse off than z through his own fault or choice, (ii) it is not the case that y is worse off than z through his own fault or choice, and (iii) it is not the case that the group consisting of x and y is worse off than z through the choice or fault of x and y.

This formula gives intuitively plausible responses to my two counterexamples. Because of (iii), it implies that it is not bad from the point of equality that Adam is worse off or bad that Betty is worse off—despite each being worse off through no fault or choice of his or her own. Also, because of (i) and (ii), it implies that it is not bad that Eric is worse off, nor that Fred is worse off—despite the fact that they constitute a group that is worse off through no fault or choice of its members.

The revised formula may well stand in need of further tinkering. Some might argue that only in cases involving collective group choice that leads its members to end up worse off is it not bad that some particular member of this group are worse off through no fault or choice of their own. This particular objection, I think, can be answered.[20]

---

[19] Thanks to Zofia Stemplowska for rebutting the argument previously contained in this paragraph.

[20] Interestingly, G. A. Cohen in his critique of incentives-based arguments for inequality denies that talented people demanding inequality-inducing incentives in return for being optimally productive are not responsible for their collectively produced result on the ground that they do not constitute an 'organized

I find it hard to see why we should care less about inequality involving a group of people who are preoccupied with fairness and separately decide to abstain from gaining a benefit that only some members of the group can enjoy than we should care about inequality involving a group of people who by way of collective group choice decide to abstain from gaining a benefit that only some members of the group can enjoy. However, there are other objections to (5) that I am less comfortable about dismissing. Specifically, it might be argued that (5) condemns too few inequalities as being in themselves bad. First, consider a prisoner's dilemma-like situation in which an individual actually cooperates, but to no avail, or was willing to cooperate provided that enough others signalled the same intent, but refrained from so doing because not enough signalled intent to cooperate, and ends up worse off. It might plausibly be argued that this individual is worse off in a way that is bad from the point of view of equality.[21]

Second, (5) in its present form fails to accommodate cases where it is unreasonably difficult or costly for people to act in such a way that the relevant individuals do not end up worse off, e.g. as when an equal outcome is only brought about by a few out of millions of possible combinations of actions by a large number of people and it is very difficult for each of these people to know what the other persons will be doing.

Finally, (5) arguably fails to accommodate cases where, in a spirit of equality, people choose to act in such a way that they end up worse off. Suppose that Eric and Fred both abstain from appropriating the treasure, not because of laziness, but because each finds it unfair to the other person to do so, say, because of how they understand luck egalitarianism or because of how they understand the requirements of their special relationship. They would prefer to share the treasure equally were this possible, but, given that it is not possible, both prefer not to be the one who gains an unfair advantage over the other. I submit that, from the point of view of egalitarian justice, the resulting inequality between Eric and Doris and between Fred and Doris is bad despite the fact that it is true of Eric and Fred that he is worse off through a choice or fault of his own.

If we accept all three objections we might end up with a somewhat complicated formula:

(6) For all individuals, x, y, and z, it is bad if x is worse off than z and it is bad if y is worse off than z if, and only if, (i) either it is not the case that x is worse off than z through his own fault or choice, or x is worse off than z because x acted out of egalitarian solidarity,[22] (ii) either it is not the case that y is worse off than z through

group' (G. A. Cohen, 'Incentives, Inequality, and Community' in G. B. Petersen (ed.), *The Tanner Lectures on Human Values*, volume 13 (Salt Lake City: University of Utah Press, 1992), 263–329, at 294).

[21] In cases involving cooperation between large numbers of individuals it will almost always be the case that each individual has no influence on whether an agreement to cooperate is reached and, thus, no influence on whether he himself ends up worse off.

[22] I ignore here the other praiseworthy motivations possibly rendering choice-induced inequality bad, which I mentioned in section 4.2. By 'egalitarian solidarity' I mean solidarity with people whom the agent reasonably believes to be worse off than others because they, so he believes, are worse off than others. Hence,

his own fault or choice, or y is worse off than z because y acted out of egalitarian solidarity, and (iii) either it is not the case that the group consisting of x and y is worse off than z through the choice or fault of x and y or at least one of the following three claims were true: (a) x and y tried, but failed, to cooperate, (b) x and y were suitably disposed to cooperate to bring an outcome in which none of them was worse off, or (c) it was unreasonably costly or difficult for x and y to act in such a way that neither x, nor y, would be worse off than z.

Not all may be persuaded that these revisions are all necessary. But whether or not we settle for (5), (6), or something in between, it follows that responsibility plays a different role in egalitarian theory than has so far been assumed by luck egalitarians, since there are cases in which it is not bad that someone is worse off through no fault or choice of his own and cases in which it is bad that someone is worse off through his own fault or choice. The revisions incorporated in (6) merely reduce and do not empty the set of such cases. While my argument has shown responsibility to play a different role in luck egalitarian theory from that it is assumed to play, it has not relegated responsibility to utter irrelevance. First, both (5) and (6) imply that collective responsibility for being worse off matters. Second, arguably some of the revisions incorporated in (6) reflect a concern for responsibility. For instance, the fact that it matters whether one signalled intent to cooperate may suggest that responsibility matters to the badness of a resulting inequality. However, the relevant object of responsibility is slightly different from that suggested by the standard luck egalitarian formula—i.e. whether one is responsible for being worse off. The relevant object is whether one has signalled intent to cooperate.

While I think the first point simply must be conceded, the second point deserves some further thought. If what renders it not bad that someone is worse off is that this person did not signal intent to cooperate even if this is causally irrelevant to his being worse off, then this raises the question of why exactly responsibility for this fact rather than responsibility for some of the countless other facts that are causally irrelevant for this person's being worse off is relevant to the badness from an egalitarian point of view of his being worse off. Normally, we would not accept the inference from someone's being responsible for any old fact other than his being worse off, e.g. his allowing himself to cultivate a taste for football rather than an equally expensive taste for badminton, to its not being bad that he is worse off.

One plausible explanation here is that responsibility for signalling intent to cooperate matters, not because it matters in itself, but because it matters as a reliable indicator of something else that matters in itself, namely one's moral deservingness where that is determined by, say, the moral quality of one's will. So the thought here might be that it

---

I would allow that if x falsely believes that y is worse off than z and for that reason refrains from acquiring some benefit that y could not then enjoy, then it is bad that x is worse off than z even though he is worse off through his own choice.

is not the case that each individual of a group of people who failed to cooperate deserve to be better off—for this to have been the case, they would have had to have made a serious attempt at cooperating. This is why we ought to benefit Al and Beatrice rather than Adam and Betty despite the fact that it is true of each of these four persons that they are worse off through no fault or choice of their own. On the plausible assumption that how well off someone deserves to be depends no less on that part of his conduct which is causally irrelevant to how well off he is than on that part of his conduct which is so relevant, this explains why responsibility for something that is causally irrelevant for one's being worse off may nevertheless affect the badness of inequality.[23]

Unfortunately, this explanation fails. First, suppose that we know that Adam and Betty are overall much more deserving than Al and Beatrice. Hence, we know that their being responsible for not signalling intent to cooperate—supposing for a moment that such signalling is possible and believed to be possibly consequential—does not alter our overall picture of the comparative deservingness of Adam and Betty, on the one hand, and Al and Beatrice, on the other. I submit that even in this case there is a strong egalitarian reason to benefit Adam and Betty rather than Al and Beatrice. If so, responsibility matters not simply as a reliable indicator of deservingness, although, of course, it may also matter as such. Second, arguably there are cases not involving moral deservingness where we may want to reward on the basis of responsibility. Consider a world inhabited by two Robinson Crusoes living oceans apart on small islands. One is lazy, the other is not. On the assumption that they do not differ in terms of moral deservingness—neither of them interacts with other people and we can assume that had they done so, they would have been identically disposed—egalitarians should be indifferent as to who is worse off than the other, if responsibility matters only as a reliable indicator of moral deservingness. Arguably, however, luck egalitarians might think it would be preferable from the point of view of egalitarian justice that the lazy Robinson Crusoe is the worse-off person rather than the diligent one. For these reasons, I conclude that while responsibility plays a different and less prominent role in the revised luck egalitarian formula than in the standard formulation, the present line of argument does not show that it plays no role at all.

4.4 A sophisticated group-based account

Let me conclude this chapter by briefly suggesting a sophisticated multilevel response to the two counterexamples offered above. The response is inspired by an analogous move concerning moral wrongness in situations such as one in which, say, exactly five out of ten need to act in a certain way in order to avoid a disastrous result and no one acts in this way. Such cases clearly seem to involve wrongdoing yet it is not clear

---

[23] R. Arneson, 'Egalitarianism and Responsibility', *The Journal of Ethics*, 3 (1999), 225–247.

who acts wrongly. Some have argued that in such cases each person acts morally right, since given how the others acted it would have been no use to act otherwise.[24] This, however, does not mean that no moral wrongdoing took place. Each group of people who could have prevented the disastrous result, but failed to do so, acted morally wrong. So there is no wrongdoing at an individual level, but wrongdoing at a collective level. An analogous axiological view regarding the badness of inequality would say that in my first example in section 4.2 it is bad that Adam is worse off and bad that Betty is worse off, but not bad that the group consisting of Adam and Betty is worse off. Neither Adam, nor Betty, is worse off through a fault or choice of their own, but Adam and Betty are worse off as a result of how they chose to act. In the second example, the proposed view would imply that while it is bad that the group consisting of Eric and Fred is worse off, it is not bad that each of them is worse off, since each of them is worse off through a choice or fault of their own. More generally, on the proposed view there are no entailments between judgements about the badness of inequality at a group level and judgements about the badness of inequality at an individual level. Ignoring the complications motivating the move from (5) to (6), the view I entertain here is a conjunction of (1) and (2):

(7) For all individuals, x, y, and z, it is bad if x is worse off than z and it is bad if y is worse off than z if, and only if, (i) it is not the case that x is worse off than z through his own fault or choice and (ii) it is not the case that y is worse off than z through his own fault or choice; and for all individuals, x, y, and z, it is bad that the group consisting of x and y is worse off than z if, and only if, it is not the case that the group consisting of x and y is worse off than z through the choice or fault of x and y.

While initially attractive and pleasingly systematic, I believe that the suggested multi-level account is inferior to the revised formula that I offered above. Presumably, if egalitarians should care about inequalities at individual levels as well as at group levels, situations may arise in which there is a trade-off between reducing inequality at either level.[25] So, in my second example, multilevel egalitarians will want to eliminate the undesirable inequality that exists at group level. Hence, on the multilevel theory it would, implausibly, be in one way better from the point of view of equality to transfer resources to those people who out of laziness failed to acquire the benefit that only one

---

[24] F. Jackson, 'Group Morality', in P. Pettit, R. Sylvan, and J. Norman (eds), *Metaphysics and Morality* (Oxford: Basil Blackwell, 1987), 91–110; T. Tännsjö, 'The Morality of Collective Actions', *Philosophical Quarterly*, 9 (1989), 221–228.

[25] In some cases this might be avoided if there are pure collective benefits and harms, i.e. benefits and harms that make a group better or worse off but whose presence or absence does not affect how well off those individuals of which the group consists are. I take the view that there are no pure collective goods and, hence, that egalitarians cannot defend the possibility of the simultaneous elimination of luck at an individual as well as at a collective level by appeal to them.

of them could acquire.[26] Also, in my first example, multilevel egalitarians are committed—again implausibly—to holding that it would be in one way better to benefit those who are worse off through no individual choice or fault of their own but worse off through their collective choice not to cooperate.

Unlike the proposed multilevel theory, (5) and (6) tie the badness of inequality at the individual level and the group level together. Choices at either level may affect the badness of inequality at the other level. This I take to be more intuitive. By way of further support for this claim consider a case where Geoff is worse off (than average) through no fault or choice of his own and responsible for Ingrid's being worse off (than average) and Ingrid is worse off through no fault or choice of her own and responsible for Geoff's being worse off. They both act independently of one another, have no way of communicating, and both knowingly let an option to raise the other person to the level of the better-off pass by out of sheer laziness. Hence, while they are responsible for their being worse off, considered as a group, each of them is not responsible for his or her being worse off. If luck egalitarians would deny compensation in an otherwise comparable case where each of them let an option to raise him- or herself to the level of the better-off pass by out of sheer laziness, then it strikes me as odd to recommend compensation for Geoff and Ingrid on the ground that each of them is not responsible for him- or herself being worse off when *they* are worse off due to *their* laziness. In the former case, luck egalitarians think that it is unreasonable to expect others to bear the costs of the worse-off people's laziness. If they think it is not unreasonable in the latter case, then it must be because they think that it is not unreasonable to expect people to make themselves better off, but unreasonable to expect them to make others better off, thereby making them as well off as others. But why should egalitarians not consider it reasonable to expect people to act on motivations other than that of benefiting themselves?

To the extent that we agree about the absence of a luck egalitarian case for compensating Geoff and Ingrid this speaks against (7), which wrongly recommends that each of them receive compensation while the group consisting of Geoff and Ingrid does not. It speaks in favour of (5) and (6), which rightly, in my view, recommends that there is no egalitarian case for compensation. This is so because the group consisting of x and y is worse off than z through the choice or fault of its members for the special reason that y is worse off than z through the choice or fault of x and x is worse off than z through the choice or fault of y.

In the light of the sort of cases considered, where being worse off through one's own individual choice or fault, being worse off through some other individual's choice or fault, or being worse off through the choice or fault of a group of which one is a member are pried apart, I conclude that considerations about responsibility must play

---

[26] Admittedly, one could care about inequality at the group level only as a tiebreaker. However, such a multilevel theory would in effect be extensionally equivalent to a view that is simply concerned with the badness of inequality at an individual level.

a different and less prominent role in egalitarian theory than is normally assumed. G. A. Cohen writes in his very influential study of the currency of egalitarian justice that the purpose of egalitarianism 'is to eliminate *involuntary disadvantage*, by which I (stipulatively) mean disadvantage for which the sufferer cannot be held responsible, since it does not appropriately reflect choices that he has made or is making or would make'.[27] I have argued that some such disadvantages are of no concern from an egalitarian point of view and that some disadvantages for which the sufferer can be held responsible since it reflects choices he made are nevertheless something that is bad from the point of view of equality.[28] Moreover, in some cases where choice, fault, or responsibility plays a role, they play a different role from that assumed by luck egalitarians. The object of choice, fault, or responsibility is not always and not merely the fact that the individual is worse off, but sometimes the fact that the individual does not want to gain unfair advantages or the fact that the individual has tried to cooperate to bring about an equal distribution. Hence to some extent, choice, fault, and responsibility may matter, not because they matter in themselves, but because they matter as reliable indicators of something else, e.g. moral deservingness. As I have pointed out, none of this implies that it does not matter at all from an egalitarian point of view whether an individual is worse through his own fault or choice.

Appendix

Let:

'B(. . .)' mean 'It is [in itself] bad that . . .'

'xWz' mean 'x is worse off than z'

'xN(. . .)' mean 'It is not through x's fault or choice that . . .'

'xUy' mean 'The group of x and y'.

We can then distinguish between the following two readings of the location of badness component—'it is [in itself] bad . . . for some to be worse off than others'—in 'it is [in itself] bad—unjust and unfair—for some to be worse off than others [through no fault or choice of their own]':

(a) B(xWz) and B(yWz)

(b) B((xUy)Wz)

---

[27] Cohen, 'On the Currency of Egalitarian Justice', 916.

[28] 'Appropriately' can cover a lot of things and, of course, it might be said that when someone chooses not to render himself equally well off out of solidarity with others the disadvantage he suffers does not appropriately reflect his choice. Since Cohen does not discuss the sort of cases I discuss here, nothing in his article suggests that this is how he intends the qualification to be understood, but should anyone insist on this reading I am happy to regard my second criticism as a specification of Cohen's formulation rather than as a criticism of the narrower reading of it.

Let us similarly allow the following eight readings of the responsibility component—'worse off than others [through no fault or choice of their own]'—of the canonical luck egalitarian formulation:[29]

(i) xN(xWz) and yN(yWz)
(ii) yN(xWz) and xN(yWz)
(iii) xN((xUy)Wz) and yN((xUy)Wz)
(iv) xN(xWz) and yN((xUy)Wz)
(v) xN((xUy)Wz) and yN(yWz)
(vi) (xUy)N(xWz) and (xUy)N(yWz)
(vii) (xUy)N((xUy)Wz)
(viii) (xUy)N(xWz) and (xUy)N(yWz) and (xUy)N((xUy)Wz)

Putting together the two different readings of the location of the badness component and the eight different readings of the responsibility component to form bi-conditionals like (1) to (4) gives us sixteen different readings of the canonical luck egalitarian formula.[30] Even more readings are possible if we allow more complex readings of the location of badness component, e.g. as in (7); readings of the responsibility component, which contain more than three conjuncts, e.g. '(xUy)N(xWz) and (xUy)N(yWz) and (xUy)N((xUy)Wz) and xN(xWz) and yN(yWz)'; or readings of the responsibility component containing disjunctions, e.g. '(xUy)N(xWz) or (xUy)N(yWz)'. Obviously, not all of these readings give us luck egalitarian positions that are equally plausible or positions that represent equally plausible interpretations of what leading luck egalitarians may have had in mind.

---

[29] The responsibility component so construed covers both what in section 4.1 I called the subject of choice or fault—whose choice or fault matters—and the object of choice or fault—the choice of or fault for what matters.

[30] The combination of (a) and (i) corresponds to (1); the combination of (a) and (vii) to (3); the combination of (b) and (vii) to (2); and, finally, the combination of (b) and (i) to (4).

5

Responsibility and Respect: Reconciling Two Egalitarian Visions[1]

Zofia Stemplowska

Are those who suffer disadvantage due to their own choices entitled to assistance from others as a matter of justice? Or do they lose any claim to such assistance on the grounds that they are responsible for bringing their disadvantage about? Attempts to render justice responsibility-sensitive continue to raise controversy even as they gain acceptance among policy makers in an increasing range of settings including, for instance, health-care provision.[2] Of course there is nothing surprising about the reluctance of political philosophers to line up behind one position but, as I will try to show in this chapter, some of the philosophical disagreement over the grounds and policies of responsibility sensitivity stems from a failure to draw explicit distinctions between the different ways in which justice—and especially egalitarian justice—could be rendered responsibility-sensitive.

One of the main aims of this chapter, then, is to distinguish between three key ways of making egalitarian justice responsibility-sensitive, and to emphasize the relative advantages of one of them. Specifically, I will suggest that egalitarian responsibility

[1] I am grateful for comments and/or discussion to Richard Arneson, Ian Carter, Cécile Fabre, Gerald Gaus, Ben Jackson, Daniel McDermott, David Miller, Jonathan Quong, Avia Pasternak, Roland Pierik, Rob Reich, Debra Satz, Hillel Steiner, Andrew Williams, and two anonymous referees. I am also grateful to the audiences of the Edinburgh Political Theory Workshop 2008, the Luck Egalitarianism in Practice session at the American Political Science Association Annual Conference 2008, and the Stanford Center for Ethics Postdoctoral Workshop 2009.

[2] See, for example, D. Wikler, 'Personal and Social Responsibility for Health' in S. Anand, F. Peter, and A. Sen (eds), *Public Health, Ethics and Equality* (Oxford: Oxford University Press, 2004), 109–134; H. Schmidt, 'Charters and Health Responsibilities', *British Medical Journal*, 335 (2007), 1187–1189; 'Personal Responsibility for Health', *European Journal of Health Law*, 14 (2007), 241–250. For a general discussion of conditionality in welfare regimes in Europe and North America see, for example, D. King, *In the Name of Liberalism: Illiberal Social Policy in Britain and the United States* (Oxford: Oxford University Press, 1999), especially 219–286; S. White, *The Civic Minimum* (Oxford: Oxford University Press, 2003), especially 129–152; D. Gallie, *Resisting Marginalization: Unemployment Experience and Social Policy in the European Union* (Oxford: Oxford University Press, 2004), especially 197–200, 220–222.

sensitivity should be grounded in the need for everyone to treat others as their moral equals (to respect their equal moral status). I will show why adopting such a ground for responsibility-sensitive egalitarianism makes it into a less harsh doctrine than it is usually thought to be. I will also suggest that conceiving of responsibility-sensitive egalitarianism the way I suggest makes it better equipped to respond to some of the challenges set for it by social egalitarians. In post-Rawlsian egalitarian thought two egalitarian visions—responsibility-sensitive egalitarianism and social egalitarianism—have been struggling not only for the hearts and minds of egalitarians but also for the mantle of the true followers of Rawls. In what follows I hope to show that the extent of conflict between them has been exaggerated and that we may not even have to conceive of them as rivals with regard to what each should accept as an egalitarian solution to the problem of compensation for avoidable disadvantage.

In section 5.1 I will briefly characterize responsibility-sensitive egalitarianism and social egalitarianism and explain why they might be thought to conflict over the question of compensation for avoidable disadvantages. I will then, in section 5.2, distinguish between three ways of modelling responsibility-sensitive egalitarianism and explain why they would each take a different stance on the issue of compensation for avoidable disadvantages. I will try to show not only that a widespread interpretation of the ideal is unattractive but also that it is not essential for those who wish to make egalitarianism responsibility-sensitive, and that some of the support for the ideal may simply be the result of philosophical confusion. I will suggest how the ideal of responsibility-sensitive egalitarianism should be modelled instead to allow it to capture the normative truth that all persons enjoy equal moral status. Armed with such an account of responsibility-sensitive egalitarianism, in section 5.3 I will try to show why *social* egalitarianism should in fact adopt responsibility sensitivity as a side constraint on its own egalitarian recommendations. I will conclude by pointing to a general policy implication of my argument.

5.1 Two egalitarian visions

Egalitarian thought is divided over what should be the currency of egalitarian justice and thus what should be subject to egalitarian distribution. Crudely speaking, social egalitarianism concerns itself exclusively with the distribution of relational goods and, specifically, the relational good of social status, while responsibility-sensitive egalitarianism insists that the distribution of (access to) non-relational goods is important in its own right. Non-relational goods are understood in this debate to be goods that people can have independently of how others relate to them, in the specific sense that how others relate to them is not part of the definition of having the good. Paradigm examples of such goods are money or welfare. Relational goods, on the other hand, are goods that consist in certain relationships. Social status or friendship are paradigm examples of such goods.

According to responsibility-sensitive egalitarianism, then, achieving genuine equality (or egalitarian fairness, or egalitarian justice—I will use them interchangeably here) requires achieving an egalitarian distribution of non-relational goods, where the measure of whether the distribution is egalitarian, and in this sense fair, is not merely a function of whether people can enjoy an egalitarian distribution of *relational* goods. In other words, responsibility-sensitive egalitarianism is concerned that the distribution of non-relational goods be egalitarian in its own right. Moreover, genuine equality is thought to require equality of opportunity rather than equality of outcome. That is, the presence of outcome inequality is not necessarily taken to signal unfairly inegalitarian resource distribution, in line with the familiar thought that if two people have been given equal slices of cake to begin with, the one who eats his slice first cannot then demand the redistribution of part of the other person's slice as a matter of egalitarian justice on the grounds that he alone now has no cake. The resulting inequality of outcome signals only that the two people made different choices regarding their initial share of cake, not that their share of cake was unequal. Of course it is not always easy to judge whether opportunities have been equalized and thus whether everyone has been given their fair share of resources.[3] But the general idea is that equalizing opportunities requires the elimination of the differential impact of brute luck on whatever is considered to be distributively important or, at least, the elimination of differential and unavoidable exposure to the risk of suffering bad brute luck.[4]

Conceiving of egalitarianism in the terms set out above is, of course, immediately recognizable as 'luck egalitarianism' or, as I have already been referring to it, 'responsibility-sensitive egalitarianism' (RSE).[5] As I will argue in the following section,

---

[3] Specific accounts of responsibility-sensitive egalitarianism must take a stance on the currency in which to measure whether the distribution of non-relational goods meets the requirement of equality of opportunity but my argument here will not depend on whether people are thought to be owed equal opportunity for welfare, advantage, equal resources, or anything else. When referring to an (un)equal distribution of resources or advantage I do not thereby mean to imply that it is equality of resources or advantage that must be adopted as the currency of egalitarian justice; whichever currency is adopted, resources and advantage will need to be redistributed to meet its demands. Incidentally, it is possible to construct mixed currencies of egalitarian justice that, for example, insist on providing all with resources that suffice to secure *relational* goods up to some threshold and then proceed to equalize the distribution of *non-relational* goods above the threshold. For mixed-currency proposals see N. Barry, 'Defending Luck Egalitarianism', *Journal of Applied Philosophy*, 23 (2006), 89–107; and J. Wolff and A. de-Shalit, *Disadvantage* (Oxford: Oxford University Press, 2007), ch. 10.

[4] R. Arneson, 'Equality and Equal Opportunity for Welfare', *Philosophical Studies*, 56 (1989), 77–93; 'Egalitarianism and Responsibility', *The Journal of Ethics*, 3 (1999), 225–247; 'Equality of Opportunity for Welfare Defended and Recanted', *Journal of Political Philosophy*, 7 (1999), 488–497; his chapter in this volume; G. A. Cohen, 'On the Currency of Egalitarian Justice', *Ethics*, 99 (1989), 906–944, at 931; 'Joint Session 2001: Reply to Hurley and Arneson', unpublished manuscript; L. Temkin, *Inequality* (Oxford: Oxford University Press, 1993), 13; 'Egalitarianism Defended', *Ethics*, 113 (2003), 764–782; J. Wolff, 'Fairness, Respect, and the Egalitarian Ethos', *Philosophy and Public Affairs*, 27 (1998), 97–122, at 106. This list is in no way exhaustive.

[5] All those mentioned in footnote 4, except Wolff, can be classified as luck egalitarians (or responsibility-sensitive egalitarians), as well as, to name just a few others, J. E. Roemer, *Egalitarian Perspectives* (Cambridge: Cambridge University Press, 1994); and his *Theories of Distributive Justice* (Cambridge, MA: Harvard University Press, 1996); and E. Rakowski, *Equal Justice* (Oxford: Oxford University Press, 1991). I would also include R. Dworkin, *Sovereign Virtue* (Cambridge, MA: Harvard University Press, 2000), who rejects the

there are in fact at least three different ways of making equality sensitive to responsibility and thus three different models of RSE. For now let me emphasize, however, that the standard interpretation of RSE sees it as unable to condemn as unfair a situation in which no assistance is offered to someone who ends up disadvantaged—even severely disadvantaged—as a result of his own genuine choice.[6] This harsh conclusion is thought to be necessitated by the RSE twin commitment to secure initial equality of opportunity for all and to resist upsetting this equality on account of the fact that some individuals have subsequently chosen to waste their opportunities and are thereby in need of assistance if they are to avoid severe disadvantage. The standard example used to illustrate the (in)famous harshness of RSE involves an uninsured reckless driver. The driver, we are asked to imagine, while no worse off than anyone else, makes a genuine choice both not to insure and to drive dangerously. As a result of his choices he suffers an accident and requires an expensive medical operation.[7] If we further assume that this operation would leave him unable to work in order to repay its costs, he can have no *egalitarian* complaint against others if they choose not to offer it to him (even if he can certainly complain that they lack charity).

The harshness of RSE is often contrasted with the more accommodating vision of egalitarianism offered by social egalitarianism (SE). Social egalitarianism self-identifies as concerned with creating a society of equals.[8] A society of equals is understood

label in 'Equality, Luck and Hierarchy', *Philosophy and Public Affairs*, 31 (2003), 190–198, at 190–191. Dworkin grounds the importance of an egalitarian distribution of non-relational goods in equality of concern. Concern, admittedly, is a relational good but, strictly speaking, the egalitarian distribution of non-relational goods is not derived from the ideal of equal concern but, in part, defines what the ideal consists in.

[6] I leave aside the complex question of which outcomes can be said to result from a given choice; I assume that some outcomes of risky choices can be appropriately attributed to these choices. On this question see Peter Vallentyne's chapter in this volume and his 'Brute Luck and Responsibility', *Politics, Philosophy and Economics*, 7 (2008), 57–80. I also leave aside here how to interpret the idea of genuine choice—the use of the adjective signals only that what might at first appear to be a choice could, on closer examination, turn out to be no such thing. I will also not explore the argument that there may be no such thing as genuine choice and so equality of opportunity must inevitably collapse into equality of outcome. For discussion of this possibility, see G. A. Cohen, 'Equality of What? On Welfare, Goods, and Capabilities' in M. Nussbaum and A. Sen (eds), *The Quality of Life* (Oxford: Oxford University Press, 1993), 9–29. For an argument aimed at showing why responsibility-sensitive egalitarians should not, by their own standards, aim at equality of outcomes even if there is no such thing as genuine choice, see my 'Holding People Responsible For What They Do Not Control', *Politics, Philosophy and Economics*, 7 (2008), 355–377.

[7] M. Fleurbaey, 'Equal Opportunity or Equal Social Outcome?', *Economics and Philosophy*, 11 (1995), 25–55. That such choice can or is likely to be genuine has been questioned and so has the idea that option luck (luck brought about by choice) should be seen as unobjectionable by luck egalitarians, K. Lippert-Rasmussen, 'Egalitarianism, Option Luck, and Responsibility', *Ethics*, 111 (2001), 548–579. I remain agnostic in this chapter on whether the differential pay-offs of option luck should be redistributed among those who made equivalent risky choices.

[8] Wolff, 'Fairness', 103–110; D. Miller, *Principles of Social Justice* (Cambridge, MA: Harvard University Press, 1999), 232, 230–244; E. S. Anderson, 'What is the Point of Equality?', *Ethics*, 109 (1999), 287–337, at 312–337; T. Hinton, 'Must Egalitarians Choose Between Fairness and Respect?', *Philosophy and Public Affairs*, 30 (2001), 72–87, at 80–81 [Hinton does not offer a pure account of social egalitarianism as he is also concerned with the distribution of 'the resources of the external world' in its own right (p. 85)]; S. Scheffler, 'What is Egalitarianism?', *Philosophy and Public Affairs*, 31 (2003), 5–39, at 21–24; 'Choice, Circumstance, and

(in negative terms) to be free from oppression, domination, and other demeaning hierarchies of power, and (in positive terms) to be a society in which people treat each other as social (by which I will mean 'social and political') equals. This final requirement can be put in terms of respect: a society of equals is a society in which people respect other people as social equals. What does it mean to respect each other as social equals? Answers usually proceed by examples.[9] People are expected to shake hands rather than bow for instance.[10] More demandingly, people are supposed to want to cooperate with others in a democratic community. This in turn requires that people consult each other on matters pertaining to social and political arrangement, which in turn involves, as a matter of obligation, that they listen 'respectfully and respond to one's [each other's] arguments'.[11]

Importantly for my argument here, whichever specific way the ideal of social equality is elucidated, it is clear that the ideal makes some demands on the pattern of distribution of non-relational goods between people within a society (even though this distribution is emphatically not seen as the primary subject of egalitarian assessment in its own right).[12] Thus, for example, people who are without access to adequate shelter will not be able to stand as social equals in a community in which others enjoy such access.[13] And meeting basic needs is not enough. People who have not been offered education that allows them to make sense of their social world will also not stand as equals with those who have been.[14] People who cannot afford certain forms of leisure, such as travel or dining out, would also not stand as equals in societies in which many others regularly enjoy such activities. In effect, social equality requires that people do not fall below some resource threshold beyond which their limited access to resources makes it impossible for them to stand as equals with others.[15] I will not attempt to

---

the Value of Equality', *Politics, Philosophy and Economics*, 4 (2005), 5–28, at 17–23. J. Rawls's *A Theory of Justice*, revised edition (Oxford: Oxford University Press, 1999), is also associated with the development of the ideal, although while Scheffler and Hinton defend Rawls's account as offering an ideal of social egalitarianism, Anderson criticizes Rawls's difference principle as not motivated by the ideal properly understood. The idea of social egalitarianism has a long pedigree. See, for example, R. H. Tawney, *Equality* (London: Allen and Unwin, 1931); M. Young, *The Rise of Meritocracy* (London: Penguin, 1958).

[9] Probably partly because, as Miller has put it, '[i]t is possible to elucidate the ideal of social egalitarianism in various ways, but difficult to give it a sharp definition'; Miller, *Principles*, 237.

[10] Miller, *Principles*, 239. Of course bowing could be bestowed with egalitarian meaning but Miller's point, I think, is clear.

[11] Anderson, 'What is the Point', 312–314, quote at 312.

[12] Anderson, 'What is the Point', 313–314, 320; Miller, *Principles*, 241–243; Scheffler, 'What is Egalitarianism?', 22.

[13] Anderson, 'What is the Point', 317; Scheffler, 'What is Egalitarianism?', 23.

[14] Anderson, 'What is the Point', 317–318; 'Rethinking Equality of Opportunity: Comment on Adam Swift's *How Not to Be a Hypocrite*', *Theory and Research in Education*, 2 (2004), 99–110; 'Fair Opportunity in Education: A Democratic Equality Perspective', *Ethics*, 117 (2007), 595–622; D. Satz, 'Equality, Adequacy, and Education for Citizenship', *Ethics*, 117 (2007), 623–648.

[15] Social equality would also not be indifferent to the size of income and wealth inequality within a society since there is a point beyond which such inequality makes people effectively inhabit different social spaces and thus precludes equality of social status. See, for example, Miller, *Principles*, 242; Scheffler, 'What is Egalitarianism?', 23; M. Matravers, *Responsibility and Justice* (Cambridge: Polity, 2007), 110.

define where such a threshold should lie but I will assume that it should be set at a level that requires people to be able to access non-trivial amounts of resources. A society in which people respect each other as social equals is then a society in which people do not fall below such a 'social threshold' and thus a society in which people do not suffer severe disadvantage.

As far as the place of responsibility in egalitarian thought is concerned then, the main battle between RSE and SE appears to centre on their treatment of those suffering severe disadvantage as a result of the choices they made. Specifically, the disagreement seems to be the sharpest over disadvantages that were reasonably avoidable in the sense that they were reasonably foreseeable and the alternative courses of action that were open to the agent were not themselves unacceptable.[16] From now on when I refer to a disadvantage as avoidable it is this specific sense of avoidability that I have in mind. The nature of the disagreement is not hard to discern in the light of the above characterization of the two egalitarian views. SE appears committed to branding all severe disadvantage (that is, disadvantage that takes people below the social threshold) as unfair in the eyes of egalitarian justice no matter how it arose (at least if it could now be eliminated). If, on the other hand, RSE should be interpreted in the manner suggested above, then it will see nothing unfair about withholding assistance from those who could have avoided ending up severely disadvantaged but chose to act otherwise.[17]

In what follows I want to re-examine, however, this reading of RSE and the nature of the disagreement between RSE and SE. I will argue that the literature on RSE admits of at least three different ways of modelling what responsibility sensitivity should be thought to require. Distinguishing between different and conflated models of RSE is important in its own right. But my main reasons for distinguishing between the three models of RSE go beyond that. First, I want to show that one of these three models is more plausible than the other two because it can justify the move towards responsibility sensitivity with reference to the equality of moral status of persons. Second, acknowledging that RSE can be modelled this way will show not only that RSE is more aligned with SE than is often acknowledged, but that SE itself should recognize the necessity of making egalitarianism sensitive to responsibility.

---

[16] For a discussion of reasonable avoidability, see P. Vallentyne 'Brute Luck, Option Luck, and Equality of Initial Opportunities', *Ethics*, 112 (2002), 529–557; White, *The Civic Minimum*, 47.

[17] That such a conflict would arise has usually been noted by those critical (if not always entirely) of the ideal of egalitarian fairness. This is perhaps unsurprising since not many proponents of RSE would want to go out of their way to point out that their ideal conflicts with creating a society of equals. As Jonathan Wolff has put it: 'a society which attempts to realize exact egalitarian fairness will undermine the respect of at least some of its citizens by treating them precisely in the way that is inconsistent with respecting them [as social equals]' (Wolff, 'Fairness', 107). As Hinton has reasserted: 'a properly egalitarian understanding of respect [in terms of social equality] is indeed inconsistent with implementing such a view [i.e. egalitarian fairness]' (Hinton, 'Must Egalitarians Choose', 73). Others who have stressed the conflict include Anderson, 'What is the Point', and Scheffler, 'What is Egalitarianism?'; 'Equality as the Virtue of Sovereigns: A Reply to Ronald Dworkin', *Philosophy and Public Affairs*, 31 (2003), 199–206. To be precise, the literature points towards two key dimensions across which SE and RSE are said to conflict: (1) their treatment of brute luck inequality in the distribution of non-relational goods, and (2) their treatment of disadvantage that arises due to choice.

Before I proceed, however, let me tidy up a few definitional issues. Debates about egalitarianism are often unnecessarily confusing on account of the fact that the mention of inequality, or disadvantage, can be read either as a normative claim (about unfair inequality) or a descriptive claim about the presence of different outcomes which may or may not also be normatively unequal (i.e. unfair). Let me then reserve the qualifications 'unfair' or 'genuine' to refer to the former type of disadvantage, while using the term 'disadvantage' (or disadvantageous outcome, or inequality, etc.) without the qualification to refer to the latter. Second, I will not attempt to provide here a detailed definition of choice or responsibility. When I say that a disadvantage has been chosen, or that one *is* responsible for a disadvantage, I mean by it that one is to be thought to be the (agent responsible) author of that disadvantage according to whichever plausible account of choice is adopted.[18] When I say that someone is to be *held* responsible for a disadvantage, however, I use 'responsibility' in an entirely different sense to mean that the person has no claim of egalitarian justice against others to be provided with assistance (whether full or partial) with the disadvantage in question. Finally, when I talk of assistance (or compensation) being allowed or disallowed I am concerned only with it being allowed or disallowed solely by the standards of egalitarian justice and only on the assumption that the provision of such assistance is made compulsory. That is, I do not mean to imply anything about the (un)desirability of such assistance, or about the (im)permissibility of offering it voluntarily.

5.2 Three models of responsibility-sensitive egalitarianism

The literature on RSE usually refers to RSE by the term 'luck egalitarianism' and hides under this common label various models of making egalitarianism responsibility-sensitive. Three of these merit a closer look on account of their different assessments of the fairness or unfairness of withholding assistance in various cases of avoidable disadvantage.

5.2.1 Equality of opportunity

How can we make egalitarianism responsibility-sensitive? The answer will surely depend on what is found wanting in egalitarian distributions that are not sensitive to responsibility. One of the most straightforward answers, and one often given or implied by the pioneering luck egalitarians, is that not making distributions sensitive to responsibility means forcing some to subsidize the choices of others in a way that upsets egalitarian fairness understood as equality of opportunity.[19] The requirement of

---

[18] For discussion of agent responsibility, see 'Introduction', section 2.1.
[19] R. J. Arneson, 'Equality and Equal Opportunity for Welfare'; G. A. Cohen, 'On the Currency of Egalitarian Justice'.

responsibility sensitivity then becomes a way of ensuring that there is genuine equality of opportunity.

The first model of RSE is then very simple: RSE consists in the provision of equality of opportunity. Once this model is adopted it quickly becomes apparent that there is no need to disallow all instances of compensation for avoidable disadvantage. This is because compensation would not upset equality of opportunity if the provision of compensation was itself included as part of an equal opportunity set to begin with. After all, there is a number of ways of structuring the opportunity sets open to people. Such sets might exclude all forms of compensation for avoidable disadvantage but they might also include the provision of some such assistance. In so far as the opportunities that people enjoy are structured in such a way that equality of opportunity is compatible with some compensation (or, in other words, compatible with insuring people against some forms of avoidable disadvantage), then such compensation (insurance) would *not* amount to an inegalitarian subsidy. Of course, we are all familiar with arguments about the undesirable incentive effects of insurance, but my point here is only that in order to secure equality of opportunity for all we are not forced to adopt a strict no-compensation policy towards the disadvantaged and hence rendering egalitarianism responsibility-sensitive does not require us to adopt such a policy.[20]

Given, however, that this model of RSE has the potential to transform what has normally been seen as a harsh doctrine into a more gentle doctrine of accommodation, it would be reasonable to wonder if the model is, after all, an accurate reading of what responsibility sensitivity must require. For reasons of space, I will sidestep here the interesting question of whether modelling the requirements of RSE this way is in line with the intentions of the leading luck egalitarians. I will also put aside the above-mentioned problem of how to deal with the costs of providing insurance for avoidable disadvantage to all given the problematic incentive effects. I want to concentrate instead on another worry arising in this context, namely that the above model is simply wrong when it assumes that compensation for avoidable disadvantage need not upset equality of opportunity.

This objection can be developed as follows. Providing people with compensation for avoidable disadvantage means erasing inequalities that are due to choice: the choice

---

[20] See Marc Fleurbaey in this volume; 'Equal Opportunity'; as well as his *Fairness, Responsibility and Welfare* (Oxford: Oxford University Press, 2008), especially chs 2–3; M. Hild and A. Voorhoeve, 'Equal Opportunity and Opportunity Dominance', *Economics and Philosophy*, 20 (2004), 117–145, especially 124. Put more generally, the ideal of equality of opportunity prohibits differential treatment of individuals who make the same choices but does not require that individuals be held responsible for anything over and above that. There remains a further question whether individuals would have the option to forgo or sell any insurance for avoidable disadvantage that is part of their equal opportunity sets. Responsibility-sensitive egalitarianism that takes freedom as its currency (or is otherwise attempting to reconcile equality and freedom) might appear incompatible with compulsory insurance. See I. Carter, 'Is There a Freedom-based Justification for the Safety-net?', unpublished paper, 2009. See also M. Fleurbaey, 'Equal Opportunity', and Z. Stemplowska 'Making Justice Sensitive to Responsibility', *Political Studies*, 57 (2009), 237–259. I am grateful to Hillel Steiner and an anonymous referee for pressing me to clarify this point.

to act in such a way that leads to or avoids the disadvantageous outcome. For simplicity, and despite the unfortunate and potentially misleading implications, I will from now on refer to choices that lead to disadvantage (absent insurance) as *imprudent* and to choices that do not as *prudent*. The objection insists that erasing avoidable disadvantage means forcing the prudent to subsidize the imprudent. This is because the resources needed to offer compensation must come from somewhere and so they must come from the prudent. For example, providing unemployment insurance to the imprudent, who lose their jobs as a result of (avoidably) arriving late at work, means asking those who prudently get up early to subsidize the imprudent. Importantly, such subsidies necessarily shrink the relative share of resources that would be available to the prudent had no such insurance been provided. For this reason offering compensation to the imprudent must upset equality of opportunity.

Notice, however, that the conclusion of the above argument depends on accepting the incorrect premise that the *relative share of resources* available to the prudent is shrunk as a result of offering compensation for avoidable disadvantage. This is not the case, as Scenarios 5.1 and 5.2 illustrate by setting out the assets and liabilities of the prudent and imprudent under the two relevant scenarios: first, when those who end up avoidably disadvantaged do receive compensation and second, when those who end up avoidably disadvantaged receive no compensation (unless they had chosen to purchase private insurance cover for themselves).

Scenario 5.1 (Compensation/Public insurance)

	Prudent	Imprudent
Insured	+ Resources X + insurance cover − the cost C1 of public insurance cover	+ Resources X + insurance cover − the cost C1 of public insurance cover [+ **insurance pay-off**]
Uninsured	N/A	N/A

Scenario 5.2 (No compensation/No public insurance)

	Prudent	Imprudent
Insured	+ Resources X + insurance cover + C1 − the cost C2 of private insurance cover	+ Resources X + insurance cover + C1 − the cost C2 of private insurance cover [+ **insurance pay-off**]
Uninsured	+ Resources X + C1	+ Resources X + C1

Examining the two scenarios, the prudent might try to argue that their share of resources in Scenario 5.1 is less than that of the imprudent since the imprudent enjoy all that the prudent enjoy and, in addition, enjoy the insurance pay-off they receive when disadvantage strikes. This argument will not work, however, since it would also commit them to the claim that, in Scenario 5.2, the prudent who insure and do not receive the insurance pay-off (because their prudent choices shield them from disadvantage) are worse off than the imprudent who insure and do get the insurance pay-off. If correct, the argument would simply show that neither scenario offers equality of opportunity. The prudent might therefore try to compare the relative share of their resources in Scenario 5.1 with what they themselves would get in Scenario 5.2, pointing out that the cost C1 of the public insurance cover that they must buy in Scenario 5.1 would doubtless be greater than the cost C2 of the private insurance cover they would buy in Scenario 5.2. This strategy succeeds in showing that the prudent would be worse off if Scenario 5.1 is adopted rather than Scenario 5.2 but it would not succeed in showing what is at stake here, namely that the prudent face worse rather than equal options *under* Scenario 5.1. After all, equality of opportunity should be measured within rather than across different distributive regimes.

We might nonetheless find it troubling *if* the prudent end up worse off under Scenario 5.1 than they would under Scenario 5.2. If we do find it troubling this must be because we expect responsibility sensitivity not only to ensure that compensation does not derail equality of opportunity but also to perform some additional function. What this additional function might be is the subject of the rest of this section. The point of my discussion so far has only been to emphasize the sometimes overlooked fact that compensating people for avoidable disadvantages cannot be ruled out simply on the grounds that there should be equality of opportunity. Hence, when the requirement of responsibility sensitivity is interpreted as a way of protecting equality of opportunity it is, at least in principle, reconcilable with the provision of insurance to those who fall below the social threshold.

It is worth emphasizing here that this first model of responsibility sensitivity makes RSE into a doctrine that cannot pretend to offer a full account of what it takes to achieve just distributions. After all, just as it cannot rule out insurance as impermissible, it also cannot rule out many obviously unacceptable ways of structuring everyone's equal opportunities. For example, it has no conceptual tools to condemn arrangements in which everyone is equally exposed to stoning as a result of having sex outside marriage, or arrangements in which anyone who defaults on a payment is condemned to a lifetime of slavery. It is therefore all the more important to ask if the other two models of RSE can provide a more attractive and complete account of egalitarian justice.

5.2.2 Equality of opportunity for maximum advantage

Responsibility sensitivity might be understood to require not simply the ban on compensation for avoidable disadvantages *when such compensation would upset equality of opportunity* but, *in addition*, that equality of opportunity takes a certain shape; that it should be fair as judged by some additional concern or principle. What shape might that be? Put somewhat imprecisely for now, the demand can be understood to require that opportunities should be structured in such a way that people who make different—better or worse—choices end up with different—better or worse—outcomes. Ensuring that outcomes necessarily vary with choices would make equality choice-sensitive by anyone's standards. And, importantly for this discussion, adopting this interpretation of responsibility-sensitive egalitarianism would rule out the provision of full compensation for avoidable choices: such compensation, after all, would make it the case that people who had in fact made different choices ended up with the same rather than different outcomes.

Before this second model of RSE can be assessed, let me make it more precise. Clearly, it cannot simply require that different choices lead to different outcomes without specifying what should count as different choices. For example, if we are both facing the option of spending an afternoon reading in a library or flying kites and I enter the library by the west entrance and you by the east, our choices should not qualify as different in the relevant sense. Moreover, the demand needs to be rephrased in such a way as to block the possibility that a person whose choice has been to work hard ends up worse off than a person whose choice has been to do nothing; this would make the final distribution choice-sensitive but not in the sense normally envisaged by the proponents and critics of RSE.

There are various ways in which this second model of RSE could be rendered more precise. One obvious way involves allocating outcomes to choices on the basis of desert[21] but I want to consider here instead a 'non-desert' model, partly because it is this 'non-desert' way of matching outcomes to choices that has been under-explored and conflated with RSE understood simply as equality of opportunity. Such a model would require that those whose choices are somehow better (more productive, more ambitious, more successful, or more prudent—and for simplicity I will continue referring to prudence only) end up better off than those whose choices are in the relevant sense worse. The provision of compensation for avoidable disadvantage would be entirely disallowed if it was specified that those whose choices are better (in the above sense) must be able to maximize the advantage they achieve over those whose choices are (in the relevant sense) worse. The core idea behind this move seems to be that this would prevent the imposition of any costs on those who choose to behave prudently (or in some other productive or successful way) by those whose choices are not equally prudent. Requiring compensation for avoidable disadvantage, the explanation proceeds, means that the prudent lose out on the relative advantage that they could gain (vis-à-vis the imprudent) by behaving prudently, or, when the costs are measured in non-relative terms, that they lose some ability to convert resources, that are now reserved for the insurance fund, into a benefit they would most prefer.

---

[21] See the chapters in this volume by Richard J. Arneson, Carl Knight, and Larry Temkin.

Interpreting the demands of RSE this way brings to the foreground some of the implicit assumptions underpinning many recent interpretations of luck egalitarianism. It thus allows us to makes sense of the range of examples used in the literature to illustrate the harsh consequences of making egalitarianism responsibility-sensitive. After all, this model of RSE, in contrast to the first one, really *is* hostile to compensation for the imprudent uninsured driver and, in general, hostile to the possibility that those who made mistakes be entitled to another chance. To emphasize, this hostility is not simply the result of an acceptance that people ought to face equal options in life but requires the further acceptance of an additional principle constraining the shape that such options must take. Given the need for this additional principle, it is in fact striking that (with the exception of debates about desert-sensitive egalitarianism) there has been very little explicit discussion in the literature over the content and grounds of this additional principle. It is puzzling until we realize that the reason why much of the luck egalitarian literature has been interpreted in line with this second model, but without much explicit acknowledgement of the content of this additional principle, might be a result of conflating the first and second models of responsibility sensitivity.

Why might responsibility-sensitive egalitarianism be interpreted simultaneously as a call to equality of opportunity and a call to ensure that different choices lead to different outcomes without much explicit discussion of the differences between these two positions?[22] Because both can be formulated using the same vocabulary. Thus the call to use responsibility sensitivity to equalize opportunities, in line with the first model, can be formulated as a principle that *inequalities that arise due to different choices operating against the background of equality of opportunity are just.* And the no-insurance call of the second model can be formulated as a principle that *justice requires that equal opportunities must be structured so that different choices lead to inequalities.* Of course only the second principle tells us how we must design the structure of equal opportunities, namely to ensure that different choices do lead to inequalities, but it does not help to disambiguate the two principles when the luck egalitarian mantra is formulated as *inequalities, or parts thereof, are just* [fair] *if and only if they are traceable to choice, rather than chance,* since this leaves it unclear whether any directions are issued regarding how to design the structure of equal opportunities.[23] Finally, notice that both principles can be

---

[22] Marc Fleurbaey's writings are a notable exception. See, for example, his chapter in this volume. For a general discussion of the need to be more explicit about how to match outcomes to different choices (to use my vocabulary), see S. Olsaretti, 'Responsibility and the Consequences of Choice', *Proceedings of the Aristotelian Society*, 109 (2009), 165–188.

[23] M. Seligman, 'Luck, Leverage, and Equality: A Bargaining Problem for Luck Egalitarians', *Philosophy and Public Affairs*, 35 (2007), 267–292, at 268. Seligman couples this principle with the following two: '(1) Distributions are the result of people's choices, and of chance. All factors that affect the distribution are either choices or chance. (2) Any inequality in the distribution is separable into parts traceable to a choice, and parts traceable to chance.' Compare N. Eyal, 'Egalitarian Justice and Innocent Choice', *Journal of Ethics and Social Philosophy*, 2 (2007), 1–18; Kristin Voigt, 'The Harshness Objection: Is Luck Egalitarianism Too Harsh on the Victims of Option Luck?', *Ethical Theory and Moral Practice*, 10 (2007), 389–407.

used to attack equality of outcomes—the original target of luck egalitarianism—which might further account for why they are not always adequately distinguished.

Let me return, however, to the more pressing question of how we should assess this model of RSE. How can those wishing to adopt this model defend the requirement that the prudent be allowed to maximize their advantage? The most natural defence will likely make an appeal to the value of freedom. It is not just advantage, the argument goes, that the prudent are allowed to maximize when this model is adopted, it is freedom for all that is being maximized. This is because, the argument proceeds, getting rid of compensation for avoidable disadvantage amounts, by definition, to getting rid of compulsory insurance schemes, and getting rid of compulsory insurance schemes maximizes the freedom people enjoy with regard to the various options they can pursue: after all, they can still insure on the private market if they wish to but, if they prefer instead to use the resources differently, for example to buy a piano instead of insurance cover, they can do so too.

Notice, however, that this argument cannot work as a general defence of this model of RSE. There can, after all, be no guarantee that freedom would be maximized by scrapping the common insurance fund. This is because once the insurance fund is scrapped, some people will either be left without a safety net in circumstances where it was present before or they may have to pay a higher premium than before in order to retain it (thus facing a steeper trade-off between a safety net and other options).[24] Having a safety net is, however, itself a form of freedom: it increases the range of choices available to people at no extra risk of disadvantage (which for some at least translates, in addition, into a very tangible freedom from worry).[25] It is therefore not clear that equal freedom would be maximized for all were all insurance funds to be eliminated. But even if freedom would be maximized if this second model of RSE were adopted, we should still reject it as an unattractive account of egalitarian justice.

My reservations about the model (as a normative recommendation) are best illustrated with the help of a few examples. Imagine, then, that we are considering whether to offer general compensation for a certain disease or whether to adopt the second model of RSE and insist that any compensation would have to come out of each individual's private insurance. Imagine further that the effects of the disease, if untreated, are debilitating, while the treatment for it is very expensive. Moreover, the disease is only caught following attendance at crowded places and the only effective way to prevent infection is to avoid any big gatherings of people, such as concerts,

---

[24] For an argument of why this might be the case, see C. M. Macleod, *Liberalism, Justice, and Markets—A Critique of Liberal Equality* (Oxford: Oxford University Press, 1998), especially 100–101.

[25] See A. Ripstein, *Equality, Responsibility, and the Law* (Cambridge: Cambridge University Press, 1999); S. V. Shiffrin, 'Egalitarianism, Choice-Sensitivity, and Accommodation' in P. Pettit, S. Scheffler, M. Smith, and R. J. Wallace (eds), *Reason and Values: Themes from the Moral Philosophy of Joseph Raz* (Oxford: Oxford University Press, 2004), 270–302, at 287–288; M. Fleurbaey, 'Freedom with Forgiveness', *Politics, Philosophy and Economics*, 4 (2005), 29–67, at 39–41; A. Williams, 'Living as Equals: Right or Responsibility?', paper presented to the Political Theory Research Seminar, Department of Politics, Oxford University, 8 June 2005.

football games, lecture halls, conferences. It so happens, however, that the risk of catching the disease, even for those who do not avoid crowded places, is low enough to prevent the development of a well-functioning private insurance market.[26] Clearly, catching the disease can be seen as reasonably avoidable and yet it seems to me that the costs of avoiding it are so high that to withhold treatment from those who develop the disease as a result of hanging out in crowded places would be unreasonable. Of course, whether compensation should be provided would depend on the costs of offering such compensation, but the point of the above example is to show that the mere fact of reasonable avoidability does not render the claim for compensation mute.

Or imagine that we could set up the courts and the police in such a way that priority would always be given to the claims of those who did not avoidably expose themselves to any risk of crime or court action. Those whose locks were a bit flimsy, or who married potential gamblers, or who opened their door to strangers that turned out to be robbers, or those who dressed 'provocatively' when going out late at night and were sexually assaulted, would have to wait in line until the claims of all the more prudent citizens facing similar problems were met. Surely this is not a policy that we should adopt since all those people should be seen as having the right to equal protection from the courts and police.

There are, admittedly, many possible reasons why we may want to reject this policy of prioritizing the claims of the more prudent citizens (we may worry that it would make crime too hard to police, that it would grant the police too much arbitrary power, that it would be administratively costly to administer, etc.), but one of those reasons should be that the mere fact that a disadvantage is reasonably avoidable does not need to render compensation for it unfair. Rather, we should look for a principle of egalitarian justice that would allow us to offer some insurance and would tell us when this should be done. This is what I hope to do below by outlining a third model of responsibility-sensitive egalitarianism.[27]

5.2.3 Equality of opportunity for equal interests

How might we render egalitarianism sensitive to responsibility without committing ourselves to the view that it is always impermissible to provide compensation for avoidable disadvantage, even when such disadvantage takes people below the social threshold and even when the price to pay for avoiding the course of action that led to the disadvantage is very high?[28] What the above examples of people who avoid

---

[26] This may strike some as improbable without further assumptions about imperfectly functioning markets. I am grateful to Hillel Steiner for this point.

[27] The rationale for searching for the third model can also be put as follows. We can think of the second model of responsibility sensitivity as one that offers people a bundle of choices that favours the preferences of the prudent, and of the first model as one that does not tell us at all how to resolve the dispute between the prudent and the imprudent over which bundle of choices should be offered. The search for the third model is therefore motivated by the fact that we need to be able to resolve such disputes without favouring the preferences of one set of people over another.

[28] This subsection draws on an argument I develop in 'Making Justice Sensitive to Responsibility'.

infection through social seclusion, or who screen marriage partners for any signs of weakness, or who avoid any risk of robbery by not opening their door to strangers, are meant to illustrate is that sometimes the costs of avoiding the course of action that will (or might) lead to disadvantage is very high for the agent in question. At the same time, providing compensation for the resulting disadvantage may not make a comparable difference to our ability to pursue our life plans.

My general suggestion—and the third way of rendering egalitarianism responsibility-sensitive—is this. Sometimes needing to act prudently lest it lead to a disadvantage would require a sacrifice that is greater than whatever sacrifice is necessary to provide compensation should the disadvantage arise. This is usually the case when essential interests are served by not needing to act prudently and assistance is not prohibitively expensive. An example might be helpful. Imagine then that criminal insurance policy is introduced instead of the universal (at least in aspiration) police protection we are familiar with. According to the second model of RSE I rejected, there would be nothing objectionable about providing police protection only to the insurance holders; indeed the prudent might even have a claim that such a scheme be introduced and universal protection scrapped. According to my model, however, we can resist this conclusion. We can argue that even if people did not purchase criminal insurance they should be provided with equal police protection and assistance because, for example, it is important to be able to go about one's life without erecting barriers between ourselves and other people; and that this freedom is more important than whatever would be sacrificed by financing it.

More technically, my suggestion is that people should be provided with insurance against a given type of avoidable disadvantage just as long as the interests that are served by not needing to avoid a given conduct (lest it leads to a disadvantage), or not needing to purchase private insurance against the disadvantage, outweigh the interests that would be served if such compensation did not have to be provided. Thus, for example, if private insurance is prohibitively expensive and the interests people have in not needing to avoid crowded places (lest it leads to infection) or opening their houses to strangers (lest it leads to squatting) or walking briskly on high hills (lest it leads to costly leg-mending operations) or cycling on an old bike (lest it leads to costly accident rescue) are more important than the interest people have in retaining the resources that are needed to offer public insurance for such avoidable disadvantages, then the insurance should be offered as a matter of policy. Notice that, most likely, this would still *not* lead us to offer compensation to those whose disadvantage is the result of drunk driving or going bungee jumping uninsured. With regard to smoking, the standard example of imprudent conduct, it depends whether we agree with John Reid who suggested—when he was the British Secretary of State for Health—that for many very poor people (in fact he singled out single mothers on council estates)—smoking is an essential and rare escape from stress.[29] My point here is only that this is exactly the

---

[29] 'Let Poor Smoke, Says Health Secretary', *Guardian*, 9 June 2004.

right question to ask: Does prudence in a given case require an unreasonable sacrifice given the various interests at stake?

Judging when one set of interests outweighs another is not going to be easy.[30] Notice, however, that we would only need to make such assessments in cases when we suspect that the private insurance market is unable to deliver a reasonable insurance rate because there exists a minority that is disadvantaged on account of the preferences of the majority in not having access to reasonable insurance rates. Moreover, I do not mean to suggest that we must assess such trade-offs between interests in the case of each separate activity (however we individuate them). Rather, we can simply be on the lookout for troubling cases of disadvantage and when they arise, or when we can anticipate them, we will need to ask if the way to avoid the disadvantage was particularly difficult or otherwise demanding on the disadvantaged agents.[31]

The above model of responsibility-sensitive egalitarianism is in fact meant to capture the idea that we must respect each other as beings with equal moral status and our own lives to lead. To lead their own lives, and thus carry out their projects, people need access to resources. But because of scarcity of resources, the choices one person makes can affect the amount of resources available for others. So, because we are beings with separate lives in circumstances of scarcity, we must respect each other as holders of entitlements that offer us *some* protection against the choices of others, especially those that are unreasonably wasteful or reckless or would be so had compensation been offered to them as a matter of predictable policy. It is for this reason that not all avoidable disadvantage should be compensatable. But, at the same time, the ideal of equal moral respect does not require that the prudent be presented with the option to maximize their advantage and indeed it cannot do so if providing such opportunities means that some people had to sacrifice their more important interests lest their actions led them to suffer severe disadvantage.[32] This, admittedly, does not deliver the conclusion that people ought to enjoy equality of access to non-relational goods, but

---

[30] For one, we will need to decide whether to adopt a subjective or objective view of interests. Although I do not have space to argue for this conclusion, the account of interests that best fits with this third model of responsibility sensitivity is, I would like to suggest, a non-perfectionist objective account. It needs to be non-perfectionist and objective in order to accommodate the ideal of equal moral status. The fact of equal moral status limits the extent to which we can tell people that they are mistaken about what makes life good (hence non-perfectionism) but it also calls for the protection of certain essential interests (hence objectivism). I am grateful to Jonathan Quong for discussion of this point.

[31] I say nothing above about how to resolve the issue of aggregation, namely, whether to take into account how many people actually have a given interest in pursuing and/or not bailing out those who engage in a given conduct. I am inclined to follow a modified version of Scanlonian intrapersonal aggregation, and, when deciding which policies to adopt, to add up their impact, as measured by people's ability to satisfy their interests, not across different individuals but within the lives of the (most) affected persons. I am grateful to Jonathan Quong for discussion of this point. T. M. Scanlon, *What We Owe to Each Other* (Cambridge, MA: Harvard University Press, 1998), 229–241, especially 236–237.

[32] It a form of *equal* respect when we acknowledge that all those who are capable of formulating their own (better or worse) life plans are entitled to this form of respect; that is, such respect is owed to all who can lead their lives according to some minimally reasonable criteria and is not dependent on formulating especially ambitious or challenging or otherwise rewarding life plans.

it does deliver the conclusion that it is possible to offer a rationale for expecting more of responsibility sensitivity than a mere protection of equality of opportunity without signing up to the idea that such opportunities must be structured in a way that would maximize the advantage of the prudent.

In a nutshell then, it is because all persons have equal moral status and their own lives to lead that no one's interests should be unfairly privileged over the interests of others and why an acceptable theory of egalitarian justice must be careful not to allow situations when this is so. I do not mean to suggest here that this is the only way of interpreting what equality of moral status consists in or requires, or that this is the only way of interpreting what it means to treat others with respect on account of their equal moral status. But I do mean to suggest that there is a sense of respect for equal moral status that can underpin this third model of RSE. If I am correct, then there is a sense of equal respect for persons that explains the move towards responsibility-sensitive egalitarianism interpreted as combining the demand for equality of opportunity with some—but not full—prohibition on unconditional insurance.[33]

5.3 A responsibility-sensitive society of equals

Armed with the above interpretation of what is required by responsibility sensitivity and how to ground moves to achieve it, let me finally tackle, as advertised earlier, the issue of showing how responsibility sensitivity can be reconciled with social egalitarianism in their treatment of severe avoidable disadvantage.

Understanding RSE according to the third model clearly eliminates some points of conflict between RSE and SE by allowing that compensation sometimes be given to those below the social threshold. But RSE still does not allow unlimited compensation of this type. Where does it leave us, then, with regard to the conflict? To answer this, let me look again at the ideal of equal respect. As argued above, the third model of RSE, and specifically its treatment of compensation, is meant to capture what it takes to respect persons as moral equals. SE, in turn, tells us what it takes to respect persons as social equals, that is, as members of a society of equals. Once things are put this way, however, we can see why the recommendations of the third model of RSE vis-à-vis compensation should be accommodated by SE: we should recognize that being owed respect as a *social* equal is conditional upon respecting others as one's *moral* equals. That is, only those who respect equality of moral status should themselves be recognized as being owed respect as social equals. But if this is so, then the demands of SE vis-à-vis insurance should not be seen as competing with the demands of RSE, but rather the demands of the former should be seen as presupposing that the demands of RSE have already been met.

---

[33] This is an attempt to answer the challenge posed by Scheffler, who has argued that luck egalitarianism cannot be grounded in an 'appeal either to the equal worth of persons or to the idea of equal treatment', 'Choice', 21.

Of course, social status is a multifaceted notion: losing one's status as a social equal would not mean that one was automatically to be denied all the privileges that social equals enjoy. The prudent may not be under an obligation to subsidize the unreasonably reckless or wasteful (i.e. those whose interests would be unreasonably privileged by compensation), but this would not mean that the unreasonably reckless or wasteful should also lose their right to vote or their right to a fair trial.[34] My point here is not that once someone fails to respect others as moral equals that person should be banished from society for ever or that anything goes. My point is rather that such a person is no longer entitled to compensation for her disadvantage *on account of her equal social status*.

Is this suggestion of conditionality plausible? The very notion of equal social respect as conditional may strike some as in tension with the rationale behind the ideal of *equal* respect. After all, the ideal of equal respect is of value if we recognize people as equals but, it could be argued, recognizing people as equals means that we should not differentiate between people by asking who can qualify for respect as a social equal. But this objection is too quick. The proponents of the ideal of equal social respect would not want to (and, in fact, do not) argue that even the perpetrators of hideous crimes must be respected as social equals by others. If it is to remain plausible, therefore, the ideal of respect for people as social equals must be able to accommodate conditionality. At the same time, of course, the conditions that are put in place must be such that everyone can meet them. But requiring that people respect each other as moral equals is precisely this type of requirement.

There is in fact ample textual evidence suggesting that the proponents of social equality do appeal to intuitions that support some such conditionality of social respect. Thus Anderson notes that people 'do not owe one another the real freedom to function as beach bums'. Indeed, she insists that '[i]n the typical case of an able-bodied adult, for instance, access to a decent income would be conditioned on responsible performance of one's duties in one's job, assuming a job was available'.[35] Conditionality is also endorsed by Anderson in cases where people insist (and I use the word advisedly) on living in disaster-prone areas; social equality may forbid such choice altogether or may require co-payment for disaster relief.[36] These ideas are echoed by Scheffler who, approvingly explaining Rawls's view, notes that '[p]eople are asked to accept responsibility for their ends, in Rawls's sense . . . because it is reasonable to expect people to make do with their fair shares'.[37]

It could be argued that all these requirements—to work, to make do with one's fair share—are simply requirements to treat others as social equals. Even if this is so, presumably the compelling reason why work and avoiding expensive choices such as building houses in disaster-prone areas are recognized as required by social equality is that

---

[34] Scheffler offers a discussion of this issue in the context of assessing RSE: Scheffler, 'Choice', 15.
[35] Anderson, 'What is the Point', 321 and 328.
[36] Anderson, 'What is the Point', 323 n. 82.
[37] Scheffler, 'Choice', 27.

they are dictated by the more basic ideal of equal respect for others that captures the fact that people have their own lives to lead and no one is morally inferior to anyone else.

At the same time it does not strike me as plausible to argue that equal respect for people as beings with equal moral status is owed only to those who treat others as their social equals. This is because not shaking hands, feeling superior, not listening, and even—barring criminal behaviour—not consulting on matters of importance for the whole community or acting in a demeaning way should not, in my view, translate into a loss of entitlements over resources that would otherwise be one's to use. It would be unfair to deprive someone of, say, a portion of her income (or, in effect, to fine her) if she did all that treating others as moral equals requires but not all that social equality does—if, for example, she sneered at the political proposals of others in a patronizing manner, ridiculed their views in public, or tried to manipulate people into accepting her own political proposals. Of course, certain forms of conduct that go against the requirements of social equality might be thought to be 'punishable' by the loss of certain opportunities (for instance, those who do not listen to others might not be allowed to become councillors), but this idea can be accommodated by RSE; after all such a view must in general be able to accommodate the thought that certain jobs and opportunities are only open to people with certain qualities.

The above argument, however, should not be taken to suggest a simple normative ordering of the two ideals of respect. I am not claiming, for example, that we must always *prefer* to be respected first and foremost in the way demanded by RSE, i.e. as moral equals before we are respected as social equals, or that *showing* the first type of respect must always be given priority over showing the second type of respect. Rather, I am suggesting that being recognized as someone to whom equal social respect is due requires that the person has not violated the requirement to treat others with the respect they are owed on account of their equal moral status. I am also not claiming that failing to respect others in the way required by RSE means that the culprit should not be given assistance if he finds himself below the social threshold. Rather, I am suggesting that any assistance in such cases would not be owed as a matter of that person's equal social status but for other reasons: for example, because we think—in my view correctly—that giving people the opportunity to regain their status as social equals is worth a sacrifice in terms of equality.

Let me note one surprising upshot of the above discussion. Luck egalitarianism has been frequently accused of being too preoccupied with so-called ideal theory (theory that is not directly focused on real-world problems).[38] However, if I am correct, then across one crucial dimension, luck egalitarianism seems to be more concerned with the non-ideal than social egalitarianism: it tell us what equality demands when people fail to follow the requirements of equal respect. It tells us, in other words, what to do when some people have not complied with the duties that social egalitarianism places upon

---

[38] S. Hurley, 'Choice and Incentive Inequality' in C. Sypnowich (ed.), *The Egalitarian Conscience* (Oxford: Oxford University Press, 2006), 130–153.

them. Since such compliance cannot be taken for granted, social equality must either make access to resources responsibility-sensitive, or it opens itself to the objection that it assigns equal social status to those who in fact treat others as their moral inferior and thereby undermine their standing in a society of equals.

5.4 Conclusion

One of my main aims in this chapter has been to show that there is less of a conflict than has been usually identified between social egalitarians and responsibility-sensitive egalitarians regarding compensation for those whose severe disadvantage has been the result of avoidable choices. The conflict is less acute than is often perceived because, as I argued, responsibility-sensitive egalitarians, in line with social egalitarians, can and should compensate people for some such disadvantages. At the same time, social egalitarians cannot themselves offer compensation where it has been denied by responsibility-sensitive egalitarians *on egalitarian grounds*. Of course it may be that, all things considered, compensation should still be offered in such cases but unless we are clear about the grounds on which compensation can be offered, we risk not being able to justify it when policies supporting such transfers are challenged.

I have not concentrated here on the issue of policy design but my argument does have some implications for policy. First, the discussion illustrates that providing some insurance for those whose choices lead to disadvantage does not require abandoning the ideal and prescriptions of responsibility-sensitive egalitarianism. Second, it suggests that the basis on which a decision about compensation ought to be made should not be the assessment of the degree of responsibility of a person for her disadvantage but rather the assessment of how good an opportunity the person in question had to avoid the disadvantage and thus how costly it would have been for her to do what was necessary to avoid ending up disadvantaged.[39] This is, in one sense, only a subtle difference since both assessments will feed off each other. But, in another sense, the difference is enormous as policy makers are asked to focus, in the first case, on assessing people's contribution to their disadvantage while, in the second case, they are asked to focus on assessing the value of opportunities a person enjoys to avoid ending up disadvantaged. And once we begin to focus on the latter we will surely sometimes conclude that although a given disadvantage was avoidable, even reasonably avoidable, it would still be unreasonable to ask the person to take the steps to avoid it (or bear its full costs).

It might seem to the sceptics, however, that I am putting the cart before the horse here by examining how to make egalitarianism responsibility-sensitive without

---

[39] The usefulness of phrasing the problem in this way has been impressed upon me by Andrew Williams. The argument of this chapter is greatly indebted to my conversations with him, even though this should not be taken to suggest that he would agree with it. For a brief statement of his views see 'Liberty, Equality, and Property' in John S. Dryzek, Bonnie Honig, and Anne Phillips (eds), *The Oxford Handbook of Political Theory* (Oxford: Oxford University Press, 2006), 488–506.

examining (or indeed justifying) how to make equality of opportunity a reality to begin with. Putting this second question aside might seem puzzling given the fact that responsibility sensitivity is supposed to constrain our design of equal opportunities: presumably, then, as long as equality of opportunity is only a dim prospect, there can be no or very little point in designing policies that would make such equality of opportunity responsibility-sensitive. But this conclusion is too quick. It assumes, wrongly, that people who enjoy worse opportunities than others cannot be held responsible for their choices (in the sense of being denied compensation for some avoidable disadvantages)—presumably on the grounds that they themselves are still owed additional resources from the better-off. The reason why this assumption is wrong is that it proceeds as if the second best solution to the problem of holding people responsible (the solution we need, that is, when equality of opportunity does not obtain) is just an extension of the first best solution. Notice, however, that once we assume that inequality of opportunity is fixed in the medium term, then those who fare better than some but worse than others may still need to adjust their conduct to take account of the fact that fewer resources can be shared between them and the worst-off. For example, given a meagre welfare state budget and medium-term budgetary constraints, people who do not enjoy equal opportunity with others may still be asked to take greater care not to become unemployable than if the budgetary constraints had been more relaxed. This is because, to continue the example, the fewer resources are available for unemployment insurance the more weighty are the interests that get sacrificed when such insurance has to be extended to cover a wider range of avoidable unemployment. This is of course a pretty unremarkable conclusion in policy terms but my precise point here is that responsibility-sensitive egalitarianism can inform our policy even when equality of opportunity is out of reach. These very brief remarks leave a whole host of policy issues unexplored but they suffice, I hope, to establish why it is important to ask what responsibility sensitivity might require even when equality of opportunity for all is nowhere on the horizon.

My other key aim in this chapter has been to show that we must be careful to distinguish between various models of responsibility sensitivity. This is essential not only to avoid confusion about policy recommendations but also to allow us to assess the grounds for adopting responsibility sensitivity as a goal. I argued that the most plausible model of responsibility-sensitive egalitarianism is the one that sees responsibility sensitivity as a way of ensuring that people respect each other as moral equals. Thus, while social egalitarianism aims to elucidate a society in which people, who are presumed to treat each other with equal respect on account of their equal moral status, can stand in a relationship of social equality to one another, responsibility-sensitive egalitarianism addresses a different problem: it tells us what egalitarianism requires in circumstances in which we cannot take for granted that people will respect each other as they should on account of their equal moral status.

6

Mad, Bad, or Faulty? Desert in Distributive and Retributive Justice[1]

Matt Matravers

6.1 Introduction

Rawls says only a few things about punishment in *A Theory of Justice*, but two of them in particular have caused both controversy and puzzlement amongst philosophers of both distributive and retributive justice. Towards the end of the book, Rawls writes of those for whom acting justly is 'not a good for them' that 'one can only say: their nature is their misfortune'. This has struck many commentators as quixotic given that it comes eleven pages from the end of a very long book much of which is dedicated to removing misfortune and chance from justice. The explanation—at least of why Rawls did not think his remark in conflict with the rest of his theory—lies earlier in the text, where he explicitly denies that 'retributive justice' is like 'distributive justice'. In particular, in the latter, personal characteristics such as natural and socially developed talents are morally arbitrary whereas in the former 'legal punishments' rightly fall on those of 'bad character' who violate penal statutes.[2]

Although Rawls provides the starting point of this chapter, and his arguments act as the hook on which much of the rest of the chapter hangs, my interest here is not in Rawls exegesis or in contributing to the discussion of whether Rawls is consistent.[3] Rather, I am interested, first, in beginning to develop a broadly Rawlsian-inspired approach to some aspects of crime and criminal justice and, second, in defending this

[1] Versions of this chapter, and related papers, have been given at the Morrell Theory Workshop at York; at the LSE Forum in Legal and Political Theory; at the Northern Political Thought Conference at Edinburgh; and at the UK ALPPC. I am grateful to my colleagues, to Philip Cook, Cécile Fabre, and Matthew Kramer, for the invitations, and to them and all the other members of these gatherings for their comments. In addition, I am particularly grateful to Annabelle Lever for written comments, and to Samuel Scheffler—whose work is discussed at length here—for taking the time to read and to give me feedback on an earlier version of this chapter.

[2] All quotations from J. Rawls, *A Theory of Justice* (Cambridge, MA: Harvard University Press, 1971), 576, and 314–315.

[3] I have said a fair bit about that elsewhere: M. Matravers, *Responsibility and Justice*, (Cambridge: Polity Press, 2007); *Justice and Punishment: The Rationale of Coercion*, (Oxford: Oxford University Press, 2000).

against the most sophisticated version of the argument that to attempt to adapt Rawlsianism to retributive justice is a mistake because Rawls's arguments in relation to distributive justice do not generalize to the retributive case. Finally, I make some general, and highly speculative, remarks about where a Rawlsian-inspired argument might end up if I am right in thinking it can be pursued at all.

If Rawls provides the starting point in distributive justice, one motivator in the retributive sphere is the recent re-emergence of non-desert based responses to crime such as 'therapeutic jurisprudence'.[4] Or, as the evolutionary biologist Richard Dawkins has put it: 'isn't the murderer just a machine with a defective component? Or a defective upbringing? Defective genes? Why do we vent hatred on murderers when we should regard them as faulty units that need fixing or replacing?'[5]

This is a recognizable—albeit unfashionable—position in criminal justice. It may be that the problem with the murderer is that he is wicked, or it may be that he is weak-minded or personality disordered. The purpose of the criminal trial ought to be to establish whether the accused is guilty, and if so, to find out what drove him to act. The focus is not on the offender's responsibility or culpability, but on discovering how best to fix him. The purpose of punishment, then, is to try to achieve this 'fix' and to 'set him on the road to virtue' as Barbara Wootton puts it.[6] Society might then deploy moral education in the case of the wicked, therapeutic interventions in the cases of the weak-minded or personality disordered, and so on.

Liberals tend to recoil at this kind of argument. They do so in part because of its association with paternalism and with dystopian visions in which offenders are locked away and forgotten in mental health institutions. However, this seems to me too quick, and to lead to the possibility that we are overlooking interesting philosophical arguments because of their possible political implications. Indeed, one of those arguments has impeccable liberal credentials for surely one way in which Dawkins's thought unsettles us is through a background appeal to fairness.

This argument might be thought to have weight only for a very small number of those who come before the criminal justice system. A judge punishing a child, or someone who is insane, would be acting unfairly precisely because we think that the insane and those under the age of 'reason' lack the capacity for responsibility. Thus, we discipline children to set them on the road to virtue; we do not—or should not—punish them.

In order for the argument to have any general applicability, we have to accept some relevant similarity between children, the insane, and sane rational adults. Wootton, for example, thought that science and psychiatry had sufficiently blurred the line between

---

[4] See generally, D. B. Wexler and B. J. Winick, *Law in Therapeutic Key: Developments in Therapeutic Jurisprudence* (Durham, NC: Carolina Academic Press, 1996).

[5] *Daily Telegraph*, 3 January 2006.

[6] B. Wootton, *Crime and the Criminal Law: Reflections of a Magistrate and Social Scientist* (London: Stevens and Sons, 1963), 79.

mental health and illness to a degree that made it impossible to distinguish between 'the wicked and the weak-minded'.[7] This, of course, is what the liberal rejects; paternalistic treatment and (coerced) therapeutic interventions are acceptable for children and the insane because children and the insane are different from the rest of us.

One way to take this argument forward would be to consider the idea of responsibility and the capacities needed by individuals for them to be properly held responsible. Such an argument might take the form of first trying to get the idea of responsibility right and then, having done so, asking whether or not this or that class of people is properly held responsible. For reasons given elsewhere, I do not think this strategy will work.[8] Rather, I think we have to put our practices of 'holding responsible' at the centre of the enquiry. What I mean by this will (I hope) become clear below. That said, it is necessary to say something about human beings if the argument is to have any purchase at all. In short, is there any interesting sense in which ordinary human beings can be talked of as 'faulty'? I believe that there is, but that it is a very different sense from that which drives Wootton (and Dawkins).

Consider the following, very weak, claim. What, for the sake of brevity I shall call 'the constitution' of individual agents—that is some notional complete account of their biological and personal characteristics (including their personalities)—in interaction with environmental factors has a profound effect on the behaviour of those agents. For example, some people find it easy to control their aggression, others find it difficult, and some find it impossible. No doubt the full explanation of that would be enormously complex, but one part of it is undoubtedly down to different brain function, just as another part is down to environmental factors. Whatever the mix, a person's constitution, interacting with her environment, will have a significant effect on her behaviour.[9]

I take the above claim to be so weak as to be uncontroversial. Nevertheless, it allows for the introduction of the idea of a faulty constitution: a faulty constitution (or a faulty element of one's constitution) is one that is either or both harmful and/or a handicap.

The distinction between a *harmful* element and one that is a *handicap* is rough and ready, but not in a way that damages the argument. It is meant to capture the thought that there are elements of a person's constitution that are straightforwardly *harmful* given the kind of organisms that human beings are and elements that are a *handicap* given prevailing social norms and structures. For example, being born with spina bifida is always harmful whereas a predisposition to violence and a reduced ability to

[7] Wootton, *Crime and the Criminal Law*, 73.

[8] Matravers, *Responsibility and Justice*.

[9] For a discussion of some of the ways in which the environment interacts with the constitution, see Susan Hurley's chapter in this volume. For discussion of the epistemic difficulties of disentangling constitution from the environment, see Marc Fleurbaey's chapter in this volume, especially section 3.9.

recognize risk may be a handicap in one society (or social setting) but not in another (for example, it may not be a handicap in a martial society or in conditions of war).[10]

To summarize: there is a way we are, the way we are has a profound effect on what we do, and both have a similarly significant effect on whether we flourish given certain biological and social standards. That claim is too weak to underpin incompatibilism, and nothing in what follows rests on a commitment to denying the possibility of individual responsibility. So, the question is, what if anything follows from the basic position outlined above; from the idea that human beings can have faulty constitutions?

6.2 Natural assets

In one of the most passionate of the arguments in *A Theory of Justice*, Rawls takes to task those who think that injustice is inevitable given that human beings differ in their natural assets and social starting points and that a refusal to accept this 'is on a par with being unable to accept death'. That is to say, some might point to the obvious differences between people—differences in height, intelligence, and so on—and say that it is pointless to rail against the injustice of these unequal starting points (just as it is pointless to object to the fact that we are mortal). Rawls agrees, but thinks it beside the point. The critic is right to think the 'distribution of natural talents and the contingencies of social circumstance are [*not themselves*] unjust'. Rather, they are 'neither just nor unjust' given that they are 'simply natural facts'. However, 'what is just and unjust', Rawls argues, 'is the way that institutions deal with these facts'. The critical point is that we need not resign ourselves to the translation of these facts into an inegalitarian social structure. We must recognize that 'the social system is not an unchangeable order beyond human control but a pattern of human action'. That system can be just or unjust and it is up to us which it is. Given that the simple natural facts include inequalities between people, and that, in a just society, these inequalities are not allowed to dictate the shape of the social system, in justice as fairness, we (in one of Rawls's more memorable phrases) 'agree to share one another's fate'.[11]

I want to hang on to this central claim—justice requires that we 'agree to share one another's fate'—whilst putting all technical, and exegetical, questions about Rawls to one side (for example, about his use of primary social goods as the currency of justice). An example of how the central claim works is as follows: people are born with different and unequal natural assets. For example, some people are born blind. Whilst that is certainly unlucky, it is not unjust. However, it *is* unjust if society fails to adjust its institutions and social systems to accommodate the fact that some of its members are blind. Of course, those of us who are not blind could advance our own interests better by ignoring, or expelling, the blind, but we do not do so because it would be unjust.

---

[10] Arguments over deafness show the importance, but also the controversial nature, of this distinction. For some, deafness is not harmful, and is only a handicap because of discriminatory social norms and structures.

[11] All quotations from Rawls, *A Theory of Justice*, 102.

It is in this sense that we share one another's fate (not as some criticisms of egalitarianism would have it by levelling down, or by redistributing one good eye from the sighted to the blind, but by using joint resources to advance the position of those less able).

Famously, Rawls extends this argument by adopting a fairly broad account of natural talents and assets (including the capacity to work hard).[12] The point is that such things are not only neither just nor unjust, they have no moral status whatsoever. Thus, they have no moral authority when it comes to the design of the social system—no claim to be translated into that system—and so desert tied to moral worth must be rejected as the basis for distribution.

To put this in the language used above, in a modern developed economy having a constitution that includes low intelligence is a handicap. The social structures of such economies systematically favour intelligence. There may be good reasons for this—for example, we have good reason to want intelligent people in certain jobs—but those reasons have nothing to do with translating the natural fact that intelligence is unequally distributed into the social fact of an inegalitarian, intelligence-tracking, system of distributive justice. Those without this handicap could, of course, better advance their interests by excluding or discriminating against the less intelligent, but to do so would be to refuse to share one another's fate; that is, it would be to refuse to be just.[13]

I take what I am calling Rawls's central claim to have a very powerful moral appeal. The question that drives this chapter is whether a similar story can be told for those natural facts that are connected to some criminal behaviour. If so, some people might conclude that we should reject the Rawlsian argument whilst others might embrace the further extension of it. For the purposes of the argument here, that does not make a difference.

Consider a brief application of the central claim to the retributive sphere: in contemporary developed societies, given the need for social order and the circumstances of justice, a disposition to react aggressively to minor slights, and difficulty with controlling one's aggression once triggered, are *handicaps*. If so, and if Rawls's central claim has the kind of moral appeal that I think it does, then justice requires that we agree to share one another's fate and refuse to translate these unequal starting points into an inegalitarian system of retributive justice.

For this argument to work, Rawls's central claim must generalize from the distributive to the retributive realm. In what follows, I first try to counter the argument that it does not. I then briefly consider what it would mean to 'to agree to share one another's fate' in the retributive sphere.

---

[12] Rawls, *A Theory of Justice*, 312.

[13] Cf. T. Nagel, 'Equal Treatment and Compensatory Discrimination', *Philosophy and Public Affairs*, 2 (1973), 348–363.

6.3 Distributive and retributive justice: one thing or two?

One immediate response to the argument of the last section might be to say that it rests on the mistake of thinking that distributive and retributive justice are relevantly similar (indeed, are both aspects of the one thing: namely, justice) in particular with reference to desert. This is Rawls's response: 'to think of distributive and retributive justice as converses of one another', he writes, 'is completely misleading'.[14]

It is clear that it is possible to distinguish between distributive and retributive justice in the way envisaged by Rawls. Critically, one can say that distributive justice, on the one hand, does not aim at giving people what they (prejusticially) deserve. Rather, people deserve (are entitled to) whatever the account of distributive justice determines that they are entitled to. In short, the institutions of distributive justice are not there to ensure that when they operate they give people what they deserve. Rather, what people deserve is established by justice and just institutions will ensure that they get whatever it is that they deserve. Retributive justice, on the other hand, does appeal to an independent notion of desert and just institutions will operate, other things equal, so as to ensure that people get what they deserve.[15]

In terms of the language I have used above, in distributive justice we accept that people's constitutions do not establish a 'desert basis'—that is they do not provide the basis for differentiating between people in terms of desert—but in retributive justice they do.[16] The question, of course, is why should one think that there is this asymmetry between distributive and retributive justice?

One answer to that question is given by Samuel Scheffler in 'Justice and Desert in Liberal Theory'.[17] Scheffler argues that distributive justice is *holistic* and this contrasts with both desert and retributive justice. What Scheffler means by 'holistic' is that 'the justice of any assignment of economic benefits to a particular individual always depends—directly or indirectly—on the justice of the larger distribution of benefits in society'.[18] Why should we think that distributive justice is like this? Because, Scheffler says, of certain empirical conditions that ally with the liberal egalitarian's commitment to the moral equality of persons. Those empirical conditions concern the interconnections that effect people's productive prospects. In short, a given individual's capacity to contribute depends on others, as does the value of that contribution, and both depend on the overall distribution of economic benefits throughout the system.[19]

---

[14] Rawls, *A Theory of Justice*, 315.

[15] Rawls, *A Theory of Justice*, §48; S. Scheffler, *Boundaries and Allegiances: Problems of Justice and Responsibility in Liberal Thought* (Oxford: Oxford University Press, 2001), 184–185.

[16] J. Feinberg, *Doing and Deserving: Essays in the Theory of Responsibility* (Princeton, NJ: Princeton University Press, 1979).

[17] Scheffler, *Boundaries and Allegiances*, ch. 10. Scheffler's concern, as he has noted to me in correspondence, is not with defending retributivism or a prejusticial account of desert on which it might rest, but is with showing that Rawls's arguments in distributive justice need not generalize to the retributive sphere.

[18] Scheffler, *Boundaries and Allegiances*, 190.

[19] Scheffler, *Boundaries and Allegiances*, 191.

Combine these features with the background that distributive justice is concerned with the distribution of goods that are moderately scarce and distributive justice does indeed look holistic. That is to say, more succinctly, that a theory of distributive justice is a theory of distributive *shares* (of some moderately scarce goods) and so is a theory in which one person's proper share will be a factor of the overall distribution of shares.

Contrast this with retributive justice. Here it is worth quoting Scheffler:

The problem of retributive justice is not the problem of how to allocate a limited supply of benefits among equally worthy citizens but rather the problem of how society can ever be justified in imposing the special burden of punishment on a particular human being. To put it another way, the establishment of penal institutions is a social response, not to allocative concerns, but rather to exercises of individual agency that society deems intolerable.[20]

All of this is pretty abstract, so perhaps an example of both the holistic nature of distributive justice and its lack of connection with desert will help. Consider a society in which the production of some good is in surplus and/or there are independent reasons to wish to reduce production. It might be, for example, that agriculture is producing too much food and damaging the environment or that in general we need to reduce production and consumption to secure decent living conditions for future generations. In these cases, a just social system might allow or determine that farmers should be paid not to work their land, or that people in general should be paid disproportionately for job sharing so that those who wish to keep in full time employment are comparatively worse off.

In both these cases, what is due to people is determined by justice and depends on solving an overall allocation problem. Moreover, in both cases, the hard-working and talented may actually be entitled to less if they do not do what the system announces will be rewarded. Of course, the farmer or anyone else may use their spare time to do voluntary work, say, in assisting at their local youth centre. In such cases, they would be due praise and moral approbation, but there is no translation here of natural assets into distributive desert.

It is worth noting that the deserving of praise is only possible if one does not go down the route of arguing that Rawls derives his position on desert from a commitment to incompatibilism (there are many additional reasons not to go down this route, but it is worth making this clear as many people seem to be attracted to an interpretation of Rawls that has it that he denies that people deserve anything because he denies that people can ever be responsible for their natural or social characteristics). The incompatibilist claim that no differences between persons can be the basis for different desert claims *because* all differences between people are themselves undeserved does of course deliver the irrelevance of desert to distributive justice, but it delivers far too much. It is both generalizable to retributive justice (which is what the argument of this section is trying to avoid), and it would rule out all claims for praise and blame on the

---

[20] Scheffler, *Boundaries and Allegiances*, 162–163.

basis of natural talents and assets such as generosity or the capacity to work hard. Such a position is, of course, both possible and coherent, but it is not one embraced by Rawls and it is not one being considered here.[21]

To summarize: Scheffler's claim is that distributive and retributive justice are asymmetrical because the former is holistic and the latter individualistic. Retributive justice finds its desert basis in some fact about the subject. That is:

No assessment of the overall distribution of benefits and burdens in society or of the institutions that produced that distribution is normally required in order to decide whether a particular individual deserves a certain [punishment]. Instead, it is a constraint on the justice of distributions and institutions that they should give each individual what that individual independently deserves in virtue of the relevant facts about him or her.[22]

This contrasts with holistic distributive justice, as noted earlier, in which 'the justice of any particular assignment of benefits always depends—directly or indirectly—on the justice of the larger distribution of benefits and burdens in society'.[23]

6.3.1 Is distributive justice holistic?

In order to assess this argument, we can ask whether it is plausible that distributive justice is holistic, and if so why, and whether it is plausible that retributive justice is individualistic, and if so why.

As we have seen, Scheffler offers two arguments for the holism of distributive justice: the *moral* argument is that, given a commitment to the fundamental equality of persons, there is no '"natural" baseline' of differentially deserving people. This is, of course, where the argument connects with the moral arbitrariness of natural fortune. From the perspective of distributive justice there is no 'pre-social' order of persons distinguished by facts that relate to desert.[24] The *empirical* argument is that 'the life prospects of individuals are so densely and variously interrelated...that virtually any allocation of resources to one person has morally relevant implications for other people'.[25]

Clearly, both Scheffler's arguments for distributive holism could be challenged. People have, and do, believe that the institutions of distributive justice ought to ensure that people get what they prejusticially deserve (because people are differentially virtuous, hard-working, capable, and so on). However, I want to grant that distributive justice is holistic in the way described by Scheffler both because my main concern is with retributive justice and because I think Scheffler is largely right.

6.3.2 Is retributive justice individualistic?

That leaves the question of whether retributive justice is individualistic, which I am going to approach by asking whether the arguments for the holism of distributive justice apply to retributive justice.

---

[21] See, however, Larry Temkin's chapter in this volume.
[22] Scheffler, *Boundaries and Allegiances*, 168.
[23] Scheffler, *Boundaries and Allegiances*, 166.
[24] Scheffler, *Boundaries and Allegiances*, 167.
[25] Scheffler, *Boundaries and Allegiances*, 132.

First, then, consider the moral argument: Is there a 'pre-social' baseline in which persons can be differentiated in terms of desert by facts about them? One reason to think the answer to that is 'yes', is to think about the standard distinction between *mala prohibita* and *mala in se* crimes. The latter would be wrong even in the absence of a criminal system that makes them illegal. So, if Bert intentionally kills another person without justification or excuse and Ernie does not, then Bert deserves punishment even in the absence of a system of justice that will give it to him. The purpose of the system of justice, when established, is to translate Bert's individual desert standing into the world by giving him what he deserves.

Second, consider the empirical argument: Is there a difficulty in identifying the contribution of a given agent to a given outcome? Clearly there may be in certain cases, but it is not hard to devise a core example in which no empirical difficulties arise. Assuming Bert did not have an accomplice, etc., then he (and he alone) is the murderer. There is no complex system of production and exchange here such that it is impossible to distinguish one person's contribution, or the value of that contribution, from another's. In short, the empirical argument that appeals to the interconnections between people within the structures of distributive justice does not seem to hold.

Thus, Scheffler's position seems to be vindicated and the force of the question about what it would mean 'to share one another's fate' in retributive justice is blunted. However, in the next section I argue that neither the moral nor the empirical argument is so straightforward.

6.4 Retributive holism: the moral argument

Scheffler's moral argument depends on the Rawlsian position identified at the start of this chapter. People's natural assets are merely natural facts that are neither just nor unjust. They do *not* determine the 'deservingness' of the person, and they have no moral authority such that the institutions of justice should translate them into unequal distributive shares. We start with a commitment to an egalitarian moral baseline in which each individual is thought of as fundamentally equal; that is, equal once abstracted from particular contingencies such as his or her talents, abilities, natural assets, and so on. The question with which I began, though, was why this argument should not apply to, say, the unequal distribution of the ease with which people can control their aggression. That is to say, what is the difference between thinking, prejudicially, about a person disposed to hard work and one disposed to anger?

Scheffler's answer—that we expect the systems of (retributive) justice to punish those who act on their anger (because they deserve it), but we do not expect the systems of (distributive) justice to reward those who work hard (unless there are other, non-desert related reasons to do so)—begs the question. *That* is the conclusion that Scheffler needs in order to distinguish holistic distributive justice from individualistic retributive justice, so it can hardly be the argument for that conclusion. In short, the moral argument seems to be largely stipulative in distinguishing certain features of people's constitutions that ought to be considered prejusticially relevant from those held to be irrelevant. If this is to be defended, then Scheffler needs to import an argument. There are three possibilities that are worth distinguishing.

Undeserved all the way down. Of course, one possibility is to say that assets such as intelligence and the capacity to work hard are not themselves deserved. However, that is true of all features of our constitutions and, if relevant, delivers incompatibilism (moreover, it is that interpretation of Rawls's account that Scheffler is trying to avoid).

Compatibilism. Another, more plausible, but more complex, position would be to distinguish between, say, the capacity for hard work (or, to make it easier, height) and, say the disposition to be quick to anger by arguing that the latter is morally relevant for all the reasons usually given by compatibilists.

Scheffler does not explicitly endorse this strategy, but it may well be that it sits in the background to do the necessary work. What is needed is some plausible compatibilists account. Take, for example, Fischer and Ravizza's reasons-responsiveness account. This holds that 'an agent must *control* his behavior in a suitable sense, in order to be morally responsible for it' where the suitable sense of control is one linked to the agent's ability to act in a way that is responsive to reasons.[26] In short, the compatibilist holds that whilst it (usually) makes no sense to hold a person responsible for her height, gender, or skin colour, it does (usually) make sense to hold her responsible for acting aggressively. Some characteristics, relevant to morality, are thus properly the basis for prejusticial distinctions between people.

For reasons given elsewhere (and that would take too long to repeat here), I think compatibilist strategies of this kind are problematic.[27] However, assume that some such strategy can be successful. Does it, then, underwrite the distinction that Scheffler needs between those natural facts, like intelligence and the capacity to work hard, that are irrelevant to distributive justice and those, like a disposition to anger, that are relevant to retributive justice? Perhaps in core cases it does. The natural facts that some people are stronger or taller than others, and that some are blind, are morally arbitrary. We agree to share one another's fate by refusing to organize society in a way that translates these inequalities into distributive shares. The account that we now have of their moral arbitrariness is that these facts are not under the control of the agent in the relevant sense. It would make no sense to ask the agent to give a reasoned account of himself and his strength, height, and capacity to see. In organizing society so that we do *not* agree to share the fates of those with tendencies to aggression, we hold that tendency to be morally relevant because (assuming the tendency is not irresistible), it is under the control of the agent in the relevant sense. It does make sense to demand to know of

[26] J. M. Fischer and M. Ravizza, *Responsibility and Control: A Theory of Moral Responsibility* (Cambridge: Cambridge University Press, 1998), 13.

[27] Matravers, *Responsibility and Justice.*

the agent, 'why did you do that?' when he acts aggressively and to expect an answer in terms of reasons.

This is a familiar and, to many, a plausible, account. Yet it is problematic to apply it to rescue the distinction to which Scheffler is appealing for three reasons. First, although it seems clear in a case such as blindness, it seems far less clear in a case such as the willingness, or capacity, to work hard. Moreover, although 'native intelligence' (or its absence) may be akin to blindness, the disposition to develop that intelligence through schooling and application seem more like the disposition to be easily angered. In other words, by treating all contingent aspects of the person as arbitrary, we cut through all the problems of defining desert and reassert the liberal commitment to an egalitarian prejusticial baseline. By unpacking that and redefining the baseline in accordance with some or other compatibilist theory, we risk both impractical complexity and the egalitarian commitment.

Second, for all that compatibilist theories are technically adept marvels of the modern philosophical imagination, it is not clear that they go far enough to rescue the broad intuition that we have about fairness that underwrites some of Rawls's appeal. When Rawls writes in response to the argument that moral desert can be understood in terms of conscientious effort, that 'the effort a person is willing to make is influenced by his natural abilities and skills', he is not making a claim about the metaphysics of responsibility or about whether 'effort' is responsive to reasons; he is making a claim about fairness. It is unfair to translate natural facts into distributive outcomes. My question is, why is it not unfair to do the same in the sphere of retributive justice?

Third, and finally, even if one grants that there is a differential desert basis in the retributive case that does not apply to the distributive sphere, that is not the whole story. One point of Rawls's central claim is that some things are handicaps in a given social structure that might not be handicaps in some alternative structure. If so, then those who benefit from the structure owe a justification for it to those who are disadvantaged by it. Thus, although it may make sense for us to call the aggressive person to account for his behaviour in a way that it does not in the case of the very tall or the blind, it is also possible for him to ask for a justification from us of the social structures that have converted some natural fact about him into a handicap; after all, a tendency to be quick to anger is not a *harmful* characteristic (in the sense defined above), it is a natural fact that is turned into a *handicap* by social structures of a certain kind.

6.4.1 Holism

Scheffler has one other route available, which is to appeal directly to the idea that distributive justice is holistic and argue that this means that there is no 'thing'—no reward or penalty—that is such that it would relate in the right kind of way to difference in the prejusticial desert of persons. This is, in a sense, to turn the argument around. Rather than say that individuals are all equal, in that the differences between them are morally arbitrary, and so distributive justice ought not to reflect those differences, it says that since distributive justice is holistic there is no point in distinguishing prejusticially between people because no distinction could be a desert basis; there is nothing to be 'deserved'.

I think this argument is right. Even, say, were we to hold 'being hard-working' as morally relevant—say, the desert basis for praise—there is nothing that can be said about, for example, the income level that should be attached to being hard-working. Indeed, as we saw above in the case of the over-supply of some good, there may be cases in which the appropriate 'reward' for hard work is a smaller share (albeit that we might otherwise praise and admire the hard-working). The problem for those who would distinguish between retributive and distributive justice is that this applies in exactly the same way to retributive justice. *Pace* Kant, there is no unique fitting and deserved punishment for a given offence. There are no 'celestial mechanics' that require that murderers are punished with death.[28]

6.5 Retributive holism: the empirical argument

The argument from holism above connects to Scheffler's empirical argument. This, recall, rests on the claim that 'the life prospects of individuals are so densely and variously interrelated...that virtually any allocation of resources to one person has morally relevant implications for other people'. Does this holism apply to retributive justice?

In order to answer that question, it is necessary to unpack the term 'retributive justice', which I have used carelessly up to now to refer to the system of criminal justice and the social practice of imposing punishment on a particular offender. Clearly, for present purposes, the critical question is that of punishment. What, if anything, justifies imposing this punishment on this offender?

We have seen that the equivalent distributive question—What, if anything, justifies rewarding this person with this benefit?—is said to be answerable only by reference to the entire system of distributive shares (by reference to what others have got in the system). Whereas, Scheffler claims, we can consider whether this particular punishment can be deserved by this particular offender without considering the overall system of punishment and what it has delivered to others.

As noted above, there are punishment theorists who believe that there is some prejusticially given punishment that is uniquely suited to each crime and that it is the job of our system of criminal justice to ensure that people get what they deserve (and neither more nor less), but this does not seem to me to be a plausible position.[29] Instead, it seems to me—and here I do not have space to defend what follows so offer it only as a conclusion—that a plausible account of punishment will separate the element

---

[28] The phrase 'celestial mechanics' is taken from M. Cohen, 'A Critique of Kant's Philosophy of Law' in G. T. Whitney and D. F. Bowers (eds), *The Heritage of Kant* (Princeton, NJ: Princeton University Press, 1939), 279–302.

[29] See M. Matravers, *Justice and Punishment*, ch. 3.

of criticism or communication from the element of hard treatment (a fine, prison, or whatever). For the sake of brevity—and at the risk of some inaccuracy—let us say that it will separate issues of criticism from issues of penal hard treatment.

Is criticism, understood as above, individualistic? The answer to that is 'yes', but only given the restriction on the meaning of the term. Other things equal, people who commit wrong acts (*mala in se*) deserve moral condemnation. In the same way, though, people who do morally good acts—including in the distributive sphere—deserve moral praise.

What of penal hard treatment? Clearly, the just, or deserved, sentence for a particular individual for a particular crime depends on the overall system of penalties both in the sense that it needs to be ordinally and cardinally proportional, and in the sense that the overall pattern of sentencing needs to be determined by reference to social circumstances. Note, this is *not* to say that it is unjust to sentence one murderer to twenty years unless one can sentence all murderers to twenty years (which one clearly cannot since not all murderers are convicted). It is to say that *this* murderer only deserves twenty years if that is the tariff for murders of this seriousness and with this degree of culpability. However, this is not enough to establish holism.[30] This is because the principle of treating like cases alike is not sufficient for holism (for example, it is a principle that could be incorporated into an individualistic account of distributive justice).

On one account sentencing is not holistic. This account would have it that if we grant that offenders deserve moral criticism *and* there is an intrinsically connected amount of hard treatment that is deserved as the unique means to express that criticism, then individual hard treatment is deserved and the level of it does not depend on the allocation of criticism and hard treatment to others. Of course, given limited resources, it may be that no one gets their fair share (because, after all, the supply of hard treatment in a given society is not actually likely to be endless), but that does not mean that the share that each deserves is not fixed individually.

For independent reasons, I think any such account is unlikely to be successful. Particular levels of hard treatment simply do not have that kind of internal connection to criticism. Rather, levels of hard treatment are likely to be set for broadly conse-quentialist reasons (constrained, of course, by the need not to contradict the message of deserved criticism). If so, then hard treatment is indeed likely to be an allocative question; it is a matter of how much the society can afford and the just distribution of one share of that allocation to one individual will be a factor of the overall effect of allocations to all relevant individuals. This, though, is not a fully satisfactory argument. In so far as it relies on detaching hard treatment from punishment, and then associating the distribution of hard treatment with consequentialism, it shows that the distribution of hard treatment *rather than* the distribution of punishment is holistic.

---

[30] In the first version of this chapter, I thought it was. However, Scheffler convinced me that this was wrong for the reasons that follow.

However, the key is not to detach criticism and hard treatment, but rather to appeal to the very complexity that underpins Scheffler's empirical argument for distributive holism. One can do this in two ways: first, the supply of punishment understood as consisting of both moral criticism and penal hard treatment is not endless and its distribution will not be fixed only by individual desert. Offenders may deserve individually fixed levels of criticism, but the levels of penal hard treatment they deserve will be a complex matter determined in part by what is decided to be just overall and thus, within that overall system, to what level of hard treatment the individual offender is entitled (where entitlement is a holistic idea). Second, we have reason to be cautious in thinking about the desert of individual offenders given that, as Scheffler puts it, 'the life prospects of individuals are so densely and variously interrelated'. Recall that this chapter began by pointing out that some things related to criminality are *handicaps*. It is, in part, the social structure that has made it the case that some natural facts have been converted into handicaps. The tendency to act aggressively, and the tendency to work hard, are not only 'influenced by…natural abilities and skills', but are also both related to certain kinds of outcomes only because of arbitrary circumstances that converted one into an advantage and the other into a handicap.[31]

6.6 Concluding remarks

The basic issue at stake here is as follows: there is something enormously attractive about Rawls's vision of justice as an agreement 'to share one another's fates'. We establish social practices and are accountable for them. Those practices could simply reflect the inequalities between people—at the limit the most able could enslave the least able—but (on the liberal egalitarian model) that would be unjust. Instead, social practices should abstract from 'natural facts' and treat people as equals. This is not because natural facts are themselves undeserved, or because Rawls has doubts about the metaphysics of responsibility, it is because those natural facts have no moral authority when it comes to the construction of principles of justice.

This vision has set the agenda for liberal egalitarian political philosophy and it has been developed and refined in millions of words. Yet the argument is limited to distributive justice. Many philosophers do not even note that limitation. What drives this chapter is the thought that this argument might apply also to retributive justice.

One of the few philosophers who has been troubled by this is Scheffler. As we have seen, he thinks we can distinguish between distributive and retributive justice because the former is holistic and the latter individualistic. The case is in two parts: a moral argument that says that there are no relevant prejusticial differences between people,

---

[31] There is an additional argument suggested to me by John Gardner, which is that in the non-ideal world we inhabit, punishment—and, in particular, penal hard treatment—spills over from the person punished to his relatives, children, partner, and so on. That is, punishment has a devastating effect on the life prospects of related persons.

and an empirical argument that says that the distributive case is so complex that it would, in any case, be impossible to establish who individually deserved what, even if it made sense to think of people as differentially deserving.

My argument is that the reasons we have to endorse prejusticial egalitarianism apply equally to the retributive case. Whilst a distinction can be drawn using some or other compatibilist theory of moral responsibility, I do not believe that the distinction would mirror the distributive/retributive divide and nor do I believe that it is the appropriate *kind* of argument. As for the empirical argument, I do not think that this distinguishes distributive rewards and penalties from deserved hard treatment imposed as punishment.

It is important to note that this is not an incompatibilist argument (it would be much easier if it were). The claim is not that persons are not responsible for any individual features of themselves because none of those features is deserved. Rawls nowhere denies the appropriateness of prejusticial notions of deserved moral praise and blame. The argument is rather that what we should *do* beyond praise and blame, in both the distributive and retributive spheres, depends on what the account(s) of justice that we endorse tells us we should do. There is no prejusticially given suffering that is deserved by the criminal offender that it is the job of our system of retributive justice to ensure he gets, just as there is no prejusticially given distributive share deserved by the intelligent and able that it is the job of our system of distributive justice to hand out.

Finally, then, what follows from the (no doubt counter-intuitive) idea that when it comes to those who have a tendency to aggression and those who do not we should 'agree to share one another's fates'? Clearly, nothing follows at the individual level. We are not required by distributive justice to employ lazy and inept builders to do our construction projects because their laziness and natural disadvantages are morally arbitrary in the construction of the system of justice. Similarly, we are not required to volunteer to be mugging victims for those disposed to violence.

Rather, we share one another's fate in the retributive sphere by thinking about the impact of social structures on those who might fall foul of the criminal law. Take just one example: the social system we have established means that there are strong economic pressures for people to live in reasonably large towns and cities, and to engage with modern productive technologies (using that word in the broadest sense). These things make life more difficult for the blind, for example, than they might otherwise be (they make blindness more of a handicap than it would be in some alternative sets of arrangements). The requirement that we share one another's fates means that we build into our towns and cities, and into our productive technologies, things that are expensive, but that make it easier for the blind to live fulfilled lives. There are limits to what justice requires, but it requires us to do something.

Similarly, we know that living in towns and cities with relatively dense populations and stressful, intensive, productive technologies is difficult for those who find it hard to control their aggression. A disposition to respond aggressively to situations is more of a handicap in our society than it would be otherwise. The requirement to share one another's fate might mean, for example, that we think differently about avoiding criminogenic situations. The point is not simply to protect the potential victims, but also to minimize the chances of the offender acting in ways that may well come to disadvantage him.

7

Responsibility, Desert, and Justice[1]

Carl Knight

7.1 Introduction

One strand of contemporary theorizing about distributive justice attempts to accommodate considerations of individual responsibility. This strand holds that the character of persons' responsible acts can legitimately influence welfare and/or resource levels. Attention has particularly focused on attempts to accommodate considerations of responsibility within egalitarian theory.[2] According to *responsibility-sensitive egalitarianism* (or 'luck egalitarianism'), departures from equality are justified, provided that they reflect differential exercises of responsibility.

In this chapter I focus on a more generic position, which we might call *responsibility-sensitive justice*. This view also bases distributions on responsibility considerations. But unlike responsibility-sensitive egalitarianism, it is not committed to an egalitarian baseline. This might mean, for instance, that where there are no responsible acts it shows indifference towards the various possible states of affairs. I seek to establish just what kind of responsibility this view responds to, and how the nature of that response is established.

I contrast the structure of responsibility-sensitive justice with that of an older view which we might call *desert-sensitive justice*. This view holds, as Mill puts it, 'that each person should obtain that (whether good or evil) which he *deserves* . . .'.[3] I show that, while responsibility considerations feature prominently among desert considerations, desert considerations are in two regards narrower and in one regard wider than responsibility considerations. Each of these differences has important implications for the relative success of the two competing accounts of justice.

[1] Earlier versions of this chapter were presented at a Historical, International, Normative Theory meeting at the University of Glasgow in February 2008 and at a Northern Political Theory Association meeting at the University of Edinburgh in the same month. I thank the participants on both occasions, two anonymous referees, and Zofia Stemplowska for their helpful comments.

[2] R. J. Arneson, 'Equality and Equal Opportunity for Welfare', *Philosophical Studies*, 56 (1989), 77–93; G. A. Cohen, 'On the Currency of Egalitarian Justice', *Ethics*, 99 (1989), 906–944.

[3] J. S. Mill, *Utilitarianism* in *On Liberty and Other Essays*, J. Dunn (ed.) (Oxford: Oxford University Press, 1991), 179.

The main argument is that desert sensitivity is a better approximation of our intuitions about justice. First, I demonstrate that, while responsibility may be judged on prudential or moral grounds, desert is necessarily moral. As a plausible responsibility- or desert-based account of justice must involve moral appraisal, responsibility sensitivity is only prima facie plausible in one of its two broad formulations. The narrowness of desert in this regard is preferable. Second, I distinguish responsibility sensitivity *in the strict sense*—the view that distributions should be shaped by responsibility factors alone. This position has been overlooked in the literature, which is surprising given that it is most faithful to the idea of responsibility sensitivity. Strict responsibility sensitivity is implausible on account of its reliance on a morally arbitrary distinction between different kinds of non-responsibility (or brute luck). Desert-sensitive justice makes no such distinction, and so avoids moral arbitrariness. Finally, I identify the more familiar, less strict form of responsibility sensitivity that would really be better described as *non-responsibility negation*. While this is undoubtedly an improvement on strict responsibility sensitivity, in that it does not make distributive decisions on morally arbitrary grounds, it faces a different problem in that it refuses to provide for those whose basic needs are unsatisfied due to their own negligent actions. Desert sensitivity can provide such compensation since it does not view an individual's responsibility for their severely disadvantaged state as sufficient grounds for ruling out alleviation of that state.

The first two points suggest that desert sensitivity is a tighter fit with our considered judgements about justice in the weak sense that, while responsibility sensitivity *can* be conceived as in accord with them, desert sensitivity is necessarily in accord with them. The final point supports the stronger claim that desert-sensitive justice comports better with our justice intuitions than any construal of full responsibility sensitivity.

None of my claims are intended to show that desert-sensitive justice is itself the best account of justice. Indeed, I will mention a reason for thinking that this is not the case (a reason that is at least as relevant to responsibility-sensitive justice). The principal purpose is rather to show its comparative advantage over responsibility-sensitive justice. I begin by clarifying the concepts at the heart of responsibility. These, and desert's equivalent concepts, feature prominently in what follows.

7.2 Responsible acts

When we say that an individual has performed a *responsible act* we might mean one of two things,[4] either of which may be greatly relevant to the response of institutions guided towards realizing responsibility-sensitive outcomes. We might, in the first place, mean only that the act is one which is responsible in the sense of being an

---

[4] There are several ways in which a person might act responsibly that I do not go into here. A famous taxonomy of responsibility is provided in H. L. A. Hart, *Punishment and Responsibility* (Oxford: Clarendon Press, 1968), 211–230.

appropriate basis for praise, blame, reward, or penalty. This sense implies that the *grounds of responsibility* have been established—that a full-blown act of free will is at hand, or that there are sufficient reasons of a less metaphysical character for holding the individual to account, even though his actions may have been beyond his control or otherwise unfree. This first sense in which an act might be responsible is in it being a *responsibility basis*.

That an act is a responsibility basis does not itself tell us anything about whether it is a good act or a bad act. When my neighbour goes away on holiday for a month and I agree to feed his cat, following through fully on that agreement, making some attempt to follow through on that agreement but negligently failing to feed the cat on some occasions, and deliberately reneging on the agreement may equally be responsibility bases, despite the differing character of each of these courses of action. The second, stronger sense in which we might say an act is responsible is sensitive to these differences of character. It assumes that the act in question is a responsibility basis, but adds the judgement that that responsible act is worthy of praise or reward. This second sense in which an act might be responsible is in it being a *positive responsibility basis*.

An irresponsible act may also be irresponsible in either of two corresponding senses. In the first sense, an irresponsible act is one which is inappropriate grounds for praise, blame, reward, or punishment. It is a *non-responsibility basis*. In the second sense, an irresponsible act is one which forms a responsibility basis, and which is worthy of blame or penalty. It is a *negative responsibility basis*. The idea at work in the first sense of responsibility and the first sense of irresponsibility might be referred to as *basal responsibility*, while the notion at work in the second sense might be called *appraisal responsibility*.[5]

In order to get from basal responsibility to appraisal responsibility one needs reference to *grounds of appraisal*. One possible ground is *prudential:* a responsibility basis is to be positively assessed in so far as it furthers the interests or welfare of the actor. Another possible ground is *moral:* a responsibility basis is to be positively assessed in so far as it is morally right. And there are many grounds of appraisal between self-interest and all-things-considered moral rightness. Positive assessments may, for instance, depend on the extent to which the responsibility basis promotes the interests of the actor's family, employer, or society. A confluence of instances of one class of such acts may form the basis for the assessments that 'she is prudentially responsible', 'she is ethically responsible', 'she is a responsible mother', 'she is a responsible worker', and

---

[5] These roughly correspond to what Thomas Scanlon calls 'responsibility as attributability' and 'substantive responsibility'; see Scanlon, *What We Owe To Each Other* (Cambridge, MA: Harvard University Press, 1998), 248. For discussion using the terminology of 'agent responsibility' and 'consequential responsibility', see the 'Introduction' to this volume and Peter Vallentyne's chapter. Here I prefer 'basal responsibility' and 'appraisal responsibility' in order to (1) make the role of bases of responsibility more apparent, especially as regards their similarities and differences with desert bases, and to (2) disambiguate the grounds of appraisal from the resulting appraisal responsibility.

'she is a responsible member of society'. Very often a responsibility basis may be assessed as positive on some grounds, but negative on others.

Even limiting our attention to just the pure prudential and moral views, there are a huge range of possible grounds of appraisal. Prudential views must in the first place decide on some account of advantage (usually welfare and/or resource based) and then decide on the appropriate prudential strategy (for instance, maximization of expected outcome or maximin). Evidently, many combinations of these two criteria are possible. Moral views are, if anything, even more diverse. They too must decide on an account of advantage, but they must also decide on a moral principle or set of such principles, as may be brought together in a theory. Positions include egalitarianism, Kantianism, utilitarianism, libertarianism, prioritarianism, and sufficientarianism, as well as theories based on responsibility and desert. These are of course really schools of thought, each containing many principles and theories, some of which overlap with principles and theories from other schools.

Notice that each of the various grounds of appraisal are sensitive to the *degree* of goodness or badness (in the stated regard) of each basally responsible act. In the case of positive responsibility bases, this will indicate whether praise is sufficient, or if material reward of some kind is appropriate, as well as the degrees of praise and reward that are appropriate. For negative responsibility bases, the appropriateness and degrees of blame and penalty are similarly decided. Where the negativity of a responsibility basis is sufficiently strong, as indicated by one of the more morally significant grounds of appraisal, the penalties may be penal in character, or take other severe forms.[6]

It may also be possible that the grounds of appraisal specify particular other agents as appropriate sources of praise and/or reward on the basis that they in particular have benefited from the act in question. Similarly, those who have suffered as a result of the basally responsible act may be picked out as privileged sources of blame and/or penalty. I do not take a view on whether being appraisal responsible for some good or bad thing implies such things as rights to expressions of gratitude from specific persons or liabilities to compensate specific persons, but if responsibility does have these kinds of interpersonal implications it seems sensible to think that they would be identified by the appraisal grounds.[7]

In my view, these relationships between the grounds of responsibility, basal responsibility, appraisal responsibility, and the grounds of appraisal explain how responsibility considerations function, at least as regards distributive justice. It is in every case true

---

[6] Severe punishments are generally, and quite rightly, acknowledged by law as inappropriate responses to even serious *prudential* failures of an individual. Similarly, someone's failure to be a responsible mother, or to be a responsible worker, is no grounds for such punishment, except where such an act is also contrary to morality or the interests of society.

[7] Although I do not give the matter separate discussion, if there is such a thing as interpersonal *desert*, it too would seem to rely upon moral appraisal grounds. 'Speaking in a general way, a person is understood to deserve good if he does right, evil if he does wrong; and in a more particular sense, to deserve good from those to whom he does or has done good, and evil from those to whom he does or has done evil' (Mill, *Utilitarianism*, 179).

(1) that an act is defined as basally responsible on the basis of the basal grounds, (2) that basal responsibility is a necessary condition for appraisal responsibility, (3) that an act is defined as appraisal responsible on the basis of the appraisal grounds, and (4) that appraisal responsibility is a necessary condition for any particular response of praise, blame, reward, or penalty on grounds of responsibility. Responsibility considerations function in this way regardless of the content given to basal responsibility—irrespective of whether metaphysical libertarianism, hard determinism, or compatibilism are true,[8] and irrespective of which responsibilities are actually assigned in practice—and regardless of the grounds of appraisal in operation—irrespective of whether the basis of appraisal is prudential or moral, and irrespective of how prudential or moral goodness is to be judged. The same structure would be in place even if we were to take J. J. C. Smart's 'hard compatibilist' position that an act is basally responsible where treating it as such—praising, blaming, rewarding, or penalizing it—produces good consequences, typically through affecting others' behaviour.[9] Admittedly, the basal grounds and the appraisal grounds may be thought to be both dubious in their own terms and uncomfortably close to one another—consideration of the consequences of one's being held responsible enters at both stages, while the origin of such consequences, and their 'intrinsic' goodness or badness, does not get a look in—but that simply reflects the struggle this version of compatibilism faces in trying to square its account of responsibility with more commonplace notions. The structure remains the same even where some of its component parts have gone through such contortions.

It is sometimes claimed that those who advocate responsibility-sensitive accounts of justice—typically, luck egalitarians—equivocate between basal and appraisal responsibility. Susan Hurley, for example, suggests that John Roemer's account of equality of opportunity fails to distinguish between, on the one hand, what persons are responsible for, and on the other, whether persons are prudentially, socially, or ethically responsible.[10] To avoid this conflation of the various senses of responsibility, Hurley restricts her use of 'responsibility' to what I am calling basal responsibility, and prefers 'desert' when referring to, roughly, appraisal responsibility. But this seems to rather gloss over whether appraisal responsibility and desert are the same thing, and in particular whether desert takes things other than positive and negative responsibility bases into account. I will now suggest how responsibility may be accommodated by an account of justice without any equivocation over the intended sense of responsibility. In the next section I will suggest how desert may be so accommodated. It turns out that the results in each case are importantly different.

[8] For discussion of the distributive implications that the truth of these accounts would have, see C. Knight, 'The Metaphysical Case for Luck Egalitarianism', *Social Theory and Practice*, 32 (2006), 173–189.

[9] J. J. C. Smart, 'Free Will, Praise, and Blame', *Mind*, 70 (1961), 291–306; see also R. J. Arneson, 'The Smart Theory of Moral Responsibility and Desert' in S. Olsaretti (ed.), *Desert and Justice* (Oxford: Clarendon Press, 2003), 233–258; D. C. Dennett, *Elbow Room: The Varieties of Free Will Worth Wanting* (Oxford: Clarendon Press, 1984).

[10] S. Hurley, *Justice, Luck, and Knowledge* (Cambridge, MA: Harvard University Press, 2003), ch. 6.

Responsibility-sensitive justice cannot be based purely on considerations of basal responsibility. To be sure, that my act is responsible in the sense of it being a responsibility base is a necessary condition for distributions to be sensitive to that act. But it is not a sufficient condition. The appropriate response to many basally responsible acts is non-distributive. I may be responsible for performing particularly well in an informal game of tennis, or particularly badly in an informal game of golf, but in the absence of specific prior arrangements the appropriate responses are at most those of praise and blame. Certainly it would be unjust for the state to take measures to increase or decrease my level of income or my level of well-being on that score.[11]

More seriously still, even where the appropriate response to some basally responsible act is one of rewarding or penalizing, the basal responsibility tells us neither whether rewarding or penalizing is appropriate, nor the correct form of the reward or penalty. Being sensitive to responsibility cannot mean simply leaving the consequences of responsible acts to stand. On that view, if I am basally responsible for my act of stealing someone's wallet, this redistribution of money is just precisely because of my act of theft. Bizarrely, there would only be a case for compulsory return of the money if my basal responsibility for the act was in doubt. An obvious solution to this sort of problem is to hold that consequences should only stand where they have been arrived at in ways consistent with the law. But for these laws to deal with the problem at hand—the non-punishment of successful and basally responsible thieves, murderers, rapists, and so on—they must be derived from morality. In this way responsibility-sensitive justice is constrained by morality, so there is little departure from the version of responsibility-sensitive justice that brings in relevant moral considerations at an earlier stage as grounds of appraisal.[12]

I will, for the sake of brevity, focus only on the latter of these roughly equivalent views in what follows. That is, I will describe responsibility-sensitive justice as sensitive to appraisal responsibility, rather than to constrained basal responsibility. Since appraisal responsibility is in part based on basal responsibility, both varieties have their role, and it is even arguable that basal responsibility is the more fundamental of the two. But on the construal at hand, distributive justice only refers directly to appraisal responsibility.

7.3 Deserving acts

To say that some act is a *deserving act* is to introduce an ambiguity that is formally very much parallel to that involved in talking of responsible acts. A deserving act may be so

---

[11] On some compatibilist accounts of responsibility there are circumstances where praising and blaming are the most we should do even where the consequences of the responsible act in question are very significant; see Scanlon, *What We Owe To Each Other*, ch. 6.

[12] A gap between the views' recommendations would open up where the law failed to fully coincide with morality. In such a case appraisal responsibility-sensitive justice is more plausible, since it would not allow persons to exploit such legal oversights. Of course, someone endorsing constrained basal responsibility sensitivity might reply that this shows only that morality itself, rather than its imperfect reflection in the law, is the appropriate constraint. This may be true, but in that case the space between the two views is very hard to discern.

either in the sense of being a *desert basis*, or in the sense of being a *positive desert basis*. A desert basis is simply grounds for someone or something to be deserving of some response or other (praise, blame, reward, or punishment). A good job performance may be a key factor in one deserving a promotion, just as a poor job performance may be a key factor in one deserving a demotion. Both types of performance are then a desert base. A positive desert basis is grounds for someone or something to be deserving of praise or reward. A good job performance is deserving in the positive sense, but a bad job performance is not. The poor job performance is, let us say, basally deserving, but the character of that desert is diametrically opposed to that which attaches to the good job performance. That is, the poor job performance is a *negative desert basis*. The structure of a deserving act appears to be very much parallel to that of a responsible act: (1★) an act is defined as basally deserving on the basis of the basal grounds; (2★) basal desert is a necessary condition for appraisal desert; (3★) an act is defined as appraisal deserving on the basis of the appraisal grounds; and (4★) appraisal desert is a necessary condition for any particular response of praise, blame, reward, or penalty on grounds of desert. But this seeming similarity between desert and responsibility glosses over significant differences of content. In this section I focus on a key difference in the appraisal grounds which apply to responsibility and those which apply to desert.

As with responsibility bases, desert bases are identified as positive or negative by grounds of appraisal. But desert is far less promiscuous in its view of what can count as a ground of appraisal, being limited to *moral* grounds of appraisal. Here it may seem that I have committed what David Miller has identified as 'a characteristic mistake of philosophers writing on this topic', which is 'to suppose that deserving agents must have moral motives for their performances—that to deserve on the basis of P, one must have performed P out of a sense of duty, or in order to confer benefits on others'.[13] As we will see, my position differs from that of Miller, but our difference on this point is not as pronounced as it may seem because on my view it is possible for one to be deserving on the basis of self-interested action. Where one's interests coincide with those of others, or where one's actions do not impact upon others' legitimate interests, a person's wholly self-interested act may be positively deserving.[14] These circumstances are precisely those in which prudence and morality are consistent with one another. My position is then different from Miller's, as he requires no such confluence for desert to arise from self-interested action. When prudence and morality are in conflict, Miller holds that acts supportive of both might be positively deserving, whereas I hold that the only positively deserving acts will be those which comport with morality.

To illustrate my position, suppose, for instance, that I have the choice of taking either a poorly paid and time-intensive job as a teacher in a developing country, or a well paid job with short working hours and long holidays in a private school in my own

[13] D. Miller, *Principles of Social Justice* (Cambridge, MA: Harvard University Press, 1999), 134.

[14] Hence I believe that there is differential desert in Kasper Lippert-Rasmussen's example of a lazy Robinson Crusoe and a diligent one; see his chapter in this volume, section 4.3.

developed country. We stipulate that I am basally responsible for my choice, and also that the first choice is the morally best choice—maybe we are welfarist utilitarians and this promotes total or average welfare, maybe we are resource egalitarians and this promotes equality of resources, or maybe even we are right libertarians, and this is demanded by our contractual agreements (which will not be enforced)—and that the second choice is the prudentially best choice (it increases my resources, and my welfare levels are strongly determined by my resource levels, say). So stipulated, were I to take the first job, and stick to it, and someone was to claim that I had been irresponsible in so acting, I could complain of the ambiguity of the claim, or even counterclaim that, from my perspective, my actions were responsible. But I could not object that they were mistaken in their belief that I had acted irresponsibly, since, from at least one broad range of perspectives—that of prudence—I have indeed acted irresponsibly. Even some non-prudential (though also non-all-things-considered moral) accounts of responsibility might agree that I have acted irresponsibly. If my time abroad has been bad for my family, I may be considered an irresponsible parent, or if my country has a shortage of teachers, I may be considered an irresponsible citizen. But for all this, it would be not merely ambiguous but outright wrong for my interlocutor to claim that, in acting as I have, I have become undeserving, in the sense of my fulfilment of my job's duties constituting a negative desert basis. This is because desert is necessarily a moral notion in a way that responsibility is not. It does not seek to reward mere prudence, nor even any sub-set of moral considerations (those pertaining to the family, say); it is concerned with all-things-considered moral goodness.

Now it might be objected that I have drawn this line between responsibility and desert too starkly, and that in fact it does make sense to compartmentalize our desert judgements. It might be thought, for instance, that in taking the foreign teaching post I have become deserving all-things-considered, but that I have also become an undeserving parent. There will be different moral responses to each of these phenomena from different moral agents. Those who have been looking after my children (my parents or estranged spouse, say) may complain of my actions, or even refuse to let me see my own children, on the basis that I have become deserving of this censure and undeserving of this privilege, even whilst acknowledging that I have become deserving of other forms of praise and, maybe, reward from other persons. It might be claimed, then, that my account fails to account for the complexity of the structure of desert.

My reply is that this objection conflates desert with something like interest. The specific responses it describes are better understood by reference to the wants or needs of the family than by reference to their deserts. In acting as I have, I have (we allow) acted contrary to the interests of my children, and can for that reason not in practice expect to be well-spoken of or favourably treated by my family, regardless of my desert. But it is, I submit, stretching the language of desert to breaking point to talk of someone who is deserving simpliciter as also being an undeserving (i.e. negatively deserving) parent, or even as being undeserving as a parent. There is usually no need to specify that the desert one has in mind is moral desert. The 'moral' of 'moral responsibility' is not redundant in the same way. The adjective 'deserving' accordingly tells us much more about the nouns which it precedes than does 'responsible'. One can be a responsible concentration camp guard by staying at one's post in spite of the horrors that this facilitates. But one cannot thereby become a *deserving* concentration camp guard; to earn that peculiar title one must perform feats that are peculiar in equal measure. To return to the more commonplace example, then, I can only become an undeserving parent by becoming undeserving simpliciter. My parents or my estranged spouse may understandably vent their anger at my actions through the grammar and vocabulary of desert. But circumstance—which puts my family's wants and needs at odds with broader and weightier moral demands—is the more appropriate target, and interest or responsibility the more appropriate language.

Miller's position on desert places it much closer to interest and responsibility than I am willing to allow. Miller writes that, for a performance sufficiently within one's control to count as a positive desert base, it 'must be something that is positively appraised or valued by the surrounding community, but . . . this need not amount to moral evaluation'.[15] While acknowledging that 'in the background there often stands some idea of social utility', Miller holds that 'it does not seem to me essential to the idea of desert itself that this should be so'.[16] Two examples are given to illustrate this point:

Although athletic competitions may create benefits (as entertaining spectacles, for instance), the performances that form the basis of athletes' deserts, such as running down a track very fast, have no social utility in themselves. And to take a case where the performance is in fact socially harmful, there seems nothing incoherent or bizarre in saying that the man who masterminded the bank robbery deserves a larger share of the loot than the guy who merely drove the getaway car.[17]

The obvious way to approach the first example is to consider what we would say in the event that athletic competitions did not create social benefits, but sprinters nevertheless ran down tracks in empty stadiums extremely quickly. It might seem that some positive desert would still remain, just with much lower accompanying awards. I suspect, however, that this is because, as the case has been described, some small benefit to society remains. The runners themselves are presumably happier running than not, as they continue to run in the absence of the adulation of the crowd and general public, so this seems to fit the case of self-interested action consistent with morality that I have already described as one sort of positive desert base. To make it a case where we are really testing whether a performance can be the basis of positive desert even though it receives no support from morality we would need to stipulate that, alongside the small benefit to the runners, there are morally adverse effects. So suppose that the runners wear shoes manufactured in a sweatshop which fails to recognize the human rights of its employees, and that the athletes know that without

---

[15]   Miller, *Principles of Social Justice*, 135.
[16]   Miller, *Principles of Social Justice*, 135.
[17]   Miller, *Principles of Social Justice*, 135.

their custom the sweatshop would close to be replaced by a business offering much more favourable terms to its employees. In such conditions I do not see how the winning athletes could claim any positive desert. We might still make evaluative judgements about the excellence of the athletes and their performances, but these judgements would be stripped of their connection to positive desert by the immoral means deployed by the athletes. Running down a track very fast only seems to form a positive desert base where we have moral reasons to appraise that performance positively.

The sweatshop variant of the athlete example is similar to the bank robbery example, which is especially interesting as it is here that Miller believes he is describing a case where morality and desert actually conflict. But he does not explicitly tell us why we might think the mastermind more deserving than the getaway driver. The most likely explanation, given Miller's focus on the appraisal of the community, is that the mastermind's display of cunning is valued by the criminal fraternity. This does not strike me as a plausible way to ground desert. In a slightly different context in the same discussion Miller acknowledges that 'revealing a bad moral character may generate negative desert, which has to be set against the positive desert of the performance itself'.[18] But when considering the desert arising from a criminal act we do not view the badness of the motive as being open to being offset by exceptional flair or technical expertise deployed in support of it. The opposite is true. It would of course be quite perverse for a judge to acknowledge that the bank robbery was a grave case of wrongdoing, but to accept as a mitigating consideration that the mastermind was the lynchpin of the whole operation, which would have been quite impossible without him. More usual sentencing practice, where the expendable getaway driver's offence is mitigated and the mastermind's offence aggravated, appears to reflect desert appropriately. So why should things be different when we shift our attention from sentencing to dividing loot?

Distributing the proceeds of crime in proportion to contribution may seem like a natural idea, as reward in proportion to contribution is roughly consistent with desert when the benefits are legitimately up for distribution between the participants. But in my view the shift from legitimate gains to ill-gotten gains eradicates any positive desert, and Miller has not tried to explain why this is not the case. Indeed, I would go further and say that that shift actually makes it more appropriate for those who have made lesser contributions to get more, since their negative desert is smaller. The mastermind is due less than the getaway driver, who is in turn due less than the safe-cracker who pulled out of the job at the last minute. This seems to me to be the most plausible account of distribution among thieves, being consistent as it is with the intuition that greater wrongdoing should not receive greater rewards, and it is clearly consistent with my position that desert can only be appraised morally.

---

[18] Miller, *Principles of Social Justice*, 134.

We have seen that appraisal desert is a narrower concept than appraisal responsibility, being grounded in all-things-considered morality alone. One cannot be deserving simply because one's desert bases accord with prudence, nor because those bases accord with some prima facie moral duty (to contribute to the upbringing of one's children, for instance). Where prudence or prima facie moral duties come into conflict with all-things-considered morality, it is clear where desert's loyalty lies. But what about basal desert? How do we establish whether an act is a candidate for appraisal along the lines indicated above? How do basally deserving acts differ from basally responsible acts?

The answer is, I think, that there is no difference. The question of whether an act is basally deserving or not is the same as the question of whether it is basally responsible. The basal grounds are identical in the two cases. The difference between a responsible act and a deserving act comes only at the level of appraisal. Moreover, even there, the same grounds of appraisal may be used. An all-things-considered morally responsible act amounts to the same as an (all-things-considered) deserving act where the same comprehensive account of morality is in play.

Desert-sensitive justice and responsibility-sensitive justice are distinctly different from one another, since the latter can be conceived as being concerned only with the prudential version of responsibility.[19] Indeed, this appears to be the position most commonly taken.[20] But it is not a plausible position. If my basally responsible act has placed me in some disadvantageous position, the correct response will take into account whether the act was required or commended by morality. There is no equivalence between a basally responsible refusal to get a job on the grounds of a preference for leisure, and a similar refusal grounded in the obligations one has to look after one's sick child, or even such a refusal grounded in the performance of super-erogatory acts. Indeed, it seems doubtful whether the prudential value of an act is at all relevant. Of course, often morality and self-interest coincide with one another—this is typically the case where there is a choice between being productive or non-productive—and it is natural to reward in these cases, but where morality and self-interest come apart—as where the thing being produced is socially harmful—justice demands only that the morally praiseworthy acts are rewarded.

To illustrate, consider a salesperson facing three options: (a) she can sell food to the poor, which will provide only a subsistence level income, but which will make the lot of the worst-off considerably better (which happens to be good in terms of utilitarianism, Kantianism, etc.); (b) she can sell medicine to the poor, which will provide a

---

[19] It might also be conceived as being concerned with one or other of the prima facie moral responsibilities (for example, parental responsibilities). But it is hard to see any motivation for such a position.

[20] See Arneson, 'Equality and Equal Opportunity for Welfare' and J. Roemer, 'A Pragmatic Theory of Responsibility for the Egalitarian Planner', *Philosophy and Public Affairs*, 22 (1993) 146–166. For comparison of the prudential and moral versions of responsibility-sensitive egalitarianism, see P. Vallentyne, 'Brute Luck Equality and Desert' in S. Olsaretti (ed.), *Desert and Justice* (Oxford: Clarendon Press, 2003), 169–185; R. J. Arneson, 'Luck and Equality', *Proceedings of the Aristotelian Society*, Supplement, 75 (2001), 73–90; and Richard J. Arneson's chapter in this volume, section 1.3.

moderate level of income, and make the lot of the worst-off considerably better; (c) she can sell clothing to the poor, which will provide a high level of income, and make the lot of the worst-off slightly better off. She is basally responsible for whichever choice she makes. To which choice will justice respond most favourably?

The comparison of (a) and (b) may appear to show that prudence does have a role to play, for justice surely allows that (b) should be rewarded more highly than (a), and medicine sales are only better from the perspective of self-interest. But this is not so. Medicine sales are also a morally better choice, since the increased income increases average and total levels of resources and (we suppose) utility levels. We do not need to be utilitarians to recognize this value. We could be Rawlsians or prioritarians,[21] concerned to advance the concerns of the worst-/worse-off, and to advance the interests of the better-off (such as the salesperson) where, as here, both kinds of advancement are consistent with one another. We could be quite strictly Kantian, but simply think that where all deontological duties are satisfied we ought to promote well-being. Self-interested choices, such as the choice to sell medicine rather than food, are sometimes morally praiseworthy precisely because they promote our interests. Justice rewards such choices, but only on account of their moral value.

This is further illustrated when we bring option (c) into the picture. Although selling clothes is prudentially the best of the three options, justice does not reward this because there is a concomitant decrease in the moral goodness of the option. All else being equal, a prudential improvement is also a moral improvement, and this is why (b) would give an entitlement to greater rewards than (a). But where all else is not equal, in the particular sense that the move to a prudentially sounder choice has bad effects on others that are morally weightier than the moral gains (in agent happiness, resources, etc.) associated with the prudential improvement, the just entitlement declines. Society does the salesperson the courtesy of counting her interests among what really matters, even as regards the assessment of her conduct, but has no cause to reward her where she has pursued her self-interest to the extent that even an account of morality that takes her interests into account disapproves of her choice, relative to the alternatives. (a) and (b) will receive better rewards than (c), since in this choice problem selling food and medicine are, on reasonable assumptions, morally better than selling clothes, and morality is all that matters to justicial appraisals of basally responsible acts.[22]

---

[21] J. Rawls, *A Theory of Justice*, revised edition (Oxford: Oxford University Press, 1999); D. Parfit, 'Equality and Priority' in A. Mason (ed.), *Ideals of Equality* (Oxford: Blackwell, 1996), 1–20.

[22] Note that, even on the account described here, (c) might be the best option if we abandon the reasonable assumption which the salesperson having a high level of income (as in (c)) rather than the moderate one (as in (b)) is less morally weighty than the lot of the worst-off being improved considerably (as in (b)) rather than only slightly (as in (c)). There might be some conditions under which such an abandonment would be justified. For example, it might be the case that the salesperson is such an efficient converter of resources into utility that her increased income is, on a utilitarian account of morality, more important than improving the circumstances of a relatively conversion-inefficient poor. Even were, for this sort of reason, (c) the best option, it should be clear that morality (however understood), not prudence, is carrying all the justificatory load.

In summary, desert sensitivity more closely fits our intuitive sense of justice, in that its commitment to moral grounds of appraisal is not conditional in the way that responsibility sensitivity's commitment to said grounds is. This finding is of course far from conclusive. However, the next two sections urge that this is not the only area in which responsibility sensitivity and desert sensitivity come apart in a way conducive to the latter.

7.4 Non-acts

The previous sections proceeded on the assumption, enshrined in (4) and (4★), that appraisal responsibility/desert is a necessary condition for any responsibility-/desert-based response of praise, blame, reward, or penalty. It also assumed, then, that basal desert has been established, and that basal responsibility has been established. This will all be challenged in this section, where it is maintained that one can be deserving of certain treatment, or even (in a certain class of circumstances) entitled to it on grounds of responsibility, without having performed any act at all, let alone a basally responsible one.

It is generally acknowledged that a desert basis must be some relevant fact about the (would-be) deserving person.[23] Some writers explicitly add that this fact must be something for which the person in question was at least partially (basally) responsible.[24] Others describe closely related conditions which must be satisfied: the desert base must have come about through a voluntary undertaking of the desert claimant,[25] or the claimant must have been able to do otherwise.[26]

The connection between desert and responsibility has been challenged by Fred Feldman, who gives this example of compensation for injury:

Suppose, for example, that a fast food restaurant is careless with its hamburgers. Many customers become ill with food poisoning. These customers deserve several things: an apology; some compensation for their illness; a refund for the money they spent on the hamburgers. The customers deserve these things in virtue of the fact that they are innocent victims of the restaurant's carelessness. Yet in any typical case the customers bear no responsibility for the fact they were poisoned.[27]

How do we describe this case in the terms deployed earlier? The restaurant workers are basally responsible (on account of negligence) for the dangerous state of their

---

[23] J. Feinberg, 'Justice and Personal Desert' in his *Doing and Deserving: Essays in the Theory of Responsibility* (Princeton: Princeton University Press, 1970), 55–94, especially 58–59.

[24] W. Sadurski, *Giving Desert Its Due* (Dordrecht: Reidel, 1985), 131; D. Miller, *Market, State, and Community: Theoretical Foundations of Market Socialism* (Oxford: Clarendon Press, 1989), 167–170; *Principles of Social Justice*, 133; 'Comparative and Non-Comparative Desert' in S. Olsaretti (ed.), *Desert and Justice* (Oxford: Clarendon Press, 2003), 25–44, at 27.

[25] J. Lamont, 'The Concept of Desert in Distributive Justice', *Philosophical Quarterly*, 44 (1994), 45–64, at 53.

[26] B. Barry, *Political Argument* (London: Routledge & Kegan Paul, 1965), 108.

[27] F. Feldman, 'Desert: Reconsideration of Some Received Wisdom', *Mind*, 104 (1996), 63–77, at 68.

hamburgers. Since the grounds of appraisal will (on reasonable assumptions) identify the relevant basally responsible acts as blameworthy, the workers bear appraisal responsibility for the poisoning.[28] But while the customers are basally responsible for a number of things (including entering the restaurant, ordering the burgers, and eating the burgers) it seems clear that these do not yield any significant appraisal responsibility when combined with prudential or moral grounds of appraisal (assuming, of course, that there were no obvious signs of danger). The kind of basal responsibility required for the customers to have significant appraisal responsibility is not present, since they had nothing to do with the production or serving of the harmful food. It does indeed seem to be the case, then, that a person does not always need to be basally responsible in order for a reward—or rather, compensation—to be appropriate on grounds of desert.

At first glance it may appear that this is one way in which desert-sensitive justice differs from responsibility-sensitive justice. It may seem that a person can only become entitled to anything favourable on the latter scheme on account of her responsible acts, whereas there are some ways in which she can become entitled to compensation without performing such acts on the former scheme. But further consideration suggests that the matter is more complicated.

First of all, we may note that actual theories of responsibility-sensitive justice in fact seek to compensate persons on grounds independent of their own responsible acts.[29] Often such compensation is justified on the ground that it has been caused by something that is, for the victim, *brute luck*, which is to say a 'matter of how risks fall out that are not in that sense [i.e., the sense of being anticipatable and declinable] deliberate gambles'.[30] This suggests a view that is *symmetrical as regards the origin of the disadvantaging*: whether the victim's bad brute luck issues from other persons' actions (as in the case of the burgers) or from something completely outside human control (as when someone is struck by a meteorite) does not matter for the question of whether they are owed compensation.[31] The origin of the bad brute luck does matter for the question of who is liable to provide the compensation. Where no individual is responsible for the victim's bad brute luck—that is, when it is *non-agent brute luck* — society is expected to provide the appropriate compensation, but where an individual or individuals are responsible for the victim's bad brute luck—that is, when it is *agent brute luck* — that individual or those individuals are expected to provide the compensation.[32] Standard accounts of responsibility-sensitive justice are, then, inclined to return a similar reply to that of the desert theorist in the restaurant case: the customers

---

[28] I will leave aside the obvious possibility of the restaurant owners sharing responsibility with the workers.

[29] Arneson, 'Equality and Equal Opportunity for Welfare'; Cohen, 'On the Currency of Egalitarian Justice'.

[30] R. Dworkin, 'What is Equality? Part Two: Equality of Resources', *Philosophy and Public Affairs*, 10 (1981), 283–345, at 293.

[31] I will treat the fact that something is a matter of brute luck for some person as a sufficient condition for it to be a non-responsibility basis for them.

[32] H. Steiner, 'Choice and Circumstance', *Ratio*, 10 (1997), 296–312.

are to be compensated at the expense of the workers. But the underlying rationale for the compensation applies with equal force where the victims' bad brute luck was not a result of any responsible action.

This symmetrical view is very hard to defend just by appeal to responsibility considerations. Strict responsibility-sensitive justice only responds to those things for which people are responsible. It might be thought that it is the workers' appraisal responsibility—and in particular, what I earlier called its possible 'interpersonal implications'—that demands the ex post flow of assets to the customers. In other words, the customers may become entitled to compensation on account of others' negative responsibility, rather than on account of any positive responsibility of their own. But even if this is true in cases like this, where a negatively responsible actor or actors can be identified, it seems clear that in cases where no one is responsible for the victims' bad brute luck non-acts—for example, being hit by a meteorite—there can be no responsibility-based justification for compensation. Where there is no relevant responsibility, purely responsibility-sensitive justice has no cause to compensate persons for disadvantages. Responsibility sensitivity appears at best ambivalent towards compensation for brute luck: agent brute luck may be compensable (if interpersonal implications are admitted), but non-agent brute luck is not.

The prevalence of the symmetrical view among proponents of responsibility-sensitive justice, in spite of the evident difficulty of justifying compensation on responsibility grounds where there is no relevant responsibility, is easy to explain. Such writers usually subscribe to one or another form of responsibility-sensitive *egalitarianism*, and it is the egalitarianism of their views that justifies compensation where there is brute bad luck. It does not matter whether the brute luck arose from others' responsible acts or not since it constitutes an inequality that is not itself justified by responsible acts. Responsibility-sensitive justice itself does not require inequalities to be justified on responsibility grounds, and so it sees no injustice in seeing some types of brute luck— some inequalities which are not the result of responsible action—go unaddressed.

To complete our account of the relationships that hold between non-acts and responsibility, and between non-acts and desert, one further issue needs to be addressed. What does desert make of brute luck? From the hamburger case it is clear enough that, where a person's brute bad luck is brought about by another responsible agent, there are grounds for making this agent provide compensation. But what about the case where there is no such agent? Evidently, being struck by a meteorite is not ordinarily a negative desert basis. Such a strike may be non-lethal, but impose costs on the victim—it may cause pain, reduce mobility, necessitate an expensive stay in hospital, and so on. In that case desert-sensitive justice appears unambiguously to prescribe compensation. The person has not become less deserving on account of the incident, but they have become less advantaged. Desert-sensitive justice is concerned to restore the connection between levels of desert and levels of advantage regardless of whether they have been upset by agent brute luck or non-agent brute luck. We could explain this by reference to a 'baseline of desert' similar to the egalitarian baseline of responsibility-sensitive egalitarians. Saul Smilansky maintains that '[t]he only way in which people can come not to deserve the "baseline" is through being responsible for not deserving it'.[33] Where such responsibility is absent, as with the meteorite case, there is a case for compensation.

We have found an important similarity between responsibility-sensitive egalitarianism and desert-sensitive justice, namely that they both demand compensation for all forms of brute bad luck. By extension, they also refuse to allow individuals to retain the benefits of brute luck. In other words, they both endorse the symmetrical view. Responsibility-sensitive justice, by contrast, at most only attempts to discount the advantage effects of one type of brute luck—agent brute luck. Furthermore, it is only moved to act in this case because brute luck is not all-pervasive. While the poisoning is a matter of brute luck for the restaurant customers, it is not a matter of brute luck for the workers. If the poisoning was a matter of brute luck for everyone concerned—if, say, the workers had taken all possible measures to ensure that the food was safe—there would be no case for compensating the customers. This shows that responsibility sensitivity and brute luck negation are two quite different objectives, even where matters of brute luck are treated as necessarily matters of non-responsibility. To put the point another way, making distributions respond to those things for which people are responsible is not the same as negating the distributive effects of those things for which people are not responsible.

The two objectives just described are not equally credible from the perspective of justice. To disregard the effects of non-agent brute luck, while responding to agent brute luck, seems morally arbitrary. The origin of the brute luck makes no difference to the beneficiary or victim of the brute luck. Either way they exerted no effective control over the gain or loss they have experienced. To identify one category of brute luck origin as the salient feature seems bizarre. No wonder, then, that writers have in practice rejected responsibility sensitivity and instead endorsed something more like non-responsibility sensitivity—for instance, the position that it is unfair for some to be worse off than others through no fault or choice of their own.[34] While this latter type of position delivers an appropriately even-handed treatment of different types of non-acts, it does so at the cost of replacing the simple idea of responsibility sensitivity with a less intuitive appeal to the inverse of responsibility. Desert sensitivity does not need to refer to a negation of its key concept in order to handle non-acts equally, without reference to whether they are matters of agent brute luck or non-agent brute luck.

---

[33] S. Smilansky, 'Responsibility and Desert: Defending the Connection', *Mind*, 105 (1996), 157–163, at 160; see also A. Zaitchik, 'On Deserving To Deserve', *Philosophy and Public Affairs*, 6 (1977), 370–388.

[34] L. Temkin, *Inequality* (Oxford: Oxford University Press, 1993), 13, 17, 200; see also section 2.2 of Larry Temkin's chapter in this volume.

7.5 Negative responsibility and basic needs

The preceding section showed that, for responsibility-sensitive justice to treat non-acts appropriately, it has to be construed as non-responsibility negation. This is the version of responsibility sensitivity implied by desert. In this section I will consider a familiar objection that can be modified to be applicable to this version of responsibility sensitivity. While I do not think the objection is in fact the decisive refutation of responsibility sensitivity that some suppose, it may be telling that desert sensitivity is hard-wired to resist it in a way that is not true of responsibility sensitivity.

Opponents of responsibility-sensitive egalitarianism have often questioned whether it is really egalitarian. An oft-made argument for this scepticism runs as follows:

> BASIC NEEDS PREMISE: An egalitarian account of justice attempts to provide for the basic needs of all persons.
> IRRESPONSIBILITY PREMISE: Responsibility-sensitive egalitarianism refuses to provide for the basic needs of those whose basic needs are unsatisfied due to their own irresponsibility.
> CONCLUSION: Responsibility-sensitive egalitarianism is not an egalitarian account of justice.[35]

The Basic Needs Premise of this argument is highly questionable. It is arguable that egalitarianism, understood as a position distinct from sufficientarianism, prioritarianism, or humanitarianism,[36] appears to be concerned only with the relative position of persons, and hence cannot guarantee that any individual has a given level of anything (including basic needs satisfaction) in absolute terms. I will not belabour the point, since a revision of the premise is available which avoids this problem and is more relevant to our appraisal of responsibility-sensitive justice. If we just say that a *good* account of justice provides for basic needs we admit the kind of absolute considerations that egalitarianism may preclude. The appropriate target of the revised objection is responsibility-sensitive justice, rather than responsibility-sensitive egalitarianism. These modifications, however, present a new problem, in that it is not obvious that a good account of justice seeks to satisfy basic needs *whatever the cost*. It may well be appropriate to cut off support where the basic needs can only be met at extreme cost to society, as where an extraordinarily expensive course of medical treatment is required. For our purposes the following reformulated argument will suffice to address these problems:

> REVISED BASIC NEEDS PREMISE: A good account of justice attempts to provide for the inexpensively satisfied basic needs of all persons.
> IRRESPONSIBILITY PREMISE: Responsibility-sensitive justice refuses to provide for those whose basic needs are unsatisfied due to their own irresponsibility.
> CONCLUSION: Responsibility-sensitive justice is not a good account of justice.

---

[35] See M. Fleurbaey, 'Equal Opportunity or Equal Social Outcome?', *Economics and Philosophy*, 11 (1995), 25–55; E. S. Anderson, 'What is the Point of Equality?', *Ethics*, 109 (1999), 287–337; S. Scheffler, 'What is Egalitarianism?', *Philosophy and Public Affairs*, 31 (2003), 5–39.

[36] See H. Frankfurt, 'Equality as a Moral Ideal', *Ethics*, 98 (1987), 21–43; Parfit, 'Equality and Priority'; Temkin, *Inequality*, ch. 9.

The common strength of the two arguments is the firmness—even triviality—of the Irresponsibility Premise.[37] Paired with the Revised Basic Needs Premise, which addresses the question of the adequacy of accounts of justice and acknowledges that justice does not require very costly satisfaction of basic needs, it presents a serious challenge to responsibility-sensitive justice.

An argument of this general structure might also be thought to pose a similar challenge for desert-sensitive justice. Against this new target, a further reformulation is required. With the appropriate substitutions, the argument of principal interest looks like this:

REVISED BASIC NEEDS PREMISE: A good account of justice attempts to provide for the inexpensively satisfied basic needs of all persons.

UNDESERVINGNESS PREMISE: Desert-sensitive justice refuses to provide for those who are undeserving of having their basic needs satisfied.

CONCLUSION: Desert-sensitive justice is not a good account of justice.

On some accounts, this argument may seem no less problematic than that which uses the Irresponsibility Premise, since those things which are denied to a person on the basis of their own irresponsibility may be coextensive with those things which may be denied to a person on the basis of their undeservingness. But other accounts deny such a close link between responsibility and desert. I will provide support for accounts of the latter type, and show how such accounts can be used to undermine both the Undeservingness Premise and the Revised Basic Needs Premise. I will also show why a similar strategy cannot be used by responsibility-sensitive justice.

One very permissive—in the sense that it regularly admits *responsibility-independent considerations*, i.e. factors that have nothing to do with responsibility—view of desert may simply deny the coherence, or at least practical applicability, of the Undeservingness Premise. It simply maintains that no one can ever be undeserving of having their basic needs satisfied. At least on quite minimalist views of basic needs—ones simply describing the bare essentials for survival—this seems to be a commonly held position in developed countries, at least as regards citizens of these countries. There simply are some things which are so bad that no can deserve them, no matter what they do.

A less permissive view, but one which still admits responsibility-independent considerations, might hold that, while it is possible for some people to come to deserve to have their basic needs go unmet, simply being responsible for some bad outcome in familiar ways is insufficient for such strongly negative desert. Consider, for example, the typical characterization of a negligent victim as someone in some way at fault for a road traffic accident—for instance, 'an uninsured driver who negligently makes an

---

[37] Although the premise is sound, the extent of its applicability is unclear given that responsibility-sensitive egalitarians typically place some limits on the responsibility sensitivity of their accounts of justice; see C. Knight, 'In Defence of Luck Egalitarianism', *Res Publica*, 11 (2005), 55–73.

illegal turn that causes an accident with another car'.[38] A coherent desert view might hold that the negative desert on display here—based on the basal responsibility for the crash and the appraisal of that as being worthy of blame and punishment—is not of the magnitude necessary to justify the denial of medical treatment. The driver's negative responsibility is partially (though not fully) offset by the limited but still positive desert of being a person. One taking this position might accept that the basic needs of murderers do not need to be met, since what they deserve includes deprivations sufficient to neutralize the positive desert of their personhood, but that those of everybody else must be, even where their basic needs have been endangered by self-inflicted lesser wrongs. The less permissive view, when combined with desert sensitivity, does not dispute the Undeservingness Premise—indeed, it identifies some persons as wholly undeserving. Instead it challenges the Revised Basic Needs Premise. It claims that there are in fact outlying cases where the fulfilment of even inexpensive basic needs is not a matter of justice.

Note that, if we take either of these views, the negation of advantages and disadvantages for which the holder is not responsible must be less than full. Wherever the responsibility-independent considerations support more forgiving responses than is warranted by the negatively responsible behaviour itself, the negatively responsible person is gaining at least a comparative advantage. The relative position of positively responsible persons will decline, and through no fault or choice of their own. This just confirms that desert admits of more than one value. The loss of position of responsible persons has moral disvalue, but it is justifiable provided the moral value of satisfying the negatively responsible person's basic needs is equal to or greater than this.

Analogues of the above two desert views are not open to responsibility-sensitive justice as both rely on appeal to responsibility-independent considerations. This is obvious in the first case, since the position states that certain deprivations are too harsh to be imposed on any person. The less permissive view is more complex, and it may appear as though the positive desert in play—that connected to personhood—is also a matter of responsibility, since whether it demands that basic needs be met or not is down to the individual's acts and omissions. But the positive desert is itself posited quite independently of responsibility; the only difference responsibility makes is whether the effect of the positive desert is actually felt. Full responsibility sensitivity cannot posit its equivalent—positive (appraisal) responsibility—in such basal-responsibility-free fashion.

If the Revised Basic Needs Premise is mistaken, as the less permissive view claims, its natural replacement would insist that efforts are made to satisfy the inexpensively satisfied basic needs of all *non-serious wrongdoers*. This replacement is equally problematic for responsibility-sensitive justice since that view gives no general support to satisfying the basic needs of non-serious wrongdoers. Some such persons (negligent drivers, extravagant gamblers, and so on) may become responsible for such bad outcomes that

[38] Anderson, 'What is the Point of Equality?', 295.

appraisal responsibility does not recommend basic need satisfaction. Desert-sensitive justice has the resources, which responsibility-sensitive justice lacks, to limit harsh treatment to outlying cases such as murderers and rapists (as with the less permissive argument), or to no cases at all (as with the more permissive argument).

7.6 Summary and conclusion

In this chapter I have attempted to draw out similarities and differences in responsibility sensitivity and desert sensitivity, taking our reflections on everyday ideas about responsibility and desert as the measure of which sorts of considerations fit into which category. A summary of my comparison of the two positions is provided in Table 7.1.

I argued that responsibility sensitivity and desert sensitivity have the key structural similarity of taking basal responsibility to be necessary in order for an act to be an appropriate object of appraisal (and hence the reactive attitudes of praise, blame, etc.). Beyond this, however, they are quite different positions. Desert sensitivity only allows moral grounds of appraisal, while responsibility sensitivity allows moral and prudential grounds of appraisal. I argued that the latter type of appraisal does not seem relevant to justice. Desert sensitivity treats all non-acts (excepting the special case of responsibility-independent considerations) as inappropriate grounds for advantage and disadvantage, while responsibility sensitivity, taken literally, seems to imply that some non-acts (agent brute luck) might be inappropriate grounds for (dis)advantaging while others definitely are not. I held that this position seems unsupported, and that it is little surprise that defenders of responsibility sensitivity really want to defend a similar position to desert-sensitive justice on this point. Finally, desert is not limited to rewarding and penalizing on the basis of responsibility, and so desert-sensitive justice is the better able of the two

Table 7.1. Responsibility-sensitive justice and desert-sensitive justice compared

	Responsibility-sensitive justice	Desert-sensitive justice
Basal responsibility/desert	*All appraisable acts*	*All appraisable acts*
Moral appraisal	*Possible grounds of appraisal*	*Only grounds of appraisal*
Prudential appraisal	*Possible grounds of appraisal*	*Not possible grounds of appraisal*
Appraisal responsibility/desert	*The result of the appraisal = praise, blame, reward, penalty*	*The result of the appraisal = praise, blame, reward, penalty*
Non-agent brute luck	*Resulting (dis)advantages not counteracted on strict view, counteracted on non-responsibility negating view*	*Resulting (dis)advantages counteracted except where in conflict with responsibility-independent considerations*
Responsibility-independent considerations	*No*	*Yes (e.g. based on personhood)*

to take on board the plausible suggestion that, in many cases where an individual's basic needs will, absent intervention, go unfulfilled on account of their own (negatively) responsible action, assistance is in fact appropriate.

We can explain these findings in terms of the Rawlsian *method of reflective equilibrium*.[39] According to this method we reconcile moral and political principles with our considered judgements, adjusting each in the light of all relevant facts, theories, and experiences. The arguments of this chapter suggest that, while a principle of desert sensitivity is necessarily in accord with our considered judgements about the appropriate kinds of grounds of appraisal (moral ones) and the appropriate response to disadvantaging non-acts (compensation), a principle of responsibility sensitivity is only contingently in agreement with our judgements. Furthermore, while a principle of desert sensitivity can be adjusted in line with the judgement that basic needs should (sometimes) be met in spite of responsibility considerations, a principle of responsibility sensitivity that is so adjusted is no longer a principle of responsibility sensitivity. Of course, the method allows the possibility that our particular judgements (here, those about basic needs fulfilment) should be adjusted in the light of an otherwise intuitively attractive account of justice (here, responsibility-sensitive justice), but I do not see why we would take this option, especially where an otherwise equally (or more) attractive account of justice that accommodates these particular judgements is available.

I will finish by drawing attention to a limitation of both the accounts of justice explored above. The limitation is that they are both excessively comparative and, in particular, non-aggregative in their outlook. While desert-sensitive justice can at least, as we saw in the preceding section, recognize the value of increases in absolute well-being when it comes to the very badly off, neither responsibility nor desert as they are usually conceived are capable of recognizing the value of increases in absolute well-being more generally.

Suppose we have the option of bringing about a distribution that features much higher average and total levels of resources and welfare in society. There is no way of describing these benefits in the language of responsibility and desert. This is evident in the former case, since responsibility only refers to appraisal responsibility, which in turn requires basal responsibility, and the benefits I have described do not concern responsibility at all. Desert might be thought to be a little more promising on this score, in that it can admit responsibility-independent considerations. Unfortunately these are rather limited in scope. When we say that someone deserves something we would often be basing this judgement on responsibility considerations (she has been doing her job well, say) and sometimes on considerations of humanity (she is without the means of subsistence, say); but unless we are hard compatibilists we would never be basing this

---

[39] See Rawls, *A Theory of Justice*, sec. 9; 'The Independence of Moral Theory', *Proceedings and Addresses of the American Philosophical Association*, 47 (1975), 5–22; N. Daniels, *Justice and Justification: Reflective Equilibrium in Theory and Practice* (Cambridge: Cambridge University Press, 1996); C. Knight, 'The Method of Reflective Equilibrium: Wide, Radical, Fallible, Plausible', *Philosophical Papers*, 35 (2006), 205–229.

on considerations of whether giving her that thing will increase total or average well-being. Desert is not in that way interpersonal or 'holistic'.[40]

In the light of this limitation, some defenders of desert- and responsibility-based views now endorse markedly pluralistic positions that combine principles of desert and responsibility with principles promoting welfare and giving priority to the worse-/worst-off.[41] Still, I am tentatively willing to defend desert sensitivity as an account of what is required by justice in a very strict sense that excludes efficiency-type considerations, which is sometimes referred to as 'equity' or 'fairness'.[42] I hope to have shown why even such a limited endorsement of responsibility sensitivity would be inappropriate.

---

[40] See Matt Matravers's chapter in this volume.

[41] See R. J. Arneson, 'Equality of Opportunity for Welfare Defended and Recanted', *Journal of Political Philosophy*, 7 (1999), 488–497; 'Luck Egalitarianism and Prioritarianism', *Ethics*, 110 (2000), 339–349; C. Knight, 'A Pluralistic Approach to Global Poverty', *Review of International Studies*, 34 (2008), 713–733; *Luck Egalitarianism* (Edinburgh: Edinburgh University Press, 2009), ch. 6; and Shlomi Segall's chapter in this volume.

[42] See G. A. Cohen, *Rescuing Justice and Equality* (Cambridge, MA: Harvard University Press, 2008); J. Le Grand, *Equity and Choice* (London: Routledge, 1991); and Avner de-Shalit and Jonathan Wolff's chapter in this volume.

8

Responsibility and False Beliefs[1]

Peter Vallentyne

An individual is agent responsible for an outcome just in case it flows from her autonomous agency in the right kind of way. The topic of agent responsibility is important because most people believe that agents should be held morally accountable (e.g. liable to punishment or having an obligation to compensate victims) for outcomes for which they are agent responsible and because many other people (e.g. brute luck egalitarians) hold that agents should *not* be held accountable for outcomes for which they are *not* responsible. In this chapter, I examine how false beliefs affect agent responsibility.

Unlike most of the chapters in this volume, my chapter is on the notion of agent responsibility that many believe is relevant to justice and morality generally. I do not here address the question of how, if at all, justice and morality are sensitive to agent responsibility.

8.1 The concept of agent responsibility

The term 'responsibility' is used in various ways and *agent responsibility* (or *attributive responsibility*) needs to be clearly distinguished from the others. The rough idea is that an individual is agent responsible for a choice or outcome to the extent that it suitably reflects the exercise of her autonomous agency. Being *causally responsible* for an outcome, for example, is necessary but not sufficient for agent responsibility, since an agent may reasonably have been unaware that her choice had the effect in question (e.g. when one flicks a light switch that has been secretly rigged to set off a bomb).

Moreover, an agent's being agent responsible for a choice or outcome does not entail that she is *morally accountable* (or substantively responsible) for the choice or outcome in the sense that she has certain substantive moral duties, liabilities, etc. in virtue of the occurrence of the outcome (e.g. has the duty to compensate those harmed by her actions, or is subject to permissible punishment). That is a substantive moral

---

[1] For helpful comments, I thank Dick Arneson, Carl Knight, Kasper Lippert-Rasmussen, Martin O'Neill, Shlomi Segall, Hillel Steiner, Zofia Stemplowska, Andrew Williams, and Jo Wolff.

question that will be answered in different ways by different moral theories. Agent responsibility merely establishes that the choice or outcome flows in the right kind of way from the individual's agency. It leaves open what the substantive moral implications are. Although most substantive moral theories hold agents morally accountable only for that for which they are agent responsible, some do not.[2]

An agent is agent responsible for some outcome to the extent that it suitably reflects her exercise of agency. Such an outcome is part of the agent's record (or ledger) concerning her exercise of autonomous agency and thus relevant to the creditworthiness of that exercise.[3] Reactive attitudes (blame, praise, etc.) towards an agent with respect to an outcome are appropriate in principle if and only if the agent is agent responsible for the outcome.[4] Under normal circumstances, for example, it is inappropriate to blame a person for the fact that it rained.

The mere fact that an individual is agent responsible for an outcome does not establish that any particular reactive attitude is appropriate. First, the appropriate reactive attitude will depend on the normative perspective at issue (e.g. morality vs. prudence). An agent might be prudentially praiseworthy for stealing the money (with little chance of being caught) while being morally blameworthy. Second, even from a given normative perspective (e.g. morality), the issue of what determines blameworthiness and praiseworthiness is a substantive issue. That an agent is agent responsible for an outcome merely establishes that it is not inappropriate in principle to have reactive attitudes towards the agent with respect to the outcome. It does not establish what attitudes are appropriate.[5]

Although it is not standard, we need, I believe, to distinguish between a narrow and broad concept of agent responsibility. Consider two almost identically situated agents, each of whom throws a rock at my window with the intention of breaking it. Both believe that it is certain that her rock will break the window and this belief is true for one agent but false for the other. In fact, for the second agent, it is certain that the rock

---

[2] For example, T. M. Scanlon, 'The Significance of Choice' in S. McMurrin (ed.), *The Tanner Lectures on Human Value VIII* (Cambridge: Cambridge University Press, 1988), 151–216; T. M. Scanlon, *What We Owe to Each Other* (Cambridge, MA: Harvard University Press, 1998), ch. 6.

[3] See, for example, J. Feinberg, 'Action and Responsibility' in M. Black (ed.), *Philosophy in America* (London: George Allen & Unwin, 1965), 134–160 [reprinted in J. Feinberg, *Doing and Deserving: Essays in the Theory of Responsibility* (Princeton: Princeton University Press, 1970), 119–151]; J. Glover, *Responsibility* (London: Routledge and Kegan Paul, 1970), 44; T. Nagel, 'Moral Luck', *Proceedings of the Aristotelian Society*, Supplementary Volume, 50 (1976), 137–151; M. J. Zimmerman, *An Essay on Moral Responsibility* (Totowa, NJ: Rowman and Littlefield, 1988); and I. Haji, *Moral Appraisability: Puzzles, Proposals, and Perplexities* (Oxford: Oxford University Press, 1998).

[4] On the connection between agent responsibility and reactive attitudes, see, for example, P. F. Strawson, 'Freedom and Resentment', *Proceedings of the British Academy*, 48 (1962), 187–211; and R. J. Wallace, *Responsibility and the Moral Sentiments* (Cambridge, MA: Harvard University Press, 1994).

[5] Agent responsibility for outcomes is similar to what is called 'moral responsibility' for outcomes, except that it builds in no requirement that the agent be responsive to moral reasons. See, for example, J. M. Fischer and M. Ravizza, *Responsibility and Control: A Theory of Moral Responsibility* (Cambridge: Cambridge University Press, 1999) and Zimmerman, *An Essay on Moral Responsibility*.

will not break the window (e.g. because, unbeknownst to her, the rock is too fragile). For what outcomes is each agent responsible?

If we are concerned with assessing—in the strictest sense—the merits (e.g. appropriate moral or prudential reactive attitudes) of each individual's exercise of agency, then neither agent, I would argue, is fully responsible for breaking the window. One agent did not break my window at all. The other agent did break my window, but that event depended in part on factors that do not reflect her exercise of agency (e.g. that her rock was hard enough to break my window). That difference is not a reflection of the agency of either individual. Moreover, the normatively (e.g. morally or prudentially) appropriate reactive attitudes (blame, praise, etc.), I would argue, are not sensitive to the presence or absence of factors that the agent could not reasonably have known about. In the strictest sense, I believe, agents are responsible only for the believed (intended, etc.) outcomes of their choices.[6] Call this *narrow responsibility*. In the example, the two agents have the same narrow responsibility. It is, of course, controversial that, in the strictest sense, the appropriateness of reactive attitudes (and assessment of desert) depends solely on narrow responsibility. I shall not attempt to defend this claim here. The important point to note is that, for narrow responsibility, the truth or falsity of a belief is irrelevant. Agents are responsible, at most, for the believed outcomes of their choices—whether or not they are true.[7] They are never morally narrowly responsible for objective outcomes.

Narrow responsibility is not, however, the topic that I wish to address. I am interested in the notion of responsibility that connects the exercise of autonomous agency with objective outcomes in the world. Call this *broad responsibility*. It is intermediate between narrow responsibility (based solely on the agent's mental states) and causal responsibility (based solely on the outcomes of choices). Roughly speaking, agents are broadly responsible for an outcome to the extent that they are causally responsible for it and it suitably reflects the exercise of their autonomous agency. Like casual responsibility, it is concerned with responsibility for events in the external world (as well as mental states). Like narrow responsibility, it holds that an agent's beliefs about the outcomes of her choices may limit that for which she is responsible.[8] In the above example, both agents made an autonomous choice to throw a rock at my window with the intention of breaking it. The first agent broke my window, foresaw this result, and is thus, we may suppose, broadly responsible for the breaking of

---

[6] See for example, P. Vallentyne, 'Brute Luck Equality and Desert' in S. Olsaretti (ed.), *Desert and Justice* (Oxford University Press, 2003), 169–185. This view is also held by M. J. Zimmerman, 'Taking Luck Seriously', *Journal of Philosophy*, 99 (2002), 553–576; 'Luck and Responsibility', *Ethics*, 97 (1987), 374–386; and J. J. Thomson, 'Morality and Bad Luck', *Metaphilosophy*, 20 (1989), 203–221 [reprinted in D. Statman (ed.), *Moral Luck* (Albany: State University of New York, 1993), 195–216].

[7] Some might argue that agents are responsible only for their intended outcomes and not for merely believed outcomes. For simplicity, I focus on the full believed outcome, but I allow that this may need to be further narrowed down.

[8] Broad responsibility is at least roughly what is called 'indirect responsibility' in Zimmerman, *An Essay on Moral Responsibility*.

my window. The second agent did not break my window and thus is not broadly responsible for its breaking.

Broad responsibility is the notion that most have in mind when they claim that individuals are morally accountable for those outcomes for which they are responsible.[9] In what follows, I focus on broad responsibility and all unqualified references to responsibility or agent responsibility should be so understood.

In order for an individual to be (broadly) responsible for an outcome, three general conditions must be satisfied: (1) an autonomy condition: she must make a suitably autonomous choice; (2) a causal condition: the outcome must be suitably causally related to the choice; and (3) a belief condition: she must have (or should reasonably have) a suitable belief that the outcome is so related. I shall assume throughout that the autonomy condition is satisfied. My focus below will be on the third condition. First, however, I shall briefly comment on the causal condition.

I shall assume that the causal condition restricts responsibility, relative to a choice, to the impact the choice has relative to some background baseline for the choice situation. The key point is that the agent (in the simple cases we address) is not responsible for the baseline choice situation. She is only responsible for the difference her choice makes relative to the baseline for the choice situation. Call this—the difference between the baseline and the outcome of her choice—the *impact* of her choice. I leave open how that baseline is determined, except to stipulate that it is suitably sensitive to the agent's disposition, given her beliefs and choice-making abilities, to choose and the resulting consequences. As a very crude approximation, we might think of the baseline as that which would happen if the agent made a reasonable choice (given her beliefs and choice-making abilities) in the choice situation. Thus, for example, suppose that only money matters, that one agent faces a choice between $10 and $100, that another faces a choice between $10 and $20, and that both choose the $10. Suppose that the baseline for the first agent is $90 (90 per cent of best) and that for the second agent is $18 (90 per cent of the best). The impact of choosing the $10 for the first agent would be −$80, whereas the impact of choosing the $10 for the second agent would be −$8.

Of course, agents are typically partly responsible for their choice situations (their beliefs, desires, or opportunities) in virtue of prior choices. When this is so, the agents are also partly responsible for their baseline (as well as for the impact their choices make relative to the baselines). A full account of responsibility for outcome will be historical and allocate responsibility for a given outcome on the basis of *all* the autonomous choices that an agent has made. Here, however, I shall address only the simple case where an agent is not responsible for her baseline (e.g. because it is her first choice). In particular, I assume that agents are not responsible for their false beliefs.[10] In this simple

---

[9] It is also the notion of responsibility that Fischer and Ravizza address in *Responsibility and Control*. They call it an 'externalist' account (252–253).

[10] For more on how one can be responsible for false beliefs, see M. J. Zimmerman, 'Moral Responsibility and Ignorance,' *Ethics*, 107 (1997), 410–426; C. Ginet, 'The Epistemic Requirements for Moral

case, agents are responsible, I assume, only for the impact of their choices, that is, the differences their choices make relative to their choice-context-sensitive baselines.

8.2 False beliefs

How do false beliefs affect responsibility? They do not affect *causal* responsibility, since the agent's *beliefs* are irrelevant to that topic. Nor do they affect *narrow* agent responsibility, since the *truth* of the agent's beliefs is irrelevant to that topic. For broad agent responsibility, however, false beliefs can affect responsibility. For example, an agent is not broadly agent responsible for an outcome if there was no way she could have known that her choice would produce the outcome. In what follows, I shall explore how false beliefs affect (broad agent) responsibility.

False beliefs, I claim, can affect responsibility in three distinct ways. One is that false beliefs affect an agent's disposition to choose and can thereby affect the baseline for the allocation of responsibility. The baseline for an agent who falsely believes (with no responsibility for the belief) that smoking is good for health is different (e.g. lower) than that for an identical agent but with no false beliefs (because the former is more likely to smoke). This is a very important topic, but an account of how the baseline is determined (and affected by false beliefs) is beyond the scope of this chapter.[11]

A second way that false beliefs affect responsibility is by inducing *unforeseen outcomes* (relative to the baseline). This is that part of the outcome that the agent did not foresee. Suppose, for example, that an agent, under normal conditions, flicks a light switch and thereby, unbeknownst to her, sets off a bomb. Setting off the bomb is an unforeseen outcome of her choice. It's relatively uncontroversial that, where agents do not foresee an outcome and are not responsible for the failure to foresee it, they are not responsible for that outcome. Such unforeseen outcomes play no role in choice deliberations and agents are thus not responsible for them. I have nothing to add to this case.

A third way that false beliefs affect responsibility is by inducing *imaginary outcomes*. This is that part of what the agent believes the outcome of her choice to be that was not part of the causal outcome. For example, if an agent flicks the light switch believing that it would cause the room to light up, but in fact the switch is broken, then the lighting of the room is an imaginary outcome of her choice. Imaginary outcomes are outcomes anticipated by the agent that are not real, whereas unforeseen outcomes are real outcomes that the agent did not anticipate.

It's important to distinguish imaginary outcomes from unrealized foreseen objective possibilities. When an agent makes a choice that she accurately foresees will raise the

---

Responsibility', *Philosophical Perspectives*, 14 (2000), 267–277; G. Rosen, 'Culpability and Ignorance', *Proceedings of the Aristotelian Society*, 103 (2003), 61–84; and G. Rosen, 'Skepticism about Moral Responsibility', *Philosophical Perspectives*, 18 (2004), 295–313.

[11] I develop an account of the baseline in P. Vallentyne, 'Brute Luck and Responsibility', *Politics, Philosophy and Economics*, 7 (2008), 57–80.

objective chance of winning the lottery, but she does not win, the possibility of winning is not an imaginary outcome. It is a real possibility. Whether such a possibility is realized is a matter of option luck—roughly, luck in how foreseeable and influence-able objective chances are realized. Agents who have complete and true beliefs are still subject to option luck in a world with objective chances. I address this topic elsewhere.[12] Here our topic concerns false beliefs, not unrealized foreseen objective chances. Imaginary outcomes are believed outcomes with no objective basis. They can arise independently of objective chances. For simplicity, I shall assume throughout that the outcomes of choices are objectively fully determined (with no objective chances other than 0 or 1), but similar points apply for cases where the outcomes are not so determined.

Our question concerns how imaginary outcomes affect responsibility for outcomes.

8.3 Imaginary outcomes

How is the imaginary outcome of a choice relevant for the determination of responsi-bility? Because the imaginary outcome is not part of the actual outcome, one might suppose that it is irrelevant to broad responsibility. I shall suggest that this is sometimes, but not always, so.

To see that the imaginary outcome is sometimes relevant to responsibility, consider a case in which a benevolent doctor performs an operation that she knows will be extremely painful. She performs the operation because she believes that this will save the patient's life and ultimately be good for the patient. In fact, the patient will die no matter what the doctor does, and thus the net effect of the doctor's actions is to increase very significantly the pain experienced by the patient. Is the doctor responsible for the increase in pain? On the one hand, it seems that she is, since she imposed it intentionally. On the other, she is partly excused, since she did it falsely believing that it would benefit the patient. With respect to moral blame, she is certainly less blame-worthy than she would be if she had done it without the imaginary benefit. Thus, the imaginary outcome is, at least sometimes, relevant to responsibility. At a minimum, it can sometimes mitigate responsibility for outcomes. It's not clear, however, how it does this.

In the case of unforeseen outcomes, we simply strip them away from the full causal outcome and 'record' only the foreseen impact in the responsibility account. A comparable move is not possible for imaginary outcomes. Imaginary outcomes are not real outcomes and hence cannot be stripped away. Nor can they be simply added to the foreseen outcome. That would give us the believed outcome, which is relevant for narrow responsibility but not for broad responsibility. Nor can some of the foreseen outcome be stripped away in virtue of the imaginary outcome, since there is no

---

[12] See 'Brute Luck and Responsibility'.

determinate connection between the two. For example, which pains would be stripped away in the above example in the light of the imaginary outcome?

We must, I believe, view the responsibility record as *two-dimensional*: the basic account which consists of those outcomes for which one is presumptively responsible (roughly: the foreseen impact of autonomous choices) and an imaginary impact account that can be relevant for adjusting the normative significance (e.g. blameworthiness or praiseworthiness) of the basic account. Both are relevant, but they cannot simply be merged (since imaginary impacts are not real). In the case of the doctor above, the additional pain of the patient would be in the basic account, but the imaginary benefits would be in the imaginary account. Both would be taken into consideration in determining, for example, the appropriate reactive attitudes towards the doctor.

This is a complex and important issue that deserves further analysis. Here I shall assume this two-dimensional conception of responsibility and turn to a slightly different question. Instead of focusing on what is in an agent's responsibility record, let us consider the *normative significance* of such records. Obviously, the normative significance of a record depends on the normative perspective: morality, prudence, or something else. To make the topic manageable, I shall focus on prudential assessment. Moreover, I shall focus on assessing the (prudential) *value* of the agent's record rather, for example, than determining what reactive attitudes towards the agent are appropriate with respect to the record. (The two are presumably intimately related, but I leave this open.) I focus on the prudential value of an agent's record because this is what certain standard versions of brute luck egalitarianism (and related sufficiency and priority views) do. They distinguish between the prudential value (e.g. well-being) of outcomes for which an agent is responsible and the prudential value for which the agent is not responsible.[13] They seek to equalize the prudential value of outcomes for which agents are not responsible.

I shall thus focus on the assessment of the prudential value of an agent's record for the purpose of determining what portion of the total outcome value is attributable to the agent's choice (and, for example, thus not subject to any equalization requirement). My question concerns how imaginary outcomes affect this assessment.

Consider, for example, a case where an agent intentionally undergoes a painful medical procedure because she falsely imagines that it will cure a disease she has. The foreseen impact of her choice, let us suppose, *reduces* her well-being by 10 units (relative to the relevant baseline). Relative to the agent's beliefs, however, her choice will *increase* her well-being by 20 units because of the imaginary benefits of the operation. For what impact on well-being is the agent responsible? The actual impact was to reduce well-being by 10 units and this impact was entirely foreseen by the agent. Is she thus responsible for the 10-unit reduction in well-being? Or is she

---

[13] Here and throughout I follow Susan Hurley's use of 'brute luck' in the thin sense of 'not responsible for'. See ch. 4 of S. Hurley, *Justice, Luck, and Knowledge* (Cambridge, MA: Harvard University Press, 2003).

responsible somehow for a 20-unit increase in well-being (even though that was not the actual impact)?

I shall suggest that the presence of imaginary outcomes can, relative to the value of the foreseen impact, *shrink* the value for which the agent is responsible but never *magnify* the value. Shrinking involves moving the value closer to zero (e.g. from 4 to 3 or from −4 to −3), whereas magnifying involves moving the value further away from zero (e.g. from 4 to 5 or from −4 to −5). Imaginary outcomes, that is, can mitigate, but never enhance, responsibility for value.

The analysis that follows is very speculative. The topic of how imaginary outcomes affect the value for which the agent is responsible has not, to the best of my knowledge, been systematically examined before. My aim is therefore very modest. I merely seek to sketch one seemingly promising solution to the problem of imaginary outcomes. My goal is, not to defend this solution but rather, to say enough so that we have a clear picture of the problem and of one possible solution. Even if the proposed solution is quite mistaken (and I won't be surprised if it is), my hope is that thinking about it will help us understand the problem.

8.4 Imaginary impact and responsibility for prudential value

How do imaginary outcomes affect responsibility for prudential value? A natural thought is to appeal to the prudential value of the foreseen impact of the choice that the agent *would* have made, had she not had her false beliefs about the imaginary outcome. It would be implausible, however, to hold that agents are responsible for the impact of such hypothetical choices, since this would violate the causal condition on responsibility. It would imply that agents are responsible for impacts that they did not produce (the hypothetical impacts). Instead, the appeal to the hypothetical impact must be a necessary (rather than sufficient) condition. The idea must be that agents are responsible for their actual causal impacts only if they would also have produced them in the absence of their false beliefs. Call this *the hypothetical impact requirement*. I shall now identify some problems with this requirement.

There is, of course, a general worry about whether sufficiently robust counterfactuals are well defined in most cases, but I shall not pursue this issue here. Another worry is whether counterfactuals can be made to track the right kinds of considerations for responsibility. For example, it might be that an agent who, through weakness of will, chose her believed *second best* alternative would have chosen her *first best* alternative, if she had not had the false beliefs about the imaginary impact. If this is possible, then the appeal to the counterfactual seems inappropriate.

Another problem is that the hypothetical impact requirement seems to reduce responsibility too much. Suppose, for example, that we are asking whether an agent is responsible for getting wet in the rain. Let us suppose that she had a choice between staying home, going out with an umbrella, and going out without an umbrella, and that she chose to go out without an umbrella knowing that she would get wet. Finally, suppose that the only reason that she went out in the rain was because she falsely believed that the house was going to collapse (an imaginary impact). If she had not had this false belief (or any other one concerning imaginary impacts), she would not have gone out and would not have gotten wet. According to the hypothetical impact requirement, the agent is not responsible for getting wet. This, I claim, is implausible. To see this, consider a second agent in exactly the same situation (including the same beliefs) who chooses to go out in the rain *with* an umbrella. Unlike the first agent, he makes the effort to find the umbrella so as to avoid getting wet. Clearly, in at least some situations of this sort, the first agent bears some responsibility for getting wet. Although false beliefs about imaginary outcomes may *reduce* an agent's responsibility for getting wet in such situations, they do not completely *eliminate* it, as the hypothetical impact requirement holds.

The issue is complex, but the above considerations at least motivate considering an alternative approach. I shall now sketch an approach in which, instead of appealing to the outcome of some counterfactual choice, one compares the foreseen value impact of a choice with its believed (foreseen and imaginary) value impact.[14] The latter, I shall suggest, can mitigate but never enhance responsibility for the foreseen value impact.

This analysis appeals to the notions of the foreseen value impact and of the believed value impact. In a given choice situation, the agent's beliefs about the values of the outcomes of her choices (including imaginary outcomes) and other factors determine her disposition to make various choices. Given this disposition, we can calculate two baseline values for the choice situation. One, the *foreseen value baseline*, is the value of the choice situation based on the values of the foreseen outcomes of the choices. The other, the *believed value baseline*, is the value of the choice situation based on the values of the believed outcomes of the choices. They are both based on the same choice disposition (which is based on the agent's actual beliefs) and represent the value of being in the choice situation. They differ solely with respect to the values that they associate with each choice: the value of the foreseen outcomes or that of the believed outcomes (which includes imaginary outcomes). The *foreseen value impact* of a choice is the difference between the value of its foreseen outcome and the foreseen value baseline. The *believed value impact* of a choice is the difference between the value of its believed outcome and the believed value baseline.

Consider, then, the following example. An agent confronts three possible choices, C1, C2, and C3. She (correctly) foresees the outcome of each choice (there is no unforeseen outcome), but falsely anticipates certain imaginary outcomes as well.

---

[14] I compare the value of the believed (foreseen and imaginary) impact with that of the foreseen impact rather than just comparing the value of imaginary impact with zero, because value may be holistic (so that the value of the believed impact is not the sum of the values of the foreseen and imaginary impacts).

		Outcome	
Choice	Foreseen	Imaginary	Believed
C1 (.7)	10	10	20
C2 (.2)	0	14	14
C3 (.1)	9	1	10

For this example, I shall assume that the foreseen value and believed value baselines are determined on the basis of the expected value of the outcomes, given the agent's choice disposition (given her beliefs). For illustration, we shall assume that the agent has a 70 per cent disposition to choose C1 (which has the highest believed value), a 20 per cent disposition to choose C2, and a 10 per cent disposition to choose C3 (which has the lowest believed value). The basic idea is that the agent is more disposed to choose those options that she believes have greater value, but she is not a perfect chooser: she may make mistakes, suffer from weakness of the will, and so on. The exact probability numbers used here do not matter. Moreover, I believe that my main points remain correct even if the baselines are not determined on the basis of the probabilistic dispositions of agents to choose. I have made the assumption to provide a concrete example of how the baseline might be determined.[15]

Given the assumption that baseline values are determined on the basis of expected values, and given the above probabilities, the foreseen value baseline is 7.9 (= .7 x 10 + .2 x 0 + .1 x 9) and the believed value baseline is 17.8 (= .7 x 20 + .2 x 14 + .1 x 10). Note that the same probabilities are used for both calculations. This is because we are appealing to the agent's actual choice disposition, given her false beliefs. The only difference is whether we appeal to the (correct) foreseen value or the (mistaken in this case) believed value.

Let us now ask, for each choice, what value the agent is responsible for if she makes that choice. If she makes C1, the foreseen value outcome is 10 and thus the foreseen value impact is 2.1 (= 10–7.9). The believed value outcome is 20 and thus the believed value impact is 2.2 (20–17.8). The two impacts have the same sign (both positive) and this reflects the fact that both the foreseen outcome and the believed outcome are improvements over their respective baselines. Relative to the agent's beliefs, the agent is improving things, and this is also true relative to the (actual) foreseen impact. I suggest that in this case, the agent is responsible for the foreseen value impact—and not the greater believed value impact. Because we are concerned with broad responsibility, we are interested only in the extent to which the actual impact is attributable to the agent's choice. In this case, we attribute the entire foreseen value impact to the agent. It would not make sense to attribute more than this. (Imagine a situation like

---

[15] I defend the view that the value of the baseline is the expected value of the agent's choices in 'Brute Luck and Responsibility'.

the above but where the agent falsely imagines even greater benefits. This would not increase her responsibility for the actual impact.)

More generally, where the foreseen value impact and the believed value impact *have the same sign* (e.g. both positive) and the absolute size of the believed value impact is *greater* or equal, the imaginary outcome has, I suggest, no effect on responsibility for value. The agent is simply responsible for the foreseen value impact (which is smaller or equal in absolute size). The imaginary outcome in this case neither enhances nor mitigates responsibility.

Consider now C2. Its foreseen value outcome is 0 and thus the foreseen value impact is $-7.9 (= 0-7.9)$. The believed value outcome is 14 and thus the believed value impact is $-3.8 (14-17.8)$. From both perspectives, the outcome of C2 is worse than the relevant baseline. In a case such as this, where the believed value impact and the foreseen value impact have the same sign, but where the believed value impact is *smaller* in absolute size than the foreseen value impact (-3.8 vs. -7.9 in this case), the agent is responsible, I suggest, for the believed value impact (and not the foreseen impact, as I suggested for C1). Because of the false beliefs about imaginary outcomes, the agent was not fully aware of the impact of her choice. The false beliefs do not entirely eliminate responsibility, since even relative to her beliefs her choice (C2) had a negative value impact. They do, however, mitigate responsibility by limiting responsibility to the (smaller in absolute size) believed value impact.

Finally, consider C3. If the agent chooses C3, the foreseen outcome is 9 and thus the foreseen value impact is $1.1 (= 9-7.9)$. The believed outcome is 10 and thus the believed value impact is $-7.8 (10-17.8)$. Here, unlike the previous two cases, the value of the believed value impact does not have the same sign as the foreseen value impact (-7.8 vs. 1.1). The agent is improving things from the perspective of the (actual) foreseen value impact but making things worse from the perspective of the (partially mistaken) believed value impact. Here, the agent is not, I claim, responsible for any value. Her beliefs about the outcome of her choice are too disconnected from reality for her to be responsible for the impact of her choice.

In sum, my suggestion is that agents are (1) not responsible for any value where the foreseen value impact and the believed value impact have different signs (e.g. one positive and one negative), and (2) responsible for the *smaller* absolute value where they have the same. Imaginary impacts, that is, can mitigate but never enhance responsibility for value.

On this proposed account, responsibility for the foreseen value impact is limited—not by appealing to the outcomes of a hypothetical choice but rather—by appealing to the believed value impact of the choice in question. I won't attempt to defend this view, since I am by no means convinced that it is correct even in broad outline. My goal is simply to outline a seemingly promising alternative to hypothetical accounts.

8.5 Conclusion

We have been addressing the topic of broad (agent) responsibility for outcomes. This is an important topic for any moral view—such as brute luck egalitarianism—that holds that moral accountability for outcomes depends in part on whether the agent is responsible for the outcome. Unlike narrow responsibility, broad responsibility is concerned with responsibility for outcomes outside of the agent's head. For simplicity, we have focused throughout on cases where the agent is not responsible for her beliefs (e.g. because she is making her first choice). We have been asking how false beliefs affect broad responsibility for outcomes.

False beliefs generate at least three relevant phenomena. One is that they change the agent's disposition to choose, and this, I have assumed, affects the baseline relative to which responsibility for outcomes is assessed. I have had nothing to say here about this important topic. We have simply assumed that the *impacts* of choices are measured relative to such a baseline. A second phenomenon generated by false beliefs is the existence of unforeseen outcomes—actual outcomes that the agent did not foresee. Agents are clearly not responsible for such outcomes and I have had little to say about this topic. A third phenomenon generated by false beliefs is the existence of imaginary outcomes—outcomes anticipated by the agent but with no basis in reality. This is the topic on which I have focused.

With respect to responsibility for outcomes, I have suggested that we need to think of it as two-dimensional: the foreseen impact account and the imaginary account. The two cannot be merged into one account, since broad responsibility is concerned with actual impacts and imaginary impacts are not real. Instead, the foreseen impact account gives us presumptive responsibility and the imaginary account provides the basis for adjusting such responsibility.

The above concerns the issue of what is in an agent's 'record'. That leaves open how the normative significance of a record with imaginary impact is determined. The normative significance might concern the appropriate reactive attitudes towards the agent with respect to the record or it might concern the value of the record (the value for which the agent is responsible). Such assessments will vary by normative perspective. A record, for example, may be praiseworthy from the perspective of prudence but not from that of morality. Rather than attempting to address the general issues of normative significance of an agent's record, I have focused on just one: that of determining the prudential value of an agent's record (the value attributable to the agent). This issue is central to standard forms of brute luck egalitarianism (which exclude such value from equalization).

I have suggested that imaginary outcomes (1) eliminate all responsibility for value when the believed (foreseen plus imaginary) value impact has the opposite sign from the foreseen value impact, (2) reduce responsibility for value when the believed value impact has the same sign as the foreseen value impact but has a lower absolute value, and (3) do not affect responsibility for value when the believed value impact has the same sign as the foreseen value impact but has a higher absolute value. My weaker and more general claim is that imaginary impacts sometimes eliminate responsibility for value, sometimes partially reduce it, sometimes do not affect it, and never enhance it.

The proposed analysis focused on responsibility for prudential value. I believe, but shall not argue, that the account is just as plausible as an account of responsibility for value of any sort (e.g. moral value). Moreover, although I have not addressed the question of how imaginary impacts affect the appropriate reactive attitudes (e.g. for morality), a natural extension is to say that they are determined by the (e.g. moral) *value* for which the agent is responsible. I leave this, however, as an open question.

All of this is highly speculative. My goal has been to open up an issue for further investigation rather than to resolve it conclusively.

9

The Public Ecology of Responsibility[1]

Susan Hurley

9.1 Traditional liberalism and the limits to government regulation of harmful behaviour: anti-paternalism and the principle of proximal agency

What is the appropriate role of government in influencing citizens' behaviour? How does individual responsibility enter into the answer?

Liberalism has traditionally answered the first question in a way dominated by concern to restrict governmental activity to the public realm and to protect liberty by avoiding unwarranted governmental interference in the private realm. Many liberals think government should remain *neutral* about the good: that issues about what constitutes a good life and how best to pursue it should be left to citizens' private choices. People disagree widely about how best to live their lives; this is for citizens to decide for themselves. Government should not base policies on specific assumptions about what is a good way to live, or aim to influence citizens to live better lives, as the government conceives them.

Some (perfectionist) liberals disagree with neutralist liberals about the proper role of the good in liberal policy. Nevertheless, even neutralist liberals will allow that government can and should aim to prevent certain widely recognized harms to citizens. How should we identify the harms avoidance of which is an acceptable aim of public policy? How in particular can they be publicly identified compatibly with neutrality about the good? These are important questions about ends, but they are not my focus here. Rather, my focus is on means: given some such public identification of the harms government can legitimately aim to avoid, what is the appropriate role of government in pursuing this aim by means of influencing citizens' behaviour?

[1] I'm grateful to Zachary White for research assistance and discussions which benefited this chapter. [Note from the Editors: the final version of this chapter was copy-edited after Susan Hurley's untimely death. We updated the references previously listed as forthcoming. We bear final responsibility for any mistakes.]

Traditional liberalism limits acceptable governmental means of regulating harmful behaviour in two central ways.

First, by an *anti-paternalist principle*: government should not regulate 'self-regarding actions' (as J. S. Mill called them),[2] including those that are harmful to the agent but not to third parties. If smoking is harmful only to the smoker, for example, then government should not regulate smoking; ditto an unhealthy diet. But it is generally acceptable to regulate 'other-regarding actions' if they harm third parties. If it turns out that smoking is indeed harmful to others via passive smoking, then it becomes acceptable to regulate smoking.

Second, by a *principle of proximal agency*: government should where possible avoid regulating actions that harm third parties only indirectly, via their influence on the actions of second parties. Rather, it should regulate the proximal harmful act by the second party directly. If selling alcohol enables someone to drink and then drive, leading to harm to third parties, government should regulate driving after drinking directly, not selling alcohol. If playing a violent computer game influences someone to commit similar violence, government should regulate the aggression directly, not the production or selling of the game. This preference for focusing regulation on the proximal responsible agent is part of what motivates resistance to gun control in some polities.

Liberalism goes hand in hand with responsibility. These two principles concerning the proper limits to governmental influence on harmful behaviour implicitly also answer the second of my starting questions, concerning the role of individual responsibility. For it is assumed by the anti-paternalism principle that the agent of self-regarding harmful action is responsible for his action. If he weren't so responsible—for example, if he were a child or were mentally disabled—government regulation of self-regarding harmful behaviour would be acceptable. Similarly, it is assumed by the principle of proximal agency that the second party—the proximal agent—is responsible for his act leading to harm to a third party. If he were not, then under some conditions it could be appropriate for government to regulate the actions of the first party directly. For example, if someone is already a little drunk when he arrives at a pub by car, then it may be acceptable for government to regulate the conditions under which further alcohol is sold to him. Moreover, the proximal agent's responsibility, as it were, pre-empts the responsibility of more distal agents for harm.

These principles apply most forcefully to *coercive* legal regulation of citizens' behaviour through punishment and fines. However, in diluted form they also inform liberal views about *non-coercive* governmental influences on citizen's behaviour, such as taxes and persuasive campaigns. Such views are manifest in widespread resistance to the 'nanny-state', which can reduce the effectiveness of non-coercive governmental efforts to influence citizens' behaviour. On such views, government can provide factual

---

[2] J. S. Mill, *On Liberty* in *On Liberty and Other Essays*, J. Dunn (ed.) (Oxford: Oxford University Press, 1991).

information about self-regarding harmful action so that the responsible agent can better decide for herself whether to engage in it. But ultimately it is her business whether she does or not, and government shouldn't try to cajole or nudge her into doing what is good for her. Heavy persuasion would not be compatible with respect for her responsibility for her own action. Similarly, government should not engage in non-coercive campaigns to make citizens into their brothers' keepers: to influence citizens to refrain from otherwise legitimate activity on the grounds that it may influence a second party to act in a way that is harmful to third parties. The second party or proximal agent is responsible for his own harmful action, and as such is the proper object of governmental persuasion.

These two principles operationalize traditional liberalism's concern to protect the private realm from undue public interference. In the private realm, citizens engage in actions for which they are responsible, and their responsibility limits legitimate governmental efforts to influence citizens' behaviour. The responsibility of citizens' actions in the private realm is thus prior to, a parameter of, the proper public role of governmental efforts to influence citizens' behaviour. We can sum this up by saying that traditional liberalism assumes the *priority of private responsibility*.

Critics of traditional liberalism, from feminists to socialists, have challenged its conception of the distinction between the public and the private realms and the corresponding limits to the proper role of governmental influence on citizens' behaviour. They have argued, in various ways, that the supposedly private realm is already politicized (Pateman, Moller Okin, Cohen). To ignore this is to condone the power relations embedded in the supposedly private realm, and exempt them from public review. For example, to treat domestic power relations as private and hence protected from government regulation is to render domestic exploitation and injustice invisible;[3] to regard incentive-seeking behaviour in the market as not part of the basic structure of society and so not regulated by justice is in effect to permit the talented rich to hold others hostage to their demands for extra remuneration.[4]

These are political and normative challenges to traditional liberalism's public/private distinction and its conception of government's proper limits. A different kind of challenge is naturalistic: it derives from work in the cognitive sciences that brings the priority of private responsibility into question. This work suggests that individual responsibility is not prior to the public realm, so cannot independently parameterize the limits of the public realm. Rather, individual responsibility has a public ecology. The capacity for responsible action assumed by liberalism, on this view, isn't simply a given, but has social and political conditions.[5] This second, naturalistic kind of challenge is my focus here. As a

---

[3] C. Pateman, *The Sexual Contract* (Cambridge: Polity Press, 1988); S. Moller Okin, *Justice, Gender, and the Family* (New York: Basic Books, 1989).

[4] G. A. Cohen, 'Incentives, Inequality, and Community' in Grethe Petersen (ed.), *The Tanner Lectures on Human Values*, 13 (Salt Lake City: University of Utah Press. 1992), 263–329; and his 'Where the Action Is: On the Site of Distributive Justice', *Philosophy and Public Affairs*, 26 (1997), 3–30.

[5] See and cf. C. Taylor, *Philosophy and the Human Sciences* (Cambridge: Cambridge University Press, 1985).

result, the two principles of traditional liberalism laid out above become problematic. As I'll explain, it is even harder than we thought to draw the self-regarding/other-regarding distinction required by the anti-paternalism principle, and the assumption that responsibility is restricted to the proximal agent becomes dubious.

A sidebar: in discussing the role of individual responsibility in relation to governmental influences on behaviour, it is very important to avoid a widespread confusion. This confusion flows from equivocation between two senses of 'responsibility'.[6] In the *primary sense of 'responsibility'*, we ask whether an individual is responsible for her actions or not. If she is, there is no implication that her actions are socially desirable or that she deserves any particular outcome. Someone can be responsible for acting wrongly, with very bad consequences. If someone is responsible for her action, she is accountable in principle for it; but her responsibility for her action per se tells us nothing about its moral valence, or what she deserves as a result of it. In a *secondary sense of 'responsibility'*, we speak of someone as having 'behaved responsibly' when their actions are socially desirable or deserve some reward. But the fact that someone is responsible for her action in the first sense does not entail or even suggest that she has behaved responsibly in the second sense. Responsibility for action is one thing; deservingness is another. To avoid confusion, 'responsibility' is here used only in the first sense.

9.2 Responsibility and rational agency

How then does work in cognitive science challenge the priority of private responsibility? Before I explain how it does, a few words about how it doesn't, and about the conception of responsibility I'll employ.

It is often suggested that work in cognitive science, and especially in neuroscience, reveals free will to be an illusion,[7] or shows that no one can ever do otherwise than what they do, and hence challenges the sense in which anyone is ever responsible for anything.[8] This is a big topic that I cannot treat here. But the naturalistic challenge I'll discuss is not this, and does not threaten the existence of responsibility in general.

I operate here with a conception of responsibility that is compatible with (but does not assume) determinism. If there is a sense in which responsibility requires free will, it is one in which free will is compatible with determinism. Responsibility is here understood in terms of *reason-responsiveness*, in the dominant modern tradition established by Harry Frankfurt's seminal work on responsibility and continued by

---

[6] As in J. E. Roemer, *Theories of Distributive Justice* (Cambridge, MA: Harvard University Press, 1996), discussed in S. Hurley, *Justice, Luck, and Knowledge* (Cambridge, MA: Harvard University Press, 2003), ch. 7; D. Halpern and C. Bates, *Personal Responsibility and Changing Behaviour: The State of Knowledge and Its Implications for Public Policy* (London: Prime Minister's Strategy Unit, 2004).

[7] D. M. Wegner, *The Illusion of Conscious Will* (Cambridge, MA: MIT Press, 2002).

[8] J. Greene and J. Cohen, 'For the Law, Neuroscience Changes Nothing and Everything', *Philosophical Transactions of the Royal Society B*, Biological Sciences, Special Issue on Law and the Brain, 359 (2004), 1775–1785.

John Martin Fischer and others.[9] On this type of view, responsibility for your actions requires that *you act in a reason-responsive way*: in a way that is sensitive to reasons, or to some degree rational. Just how tightly linked to reasons, and whether the reasons must be objective or can be subjective, are further questions. Moreover, *the reason-responsive way you act must be accepted by you as a way of acting on your own reasons*: for example, not the result of manipulation.[10] Acting on reasons implanted by brainwashing or hypnosis would not meet this condition. On this view, your responsibility for what you do is not hostage to issues about whether something else could have happened instead (if the universe, including you, is deterministic, it couldn't), or about whether you are also responsible for all the further-back causes leading up to your act through the ages (of course you aren't!). What matters for responsibility, rather, is the *proximal* explanation of what you *actually* did: whether you acted in a reason-responsive way that you accept as a way of acting on your own reasons.

Responsibility thus presupposes a capacity for *rational agency*. What is that? I respond to that question at two levels. At an intuitive level, I suggest, the kind of rational agency required for responsibility has three central elements.[11]

A. Publicly intelligible goals. The ultimate goals or ends that feature in the explanation of what the responsible agent did must be publicly intelligible. This is a very weak condition. It would rule out, for example, acting on an ultimate goal of avoiding pain but only on Tuesdays (though this could be a means to some other goal), or some bizarre behaviour by the mentally ill. It would not rule out acting in a weak-willed way, on goals the agent judges less important than others (eating the cake despite needing to lose weight). Nor would it rule out acting on evil or sadistic goals per se, as these are unfortunately all too publicly intelligible.

B. Instrumental sensitivity. The means by which the responsible agent pursues goals must be sensitive to instrumental information available to the agent about means/ends contingencies, i.e. about the effectiveness of different possible means to a given goal. Her action is controlled by her ends plus available information about means. Just how sensitively and just what counts as available information remain to be specified. But if an agent continues to act in a certain way even though doing so is clearly counterproductive with respect to all relevant goals, this condition is not met. Nor is it met if the agent has no capacity to be influenced prior to acting by learned information about the effectiveness of alternative possible means to a given goal.

---

[9] H. Frankfurt, *The Importance of What We Care About* (Cambridge: Cambridge University Press, 1988); J. M. Fischer and M. Ravizza, *Responsibility and Control: A Theory of Moral Responsibility* (Cambridge: Cambridge University Press, 1998); Hurley, *Justice, Luck and Knowledge*.

[10] I speak of ways of acting instead of acting on mechanisms, as the former language is less technical; but I intend to capture something very close to Fischer and Ravizza's Frankfurt-inspired account of responsibility.

[11] A fuller story about the first and third elements is told in my *Natural Reasons* (New York: Oxford University Press, 1989) and about the second element in S. Hurley and M. Nudds (eds), *Rational Animals?* (Oxford: Oxford University Press, 2006).

C. Coherent resolution of conflicts among goals. The responsible agent must have a capacity to resolve conflicts among goals coherently and to act accordingly, in a way that takes various relevant reasons into account. This is part of what it is for the reasons on which the agent acts to be her own reasons, and is the condition that probably rules out intelligent non-human animals and young children—some of whom may meet the first two conditions—as responsible. But this condition does not assume that conflicts among goals can be eliminated; they can't. Nor does it rule out responsible action on wrong or even evil resolutions of goal conflicts. Nor does it rule out weak-willed actions, on goals that the agent judges less important than others. Weak-willed action is still action for an intelligible end, and some agents are more weak-willed than others. However, a rational agent cannot be weak-willed all the time, without undermining the sense in which she has capacity to resolve goal conflicts in the first place.

In sum, a responsible rational agent acts on a range of often conflicting publicly intelligible goals, in a way that is sensitive to information about the best means for achieving those goals, and she has a capacity to resolve conflicts among those goals coherently and to act on her resolutions, despite some weakness of will. To act in a reason-responsive way that she accepts as a way of acting on her own reasons is the proximal explanation of what she actually does to meet these conditions about ends and means.

However, this generic intuitive picture of a responsible agent should also be examined at a more theoretical level, informed by the dramatic changes that our understanding of human agency and rationality has been undergoing as a result of work in the cognitive sciences. In particular I have in mind the shift from classical to situated conceptions of rational agency. Human agency and rationality are more ecological phenomena than we have traditionally thought; individual rational agency is profoundly embedded in and dependent on the individual's social environment. My task in the rest of this chapter is to explain how the public ecology of rational agency impacts on our intuitive understanding of responsibility, and in particular how it challenges the priority of private responsibility. I shall argue that private responsibility cannot unilaterally provide the limits of public action, as traditional liberalism assumes, because individual responsibility isn't private or prior to public action, but has a public ecology to which governmental action—or inaction—inevitably contributes. However, this doesn't mean that liberalism should be abandoned. Rather, it should be rethought within a more naturalistic, social framework, so as not to be hostage to implicit but problematic empirical assumptions. Digging in to ignore what we are learning about how minds are actually made up is not an effective way to defend liberalism and may eventually doom it. The proper role of government in influencing citizens' behaviour needs reformulating to recognize the public social ecology of responsibility, within an *ecological liberalism* that contrasts in this respect with traditional liberalism.

I'll explain how work in the cognitive sciences leads to a socio-ecological view of rational agency and responsibility, in three stages. First, I'll characterize a classical conception of individual rational agency. This endows the generic responsible rational agent with specifically classical features. Second, I'll review a range of empirical results that lead to scepticism about the classical conception, by casting doubt on its descriptive and explanatory adequacy. This scepticism is compatible with retaining the classical view as a normative ideal. But if responsibility requires that norms of rationality be met which human agents generally fail to meet, then scepticism about rationality will lead to scepticism about responsibility as well. Third, I'll describe a revisionist conception of rationality as situated or ecological, which has normative as well as descriptive and explanatory aspirations. This feeds into an ecological conception of responsibility and endows the generic responsible rational agency with a different set of features.

With a sketch in hand of an ecological conception of responsibility, I'll explain how it challenges the two principles of traditional liberalism described above and leads to a socio-ecological conception of liberalism. I'll illustrate the proper role of government within a public ecology of responsibility by reference to two proposed principles of ecological liberalism: the anti-manipulation principle, and the democratic public scaffolding principle.

9.3 From classical rationality through scepticism to situated rationality

9.3.1 Classical conceptions of individual rational agency

Classical conceptions of individual rational agency are characterized by a cluster of overlapping ideas. There are outcome and process versions, which can be given empirical or normative readings.

9.3.1.1 Behavioural outcomes Economists view classical rationality in terms of patterns of behavioural outcomes: to behave rationally is to behave *as if* one were maximizing expected utility.[12] The process that actually leads to such behaviour is not the primary concern. Most behavioural outcome versions of classical rationality are officially concerned only with the *consistency* of patterns of behavioural outcomes, not their substantive goodness, or with the *instrumental effectiveness* of behavioural means adopted, not the ends of behaviour. But assessing behaviour for consistency or effectiveness can require assumptions about how to individuate the consequences of behaviour, which can depend on assumptions about the value of ends,[13] hence on the public intelligibility of

---

[12] 'Chicago man' in D. McFadden, 'Rationality for Economists?', *Journal of Risk and Uncertainty*, 19 (1999), 73–105; 'e-rationality' in A. Kacelnik, 'Meanings of Rationality' in Hurley and Nudds (eds), *Rational Animals?*, 87–106.

[13] Hurley, *Natural Reasons*.

goals and on social meanings.[14] Biologically oriented applications introduce constraints deriving from evolutionary fitness.[15] Game theory addresses complications arising when the results of individuals' actions depend not only on what 'nature' does, but also on how other individuals act, so that what is rational for each to do depends on what others do; a choice in a game is seen as rational when it is the best reply to the choices made by others.

9.3.1.2 Practical and theoretical reasoning processes Psychologists and philosophers tend to understand classical rationality in terms of the kinds of processes that lead to outcomes.[16] Rational processes include theoretical as well as practical reasoning, leading to beliefs as well as action. Beliefs are not immediately observable but result from cognitive processes and are part of the processes leading to behaviour; they have multiple rational aspects. Beliefs can be assessed as outcomes themselves (for consistency and/or truth); processes leading to beliefs can be assessed for rationality; and processes leading from beliefs to action can be assessed for rationality. Beliefs can be arrived at rationally by deductive logic or probabilistic reasoning, and choices can be made rationally by applying expected utility theory to the alternatives one faces. Classically rational processes are conceived as a general-purpose cognitive interface between perceptual input from the world to the individual and behavioural output from the individual to the world.[17] Rationality primarily concerns the character of processes leading to belief and on to action, rather than the quality of resulting beliefs or actions. Rational processes do not guarantee success: rational beliefs can be false; rational actions may serve bad ends or turn out to be ineffective. Moreover, beliefs or actions that happen to succeed, but result from non-rational processes, do not count as rational. But rational processes should at least *tend* to produce true beliefs and effective actions.

9.3.1.3 Descriptive vs. normative rationality Both outcome and process versions of classical rationality can be interpreted empirically or normatively: as describing and predicting overall patterns of behaviour or processes of belief-formation and decision-making, or as characterizing what rational behaviour or processes should be like, even if they in fact fall short.

Three salient features unite various versions of classical rationality: first, the *individual* is the locus of assessment—either the consistency of her actions or beliefs, or processes *internal* to the individual. Second, classical rationality is inherently *general*, not tied to specific domains, contents, or environments. Third, in classical rationality perceptions

---

[14] See and cf. L. Lessig, 'The Regulation of Social Meaning', *University of Chicago Law Review*, 62 (1995), 943–1045.

[15] 'b-rationality' in Kacelnik, 'Meanings of Rationality'.

[16] 'pp-rationality' in Kacelnik, 'Meanings of Rationality'; D. Davidson, *Essays on Actions and Events* (Oxford: Oxford University Press, 1982).

[17] See Hurley, *Natural Reasons* on the classical sandwich.

and beliefs are *decoupled* from action in a familiar Humean way: they do not lead directly to actions, but play flexible, instrumental roles in relation to action, mediated by the individual's desires and ends. So, an individual takes in perceptions and through internal reasoning processes arrives at beliefs about the world, including other agents, and about the probable results of alternative actions; alternatives are valued instrumentally by reference to her ends to produce a pattern of choices that is consistent and instrumentally effective, relative to her beliefs and ends. For short, I'll refer to these distinctive features of classical rationality as internalism, domain-generality, and decoupling. They are exemplified in versions of expected utility theory supplemented by deductive logic and probability theory, together viewed as providing a broadly accurate description of human cognitive processes and their outcomes. This picture provides a reference point for empirically based scepticism about classical rationality.

9.3.2 Scepticism about classical rationality

Scepticism about classical rationality arises from a range of robust empirical results that challenge the descriptive and explanatory adequacy of a classical conception of rationality, even if its normative status is not challenged. Following Kahneman, Slovic, and Tversky's seminal work on heuristics and biases,[18] various systematic behavioural and cognitive 'anomalies' (from a classical perspective) have been studied; some of these specifically concern social contexts.

9.3.2.1 Behavioural anomalies In behavioural decision theory experiments, subjects tend to make choices that *violate various axioms of decision theory*. Some of these results concern individuals making *riskless choices*. Choice between two alternatives may reverse when a third 'irrelevant' alternative is added. For example, people may tend to choose a brand B model rather than a brand A model from a choice set including only these two models, but switch to brand A when the choice set is expanded to include a more expensive brand A model as well, which may make the cheaper brand A model appear a bargain.[19] Other results apply to *choices with risky or uncertain outcomes*. Preferences between two sure prospects may reverse when each is 'mixed' with the same probability of some third prospect in a gamble: people who choose A over B may, when offered a lottery, choose a p chance of B plus a (1—p) chance of C over a p chance of A plus a (1—p) chance of C. Such results violate the axioms of expected utility theory. More generally, people do not act as if they weight possible outcomes by their probabilities in a linearly consistent way, suggesting that the probabilities of outcomes do not play a purely instrumental role in guiding action. People tend to give undue weight to sure outcomes; even allowing for risk aversion, certainty seems

---

[18] D. Kahneman, P. Slovic, and A. Tversky, *Judgements under Uncertainty: Heuristics and Biases* (Cambridge: Cambridge University Press, 1982).

[19] I. Simonson and A. Tversky, 'Choice in Context: Tradeoff Contrast and Extremeness Aversion', *Journal of Marketing Research*, 29 (1992), 281–295.

to be of disproportionate value in itself, relative to high or intermediate probabilities.[20] Moreover, greater aversion is often displayed to guessing under conditions of ignorance than to facing known risks, even when tossing a coin to determine the guess would make these equivalent according to decision theory.[21]

People are unduly influenced by the way alternatives are *framed*, tending passively to adopt the formulation presented. Even experts make different choices between the same alternatives when these are presented using different but logically equivalent descriptions or formats. For example, experienced doctors respond differently when a programme to combat a disease is described in terms of 200 people out of 600 being saved as opposed to 400 people out of 600 dying. Kahneman and Tversky write:

A physician, and perhaps a presidential advisor as well, could influence the decision made by the patient or by the President, without distorting or suppressing information, merely by the framing of outcomes and contingencies. Formulation effects can occur fortuitously, without anyone being aware of the impact of the frame on the ultimate decision. They can also be exploited deliberately to manipulate the relative attractiveness of options...lobbyists for the credit card industry insisted that any price difference between cash and credit purchases be labeled a cash discount rather than a credit card surcharge...because losses loom larger than gains, consumers are less likely to accept a surcharge than to forego a discount.[22]

People tend to evaluate the results of choice in a way that is *reference-dependent*: as gains or losses compared to the status quo, rather than in terms of intrinsic outcome. They tend to weigh losses more heavily than gains, and are risk averse for gains though risk seeking for losses (as described in 'prospect theory'). Short delays in reward tend to be overweighted relative to long delays. Choices can thus be influenced by manipulation of how decisions are framed, of the perceived status quo or expected delay in reward, or of descriptions of certainty, uncertainty, and risk.[23]

9.3.2.2 Cognitive anomalies People also display a range of cognitive anomalies, in both deductive and inductive contexts. They tend to *fail to select evidence in accord with deductive logic* when asked to test conditional rules of the form 'if p then q' (the Wason effect).[24] However, it has been argued, they perform significantly better when the rule has social content relevant to the detection of cheating, suggesting the presence of *domain-specific cognitive mechanisms* rather than domain-general classically

[20] M. Allais and O. Hagen (eds), *Expected Utility Hypotheses and the Allais Paradox* (Dordrecht: Reidel, 1979); Kahneman *et al.*, *Judgements under Uncertainty*.

[21] D. Ellsberg, 'Risk, Ambiguity, and the Savage Axioms', *Quarterly Journal of Economics*, 75 (1961), 643–669; also his '[Risk, Ambiguity, and the Savage Axioms]: Reply', *Quarterly Journal of Economics*, 77 (1963), 336–342.

[22] D. Kahneman and A. Tversky, 'Choices, Values, and Frames' in D. Kahneman and A. Tversky (eds), *Choices, Values, and Frames* (Cambridge: Cambridge University Press, 2000), 1–16, at 10.

[23] D. Kahneman, 'Maps of Bounded Rationality: Psychology for Behavioural Economics', *American Economic Review*, 93 (2003), 1449–1475.

[24] P. C. Wason, 'Reasoning' in B. M. Foss (ed.), *New Horizons in Psychology I* (Harmondsworth: Penguin, 1966), 135–151.

rational processes.[25] When asked to answer questions posed in terms they find difficult, or in quantitative terms, people tend to *answer other, easier questions instead*, posed in terms of more accessible, or categorical, terms. They tend to assimilate an experimental task that is unnatural in their normal environment to a more natural task, recruiting adaptively appropriate mechanisms that work for the more natural task.[26] They *substitute readily available attributes for less accessible ones*: substitute similarity or representativeness or prototype judgements for probability judgements; substitute averages for sums; apply heuristics, rules of thumb, or exemplars even where they are not directly relevant. People also tend to *give insufficient weight to background information* and probabilities that characterize a relevant population rather than a particular case. For example, given a description of a woman in terms perceived to be typical of feminists, people tend to judge that is it more probable that she is a feminist bank teller than that she is a bank teller. They give excessive weight to the reports of eyewitnesses and of tests applied to individuals, even when these are less predictively reliable than background probabilities, thus violating Bayes' Theorem. Judgements tend to be *'anchored' by initial 'estimates'*, even when these are explicitly arbitrary, such as the output of a random device. People are also *biased to seek confirming rather than disconfirming evidence*.[27] Moreover, people tend to *overinterpret* events in causal and intentional terms,[28] and are biased to *underestimate coincidences* and random fluctuations. People tend to judge a proposition by the *motives* of its proponents rather than by evidence relevant to its truth value (the genetic fallacy), and to allow diverse judgements, including probability judgements, to be governed by their *emotional valence*.[29]

9.3.2.3 Behavioural anomalies in social contexts In social situations, people often behave in ways that cannot be explained or rationalized in classical terms. They tend to cooperate in one-shot *prisoner's dilemmas* under various conditions, when game theory says they should defect. In *ultimatum games*, one player either accepts the division of a pool of resources made by another, or rejects it so that neither party gets anything. Classical rationality recommends acceptance of any offer in one-off ultimatum games with no reputation effects. But responses across ultimatum games vary widely across cultures in a way that is not explained by classical views: in a few cultures, people tend to accept even very low offers, as they classically 'should'; but in most cultures people

---

[25] L. Cosmides and J. Tooby, 'Cognitive Adaptations for Social Exchange' in J. H. Barkow, L. Cosmides, and J. Tooby (eds), *The Adapted Mind: Evolutionary Psychology and the Generation of Culture* (New York: Oxford University Press, 1992), 163–228. But cf. alternative accounts in, for example, N. Chater and M. Oaksford, 'Human Rationality and the Psychology of Reasoning: Where Do We Go From Here?', *British Journal of Psychology*, 92 (2001), 193–216; J. Evans, *Bias in Human Reasoning* (Hove: Erlbaum, 1989).

[26] Chater and Oaksford, 'Human Rationality'; J. Henrich, R. Boyd, S. Bowles, C. Camerer, E. Fehr, and H. Gintis (eds), *Foundations of Human Sociality* (Oxford: Oxford University Press, 2004).

[27] See Kahneman *et al.*, *Judgements under Uncertainty* for discussion of many of these tendencies.

[28] R. Nisbett and L. Ross, *Human Inference: Strategies and Shortcomings of Social Judgement* (Englewood Cliffs: Prentice Hall, 1980).

[29] Kahneman, 'Maps of Bounded Rationality'.

tend to reject offers unless they are within a 'fair' range, and in a few they reject even hyperfair offers of over 50 per cent of the pool.[30]

Complex behaviour can be automatically initiated and guided by social perception. People tend automatically and unconsciously to *assimilate* their behaviour to behaviour represented around them in words or images, or to the actual behaviour of others.[31] Robust *automatic, unconscious priming* effects range from copying of specific movements by others, such as rubbing one's foot as opposed to one's chin, or copying facial expressions, to assimilation of emotions, general traits, stereotypes, and goals. Whether the stimuli that prime these automatic responses are consciously perceived or not, people are *unaware of these automatic influences* on their behaviour, and tend to resist the idea that that they themselves are subject to such influences ('maybe others, but not me'). Nevertheless, the consequences can be significant. Participants exposed to words associated with hostility tended to deliver larger 'shocks' in Milgram type experiments;[32] participants exposed to rudeness primes tend to behave more rudely while those exposed to politeness primes tend to behave more politely. Participants primed by exposure to words associated with the elderly, such as 'grey', 'sentimental', 'bingo', showed slower responses and poorer memories than controls. Merely asking someone how likely they are to perform a task in the future increases the likelihood that they will, though without the appearance of manipulation.[33] According to ideomotor theories, perceiving actions or representations of action has an automatic default tendency to induce similar actions; people unconsciously absorb behavioural tendencies from their social environment.[34] There are thus pervasive non-classical social influences on behaviour, in which *perceptions are not decoupled from resulting behavioural tendencies.*

---

[30]   Henrich *et al., Foundations of Human Sociality.*

[31]   The 'chameleon effect' in T. L. Chartrand and J. A. Bargh, 'The Chameleon Effect', *Journal of Personality and Social Psychology*, 76 (1999), 893–910.

[32]   C. Carver, R. Ganellen, W. Froming, and W. Chambers, 'Modelling: An Analysis in Terms of Category Accessibility', *Journal of Experimental Social Psychology*, 19 (1983), 403–421.

[33]   B. K. Payne and B. D. Stewart, 'Automatic and Controlled Components of Social Cognition: A Process Dissociation Approach' in J. A. Bargh (ed.), *Social Psychology and the Unconscious: The Automaticity of Higher Mental Processes* (New York, NY: Psychology Press, 2007), 293–315.

[34]   See A. Dijksterhuis, 'Why We Are Social Animals: The High Road to Imitation as Social Glue' in S. Hurley and N. Chater (eds), *Perspectives on Imitation: From Neuroscience to Social Science* 2 (Cambridge, MA: MIT Press, 2005), 207–220; A. Dijksterhuis, T. L. Chartrand, and H. Aarts, 'Effects of Priming and Perception on Social Behaviour and Goal Pursuit' in Bargh (ed.), *Social Psychology and the Unconscious*, 51–131; M. J. Ferguson and J. A. Bargh, 'How Social Perception Can Automatically Influence Judgment', *Trends in Cognitive Science*, 8 (2004), 33–39; J. A. Bargh, 'Bypassing the Will: Towards Demystifying the Nonconscious Control of Social Behaviour' in R. R. Hassin, James S. Uleman, and J. A. Bargh (eds), *The New Unconscious* (New York: Oxford University Press, 2005), 37–58; J. A. Bargh and T. L. Chartrand, 'The Unbearable Automaticity of Being', *American Psychologist*, 54 (1999), 462–479; T. L. Chatrand and J. A. Bargh, 'Automatic Activation of Impression Formation and Memorization Goals: Nonconscious Goal Priming Reproduces Effects of Explicit Task Instructions', *Journal of Personality and Social Psychology*, 71 (1996), 464–478; J. A. Bargh, M. Chen, and L. Burrows, 'Automaticity of Social Behaviour: Direct Effects of Trait Construct and Stereotype Activation on Action', *Journal of Personality and Social Psychology*, 71 (1996), 230–244.

Such automatic behaviour is often instrumentally unrelated to the agent's goals: walking relatively slowly after elderly-priming is not an agent's means to a goal. However, it can be inhibited or overridden by the agent's goals: elderly-primed participants don't walk slowly when they have independent reason to hurry. Moreover, automatic assimilative behaviour may have general social affiliative functions even if it is not used by an agent as a means to a specific goal. Participants rate confederates who mimic their posture and movements as having better ideas, being better informed, and more likeable than confederates who avoid mimicking.[35] Since people are not aware of this influence, there is scope here for manipulation; people who have been mimicked have been shown to be more likely to be helpful, to give to charity, to be persuaded by the mimicker.

9.3.2.4 Cognitive anomalies in social contexts People's judgements of others show various biases, such as a tendency to explain events by attributing dispositions to people rather than in terms of situational influences and constraints; it takes extra effort to do the latter.[36] They also tend to project their own opinions and knowledge base onto others, generating *false consensus effects.*[37]

Cognitive processes are also influenced by social priming and context in non-classical ways. Subjects primed by tasks requiring them to think about 'smart' stereotypes, such as university lecturers, performed better on general knowledge tests than did controls, and subjects primed by tasks involving 'stupid' stereotypes, such as football hooligans, did worse than controls. Black-primed participants did worse and Asian-primed participants did better on maths tests than did controls; in Asian-American women, Asian-priming improved results on maths tests while female-priming worsened results. By contrast to such *assimilative* effects of *stereotype* exposure, exposure to *exemplars*, such as a picture of Einstein, tend to induce *contrastive* effects.[38] Cognitive processes can thus be influenced in different ways, of which people are quite unaware, by exposing them to stereotypes as opposed to exemplars of certain cognitive tendencies. More scope for manipulation.

Many cognitive anomalies are influenced by statements found in the socio-cultural environment, including those carried by various media. It seems natural to suppose, with Descartes and Mill, that comprehending a statement comes first and is neutral between accepting and rejecting it. But experiments show that people tend initially to accept a statement they comprehend even when explicitly told it is false. They must go through a further cognitive process of disbelieving it, so that it is not used in making

[35] Dijksterhuis *et al.*, 'Effects of Priming'.
[36] L. L. Martin, J. J. Seta, and R. A. Crealia, 'Assimilation and Contrast as a Function of People's Willingness and Ability to Expend Effort in Forming an Impression', *Journal of Personality and Social Psychology*, 59 (1990), 27–37.
[37] W. C. Sa and K. E. Stanovich, 'The Domain Specificity and Generality of Mental Contamination: Accuracy and Projection in Judgments of Mental Content', *British Journal of Psychology*, 92 (2001), 281–302.
[38] Dijksterhuis, 'Why We Are Social Animals'.

decisions. This further process can be blocked by cognitive load or time pressure.[39] That is, *people tend to believe what they understand as well as what they perceive initially, and to assess initial beliefs in a secondary process that is subject to interference.* Under cognitive load or time pressure, people tend to default to believing statements they have understood, even when they have been told these are false, and to acting on these beliefs. More scope for manipulation: exposing people to propositions while placing them under cognitive load or time pressure makes them less likely to proceed to the second 'disbelieving' stage. For example, subjects explicitly told that certain information in crime reports was false were nevertheless influenced by this information in recommending prison sentences when pressure on cognitive resources blocked the 'disbelieving' process. Moreover, content deriving from a non-credible source tends to remain in memory longer than does information about the credibility of the source.[40] Explicitly false information thus influences people's thought and behaviour even when they do not want it to. While people tend to seek evidence that confirms a hypothesis they are considering, rather than evidence that negates it, this tendency can be blocked by also exposing them to a positive contrary hypothesis (as opposed to the denial of the original hypothesis).[41] For example, people asked to consider whether someone is an extrovert tend be biased in favour of confirming evidence, but this bias can be countered by exposing them to the thought that the person in question is an introvert.[42] Again, framing can be important: though the denial of a statement ('it's false that he's an extrovert') may be practically equivalent to the assertion of a contrary claim ('he's an introvert'), they have different effects on cognition. Lessons are here not just for those who aim to manipulate behaviour but also for those who aim to counter such manipulation. Ideas are not neutral tools, but potent entities, whose mere expression alters the behavioural propensities of those exposed to them.

Human reasoning is subject to 'mental contamination' in the sense that people may themselves *want* their beliefs or decisions *not* to be influenced in certain ways, such as being influenced by a student's attractiveness in marking the student's work. Nevertheless, people are often unaware that they have in fact been influenced in the unwanted ways, or unable to avoid the unwanted influence, or both.[43] Many cognitive processes are unconscious and automatic, and people are often not very accurate at

---

[39] D. T. Gilbert, R. W. Tafarodi, and P. S. Malone, 'You Can't Not Believe Everything You Read', *Journal of Personality and Social Psychology*, 65 (1993), 221–233; D. T. Gilbert, 'How Mental Systems Believe', *American Psychologist*, 46 (1991), 107–119; 'The Assent of Man: Mental Representation and the Control of Belief' in D. M. Wegner and J. W. Pennebaker (eds), *Handbook of Mental Control* (Englewood Cliffs, NJ: Prentice Hall, 1993), 57–87.

[40] T. D. Wilson and N. Brekke, 'Mental Contamination and Mental Correction: Unwanted Influences on Judgements and Evaluations', *Psychological Bulletin*, 116 (1994), 117–142.

[41] Gilbert, 'How Mental Systems Believe'.

[42] C. G. Lord, M. R. Lepper, and E. Preston, 'Considering the Opposite: A Corrective Strategy for Social Judgment', *Journal of Personality and Social Psychology*, 47 (1984), 1231–1243.

[43] Wilson and Brekke, 'Mental Contamination'.

identifying the source or relative power of influences on their judgements. Mental contamination can accordingly be very difficult to detect or correct.

Moreover, admitting the possibility of mental contamination conflicts with the conception many people have of themselves.[44] Avowed anti-racists along with others display automatic, unconscious effects of the racial categories of faces. Implicit association tests (IATs) show that people are faster and more accurate when asked, for example, to associate black faces and guns or white faces and tools than they are when asked to associate black faces and tools or white faces and guns. IAT results are hard to 'fake', and often contrary to participant's values; many black subjects who'd like to show positive associations with black faces fail to do so. IAT results appear to bypass deliberate intentions and introspective access, and to reflect automatic processes. Implicit associations are more malleable through indirect influences than by deliberate effort; for example, racial bias in IAT is dramatically weaker when the test is administered by a black rather than a white scientist.[45]

Debiasing procedures are most likely to avoid mental contamination if they can make people aware of it, its direction and magnitude, and motivate them to control it. But 'more, better speech' may not overcome contaminating influences, which may be very difficult to control or erase even when recognized. Effort to suppress a stereotype can actually increase the frequency of stereotyped responses. People tend to underestimate their own susceptibility to bias (unsurprisingly, when biases are unconscious) and to overestimate their ability to control the unwanted influences of information, such as the influence of gender information on a hiring decision.[46] Avoiding exposure to the contaminating information may be a more effective method of avoiding mental contamination than trying to correct its cognitive influence (as double-blind control and anonymous assessment procedures recognize), though avoiding exposure to certain information of course carries further costs.[47] Moreover, people aren't very good at self-initiated exposure avoidance, which can seem unnecessary and disempowering; they may use exposure avoidance to protect against biases in hot emotional territory, but ignore powerful biases in cold factual territory.

Empirical work shows the descriptive and predictive inadequacy of a classical conception of rational agency. As a result, we may be sceptical about human rationality, but still retain a classical conception of rationality as a normative ideal that human beings generally fail to meet. However, another response rebounds from scepticism by revising our conception of rationality in ways that have normative as well as descriptive aspirations.

---

[44] R. A. Wilson, *Boundaries of the Mind* (Cambridge: Cambridge University Press, 2004).

[45] See B. A. Nosek, A. G. Greenwald, and M. R. Banaji, 'The Implicit Association Test at Age 7: A Methodological and Conceptual Review' in Bargh (ed.), *Social Psychology and the Unconscious*, 265–292.

[46] Wilson and Brekke, 'Mental Contamination'.

[47] Research on mental contamination, it has been suggested, is on a collision course with rights to freedom of expression; Wilson and Brekke, 'Mental Contamination', 136.

9.3.3 Situated conceptions of rationality

Situated conceptions of rationality are revisionist in that they relax the three distinctive features of classical rationality (internalism, domain-generality, and decoupling). They are allied to situated conceptions of cognition more generally. The latter hold that evolution, development, and learning structure mature cognitive capacities in ways that are not inherently domain-general and content-neutral, but rather depend on interactions of individuals with relevant natural and social environments, which 'scaffold' their internal processes. Situated rational processes can be partially outsourced to individual/environment interactions, in various efficient ways that exploit environmental structure rather than duplicating it internally.[48] Individual rationality is less dependent on classical internal processes, and more on processes of ecological attunement. As Clark puts it, rationality is reinvented as an active, distributed, environment-involving achievement.[49] This can be viewed as an advance in our understanding of normative rationality as well as in our descriptions of rationality. However, since normative rationality arguably requires capacities to respond flexibly and to generalize across novel situations, a challenge for such revisionist views is to show how situated cognition can support these capacities.

One revisionist reaction to the debunking of the classical conception is represented by Gigerenzer's slogan that 'simple heuristics make us smart' and accompanying critique of the unrealistically unsituated and 'demonic' character of classical rationality.[50] His 'ecological' rationality is more radical than merely 'bounded', cost-sensitive versions of classical rationality. Gigerenzer's work shows that, in the right environments, reliance on 'fast and frugal' heuristics produces *better* results than classical rationality does, by exploiting information structures in the environment as integral parts of the problem-solving process. Chater and Oaksford contrast the revisionist, empirically grounded 'rational analysis' approach with conceptions of rationality as inherently independent of specific environmental constraints.[51] Rational analysis explains what thought or action will succeed in an agent's environment in terms of the structure of that environment. Successful cognitive processes can use short cuts to approximate optimal responses in relevant specific environments. Tasks required by psychological experiments may not be natural ones in the environments to which cognition is adapted. For example, reasoning may be adapted to the uncertainties of everyday life rather than to the certainties of deductive logic; Chater and Oaksford explain supposedly illogical responses to Wason's selection task by reinterpreting them in probabilistic terms. A related revisionist view explains various empirical results in

---

[48] Wilson, *Boundaries of the Mind*.

[49] A. Clark, 'Reason, Robots, and the Extended Mind', *Mind and Language*, 16 (2001), 121–145, at 126.

[50] G. Gigerenzer, P. M. Todd, and the ABC Group (eds), *Simple Heuristics that Make Us Smart* (New York: Oxford University Press, 1999); G. Gigerenzer, *Adaptive Thinking: Rationality in the Real World* (Oxford: Oxford University Press, 2000).

[51] Chater and Oaksford, 'Human Rationality'.

terms of 'decision by sampling', in which value, probability, and many other magnitudes associated with classical processes are not internally represented; rather, items are sampled from memory and compared to targets, in a process that adaptively reflects environmental structure.[52]

Return to the question of how situated rationality can support flexibility and generalization across different environments, despite its domain-specific basis. One type of answer views rationality as emerging from the relations among layer upon layer of domain-specific processes adapted by evolution, development, and/or learning to specific environments, 'turning each other on and off at...ecologically appropriate moments'.[53] Sperber describes the human mind as teeming with domain-specific processes to which inputs may be simultaneously available but which must compete for energetic resources.[54] As a result, some flexible, context-sensitive, efficient energy allocation procedure is needed to select inputs for processing according to their relevance (information gain less processing cost). Sperber suggests that such selection need not itself be the result of rational processes, but may emerge from non-rational physiological dynamics of brain activation; rational processes may be enabled partly by the way the mind is physically embodied.

Another prevalent type of answer distinguishes two levels of rational processing.[55] A 'lower' level has been characterized as: unintentional, unconscious, automatic, uncontrolled, associative, implicit, efficient, fast, easy, reliant on rough-and-ready heuristics rather than logic, adapted to specific domains, lacking in critical flexibility, subject to priming, environmentally driven, tending to link perception fairly directly to action, resistant to interference from concurrent processes. A 'higher' level, by contrast, has some of the features of classical rationality: it's intentional, deliberate, flexible, conscious, controlled, explicit, costly in terms of cognitive and attentional resources, slow, effortful, analytical and critical, tending to decouple perception from action, domain-general, subject to interference from other cognitive processes and to disruption by time pressure or cognitive load. Different dual process accounts emphasize different elements of this broad contrast. To illustrate: a policeman may intend not to show a bias against black suspects at one level, yet automatically respond to a black suspect who is reaching for his ID by shooting him, influenced by racial stereotypes to expect that the suspect is pulling a gun. People shown a white or a black face just before

---

[52] N. Stewart, N. Chater, and G. D. A. Brown, 'Decision by Sampling', *Cognitive Psychology*, 53 (2006), 1–26.

[53] Clark, 'Reason, Robots, and the Extended Mind', 127.

[54] D. Sperber, 'Modularity and Relevance: How Can a Massively Modular Mind be Flexible and Context-Sensitive?' in P. Carruthers, S. Laurence, and S. Stich (eds), *The Innate Mind: Structure and Content* (New York: Oxford University Press, 2005), 53–68.

[55] Kahneman, 'Maps of Bounded Rationality'; J. Evans and D. Over, *Rationality and Reasoning* (Hove: Psychology Press, 1996); Chater and Oaksford, 'Human Rationality'; R. M. Sapolsky, 'The Frontal Cortex and the Criminal Justice System', *Philosophical Transactions of the Royal Society B*, Biological Sciences, Special Issue on Law and the Brain, 359 (2004), 1787–1796; R. R. Hassin, J. S. Uleman, and J. A. Bargh (eds), *The New Unconscious* (New York: Oxford University Press, 2005).

identifying a picture as one of a gun or a tool show an unconscious tendency to mistakenly identify tools as guns when they are preceded by a black face, which increases with time pressure.

Several points about two-level views are worth noting:

- The view that there is a twofold distinction has itself been criticized as oversimple, on the grounds that the various elements of each level can dissociate. It may be more accurate to think in terms of clusters of overlapping features that come in degrees.[56]
- A great deal of human behaviour appears to be driven by processes with lower level features. Process dissociation methods allow that behaviour often results from a combination of automatic and controlled processes, and estimates the contribution made by each.[57] Overall, the capacity of the higher level to correct the output of the lower level appears more limited than a classical conception of rationality would suggest.
- In general, putting people under time pressure, cognitive load, or distraction tends to release lower level automatic processes from higher level control. The most effective techniques for bringing lower processes under the control of higher processes are not obvious; evidence rather than intuition is needed here. Techniques we may find intuitive may be ineffective or worse. For example, exhortation to avoid racial stereotyping can actually be counterproductive and enhance the accessibility of racial stereotypes;[58] asking people who are under a cognitive load to avoid sexist responses leads to more such responses.[59] By contrast, concrete action plans that link a specific environmental cue to a cognitive response do tend to overcome stereotyped associations (e.g. adopting the explicit rule 'whenever I see a black face, I'll think "safe" ').[60] But some intuitions turn out to be right: as we'd expect, people tend to exert more cognitive effort when their individual responses are identified rather than when they are submerged in the responses of a group.[61]

9.3.3.1 Situated rationality in social environments While domain-specific heuristics are generally adaptive, they may reach systematic limits in social environments. These are

---

[56] A. Moors and J. De Houwer, 'What is Automaticity? An Analysis of Its Component Features and Their Interrelations' in Bargh (ed.), *Social Psychology and the Unconscious*, 11–50.

[57] L. L. Jacoby, 'A Process Dissociation Framework: Separating Automatic from Intentional Uses of Memory', *Journal of Memory and Language*, 30 (1991), 513–541; Payne and Stewart, 'Automatic and Controlled Components'.

[58] Payne and Stewart, 'Automatic and Controlled Components'.

[59] Wilson and Brekke, 'Mental Contamination'.

[60] Payne and Stewart, 'Automatic and Controlled Components'. See also P. M. Gollwitzer *et al.*, 'The Control of the Unwanted' in R. R. Hassin *et al.* (eds), *The New Unconscious*, 485–515, at 495–496 on the use of implementation intentions to exploit automatic processes in intended ways, including to avoid prejudicial gender stereotyping.

[61] Martin *et al.*, 'Assimilation and Contrast'.

particularly demanding for several reasons. Natural environments can be relied on to go on doing more or less what they do, without changing systematically so as to get the better of an agent; but social environments cannot. In social environments, the results of each agent's action can depend on what other agents do, generating problems of mutual prediction, coordination, cooperation, and free-riding. Moreover, in social environments agents can benefit by deception and by manipulation of the information available to other agents and of their behaviour. My survey above of evidence against classical rationality noted how various opportunities for manipulation arise, especially as a result of lower level processes. The outsourcing of processes to social environments is thus fraught with danger. According to the 'Machiavellian intelligence hypothesis', the informational challenges of social life with its potential for deception and manipulation are what drive the evolution of advanced cognitive capacities.[62] Sterelny argues that the demands social life makes on cognition are unlikely to be met by 'fast and frugal' heuristics that exploit relatively transparent information structures in the environment.[63]

Perhaps the capacity for more costly, higher level processes postulated in two-level views, and some features of classical rationality, arise in response to these demands. Domain-general processes that decouple perception from action can function flexibly to defend against social manipulation. Sterelny supports Sperber's suggestion that logic and explicit, formal, meta-representative reasoning capacities emerge in the course of an informational arms race in social life: deceptive, social manipulation of information is countered by the use of norms of logic and rationality to check representations coming from others, which is in turn countered by displaying the rational credentials of representations one provides to others.[64] Domain-generality and decoupling may be overlaid by evolution on the situated foundations of rationality in response to essentially social pressures to control information: to borrow Sperber's phrase, as a means of filtering communications and of penetrating the filters of others. If so, note that these features of classical rationality have a public origin, orientation, and function.

Moreover, higher level rational processes that arise in response to the limits of domain-specific heuristics in social environments can still be outsourced in part, though now culturally, relying on public representations and meanings to provide intelligible goals and structure rational processes.[65] Domain-generality, decoupling, and other features of higher level rationality don't require that rational processes be wholly internal to the individual. So higher-level situated rationality does not reinvent classical rationality. Rather, it envisages that we create, wittingly or unwittingly, a cultural ecology of rationality that enables us, among other things, better to negotiate the informational dangers of social life.

---

[62] R. Byrne and A. Whiten, *Machiavellian Intelligence* (Oxford: Oxford University Press, 1988).

[63] K. Sterelny, *Thought in a Hostile World* (Oxford: Blackwell, 2003).

[64] K. Sterelny, 'Folk Logic and Animal Rationality' in Hurley and Nudds (eds), *Rational Animals?*, 293–312. D. Sperber, 'Metarepresentations in an Evolutionary Perspective' in D. Sperber (ed.), *Metarepresentations: A Multidisciplinary Perspective* (Oxford: Oxford University Press, 2000), 117–137.

[65] Clark, 'Reason, Robots, and the Extended Mind'.

Clark is a revisionist about rationality who doubts that human rationality can be explained as emerging incrementally from biological cognition by small evolutionary tweaks and innovations.[66] Rather, it depends on our interactions with the specifically cultural, linguistic, and technological environments that we create. These include symbolic representations that support context-free manipulation and formal, domain-general reasoning. Human brains and bodies mediate complex dynamic processes of iterated loops through such 'designer environments'; rational processes are distributed across brain, body, and cultural environments, as we learn to manipulate clunky symbols to solve problems, including problems about how to make less clunky, more powerful thinking tools. Naked biological cognition complements and dovetails with the scaffolding and props provided by our cultural environments, in a rationally enabling division of cognitive labour. In Clark's view, we should give up the idea of a 'core cognitive agent' surrounded by mere support systems; culture is not merely wrapped around biological human nature, but is as much a determiner as a product of it, in a bootstrapping process. Rationality is as much a public achievement as a private virtue of individuals. Our minds have adapted to our environments, but we have also created environments that further enable our minds beyond their biological limits by partly outsourcing rational processes.

I've explained the public ecology of features of higher level rationality: the ways they function in and exploit social and cultural forms of life. However, lower level rational processes also have a public ecology: recall that we tend to assimilate automatically traits, behaviour, and goals perceived or represented in our social environments, tend to believe statements that we comprehend, even from discredited sources, and so on. These tendencies are among those that open us to manipulation. Higher level rationality does not eliminate these lower level processes, and has only limited success in moderating them. Such lower level social-ecological processes arguably define many of the alternative actions, goals, and beliefs on which higher level rationality operates, when it does.[67]

Thus, while classical rationality was supposed to be internal to individuals, situated rationality is enabled by an agent's interactions with a public ecology, at both higher and lower levels. An arms race between manipulation and counter-manipulation in social environments leads from lower level rationality to a limited capacity, scaffolded by public representations, for higher level rationality.

9.4 From the public ecology of rationality to the public ecology of responsibility

Return to the generic intuitive conception of rational agency presupposed by responsibility sketched above in section 9.2: that of an agent who acts on a range of often

---

[66] Clark, 'Reason, Robots, and the Extended Mind'.

[67] Though of course basic biological needs also play an essential role; see and cf. Lessig, 'The Regulation of Social Meaning', on the way social meanings define available actions and induce concordant actions.

conflicting publicly intelligible goals, in a way that's sensitive to information about the instrumentally best means for achieving those goals, and with a capacity to resolve conflicts among those goals coherently and to act on her resolutions, despite some weakness of will. This generic conception of rational agency is transformed when we move from classical to situated rationality. The situated view of rationality, unlike the classical view, understands this generic conception of rational agency as deriving from and enabled by the way an agent interacts with social environments and public representations.

Moreover, the transformation also applies to responsibility, understood as a reason-responsive way of acting, which is accepted by the agent as a way of acting on her own reasons. If rationality is enabled by interactions with a public ecology, and responsibility depends on rationality, then responsibility is also enabled by interactions with a public ecology. Responsibility is likewise as much a public achievement as a private feature of individual agents or their actions.

Here's how the contrast plays out. Classical rationality, and hence responsibility in a corresponding sense, don't outsource to a public ecology; they are primarily private virtues of individuals. The constraints that determine which goals count as publicly intelligible are left undefined, and the internal processes, which are domain-general and which decouple perception from action at the individual level, enable instrumental efficiency and the capacity for coherent resolution of conflicts among reasons, thus enabling ways of acting that are reason-responsive and that are accepted by the agent as ways of acting on her own reasons. The rationality and responsibility of an action are explained by facts about the individual agent that are independent of the agent's social environment.

By contrast, situated rationality, and hence responsibility in a corresponding sense, do outsource to a public ecology; they are as much public achievements as private features of individual agents or their actions. In lower level interactions with a public ecology, an agent automatically assimilates traits, behaviour patterns, goals, meanings, and beliefs from her social environment. These processes along with internal processes enable action on publicly intelligible goals and ways of acting that count as reason-responsive. But they also render an agent susceptible to social manipulation of the ways she acts, so that they aren't in fact ways of acting she accepts as ways of acting on her own reasons. Lower level interactions with a public ecology can thus both enable or disable responsibility. Countering manipulation serves responsibility, but it isn't a purely individual achievement either. An agent's higher level interactions with a public ecology of shared culture, representations, and logic, along with internal processes, make available domain-general reasoning that decouples perception from action, enabling greater instrumental efficiency and a capacity for coherent resolution of conflicts among reasons. Higher level rationality also functions to counter social manipulation of the ways an agent acts, so that they can be ways she accepts as ways of acting on her own reasons; hence it contributes to enabling responsibility. The rationality and responsibility of an action are explained in ways that involve an agent's interactions with her social environment. Rationality and responsibility have public origins, functions, and enabling ecology.

I've just explained in general terms how a reason-responsiveness conception of responsibility is transformed by a shift from classical to situated rationality. Note as well the specific affinity between situated rationality and a reason-responsiveness view of responsibility: both are concerned with countering manipulation. Responsibility requires that an agent acts in a reason-responsive way *that he accepts as a way of acting on his own reasons*. An agent whose lower level rationality is manipulated by other agents in ways he would reject (were he aware of them) does not meet this condition for responsibility, even if his action responds to publicly intelligible reasons. Recall some of the many openings for such manipulation we found in surveying the evidence against classical rationality above. People are usually unaware of the influence on their choices of the framing of decisions, the perceived status quo, the ways certainty, uncertainty, and risk are described. They are unaware of chameleon effects and the way their cognitive processes are influenced by exposure to stereotypes as opposed to exemplars of certain cognitive tendencies. They are unaware of the way cognitive load or time pressure tends to induce uncritical acceptance of propositions they've been exposed to, even when these have been explicitly negated, or of the difference in influence between denying a proposition and asserting a contrary proposition. They are unaware of the influence of mimicry: that mimickers are thought to have better ideas, be better informed and more likeable, and those mimicked are more likely to be persuaded, give money, etc. People don't realize that their cognition and action are 'contaminated' in these ways. If they were to become aware of such lower level influences, would they find them acceptable? People tend to resist the evidence that they are subject to such influences; their reactions provide opportunities for responsibility-undermining manipulation. In particular, if such lower level influences are manipulated covertly by others for their own benefit, in ways the agent does not and would not accept, they undermine his responsibility. The public ecology of higher level rationality, by countering social manipulation, is part of what makes responsible action possible. However, an informed agent could accept the use of lower level influences as a way of better enabling him to act on his own reasons. If so, the use of lower level influences wouldn't count as responsibility-undermining manipulation, but rather as scaffolding that enables rational and responsible action. So the public ecology of lower level influences per se doesn't undermine responsibility: it depends on the way such influences are used and whether their use is acceptable to agents. Their covert, manipulative use to benefit other specific agents is not acceptable, but their open use to enable agents to act on their own reasons may well be.

The next step in the argument is to note that 'man' is not just a rational and social animal but a political animal: political arrangements no less than language, logic, and culture, are part of the public ecology we create, by means of which we protect ourselves against the dangers and manipulations of social life, and that enable rationality and responsibility. Politics is not—any more than language or culture—wrapped around a core biological human nature with the features of classical rationality and responsibility in a corresponding sense. The public ecology of rationality and responsibility includes politics.[68]

We've seen that the public ecology of responsibility can both undermine and support responsibility. If the public ecology of responsibility includes politics, how should government be compared with other agents in the social environment in this respect? Is government inherently more likely to undermine responsibility than, say, corporate agents? No. Manipulative marketing has its home in the corporate sector, though it has infiltrated political advertising also; and corporate power and influence are pervasive in modern life. If responsibility needs protection against manipulation, manipulation by corporate agents is just as relevant as manipulation by government. Can government support responsibility by countering manipulation, including corporate manipulation? Yes. Traditional liberalism tends to view government as the primary source of interference with responsible action by private individuals. Ecological liberalism should instead view government as having a counter-manipulative and positive role in the public ecology of responsibility.[69]

9.5 The priority of private responsibility revisited

In the light of this transformation in the understanding of rationality and responsibility, let's return finally to examine the principles of traditional liberalism that we started with, which express the priority of private responsibility.

The anti-paternalism principle says that government should avoid regulating self-regarding action for which its agent is responsible, even if it is harmful to the agent—so long as it is not harmful to third parties. It's long been recognized by liberals that bigotry can make it difficult to argue that an action is self-regarding. Bigoted people are often offended by the knowledge that other people are doing things in private. Are bigots thus harmed? Mill claimed that there is 'no parity' between someone's feelings about his own opinions or conduct and the feelings of someone, such as a religious bigot, who may be offended by them.[70] More recently, Sen has argued that not all preferences are equal, and that welfarism should be limited so that preferences motivated by bigotry or illiberal attitudes, even when unanimous, are politically discounted.[71]

However, the evidence surveyed above provides a more fundamental challenge to the anti-paternalism principle's protection of actions that harm only their agent, which is not avoided by making an exception for offence to bigots. For example, we've seen

---

[68] Elements of a communitarian view of the self as situated (M. Sandel, *Liberalism and the Limits of Justice* (Cambridge, MA: Cambridge University Press, 1982)) are recapitulated naturalistically by an empirically based conception of rationality as situated.

[69] See also O. Fiss, *The Irony of Free Speech* (Cambridge, MA: Harvard University Press, 1998) on government as the friend rather than the enemy of freedom of speech.

[70] Mill, *On Liberty*, 93.

[71] A. K. Sen, *Choice, Welfare, and Measurement* (Oxford: Blackwell, 1982).

that one agent's action, observed by or represented to other agents, has an automatic, unconscious tendency to prime similar goals, traits, and behaviours in those other agents. Suppose action A is responsible, though harmful to its agent, but tends automatically to prime similar behaviours B, C, D, etc. by those exposed to action A, which is harmful to them. Not all exposed agents will act similarly, of course; the effect is statistical, but nevertheless robust and significant. The well-documented phenomenon of suicide contagion is representative, and is arguably the tip of the iceberg that lends itself to proof. It looks as if A is not thus self-regarding, but results in harm to others; making an exception for offence to bigots doesn't avoid this result. Can it be argued that B, C, and D are themselves responsible actions, despite being influenced by exposure to A, so that they also fall under the anti-paternalism principle? They may be ways of responding to publicly intelligible reasons, even if harmful to their agents. But it is unlikely that these ways of responding are accepted by the agents of B, C, and D as ways of responding to their own reasons. Agents are largely unaware of such automatic social priming influences, and tend strongly to resist the idea that such influences apply to their own actions. In such cases, it's not plausible to regard B, C, and D as fully responsible actions protected by the anti-paternalism principle. Automatic social priming effects raise a fundamental and widespread challenge to the distinction between self-regarding and other-regarding action, except in cases where the former is unobserved and unrepresented. If this is hard to accept, it is because such effects are unintuitive and challenge what we think we know about ourselves; they are alien to the folk wisdom that traditional liberalism incorporates. But given their pervasiveness, I doubt that it is fruitful to try to patch up the anti-paternalism principle with more exceptions to handle this kind of problem.

The principle of proximal agency says that government should try to avoid regulating actions that harm third parties only indirectly, via their influence on the responsible actions of second parties, but should instead directly regulate the latter. An expression of this is found in a recent US Supreme Court case, *Ashworth v. Free Speech Coalition*, in which the Supreme Court struck down a law regulating child pornography because it would have applied even to virtual child pornography, created using computer graphics rather than real children.[72] Using real children to create child pornography is unacceptable because directly harmful to those children. But if using computer graphics to create child pornography does harm children, the court reasoned, it would do so only indirectly, via the actions of those exposed to the material and influenced by it to harm children directly. The agents of these latter actions are responsible for this harm, not the creators of virtual child pornography. The proximal acts of directly harming children should therefore be regulated rather than the actions of creating virtual child pornography. The issue of whether any harm does flow to children from acts of creating virtual child pornography is thus pre-empted by the

---

[72] *Ashcroft v. Free Speech Coalition* 122 S.Ct. 1389 (2002).

intervening acts;[73] the Court declines to address it. Why are the child-harming acts of those exposed to such material regarded as responsible for the harm, even if they are influenced by such material? Because any such influence would flow via the content of the 'speech', i.e. the pornography, and the hearers of speech are regarded as responsible for their responses to the content of speech, not the speakers. Under First Amendment freedom of speech jurisprudence, the physical qualities of speech may be regulated— loud talking in libraries, shouting where there is danger of avalanche—but its content should not be. Speakers are not their hearers' keepers; hearers are responsible for their own responses to speech and any harms they cause. Responsibility is fully allocated to the proximal acts of the individual agent, and not distributed across the agent and the cultural environment with which he interacts.

The Court's traditional liberal perspective fails to recognize that the content of speech has many automatic influences on agents of which they are unaware and which they would not accept as ways of acting on their own reasons. In acting under such influences, they are therefore not fully responsible for their actions, despite the fact that their actions are responding to the content of speech. Some liberals do recognize that there can be such influences. Scanlon writes that 'Expression is a bad thing if it influences us in ways that are unrelated to relevant reasons, or in ways that bypass our ability to consider those reasons'.[74] But automatic lower level influences are widespread, not limited exceptions to the norm. Their prevalence makes the challenge to the principle of proximal agency fundamental. Scanlon also writes: 'If we saw ourselves as helplessly absorbing as a belief every proposition we heard expressed, then our views of freedom of expression would be quite different from what they are.'[75] But as we've seen, under conditions of cognitive load or time pressure (which are all too common even when not deliberately imposed) we do tend automatically to believe propositions we understand, even when we have been explicitly told that they are false.[76] As a result, we can be influenced to act in ways that harm others, such as imposing more severe punishments. Again, the influence is automatic and uncon-scious, and falling under it is unlikely to be acceptable to agents as a way of acting on their own reasons. If not, the proximal agent is not fully responsible.

Return to the anti-paternalism principle, where related concerns arise about respon-sibility for self-harming actions. Consider advertising that influences people to spend money on fatty or sugary food that is harmful to themselves, using techniques that effectively manipulate automatic, unconscious, lower level influences on beliefs and

---

[73] See S. Hurley, 'Bypassing Conscious Control: Media Violence, Imitation, and Freedom of Speech' in S. Pockett, W. Banks, and S. Gallagher (eds), *Does Consciousness Cause Behaviour?* (Cambridge, MA: MIT Press, 2006), 301–337.

[74] T. M. Scanlon, 'Freedom of Expression and Categories of Expression', *University of Pittsburgh Law Review*, 40 (1979), 519–550, at 525.

[75] Scanlon, 'Freedom of Expression', 524–525.

[76] Gilbert, 'How Mental Systems Believe'; 'The Assent of Man'; Gilbert *et al.*, 'You Can't Not Believe Everything You Read'.

action. It's unlikely that people want to be influenced in these ways, or accept them as ways of acting on their own reasons.

Political advertising in election campaigns can influence the actions of voters in ways that can potentially harm both self and others. Recall Kahneman and Tversky's examples, cited above, of how lobbyists and advisors can influence political decisions, without distorting or suppressing information, merely by the framing of outcomes and contingencies; exposure to negations of propositions rather than to contrary propositions, or to stereotypes rather than to exemplars of traits, could similarly influence political decisions. Again, making decisions under such influences is unlikely to be accepted by voters as a way of acting on their own reasons, at least when these influences are deliberately manipulated to serve another's goals.

The transformation in our understanding of rationality and responsibility that I described above thus challenges the anti-paternalism principle and the principle of proximal agency of traditional liberalism. The proper role of government in influencing citizens' behaviour cannot be limited by private responsibility conceived as independent of the public domain. I doubt that patching these principles up with exceptions can solve the problem; they assume the priority of private responsibility and were not cut out to function within a public ecology of responsibility. The challenges are fundamental and require some basic rethinking about the proper role of government in influencing citizens' behaviour within a public ecology of responsibility.

9.6 Towards an ecological liberalism

This chapter has laid the groundwork for addressing the role of government in ecological liberalism, by laying out the way work in cognitive science challenges the priority of private responsibility in traditional liberalism. Ecological liberalism recognizes the public, and political, ecology of responsibility; agents' interactions with their social, cultural, and political environments are part of what makes responsibility possible. Further work is needed to characterize the appropriate roles of government in influencing citizens' behaviour within a public ecology of responsibility. But I suggest that two general principles should inform an ecologically liberal conception of the proper role of government.

The anti-manipulation principle. Government should regulate and counter manipulative influences on citizens' beliefs and behaviour, especially but not only when these lead to harm, either to self or others. When an agent acts under manipulation, he unwittingly serves the goals of the manipulator, whether or not they coincide with his own. Some ways of acting are not acceptable to their agents as ways of acting on their own reasons; action under manipulation is one of them, even when agents don't realize they are in fact being manipulated. The public ecology of responsibility includes many manipulative influences, some of which exploit automatic lower level rational processes of which agents are unaware: in advertising, entertainment, political campaigns, hiring and promotion practices, etc. These can be countered by a combination of: (a) making people aware that they are subject to a variety of automatic influences that provide openings for manipulation, with examples;[77] (b) providing effective information about counter-manipulative techniques, including ways of selectively countering lower level automatic processes and ways of strengthening higher level critical processes; (c) providing guidelines for non-manipulative practices in various spheres, in particular in advertising and in election campaigns; and (d) regulating manipulative practices, especially where these lead to harm. These are all appropriate, responsibility-enabling roles for government in influencing the behaviour of citizens for the public good.

The democratic public scaffolding principle. As well as countering manipulation within the public ecology of responsibility, government has a positive role in the design and creation of a better public ecology, by contributing to the democratic public scaffolding of rationality and responsibility.

This role can be readily understood in relation to higher level rationality. Earlier I described how cultural interactions scaffold higher level rational processes and contribute to enabling responsibility. Government should make such cultural resources as widely available as possible and encourage citizens to take them up, for example by providing incentives and support for higher education. Election campaigns should be structured and regulated in ways that support the exercise of higher level, critical rationality—demanding as it is of resources of attention, time, and effort—and that counter framing effects, cognitive load and time pressure effects, and so on.

A better public ecology doesn't just scaffold higher level rationality. Lower level influences can't be eliminated entirely; they should be pruned and cultivated so as to influence behaviour non-manipulatively for the public good.

On the pruning of lower level influences: even when an agent is not acting under manipulation, he may be influenced in ways he doesn't accept and would prefer to avoid; for example, by automatic, unconscious influences that bias hiring decisions. Moreover, such influences may run contrary to democratically decided public policy. Government has an important role in designing and regulating practices to counter such influences, even when they are not manipulative.

What about the cultivation of lower level influences? If an agent does or would accept an influence on his action as a way of better enabling him to act on his own reasons, it doesn't count as a manipulative influence. Perhaps it is dangerous to make assumptions about what influences agents *would* accept were they aware of them . . . so

---

[77] A. Dijksterhuis, H. Aarts, and P. K. Smith discuss the automatic influences of subliminally (unconsciously) perceived stimuli on attitudes, consumer behaviour, and health. Stimuli we perceive consciously can elicit control strategies that will not be available when stimuli are perceived subliminally. 'What is critical in such cases is that people are aware of how a stimulus may influence their judgments or behaviour. If people are not aware of such an influence, or if people do not know how a stimulus might influence them, these control processes are not used' ('The Power of the Subliminal: On Subliminal Persuasion and Other Potential Applications' in Hassin *et al.* (eds), *The New Unconscious*, 77–106, at 87).

make them aware of them! Informed agents can accept and use lower level rational influences in ways of acting on their own reasons, deliberately delegating control to handy automatic processes in ways that further their goals. For example, someone who doesn't wish to be influenced by gender or racial stereotypes and is discouraged to learn that deliberate efforts to suppress stereotypes can be counterproductive, may welcome the knowledge that concrete action plans linking a specific environmental cue to a cognitive response do tend to overcome stereotyped associations—and be happy to be influenced in this way. Someone who wishes to eat healthy food can pursue this goal more efficiently by forming implementation intentions that delegate control to environmental cues with automatic influences on his behaviour.[78] Members of various ethnic groups who aim to perform well on maths exams may find priming by Asian stereotypes acceptable as a way of enhancing their performance.

Can it be appropriate for government itself to use lower level influences on behaviour to reduce democratically recognized public harms, such as crime, poverty, and illness? Yes, but the trick here is for government to avoid using such influences manipulatively: their use should be overt, and be accepted by citizens through democratic procedures as a way of better enabling them to act on their own, shared reasons. For example, government can properly influence behaviour, in support of democratically endorsed public goals, in ways that take into account that people tend to weigh losses more heavily than gains,[79] that they tend to seek confirming rather than disconfirming evidence, that just asking people how likely they are to act in a certain way increases the likelihood that they will. But in all such cases, the acceptable use of lower level influences by government should meet certain conditions: the decision to use a lower level influence should be made democratically and should be in the service of democratically endorsed public goals, and actual use of a lower level influence should be accompanied by information describing the influence and how it increases the likelihood of certain behaviour that serves the public good. It is especially *improper* for an incumbent government, or any other party to an election campaign, to use lower level influences covertly to influence votes.[80] Such use does not satisfy the above conditions, but is manipulative and undemocratic.

If the priority of private responsibility is a myth and politics cannot help but contribute to the public ecology of responsibility, then better it does so wittingly rather than unwittingly. If liberalism and responsibility go hand in hand, and our understanding of responsibility needs naturalistic revision, then so does our under-

---

[78] Gollwitzer et al., 'The Control of the Unwanted', 487.

[79] Halpern and Bates, *Personal Responsibility*, explain that health messages can be more effective when worded in terms of loss rather than gain (39), that successful programmes that pay young people while they stay in school may work because losing money in your pocket is more painful than gaining money is pleasurable (48, 50), that opt-out pension contribution schemes increased savings because they took contributions only out of pay rises so avoided loss aversion (61).

[80] See Dijksterhuis et al., 'The Power of the Subliminal', 88, on the use of such techniques by the 2000 Bush campaign.

standing of liberalism. We should not try to shore up a traditional liberalism based on the priority of private responsibility against the winds of empirically based change in our understanding of human minds. This nostalgic strategy does not provide much guidance to hopes for a liberal future, as the cognitive sciences continue to advance. A progressive social liberalism should serve the public good within the public ecology of responsibility in ways that counter manipulation and support the rationality and responsibility of citizens. Such an ecological conception of liberalism is not a way of abandoning liberalism, but a way of revitalizing and strengthening it for the future.

10

The Apparent Asymmetry of Responsibility[1]

Avner de-Shalit and Jonathan Wolff

10.1 Introduction

The focus of our discussion in this chapter is the question of whether political institutions should be designed so that individuals reap the benefits of their good choices and suffer the costs of their poor choices. Answers to this question, it seems, will tend to fall into two camps, although there may be more of a continuum rather than a sharp dichotomy. At one extreme, which we can call 'the full responsibility view', individuals should pay the full social costs and receive the full social benefits of their freely made choices. At the other end—'the no responsibility view'—they should neither receive benefits nor pay the costs of their choices. On this latter view the goods one should enjoy in life have no relation to one's responsibility for creating those goods or generating one's access to them. In between full and no responsibility, there is, of course, a range of possible views.

What, then, is the correct view? Here we wish to discuss and defend what might seem a rather strange position. On the one hand, those who have made choices that turn out well should at least be allowed some significant share in the benefits to which they have contributed. On the other hand, those who have made choices that turn out badly should, at least in many cases, not have to bear the full, or even a significant share of the costs of their choices. In other words, we find ourselves reasonably sympathetic to a positive demand for responsibility (PDR), but in contrast far less sympathetic to a negative demand for responsibility (NDR). Such a combination of positions, we feel, represents a humane and tolerant perspective on responsibility, and one we feel will

[1] This chapter was presented at the Distributive Justice and Responsibility Workshop at Glasgow in January 2008. We thank the participants for their extremely helpful comments, many of which are individually acknowledged below. We would also like to thank Zofia Stemplowska and Carl Knight for their exceptionally valuable written comments, which have led to a number of changes, and also two anonymous referees for their helpful remarks.

be fairly widely shared. It is what we understand by the title phrase of this chapter, the 'asymmetry of responsibility'. What we can call 'the weak asymmetry thesis' is that people should be rewarded for their good choices to a greater extent than they should be penalised for their bad ones. This is, of course, very vague, and could be interpreted in a number of ways. Our task in this chapter is to come to see whether some such position is defensible.

It may fairly be asked what we mean by the 'full costs' of someone's choices. Any society has a system of laws and conventions in place, and on one understanding the 'full costs' are simply whatever the laws and conventions demand. It would be odd, on this understanding, to say anything other than that, except in very unusual cases, everyone should pay the full costs of their choices. Therefore the weak asymmetry thesis is not a thesis about the implementation of existing law and conventions, but rather offers to provide a critical perspective on such conventions. But this, in turn, may seem problematic, for it appears to assume something rather implausible: that there is some 'natural' sense in which choices have costs or benefits which are not in some way influenced by, or mediated through, social conventions. So it seems that the notion of not requiring people to pay the full costs of their choices is in difficulties: if full cost is socially determined, then people should pay the full costs; if it is not socially determined it is very unclear what it is.[2]

Given that the asymmetry we have in mind concerns how laws and conventions should be designed, rather than how they should be enforced, another way of putting the weak asymmetry thesis is to say that society should be arranged in such a way as to reward success but to insulate, in some greater degree, people from failure. While we accept that there are no 'natural' consequences of actions, we also feel it is easy to understand the idea that some societies make people pay more of the costs of their choices than others. Social security, for example, shields some people from the costs of their choices, and, politically, is both attacked and defended on this basis. In effect, to argue that an individual should not pay the full costs of their choices is to say that other members of society should share in the burden. The weak asymmetry thesis, therefore, can be put in the following terms: there are more, or better, reasons for all members of society to share in the costs of an individual's choices that turn out badly than there are reasons to share in the benefits of choices that turn out well. Although in a full treatment we would need to make the idea of the costs of one's choices more precise, for present purposes it will serve to rest with an intuitive understanding.

While the weak asymmetry thesis remains vague, it can easily be seen that there are several different ways in which it could be implemented. We will explain three: asymmetries of scale, cap, and scope.

Asymmetry of scale recommends a rule allowing those who do well to keep a higher proportion of the benefits they create than the proportion of the losses that have to be

---

[2] We owe this objection to Martin O'Neill.

met by those who create burdens. For example, it would allow those who earn a lot to keep more of their pre-tax gains than it requires those who do badly to pay of their pre-tax losses. Losses, therefore, would be assessed on a different scale to profits. Consider a business tax with both positive and negative rates. Businesses could, for example, pay 25 per cent tax on their net profit, but receive a 50 per cent rebate for their net losses.

'Capping' is a more familiar notion, in which there is an absolute limit to how much any individual is required to lose, but no limit to how much they could gain. An example is bankruptcy laws, where losses are capped, albeit with certain punitive conditions. There is no counterpart to bankruptcy on the positive side, where gains above a level are confiscated, or, we could put it, taxed at 100 per cent. Of course there are anomalous situations in which individuals can face a marginal tax rate of 100 per cent or even higher,[3] but these are generally the unintended consequence of the interaction between different rules, rather than any sort of deliberate policy.

Asymmetries of scope are somewhat different. For an example, consider the distinction between more and less prudent choices, albeit all of which involve some level of risk. While it may be that society is happy to allow those who make either prudent or imprudent choices that turn out well to keep all of the benefit, at the same time it could decide to shelter people against bearing the cost of prudent choices that turn out badly. So, for example, those who invest in building societies, or in low-risk investment schemes, but find that the fund collapses, will get a much more sympathetic hearing from government than those who have invested in schemes that looked implausible from the start to anyone who took care. On such a view, then, the asymmetry is this: while individuals should reap the benefits of their freely made choices that turn out well, whether those choices were prudent or imprudent, they should suffer the bad consequences only of the results of their imprudent choices that turn out badly, and should be insulated from the effects of prudent choices with bad effects.[4]

It hardly needs to be added that combinations of these theories are possible; indeed all three could be combined. First, scope asymmetry could be applied to say that people should be held responsible for the consequences of fewer sources of ill fortune than good fortune. Next, differences of scale could be applied to those sources, and then finally losses, but not gains, could be capped. Hence we hope it is clear that the notion of asymmetry of responsibility seems at least understandable.

10.2 Challenges

On the face of it, however, there are a number of obvious challenges. Here we will consider two: a familiar pair, one of feasibility, the second of desirability. The

---

[3] It is said that the Swedish novelist Selma Lagerlof earned so much that one year she was asked to pay more than 100 per cent of her income as tax.

[4] We thank David Miller for raising this possibility.

first challenge is of a practical nature: that it is simply not possible to implement such a principle, whether or not it is desirable. The second is that any possible ethical justification for one form of responsibility—the value of choice, for example—might be claimed equally to be a justification for the other form.

We will clarify and refine our position by engaging with these challenges, but first we need to say some things to set out the scope of the present enquiry. As in other joint work, our primary concern here is not ideal theory. Now, it has become very common to distinguish 'ideal' and 'non-ideal' theory, and to argue that much of contemporary egalitarian political philosophy has been too concerned with ideal theory. To say this could be to say a number of different things, but we understand it as the accusation that political philosophers argue in an unhelpfully abstract style, relying on a hugely simplified model of the world—often with just two people in it—with known variables, and highly reliable information flows. Just as importantly, in such models social rules are either automatically complied with or, if enforced, done so at little if any cost.

What, then, is non-ideal theory? Should it be ideal theory modified to take into account real-world frailties: limited information, imperfect motivation, high enforcement costs, unintended consequences, and so on? Or should it be theory designed in the first instance to apply to the real world? But what would that even mean? Without ideal theory we would have little idea of what theory would be for, or what it might achieve. Hence, it seems, non-ideal theory needs somehow to combine ideal world aspirations with an appreciation of what it is possible to achieve under real-world conditions, which might, in some cases, mean abandoning our highest aspirations and replacing them with others with a higher likelihood of successful implementation. Such observations may seem banal, but there is an important consequence. Non-ideal theory will be a theory of balance and compromise, rather than of hard principle. Hence one has to accept that it will lead to some outcomes one would rather not have. Yet the cost of changing the theory to one that avoids such difficulties would be to create new difficulties, perhaps of a more serious nature. Consequently, constructing a non-ideal theory is the secular analogue to the problem of evil: if the perfect world is impossible one must strive to create the best of all possible worlds. One message, therefore, is that to show that a real-world approach is inadequate it is not enough to point out that it has flaws or implausible consequences. In addition it needs to be shown how an alternative approach is possible; one that has fewer difficulties. However, our main reason for insisting on 'real-world' rather than 'ideal' theory is that arguments made for or against a theory using an abstract model of the world cannot always be assumed to work as well in the conditions of the real world, where the conditions of the model may not hold. We will insist on this point in the following section.

10.3 Considering the challenges to the apparent asymmetry of responsibility

So far we have expressed our sympathy for a weak version of the asymmetry of responsibility, namely accepting PDR in a wider range of cases than NDR. In other words, we believe that while it is often desirable to hold people responsible for the positive outcomes of their choices, and allow them to reap all or a significant proportion of the benefits of such choices, it is often undesirable to treat them as responsible for the negative outcomes of their choices, and require them to suffer all, or even a significant proportion of, the burdens.

The practical challenge can be formulated simply. Consider two people who choose to gamble with each other, perhaps each staking their entire fortune on the single toss of a coin. One will win and the other will lose. Yet how could any form of asymmetry—scale, cap, or scope—be applied here? It seems impossible. How could the winner keep more of the winnings than the loser has lost? There is simply nowhere else for the winnings to come from. Winnings are the mirror to losings, and there is no scope for allowing people to keep a higher proportion of winnings than losers can lose. Hence, so it appears, the asymmetry thesis is incoherent.

The natural response for the non-ideal theorist is to point out, first, that the real world has more than two people in it, and second, gambling is a very poor model even for a capitalist market. Less cryptically, the first point is that the world does not divide into those who have taken a big risk and won, and those who have taken a big risk and lost. Rather, there are those who deliberately take big risks, and win, and those who take such risks and lose, and those who do their best to avoid big risks.

Those who take big risks and win typically do not win all that they win from the losers: the economic world is not zero sum. Broadly, the central capitalist activities are trade, investment, and production. Whether or not trade and investment are productive in themselves, they facilitate production, and production, unsurprisingly, is productive. Trade, investment, and production can be very risky, yet it is in the general social interest that they take place. As everybody in society has an interest and a good reason to encourage individuals to contribute to society's wealth, it seems that they also have a good reason to encourage trade, investment, and production, at least when conducted in particular ways. In order to do so it will be helpful, perhaps even necessary, to endorse what we have called the PDR, according to which individuals who work hard and take risks should be allowed to reap a significant proportion of the fruits of their work when the risks work out. The efficiency argument is that in the real world it is better for us all, or for all members of society in general, if the PDR is applied, as it will encourage some, although not all, people to try harder, invest, and risk their wealth, all of which are likely to yield growth in society's wealth. Progress, it is often claimed, is due to people's readiness to take (calculated, reasonable) risks. If a society wants to institutionalize the right circumstances that will encourage individuals to take such risks then it has, it seems, to endorse a principle of PDR.

Everybody in society, therefore, has good reason to treat individuals' earnings from economic investments or from economic initiatives as if these achievements would not have been possible if it were not for these individuals' hard work, investment, or risk. Individuals respond to this practice by trying harder, investing energy, time, money, and so on. Therefore society's wealth grows, and there are more jobs, with better wages. This is not, however, inconsistent with taxing these productive individuals.

Consider now what we called the NDR. It is negative in the sense that it holds that individuals should be considered responsible for freely made decisions that turn out badly. Of course, this is not a demand that individuals should be held responsible for every bad situation they find themselves in, but rather only for those that are the consequences of freely made decisions they have taken. If they lost because of these decisions then it is their fault and they should be responsible. It would be unfair if other people had to share in the costs of these mistakes (assuming that the people committing these mistakes knew what risks they were taking). Such a view is one aspect of some versions of what is known as 'luck egalitarianism', as discussed in many of the other chapters in this volume, but it is also an argument put forward by right-wing politicians and theorists.[5]

Why doesn't the efficiency principle equally apply to the second arena to justify the NPR? In order for it to apply it should be the case that, on average, each member of society would be better off if everybody is to be treated as if they deserve the consequences of their bad decisions. Now, it is true that such a practice would discourage reckless risk taking. However, providing no insulation at all from the losses of any sort of risk taking would surely have a dampening effect on economic activity. Any such negative principle, in which losses could not be mitigated, would be a powerful disincentive, limiting risk taking such as investment of money, energy, or initiative in work. This is an empirical claim, for which there is evidence in history. We know, for example, that economic growth is closely related to, and explained by, the availability of insurance. In the first instance such insurance was merely a matter of risk pooling among private individuals, such as ship owners, which in itself shows the error of the zero-sum assumptions: the existence of risk pooling allowed the ship owners to trade in the confidence that while their profits would be somewhat reduced by insurance, losses to piracy and shipwreck would be capped by their insurance policy. This, in turn, generated greater wealth than would otherwise have been the case.[6]

---

[5] The main difference between luck egalitarianism and the right-wing argument is that, typically, luck egalitarians argue that people should be held responsible for their choices only against a background of some appropriate sort of equality, whereas the right-wing position makes no reference to background condition. For clarification on this we thank Zofia Stemplowska. We will return to this issue below, as the luck egalitarian restriction leaves unclear what the egalitarian should say when conditions of background equality are not met, as, of course, they never are in the actual world.

[6] See, for example, A. H. John, 'The London Assurance Company and the Marine Insurance Market of the Eighteenth Century', *Economica*, 98 (1958), 126–141.

As economies develop, so does the readiness of the state to 'insure' investors and, indeed, ordinary workers, so that in case of failure the state will cover at least some losses.[7] This is the idea behind a mechanism of public insurance, in which the state guarantees that if investors lose or entrepreneurs fail, the state will limit the losses anyone will suffer, through such things as bankruptcy laws, social security, and social services, but also free schools and hospitals, all of which cap one's losses and protect one, and one's family, from falling too far. And, of course, in the recent financial crisis we have seen this illustrated on a massive scale. It is not our purpose here to defend every such measure taken by governments to bail out companies that took reckless risks, but such measures do at least show how asymmetry is possible.

Generalizing from investors and speculators to more ordinary workers and citizens, it is feasible to claim that a significant number of people are risk averse, preferring cautious behaviour, and not investing or risking their wealth. The greater the number of such people, the less society will produce. Naturally, the more unstable the situation is, and the less the economy flourishes, the more people will become risk averse and conservative in their economic behaviour. Thus it is precisely in times when society needs investors and initiators most (because the economy is stuck), that they will be unlikely to show up. That is, as long as NDR is applied. Thus it can be safe to say that empirically the NDR cannot generally be based on considerations of efficiency.

In response, it could be argued that it *is* the case that everybody in society is better off if the efficiency principle is applied in the second arena (NDR) even if there is evidence that for some (or many) the lack of public insurance would be a reason not to invest. The argument is that protecting people from the consequences of their loss has a 'moral hazard', as it sends the message that people can rely on others rather than on themselves, and can costlessly take reckless risks. We would not deny that this does happen, and that it is certainly possible that under some social conditions, asymmetry of responsibility could be damaging. But let us ask: What is the problem here? If it is unfairness, namely that some people will free ride and exploit the system, relying on others to pay for their gambles, and benefiting when they do earn, then indeed moral hazard needs to be dealt with, perhaps by punishing those who exploit the system, or, less harshly, by scope restrictions, in which society makes it clear that the bad consequences of reckless risk taking will not be subsidized. Indeed, it is not impossible that in some societies, or some circumstances, efficiency requires such opposite asymmetry. Perhaps armies work best if there are more courts martial than medals. If, however, the problem is that such exploitation of the system would ruin it, namely that in the absence of NDR people would gamble, counting on others to cover for their losses, then this is an empirical argument which may depend entirely on how asymmetry is implemented. If, for example, people could keep all the benefits of risky choices that

---

[7] Concerning the origins of the bankruptcy law and changes in the nineteenth century, see J. Sgard, 'On Legal Origins and Bankruptcy Laws: the European Experience (1808–1914)', *CEPII Working Paper*, 26 (2006), http://www.cepii.fr/anglaisgraph/workpap/summaries/2006/wp06-26.htm.

pay off, but were completely insulated against loss, then society may well collapse through reckless risk taking. Hence we would not advocate such extreme asymmetry. However, the more modest forms, under discussion so far, with safeguards against moral hazard, could equally be modified—if further modification is needed—to prevent damaging exploitation.[8]

In any case, however, it is essential to be clear about the place of efficiency-based reasoning in our argument. At this stage it is not intended to be a moral defence of the asymmetry thesis, even if under normal circumstances it could function as such. Rather it is a response to the practical challenge: that as the resources to mitigate the losses of the unfortunate can only come from the fortunate, then the asymmetry thesis is practically impossible. The efficiency argument is designed to show that under the right social circumstances, trade, investment, and production are beneficial, and asymmetry can be funded from the extra production it facilitates. This is consistent with the possibility that in some circumstances such asymmetry would reduce total production, however unlikely that possibility may be.

We need also to look at a different type of practical challenge to the asymmetry thesis. To some degree we have tried to motivate the asymmetry thesis by making reference to existing social practices, such as bankruptcy laws, which, we suggest, are an application of a capping approach to asymmetry. However, it might be said that the asymmetry here is more apparent than real. While it is true that no society deliberately caps the benefits people can enjoy, it does, nevertheless, tax incomes. Looking purely at taxation it might be thought that for the ordinary citizen, asymmetry works in reverse. If I work harder, and earn more money, I will pay more tax, at my highest rate of tax. But if I make a consumer decision that turns out badly there is no social fund I can turn to in order to receive compensation for my loss. Hence, it could be argued, there is no deep asymmetry in real life: it is how socially shared responsibility for both losses and gains is distributed. On the positive side, shared responsibility is distributed through taxation, and on the negative side it is distributed through capping. But there is no reason in principle why the sums should not balance out.[9]

Now this is an important observation, and there are several things that need to be said here. We saw that in the casino the only way of compensating the losers was by confiscating the winnings of the winners in the same proportion. The capitalist economy, in one way, is similar. All the compensation made available must come from other people, either through taxation or by not allowing individuals to recover the full amount of what they are owed. But it does not follow from this that the winners must give up the same proportion of what they gain in order to subsidize the losers, simply because few people go bankrupt, but rather most earn and benefit. In other words, as we have already suggested, it is not a zero-sum game. For example, suppose in a country of 1,000 business people, and 1,000,000 ordinary workers, one

---

[8] Thanks to Carl Knight for helpful discussion of this point.
[9] We owe this point to Carl Knight.

business person goes bust and is bailed out by taxes paid by others. The bankrupt person in this case could be fully insulated from loss—a 100 per cent relief—while the individual impact on the others is rather small, even marginal. Note that even if all the taxes to support the bankrupt person come from the successful business people, this is not like the symmetry of redistribution in a casino, where the losers would have to be paid from the winners' winnings which they gained from the losers. Rather, the winners gain profits not from the failed business person but from ordinary workers, who work for the business people and purchase their products. Bankruptcy laws facilitate this process. Once again, growing prosperity through trade and industry, protected by bankruptcy laws, makes asymmetry possible. Whether it exists in the real world is a separate question, but there is no reason in advance to think that asymmetry is purely a matter of a convention that gains should be socially shared by taxation and losses by bankruptcy laws. It is also possible that there should be a greater social sharing of losses than there is of gains, which is another way of attempting to formulate the asymmetry thesis. Consequently, we conclude, the practical challenge can be met.

We then need to move to the ethical challenges: that for moral reasons the asymmetry thesis cannot be sustained. There are two types of powerful challenges under this head: that it is impossible to find good moral reasons for asymmetry, and that there are good moral reasons against it. There is also a weaker type of challenge: that the asymmetry thesis is an instance of a much broader pattern of moral argument, and hence has nothing especially to do with responsibility.

We will look at this final challenge first. Here the claim is that it is a very general moral truth that it is better to return good for good than evil for evil, and so the asymmetry thesis has nothing in particular to do with responsibility.[10] Now, while we are very happy to endorse this moral intuition, there are two reasons why we do not think that it renders the analysis of this chapter redundant. First, even if we think that the analysis here is subsumed under the general principle just stated, nevertheless, further specification, of the type offered here, is needed. But second, it is not so clear that the argument of this chapter does fall within the scope of such a general principle. When we endorse the PDR we do not *return* any good for any good. The person who made a decision and benefited did not necessarily do anything morally good when he made that decision. The fact that he ended up earning is also, morally speaking, neutral. Thus we as society do not return any good to him or her. We only allow them to keep what they earned. The same is true about the person who lost. She did not do anything bad, morally speaking, and therefore this is not a situation of returning bad for bad.

We now move to the first of the two strong challenges: that there are moral reasons against the asymmetry thesis. Such an argument would, most likely, be based on the idea that whatever moral considerations lead to a conclusion about positive responsibility, or negative responsibility, a mirror image set of considerations will lead to mirror

---

[10] We owe this point to Richard Arneson.

image conclusions on the other side. Consider, for example, Richard Arneson's well-known claim that:

it is morally fitting to hold individuals responsible for the foreseeable consequences of their voluntary choices, and in particular for that portion of these consequences that involves their own achievement of welfare or gain or loss of resources.[11]

Although it is sometimes thought that this is an argument for holding people responsible for their choices, we should note, however, that this is a statement of a view, rather than an argument for it. Arneson's purpose is not so much to defend this thesis as to use it as a premise to the conclusion that theories of equal opportunity for equality are preferable to straight equality theories.

It is possible, however, to try to fill out Arneson's argument, by supposing that the nature of the moral fittingness referred to by Arneson is that it is unfair for one person to have to bear the consequences of another's freely made choices. Extending such a claim, it would follow that the weak asymmetry thesis is unfair. Clearly there are examples where such a view seems intuitively plausible; if two people start with the same resources and the same opportunities, there seems no prima facie case in justice that one should pay for the costs, or share in the benefits, created by the other's choices. Two twin children, given the same pocket money at the beginning of the week, would not be expected to redistribute their wealth at the end of the week, assuming that any resulting differences are the result of freely made choices. Anything else would seem unfair.

However, an intuition in one case is not a conclusive reason for a general principle, and could be countered by other intuitions or argument. These we can group into two types: one that appeals to a value not based on fairness, which conflicts and sometimes overrides fairness; the other based on fairness. In fact we think arguments of both kinds are available. Arguments appealing to values that are not based on fairness might, for example, appeal to ideas of benevolence or generosity. While it might be unfair to force the fortunate twin to hand over some of her bounty to her sister, we might still think her mean if she does not, while recognizing that it is entirely her decision. Furthermore, we have already seen arguments based on notions of efficiency. These we introduced to show that weak asymmetry was a practical possibility; but it can also be added that they provide a normative argument for asymmetry as well, in so far as consequentialist defences of responsibility are acceptable. However, we would not wish to rest our entire case on this, as fairness in many cases seems a weightier value than efficiency.

Fairness, however, is also engaged. We want to defend asymmetry on the basis that for reasons of fairness there can be grounds for not holding individuals to the negative consequences of some of their freely made choices, while there is no mirror image

[11] R. Arneson, 'Equality and Equal Opportunity for Welfare', *Philosophical Studies*, 56 (1989), 77–93, at 88. See also his chapter in this volume.

argument from the same grounds to preclude people from enjoying the benefits of their choices. Hence, we believe, there is an argument from fairness for asymmetry of scope. The argument is based on an example we have used to motivate a distinction between what we have called 'formal opportunity' and 'genuine opportunity', but we believe that it also can be used to illustrate an argument for weak asymmetry of scope.

The example concerns an unemployed single mother who receives an offer of a low-paid full-time job, for which she has to travel quite far from her home. Suppose she chose not to accept the offer on the grounds that she feels it would be bad for her children if she was around for them less, and when around, would be too exhausted by work and travel to give them the quality of attention they need. There is no doubt in this example that she has chosen to decline the job, and a crude interpretation of 'luck egalitarian' theories of responsibility would say that once she has turned down the job offer she is unemployed by choice and should therefore bear the consequences of that choice, which in many societies would be forfeiting any unemployment benefit she currently receives. However, there seems little doubt that those sympathetic to egalitarianism would argue that such punitive measures are quite unfair, and hence she should be shielded from some consequences of some of her choices.

Many luck egalitarians will suppose that it is an easy matter to accommodate our intuitions about this case within a luck egalitarian framework. Hence, it will be said, the theory of responsibility operates only against a background of equality of opportunity, and as the single mother was already disadvantaged, with poor opportunities, then there is no case for holding her responsible to bear the adverse consequences of her choices.[12]

However, this response comes at high cost. Given that no actual society, or even one we are likely to be able to move to, is able to implement exact equality of opportunity in the favoured egalitarian sense, the luck egalitarian is left with nothing at all to say about responsibility in the real world: the background conditions for responsibility are simply not met. The distinctive thesis of luck egalitarianism, as outlined in the quotation from Arneson above, simply drains away. As no one, rich or poor, makes their choices under the right conditions, luck egalitarianism has nothing to say about whether they should bear the costs and reap the benefits of their choices.

The most obvious response is to say that those above the average level of opportunity in society are in a different position to those below. Those above average cannot complain that they lack opportunities that they should have, and thus have no complaint if they are held responsible for their choices. Those below average opportunity level should not be held responsible. Call this the 'exoneration view': those below the line are exonerated from the consequences of their choices. Hence, on such a view, luck egalitarians endorse a form of asymmetry. But note that it is a different form of asymmetry to that under discussion here, in that it bases asymmetry

---

[12] We thank Zofia Stempslowska for discussion on this point.

on who is choosing, rather than the content or outcomes of their choices. It holds those who are above average to the consequences of their choices, good or bad, and those below average to none of them, also good or bad. Strictly, then, a poor person who wins the lottery should not keep the winnings as he or she made her choice under conditions of poor opportunity.

But more importantly, we think that the exoneration view is patronizing and morally unappealing. We do not think that fairness, or other moral considerations, justify a position in which those who are below average in opportunity in society should always be shielded from all the negative consequences of all their choices. To return to the example of our single mother, suppose, knowing exactly what she was doing, she decided to gamble with a small portion of her weekly income, by buying a weekly lottery ticket. Suppose, sadly, she regularly loses. We would not argue that it would be unfair to make her pay her losses; that fairness or equality requires the refund of the ticket price, understandable though her decision to gamble may be, given her poverty.

Although it may be possible to continue to adjust the luck egalitarian position so that it generates fair outcomes in the non-ideal world, we will not attempt that exercise.[13] Rather, we will just say that in our view, the salient point that needs to be captured in the analysis is that while people can have options which, formally speaking, are open to them, it can be unreasonable to expect them to take up.[14] It is unreasonable because the costs to other aspects of their life would be too high. In such circumstances it is unreasonable, and unfair, to make them pay the costs of the choice of declining to take options. In the employment case, it is unreasonable to expect her to take the job offered (as distinct, say, from a well-paid, local, part-time job) because of what she would have to sacrifice, i.e. her relationships with her children, and hence she should not have to pay the costs of remaining unemployed by forfeiting unemployment benefit. Note that, while relevant in this case, the argument is not restricted to those who are poor and on unemployment benefit. The same reasoning might apply to a comfortably off divorced woman with young children who would forfeit alimony from her former husband if she took a job. Even under such circumstances it could be reasonable for her to refuse some, but not all, offers of employment. The question is how damaging it would be to other functionings of hers (and that of her children) rather than her baseline point of income. Of course, the baseline point is likely to make a difference—the richer she is, the less unreasonable a sacrifice might become—but it does not determine the outcome.

Our view, then, is whether it is reasonable for someone to make a choice depends on the cost to their other functionings, and that people can be excused if the consequences of their choices are that the costs in terms of risking their other functionings are too high. Not all functionings are equally important in this respect, and not all costs are too high. Research we conducted shows that most people share a view about those functionings that are more crucial and that therefore need stronger protection. In a full treatment further explanation is necessary, but for present purposes only an exposition of the outlines of the theory is required.[15]

The gambling case differs from the employment case as, generally, it is not unreasonable to expect people on low incomes to choose not to gamble for declining to gamble typically will not put any other currently enjoyed functioning at risk. Consequently there is no reason in fairness not to expect someone who gambles to pay the costs. For a compulsive gambler things could be very different, of course, or even for a non-compulsive gambler who sees no possible way out of urgent difficulties except to gamble. There are, of course, intermediate cases. Consider unhealthy diets. Is it unreasonable to expect people on low income to make healthy choices? Much depends on their situation, the cost and difficulty of obtaining and preparing healthy food, and whether it would take so much time and money it undercuts the possibility of following other valued activities.

The key point is simply that it does not always seem fair that some people should bear the costs of some of their freely made choices. The question, then, from the point of view of the asymmetry thesis, is whether similar considerations support the claim that it would be equally unfair for people to receive the benefits of some of their freely made choices. Now, we do not deny that it could be unfair for some individuals to keep (all) the benefits of their freely made choices; that, after all, is what income tax is for. However, in the negative case we have argued that there is a specific type of choice the consequences of which people should not be held to account for; effectively, if it would be unreasonable (because too risky to other functionings) to expect an individual to make an alternative choice, then socially we should behave as if that option is not there at all. It is not at all clear, however, that there is a counterpart situation on the positive side.

We conclude, therefore, that our analysis supports the claim that it can be unfair to require individuals to pay the costs of some of their choices (those choices where it would be unreasonable to expect the individual to bear the cost of a different choice) while there does not appear to be a positive counterpart where it is unfair to allow people to keep at least a significant proportion of the benefits of their choices. Hence, it seems, the argument from fairness for scope asymmetry is established.

10.4 Conclusions

This chapter has explored what we called the 'weak asymmetry thesis' that there can be reasons to protect people from the costs of some of their freely made choices, but no parallel argument to the conclusion that it is unfair to allow individuals to keep at least a

---

[15] For further discussion see J. Wolff and A. de-Shalit, *Disadvantage* (Oxford: Oxford University Press, 2007), 74–84.

significant portion of the benefits their choices bring. We have established that there are reasons of efficiency to protect people from bearing the full costs of some of their choices, as well as reasons of fairness to protect people from bearing some or all of the costs of some of their choices. We have claimed that the principle seems humane and tolerant, and we have shown that there is no practical obstacle to its implementation.

11

Taking Up the Slack? Responsibility and Justice in Situations of Partial Compliance[1]

David Miller

My aim in this chapter is to investigate what justice requires of agents who find themselves in situations that have the following general form. There are many agents who by acting together can avert some anticipated harm. Together, then, they share responsibility for avoiding that harm, but furthermore this collective responsibility can be divided fairly between them so that each knows what he or she must do to discharge that fair share. Despite this, however, some comply but others do not; the ones who do not comply could have chosen to do so, but they have shirked their share of the responsibility, and in doing so have acted unfairly. The question then arises: How should we understand the position of those who have already complied or those who have yet to decide what to do? What are their responsibilities now, in the face of partial compliance? Must they take up the slack, by doing more than they were required to do according to the original fair division of responsibility? What does justice demand in this situation?

Situations of this general kind are not merely hypothetical: one can readily think of a number of real-world circumstances that either already do or easily could take the form just described. For instance, we might think of rescue cases where there are numbers of people awaiting rescue and several potential rescuers and it is reasonably clear how much fairness requires each to contribute to the operation. Or we might think of world poverty and the position of all those who could contribute to poverty relief by

[1] Earlier versions of this chapter were presented to the London Forum on Moral and Political Philosophy, University College London, and to the Centre for the Study of Social Justice, University of Oxford. I am very grateful to both audiences for the challenging questions raised in the discussion, and especially to Jerry Cohen, Liz Kingdom, Carl Knight, Michael Otsuka, Andrew Williams, and Gabriel Wollmer for additional suggestions. Above all I should like to thank Zofia Stemplowska for a long and searching commentary on the original draft which has forced me to make a number of clarifications and concessions, although fewer than she would wish.

voluntary contributions to aid agencies.[2] Or again if we switch focus from individual agents to collective agents such as nation states, we could think of measures to conserve natural resources, such as agreements to reduce the catch of ocean fish, where each country is given a target quota such that if all countries comply, fish stocks will not be further depleted. Finally we could consider the case of global warming, and think of an agreement to cut greenhouse gas emissions with each nation being given a target to aim at, targets being set to reflect some underlying principle of fairness. In all of these cases, it is unfortunately only too easy to anticipate that because of bad faith, selfishness, weakness of will, or whatever, some agents will find reasons not to do their share, so that the goal in question—rescuing everyone at risk, keeping fish stocks at the required level, and so forth—will not be reached unless other agents take up the slack. But are they obliged, as a matter of justice, to do this?

I think that our immediate intuitions are likely to suggest different answers in different cases. If we take rescue cases, for instance, then assuming it was a matter of justice to do one's fair share in the first place—something we will need to investigate as we proceed, but assume for the moment that if the potential victims had a right to be rescued, and the costs involved in the rescue were not excessive or disproportionate to the harm averted, then justice requires that it be undertaken—many people would say that justice also requires taking up the slack if the costs stay within the same limits. If justice requires you to jump into the pond, spoiling your suit but not risking your life to pull out the first child, then if your companion declines to pull out the second child, you must at least be willing to sacrifice another suit of comparable value to you to rescue that one. On the other hand, in the case of conserving fish stocks, many would think that a nation that conscientiously sticks to its quotas has done all that justice requires, and that reducing catches still further because others have failed in their duty would be supererogation. As long as we have done our fair share, they might say, the decline in fish stocks is entirely the responsibility of the countries that haven't. But what can explain these conflicting intuitions, apart from the rather too obvious fact that one case has to do with human beings and the other with fish? Or can we restore consistency by showing that one or other intuition is mistaken?

Before I try to tackle the normative issue directly, let me expand a little on how the situations that interest me are to be characterized. First, although they are multi-agent cases, they are not standard prisoner's dilemmas, nor are they what we might call altruistic prisoner's dilemmas. By an altruistic prisoner's dilemma I mean a situation in which there is some good to be achieved or harm to be avoided but it is indeterminate which agent or agents should take action to bring that result about. So one might think of a case where there are several people standing near the pond when the child falls in,

---

[2] This is not in general a good way to think about world poverty—we should instead focus our attention on the practices and institutions that serve to reproduce it over time—but there may be cases in which it is appropriate, for example large-scale natural disasters such as the Asian tsunami where the short-term provision of aid meets basic needs for food, shelter, and so forth.

and only one person needs to jump into the pond to save him. Assuming each bystander wants the child to be saved, and would jump in if he were the only rescuer at the scene, but is reluctant to sacrifice his suit, we have a dilemma where each has a reason to hold back in the hope that someone else will carry out the rescue.[3] Or in a variant of this case, a car accident may require only a sub-set of those who witness the accident to care for the injured, but it is indeterminate who should make up that sub-set. The situations I am investigating are different from this, because by stipulation it is clear what justice requires each person to do by way of contribution. This might be because a formal agreement has been reached, on the basis of criteria that each party is willing to accept, as in the case of the fish quotas. Or it might simply be because it is evident to everyone what fairness demands in the circumstances—for example an equal sacrifice from each agent. This does not of course prevent people from acting strategically—deciding not to contribute in the hope that others will take up the slack. But it will be clear in these situations that such people are behaving unfairly, and that prima facie at least those who decide to take up the slack are doing more than justice requires.

I need to make two further clarificatory comments here. I assume that for each agent, discharging his or her fair share of responsibility is significantly costly, but not so costly that it becomes questionable whether it could be a matter of justice to contribute. Furthermore this also applies to the additional costs involved in taking up the slack—they are significant, but not so significant as to push the agent across the threshold such that it would be beyond the call of duty to contribute more. In other words, I am not going to be addressing the problem of demandingness that has occupied the attention of many philosophers—the problem of when carrying out a duty becomes so onerous that the agent in question can justifiably refuse to discharge it.[4] My interest is in questions of fairness—in how one should think about cases in which one is asked to bear additional costs only because others have failed to carry out their share of a collective responsibility. If there were no significant costs involved, this would not be an interesting problem—it would merely be pique to refuse to flick an extra switch to avoid some great harm merely because it was somebody else's job to flick that particular switch. On the other hand, when the cost becomes very high, fairness may be obliterated by the demandingness issue—that's to say, the question for each agent may simply be 'how much must I contribute to this collective task before it becomes so onerous that my personal prerogative cuts in?' I think that the examples

[3] I have explored situations of this kind, and possible responses to them, in '"Are They My Poor?": The Problem of Altruism in a World of Strangers', *Critical Review of International Social Philosophy and Policy*, 5 (2002), 106–127, reprinted in J. Seglow (ed.) *The Ethics of Altruism* (London: Frank Cass, 2004), 107–127.

[4] The voluminous literature on this topic includes S. Scheffler, *The Rejection of Consequentialism* (Oxford: Clarendon Press, 1982); J. Fishkin, *The Limits of Obligation* (New Haven: Yale University Press, 1982); S. Kagan, *The Limits of Morality* (Oxford: Oxford University Press, 1989); L. Murphy, *Moral Demands in Nonideal Theory* (Oxford: Oxford University Press, 2000); T. Mulgan, *The Demands of Consequentialism* (Oxford: Clarendon Press, 2001); G. Cullity, *The Moral Demands of Affluence* (Oxford: Clarendon Press, 2004).

I used to illustrate the fairness problem—standard rescue cases, world poverty, conserving natural resources, and combating global warming—all fall into the middle ground where the costs that agents are being asked to bear, both initially (given a fair distribution of responsibility) and as a result of non-compliance, are significant but not excessive.

One last introductory remark: someone might respond to the situations I have described by saying that what is needed is some mechanism that can oblige people to contribute their fair share, so that the question of taking up the slack need never arise. For example, we should create institutions that can supervise the behaviour of individual people, or of countries in policy areas such as resource conservation and climate change. In some cases this will be the correct response. However, I am confident that there will be other cases—many other cases, unfortunately—in which even if setting up such a mechanism were justifiable in principle, it would not be feasible. In rescue cases, for instance, you cannot in the end force human beings to perform actions they are unwilling to perform—they may simply sit on their hands and refuse to help. In the country-level cases, no international institution is likely in the foreseeable future to have either the authority or the coercive power to oblige unwilling countries to cut their greenhouse gas emissions or to conserve fish stocks or other resources (what such an institution *can* do, importantly, is to define fair shares of responsibility by setting targets for each country, but this is very different from enforcing the targets that have been set). So the problem of partial compliance as I have described it is a real one—it cannot be circumvented by ingenuity in designing institutions or other mechanisms that could guarantee full compliance.

In the situations I am considering, agents face a choice between three broad possibilities: they can discharge their original fair share of responsibility despite others' non-compliance; they can do *more* than they were originally required to do in order to compensate for the non-compliance; or they can do *less* than they were originally required to do, so that they fall more closely into line with the defaulters. Each of these options has something to be said for it, so let me elaborate a little further. The argument for the first option is that one's responsibility is only to do one's fair share regardless of what others decide. Liam Murphy, who on the whole supports this position in his book *Moral Demands in Nonideal Theory*, notes that a stricter version of the first option would require people in conditions of partial compliance to perform the best available action subject to the condition that the overall costs of doing so would not be greater than the costs they would have borne under full compliance.[5] This accommodates the fact that the world will be different in certain ways when there is only partial compliance, so what one actually has to do to discharge one's fair share of responsibility may be different than under full compliance, but the key point is that the net level of sacrifice should be the same. And, it might be said, whatever the arguments for doing more, this is all that justice specifically requires of the agent.

---

[5] Murphy, *Moral Demands in Nonideal Theory*, ch. 5.

In defence of doing more, it can be argued that because of the non-compliance of the other agents, we are now in a position where the harm we were seeking to avert will not be averted. However much we might regret the non-compliance and condemn the non-compliers, this is simply a fact of life, so what we must now do is to recalculate contributions, distributing responsibilities fairly among the coalition of the willing, so to speak. What justice requires in the new circumstances is that each agent should discharge his fair share of the responsibility as determined by these calculations. Unless he is the only willing complier, nobody is required to take up all of the slack by himself, but must contribute fairly to filling the gap left by the non-compliers. Since presumably there may be some agents who are willing to comply with the original distribution of responsibilities, but not to contribute to taking up the slack, there might have to be further iterations in which additional assignments of responsibilities are made, but to keep things simple let's assume that everyone who was originally compliant is also willing to help take up the slack. Our question will be whether this might be what justice requires of such agents.

The third possibility is that one might do less, in the face of others' non-compliance (I shall call this 'grouching'). What would doing less mean? One possibility is that one should try to place oneself at the *average* level of compliance revealed by the actions of others. This is unlikely to lead to a determinate result in the case of rescues—one can't pull half or two-thirds of a child out of the water—but in the other examples I gave it would certainly be feasible to adjust one's level of contribution to the going rate, so that if others are on average contributing one-third of what they would need to give to abolish global poverty, one would also give one-third of whatever one's full contribution was calculated to be. In defence of this policy, a person could say that he was behaving fairly given other people's actual behaviour—if they were prepared to do more he would do so as well, but justice should not require us to contribute more to a collective task than others are on average contributing. After all, to contribute the full amount in these circumstances would put the person in question at an unfair disadvantage relative to these others.[6] Of course, somebody might take this line of thinking further and refuse to contribute more than the *least* compliant of the other parties, but again to keep things simple let us have compliance at the average level on the table as our third alternative.

Having sketched these three possible responses to situations of partial compliance at a general level, let me now consider some of the factors that might affect our judgement about which response is required by justice. These in other words are factors that potentially might separate cases in the real world such as those I described earlier.[7]

---

[6] This consideration will have particular force where contribution levels cluster around a particular point, say one-third of what full compliance would require. Where they are more widely dispersed, other forms of grouching, such as taking your cue from the least compliant of the other parties, may become more defensible.

[7] The list that follows is not exhaustive. Here are two other factors that might be relevant: first, whether or not the parties have entered into a formal agreement to discharge their collective responsibility, for example

1. The first factor that might be relevant is the causal relationship between individual contributions and the result that is being sought. In other words, how far do successive contributions by different agents affect the overall outcome? One possibility is that each act of compliance has the same net effect, so that the relationship between level of compliance and outcome is linear. For example, if we take the case of conserving fish stocks, each reduction of the catch, measured in weight, say, might have more or less the same effect on the size of the long-term stock of fish in the sea. Another possibility, at the other end of the spectrum, is that each contribution taken by itself has zero effect unless all the contributions are made—one might think of a rescue that involves a human chain of rescuers such that if any one of them declines to participate the chain will not reach as far as the victims. In between there will be cases where early contributions count for more than late ones, and others where later ones count for more than early ones (early and late referring here to the position of a contribution in the sequence of contributions, not to the passage of time as such). In cases such as global warming, for example, there may be thresholds which it is important not to cross in terms of atmospheric concentrations of greenhouse gases, in which case emission cuts that would keep the world just below such a threshold would be more significant than others further below or beyond the threshold that might be desirable but not so critical.

   The relevance of this factor to our problem is relatively straightforward. Before we can decide whether justice requires us to take up the slack, or conversely permits us to reduce our contribution to the average, we should ask what the actual effect of doing so would be, in either case. In particular, would making the agreed contribution, or taking up the slack, mean crossing some significant threshold in terms of its effect? Or at the other extreme, would the contribution in either case simply be useless, given what others can be expected to do?

2. The second factor that might be relevant is whether the collective responsibility that our group of agents bear is itself a responsibility imposed by justice. Do they, in other words, owe a collective duty of justice to those who will suffer if the prospective harm is not averted? This raises the question of whether there can be such duties in situations that have the shape I am considering. I shall address that in a moment. But assuming a positive answer, it seems clearly relevant to ask whether the harm that would be averted by successful collective action is a harm that involves injustice, or merely some other kind of loss, as arguably at least

---

by signing a treaty in which each commits to contributing; second, whether the harm that collective action will avert is a harm that the parties themselves will otherwise cause (as, for example, in the case of global warming) or a harm whose causes lie elsewhere (as, for example, in the case of relief supplied to earthquake victims). I suspect that the second factor will turn out to be less important than the distinction I draw below between harms that involve injustice and those that don't.

would be the loss of fish in the sea. Where the collective responsibility we are examining is a responsibility imposed by justice, two issues of justice will arise with respect to individual compliance or non-compliance: first, justice within the collective (is each agent contributing their fair share or not?); second, justice between the collective and those to whom it is owed. Someone who contributes but refuses to take up the slack might defend herself by pointing out that she is doing her fair share and that to do more would put her at an unfair disadvantage relative to others (indeed at a double disadvantage relative to the non-compliers). But it might be said in reply that by refusing to take up the slack she is contributing to injustice against the victims, and this is a more serious form of injustice. Whatever we conclude about this, no such issue appears to arise in cases where the harm to be averted is simply a loss that does not involve injustice.[8]

So could there be a collective duty of justice towards those who will suffer the results if collective action does not succeed, or only succeeds partially, in cases of the kind I am considering? To keep things simple, let us focus on cases where the prospective victims have a right to whatever outcome the collective action would produce, and therefore, apparently, can demand it as a matter of justice.[9] This seems plainly true in the case of rescues—people have a right to life and bodily integrity—and in the case of world poverty—people have a right to a minimally decent standard of living. It may also well be true in the case of global warming, where it has plausibly been argued that among the results of un-checked global warming will be large-scale violations of the human rights of those who are unable to cope with rising sea levels, droughts, and so forth.[10] So on one side we have demands that are potentially demands of justice. But we have now to identify agents to whom the corresponding obligations can be attached. In standard cases, justice involves a claim made by one person against another, or by a person against an institution such as the state. In the present case, the obligation must attach to the whole group of potential contributors, who do

---

[8] Might there nonetheless be harms not involving injustice that are sufficiently serious that they would outweigh the unfairness involved in taking up the slack? An example might be damage to the natural environment (the loss of habitats or species) that did not infringe anyone's human rights. Preventing such damage would clearly give agents a reason to take up the slack in face of non-compliance. Whether that reason was strong enough to outweigh the unfairness must depend on the case. This, it seems to me, is something that must be left to the agents in question to decide. They cannot be required to take up the slack, even though in some circumstances this might be the right thing for them to do.

[9] I am assuming as a basic premise here that the duties that correspond to basic rights are standardly duties of justice: that is, if George has a right to be provided with some necessary good, and Helen is so placed that she has the obligation to provide it, her duty is a duty of justice. The question addressed in the text is whether this extends to cases where, instead of Helen, we have a group of agents who collectively owe a duty to George. Others argue that such duties are always better understood as humanitarian in nature. I shall not defend my assumption in this chapter, but see my *National Responsibility and Global Justice* (Oxford: Oxford University Press, 2007), ch. 9 for such a defence. I also there attempt to disentangle the circumstances in which duties of aid are duties of justice from those in which they do indeed become humanitarian in nature.

[10] See, for example, S. Caney, 'Cosmopolitan Justice, Rights and Global Climate Change', *Canadian Journal of Law and Jurisprudence*, 19 (2006), 255–278.

not together constitute an agent in the same sense: there is no collective decision to contribute or not to contribute, but rather each individual member decides whether to contribute his or her fair share, or more, or less. What we do have, on the other hand, is an agreed assignment of responsibility within the collective: by stipulation there is no dispute over what the fair share of each member amounts to. So the collective obligation to protect the rights of the potential victims does not simply hang in the air, but is translated into a series of individual obligations, and these it seems clear to me are obligations of justice. That is, if you are part of a collective group which owes something as a matter of justice to another group, and if your share in that obligation is fair and well-defined, then there is also a more specific obligation of justice that falls on you as an individual. What we should say about individual duties when there is only partial compliance remains of course to be seen, but enough has been said to establish the point that it matters whether the group's collective responsibility is a matter of justice specifically, or something less urgent.

3. The third factor that seems relevant to our question is whether the position of the non-compliers is reversible or non-reversible. Have they managed to rule themselves out of the picture altogether, so to speak, or might they be brought back into compliance? In a rescue case, for instance, we might contrast the position of those who quickly leave the scene and are then uncontactable, with those who stand around watching the rescuers but for the moment appear unwilling to contribute. More generally, we might contrast a one-off decision, where each party has to choose at a certain moment whether to opt in or opt out, with an ongoing practice where agents' behaviour can adapt over time: we might not meet our greenhouse gas emissions targets this year, but next year we can do more by way of compensation. Reversibility makes a difference for the obvious reason that where it obtains, compliers have a choice between taking up the slack themselves, and trying to persuade or cajole or force the non-compliers to make their fair contribution. But there may also be a more subtle difference, which I shall explore shortly, having to do with the assignment of responsibility. Where the non-compliers remain on the scene—they have so far chosen not to comply, but they could also choose differently—it might be thought that responsibility for the effects of partial compliance remains firmly with them. They are the ones who by doing nothing are causing some of the victims not to be rescued or some of the starving not to be fed. If they manage to rule themselves out, however, responsibility appears to shift, in some sense, to those who might take up the slack. Whether this is indeed so (and what sense of responsibility is involved here) remains to be seen, but intuitively it seems to make a difference whether the decision the non-compliers have made is reversible or not.

Having explored what seem to me to be the most salient dimensions of our problem, it's now time to begin working towards a solution. I want to argue broadly in favour of option 1—that what justice requires is contributing your fair share, neither more nor less—while conceding that there may be special circumstances in which justice overall permits option 3—grouching by doing less—and other circumstances in which there is an obligation (though, I shall argue, not an obligation of justice) to choose option 2—taking up the slack by doing more. So let me begin by looking critically at the argument in favour of grouching, which I defined as doing only as much as others are doing, *on average*, given partial compliance.

The main argument in its favour, as I suggested, is that it preserves horizontal equity within the group: I am not assuming more of the burden than others are. Another way of dressing the argument up is to say that significant non-compliance changes the meaning of a fair share of responsibility. One may be tempted into this way of thinking by considering cases such as collecting money for a colleague's leaving present where somebody might suggest an appropriate figure per head but looking into the collection box as it comes round you notice that there seem to be rather few notes and rather a lot of coins and so you swiftly revise your previous good intentions downwards. But the cases we are considering are not like this: they are cases in which the group has a collective responsibility to avoid some harm, and so if you do less than your original fair share you remain responsible for some portion of the harm that remains. Where that harm amounts to injustice towards the victims, as I have suggested it does in several of our real-world cases, this seems decisively to outweigh the relative disadvantage that a complying agent suffers with respect to the non-compliers in the group. Recall here that we are considering situations in which the cost of contributing to the collective effort is not only smaller than the cost that the victims will bear if the effort fails, but is moderate in absolute terms. So option 3 only looks plausible at all in two circumstances: one is where very little will be achieved by one agent's compliance given existing levels of non-compliance; the other is where the harm that non-compliance will produce does *not* involve injustice towards the victims, and the would-be groucher can give good reasons why doing more than others have done is unduly burdensome to her (for example, that it leaves her at a significant competitive disadvantage in some other sphere of life). Otherwise it is dominated by option 1, doing your fair share.

You might, however, think that the argument I have just given for choosing option 1 over option 3 also entails choosing option 2 over option 1: if horizontal equity among members of the group isn't such a weighty consideration, why aren't we required to take up the slack in the face of partial compliance, at least where this will have the effect of averting injustice towards the potential victims? So now I need to show that option 1, doing your fair share, is all that justice requires.

The key argument here is that because the collective responsibility to avert injustice has been fairly distributed, *ex hypothesi*, by doing my fair share I have discharged my obligation, and the injustice that remains, because of partial compliance, is the responsibility of the non-compliers, and only theirs.[11] As a general matter, we are not required as a matter of justice to correct the injustice that others perpetrate, although we may have reason to do so. If Bert steals Anne's money, justice does not require Charles to right this wrong, although if Charles happens to be so placed that he can direct the money back to Anne, this would very likely be the right thing for him to do.[12] Charles commits no injustice if he fails to secure the return of Anne's money, because responsibility for Anne's loss rests entirely with Bert.[13] How are things different in the partial compliance cases we are considering? Suppose that I am a member of a group with collective responsibility for averting some harm. Initially, then, I share in that collective responsibility. But now it is divided up so that I know what my fair share is, and I discharge it conscientiously. Others, however, do not. Does some share of the collective responsibility now revert to me, or does it remain entirely with them? One must avoid being misled here by cases in which some of the group are simply unable to discharge their share of responsibility. For example, in rescue situations, some potential rescuers might turn out to be terrified by what they were being asked to do, and become paralysed by fear. Under these circumstances, clearly, collective responsibility does return to the whole group and must be divided up afresh with each of the remaining rescuers having to carry a larger share. Similar considerations apply if external circumstances change, for example if the rescue group is alerted to the existence of a second group of potential victims, so that some of the rescuers need to hive off and form a separate party. By contrast, the cases we are considering are ones in which the non-compliers choose not to comply, even though they are able to do so and have no competing obligations that would prevent them from contributing. How can such a choice shift responsibility wholly or partly off of their shoulders and on to those of the willing compliers?

As I indicated earlier, it might seem to make a difference here whether it still remains within the power of the non-compliers to comply if they choose. If it does remain within their power, then it would be natural to say that what is causing the injustice that remains after partial compliance is the continuing unwillingness of the non-compliers to do their bit; the responsibility therefore remains wholly with them. Suppose on the other hand that they have left the scene or somehow disabled

---

[11] For further argument in support of this claim, see L. J. Cohen, 'Who is Starving Whom?', *Theoria*, 47 (1981), 65–81.

[12] Following Larry Temkin's discussion in 'Justice, Equality, Fairness, Desert, Rights, Free Will, Responsibility, and Luck' (this volume), we might say that Charles has a *reason of justice* to direct the money back to Anne. But this is different from saying that he is obliged as a matter of justice to right the wrong that Bert has caused. How weighty this reason will be depends on questions such as whether Charles is the only person other than Bert who is able to see that Anne gets her money back, how much it will cost him to do so, etc.

[13] I am treating this as a question of what particular agents are required to do as a matter of justice. We do of course have social institutions whose purpose is to rectify or offset acts of injustice, for example civil laws that may allow Anne to sue Bert for recovery of the stolen money, and insurance companies whose policies can compensate her for the loss that Bert has caused. We may be required as a matter of justice to contribute to the support of such institutions, paying taxes to cover the costs of law courts, for example. But this is clearly different from being obliged to act to remedy a specific injustice such as the one described.

themselves irreversibly from making a contribution. Clearly they are morally at fault for doing this, and if we were in the business of ascribing responsibility in order to attribute blame for the bad outcome, these are the ones we would hold responsible. Nevertheless, given that they have in fact acted in this way, the question still arises of responsibility for the ongoing injustice. Those who have already complied could if they chose take up the slack and do more; the non-compliers are out of the picture for practical purposes. Are the compliers not then responsible for the injustice if they decide not to do this?

In a purely causal sense of responsibility, this seems to be true. In other words, if we are asking what will make the difference between the remaining injustice's being remedied and its not being remedied, the answer, given the actual state of the world, is the decision by the compliers whether or not to take up the slack. But this causal sense of responsibility may not be relevant if what we are asking is whether justice requires taking up the slack. As I noted above, the fact that Charles may be able to correct the injustice that Bert has inflicted on Anne does not entail that Charles is himself required by justice to do this. After all, for each of us there are at any moment a large number of injustices that we might be able to correct if we set our minds to it. So the question that arises is what special circumstances, if any, have to obtain in order for the correction of injustice perpetrated by some other agent to be itself required by justice?

In the cases we are considering, there does seem to be one special circumstance, namely that both the compliers and the non-compliers belong to the same group of agents who were originally held collectively responsible for averting the injustice. In other words, the injustice that the compliers are being asked to redress by taking up the slack is not merely some injustice that might occur at random anywhere, but the injustice that is caused by the failure of those with whom they originally shared collective responsibility to do their bit. However, it is important here to think clearly about the nature of this collective. I have often for convenience described them as a group, but this could be misleading if it suggests a set of agents who are already bound together in some way, by identity or organization for example. But think instead of the collection of people who happen to be on the scene when a traffic accident occurs, or the much bigger collection of people who are so placed that they have a duty to contribute to the relief of global poverty. Neither of these forms a group in the stronger sense. What connects them to each other is simply the fact of being so placed that they are able by sharing responsibility to avert some harm.

This is relevant, because in groups proper we may think that responsibility passes between the members when some of them default. If a team of people has undertaken some task, for example, and some members of the team back out or become unable to continue with the work, we will often think that the rest of the team has an obligation to complete the task on their behalf. But this doesn't apply in the cases we are considering. There may or may not be some kind of signalling or communication between members of the collective—for instance a group of rescuers may need to talk to each other to divide up the necessary labour—but this will not amount to a precommitment to cover for defaulters. Indeed if anything the reverse will be the case: everyone has an incentive to send out a signal that he or she is prepared to do a fair share of the work, but nothing beyond that.

Responsibility, then, remains with the non-complying members of the collective even in cases where they are no longer in a position to contribute by virtue of earlier decisions they have made. Reversibility matters only for the practical reason that where it obtains, the compliers can choose between bending their efforts to get the non-compliers to play their part and taking up the slack themselves, whereas of course in the opposite case, only taking up the slack is an option. But in either case, compliers are not required to do more as a matter of justice.

This conclusion might, however, be challenged on the grounds that I have mis-represented the nature of collective responsibility in the situations being considered. I have relied on the idea that where collective responsibility can be fairly distributed among members of the relevant group, each has an obligation to do his fair share, but not more than that. If there are five people needing rescue, and five equally able rescuers, each rescuer's responsibility is limited to carrying out a single rescue. But there is another way of describing the situation. Suppose that the cost to each person of rescuing all five would still remain moderate, so that demandingness considerations do not enter the picture. Then it might be said that each rescuer has a responsibility to rescue all of the victims, even though, if fairness prevails, he or she will only need to discharge one-fifth of that total. In other words, the situation is more like one in which there is just a single victim in need of help and many possible rescuers—in that situation each of the rescuers has a responsibility to help, but in the event may well not have to discharge the corresponding obligation if somebody else steps in first.

What's wrong with this proposed redescription? I think it misunderstands the force of the idea of a fair division of responsibility. This is not just a convenient way of dividing up a task—each gets a specific job to do (rescue one person, say) and in that way the whole task is discharged quickly and efficiently. Instead it reflects the idea that each person is a responsibility-bearing moral agent, so that no one person is called upon to shoulder the entire burden of averting harm herself in the cases we are considering. Indeed if she does take that burden upon herself—by acknowledging in advance that she has a duty to take up the slack if others default—we might say that she does not treat the others as responsible moral agents. She would be like a mother with small children who asks for their help in clearing up the dinner table, and is pleasantly surprised when they do, but who knows that *because* they are only children all the responsibility finally rests with her. In contrast, in the five-victims, five-rescuers case, one who is left to do all the work as the others decamp can justifiably feel anger and resentment at the way she has been treated. She is not just somebody who is unlucky because as it turns out she has had to discharge her obligation in full; she has been exploited by agents whose responsibility is identical to hers but have simply chosen not to discharge it.

Where responsibility for averting a collective harm can be fairly divided, I have argued, justice can only require each agent to perform his or her fair share. But this conclusion runs up against an intuition that many people have, which is that there are situations in which justice does require more, situations in which questions about fair shares of responsibility should be set aside in favour of simply looking at the consequences of acting or not acting.[14] Rescue cases are the most frequently cited example: many think it obvious that if others are refusing to cooperate, the rescuer who has done his bit is duty-bound to jump back into the river and pull more people out, subject to the usual riders about excess cost or risk. But we might think the same applies to cases like global warming: if the world is reaching some crucial tipping point, such as the melting of a large portion of one of the polar ice-sheets for example, then the fact that other countries refuse to cut their carbon dioxide emissions in line with an agreed set of targets does not pre-empt complying countries being obliged as a matter of justice to cut back still further, given the consequences of not doing so.

What should we say about this? Everyone can agree that in these cases compliers have a strong *reason* to take up the slack, since doing so will have the effect of safeguarding basic rights otherwise under threat. We can also agree that agents who refuse to take up the slack merely because of their understandable indignation at the non-compliers are morally at fault and can be criticized and blamed for their refusal. But do they have an *obligation* to take up the slack, and if so what kind of obligation could this be?

One way to approach this question is by asking about possible enforcement. It is characteristic of obligations of justice that they are enforceable in principle by third parties, the nature of the enforcement that is justifiable depending on the case we have in mind.[15] Roughly speaking, the more urgent the duty of justice, as measured by the effects of not fulfilling it, the heavier the sanctions that may be applied by a third party to an unwilling duty-bearer. In a simple rescue case, where the only potential rescuer refuses to carry out a low-cost rescue, a third party arriving on the scene but unable to carry out the rescue herself (she can't swim, for example), can justifiably threaten to impose some fairly substantial loss, like pushing the rescuer's car into the water, for example, in order to save a life. This, it seems to me, applies also in the cases of collective responsibility we have been examining, which is why I said earlier on that if it were possible to create some mechanism that would ensure compliance that would very often be desirable. We are examining cases where no such mechanism can be

---

[14] In *The Demands of Consequentialism*, Mulgan proposes a division between two moral realms, which he calls the Realm of Reciprocity and the Realm of Necessity, and argues that in the latter realm, where we are responding to others' basic needs, simple consequentialism is the most plausible moral view, whereas in the former realm, where goals rather than needs are at issue, some form of collective consequentialism such as Murphy's is more appropriate. From Mulgan's perspective, then, to worry about questions of fairness when human lives are at stake is to fail to recognize that we have crossed into the (relatively unfamiliar) realm of necessity where we ought only to consider the actual consequences of the various actions that we might perform.

[15] I put this point cautiously, because I do not wish to claim that an obligation's enforceability is a necessary and sufficient condition for its being a duty of justice. The counterargument is made in A. Buchanan, 'Justice and Charity', *Ethics*, 97 (1987), 558–575.

created, for practical reasons, so I am appealing to enforceability only in order to test our intuitions about justice. So, consider the situation in which some have fulfilled their obligation to avert injustice but others have not. An enforcing agent arrives on the scene but is unable to get the non-compliers to act—threats of various kinds do not work. Is the enforcing agent then justified in turning his attention to the compliers and forcing them, if he can, to take up the slack? Simple consequentialism would say that he is so justified, but my intuition is that he is not. Because the compliers have already discharged their share of the responsibility, it cannot be right to force them to do more.[16] So their obligation to take up the slack is not an obligation of justice.

Let's then find a different label for this obligation—'a humanitarian obligation' would be my preferred description. Why call it an obligation at all if it is not enforceable? First of all, to distinguish it from cases of supererogation.[17] There is a moral difference between the person who refuses to go back into shallow water to pull out further victims having already done his share, and the person who declines to leap into a raging torrent for the same purpose. The first person can be blamed for his refusal while the second cannot. Second, in order to underline that the humanitarian duty in question is a weighty moral reason that can override others. Thus if the person who is taking up the slack has to disregard other duties for the time being, she could say, rightly, that in the circumstances she was obliged to do what she did. The language of obligation conveys the motivating force that the reason to take up the slack should have for the agent, while at the same time defeating the less urgent demands of others—people to whom promises have been made, or who have legitimate expect-ations of other kinds, for instance.[18] Third, to indicate that the victims have a legitimate complaint against the agent if she fails to discharge her obligation. Of course their main complaint will be against the non-compliers who have failed in their duty of justice.

---

[16] It might be said in reply here that although forcing the compliers to take up the slack is unjust, it is less unjust than leaving the victims to their fate, since it is the latter who will bear the greater costs. But consider the following case. A poor person has been robbed. I cannot force the thief to hand back what he has taken, but I can force a rich person (not involved in the robbery) to hand over an equivalent amount to the victim. The cost to the rich person, we can assume, is considerably less than the cost that the theft has inflicted on the poor person. In an outcome sense, therefore, a world in which the poor person has lost £1,000 is more unjust than a world in which the rich person has lost the same amount. How does this bear on the justice or injustice of the proposed enforcement? It would not be just to force the rich person to hand over his money. If I can persuade him to do so by appealing to his concern for the poor man, that would be good. But given that he is not responsible for the original theft, compulsion would fail to respect him as an agent. This shows what is wrong not only with simple consequentialism, but also with what we might call 'justice consequentialism' which instructs us to act so as to bring about the outcome with least injustice regardless of the means we use.

[17] Here I depart from Cohen's position in 'Who is Starving Whom?'. Cohen argues that doing more than one's fair share, even in cases where human lives are at stake, is supererogatory. I believe this fails to capture the strength of the reason one has to take up the slack in cases where this is necessary to avoid injustice—hence in place of a twofold distinction between the morally obligatory and the supererogatory I prefer a threefold distinction between obligations of justice, obligations of humanity, and supererogation.

[18] I don't mean to imply here that one obligation can only ever be overridden by another obligation. Frances Kamm has described a case in which performing a supererogatory act justifiably permits a person to breach an existing duty: donating one of your kidneys to save a life can justifiably take precedence over keeping a lunch appointment. See F. Kamm, *Morality, Mortality: Volume II* (New York: Oxford University

If restitution comes into question after the event, it is the original non-compliers who will be required to pay, not those who have merely failed to take up the slack. Nevertheless because those in the latter group have failed to act to safeguard the rights of the victims in circumstances where they could do so without incurring excessive cost, the victims do have a secondary complaint against them as well. By saying that they had a humanitarian obligation to act, we help to make sense of this complaint.

Does this also mean that compliers who decline to take up the slack are *responsible* for the harm that they fail to avert, in more than a merely causal sense? Do they *share* responsibility with the non-compliers? We need to take great care in our use of the language of responsibility here. Consider the following case. Daniel is searching for Edward with the intention of killing him. Frances knows of Daniel's intention, but can hide Edward in a place where Daniel will not find him. However, she decides not to do so and Edward is killed. In what sense, if any, is Frances responsible for Edward's death? If we were to say that she shares the responsibility with Daniel, this would be quite misleading, because it would assimilate the case to one in which Daniel and Frances have cooperated to kill Edward.[19] It is clear that the primary responsibility for Edward's death rests entirely with Daniel. Frances bears only a secondary responsibility, namely the remedial responsibility to avert harm that will otherwise be caused by another agent.[20] She is blameable for not discharging it in the absence of excusing or justifying factors. So she *is* responsible for Edward's death in a sense that is more than merely causal. However, her responsibility is of a categorically different kind from Daniel's, which is why any talk of shared responsibility is out of place. My suggestion is that this distinction applies also in the cases of partial compliance we have been considering. If the harm is not averted, primary responsibility for this lies with the non-compliers, and with them alone. If the compliers have a humanitarian obligation to take up the slack but fail to do so, they become responsible in a secondary sense. But it is incorrect to say that responsibility for the harm is *shared* by the two groups, for this neglects the categorical distinction between primary and secondary responsibility.

There is one final implication that I wish to draw out of this discussion. For reasons of simplicity I have been using examples in which it is individual people who have to decide whether to comply in situations of collective responsibility, or whether to go further by taking up the slack as well. But I said that the analysis should apply too to

---

Press, 1996), ch. 12. However, acquiring a contrary *obligation* in such cases will give the person in question an even stronger overriding reason.

[19] Note that in cases where two or more people collaborate to produce an outcome, responsibility can be shared unequally: there can, for example, be a primary instigator who carries most of the responsibility, and others who are merely his accomplices. So if we were to describe the original Daniel/Frances case as one in which Daniel bears more responsibility for Edward's death than Frances, this would still be fundamentally misleading because it would suggest that they were acting as unequal collaborators.

[20] The idea of remedial responsibility is explained and contrasted with outcome responsibility in my *National Responsibility and Global Justice*, ch. 4.

collective agents such as states, and it seems clear that problems such as resource conservation and climate change are more important than individual rescues if we are thinking about their effects on human rights and human welfare. So what does our discussion tell us about collective agents specifically? Notice here that compliance problems will often emerge at two levels: first the collective has to decide whether to discharge its fair share of responsibility, and then the individual members have to decide whether to do what they are asked to do by the collective. Thus Britain, say, has to decide whether to sign a treaty that sets limits to the overall level of greenhouse gas emissions that its population generates in any year, and then individual citizens have to decide whether to make the behavioural changes that are required of them by cutting down on the use of fossil fuels and so forth. Now I take it that where an obligation of justice is involved, the collective is justified in enforcing its decision if necessary. So if we believe that runaway climate change threatens the basic rights of people worldwide, the UK government will be justified in compelling citizens to comply with measures that are necessary to keep gas emissions below the level agreed in the treaty, such as using only low-emission vehicles for transport. On the other hand, where the harm that we are trying to avert by collective action is not one that involves injustice, or where what we are doing collectively is actually taking up the slack left by others, then internal compulsion becomes more problematic. And this raises difficult questions of political philosophy. Suppose, for example, a nation sets itself more ambitious targets in relation to climate change because of an awareness that other countries are not going to fulfil their obligations: can it be right to force citizens to change their behaviour so as to meet those targets, or must the state at this point rely upon encouraging voluntary compliance? Or to take a different case, what obligations can be compulsorily imposed on citizens in response to humanitarian disasters such as famines or civil wars occurring abroad where primary responsibility lies with the governments of those states?[21] Although there is no algorithm for answering these questions, I hope that what I have said here provides at least a partial framework for thinking about them.

---

[21] For a fuller discussion of this issue, see my chapter 'The Responsibility to Protect Human Rights' in Lukas H. Meyer (ed.), *Legitimacy, Justice and Public International Law* (Cambridge: Cambridge University Press, 2009), 232–251.

12

Luck Prioritarian Justice in Health[1]

Shlomi Segall

When are inequalities in health unjust? An initial response may be—'always'. From an egalitarian perspective, it is arguably always unacceptable that individuals do not enjoy the same level of health or that different social groups do not have the same healthy life expectancy (I shall shortly explain that term). If so, it would follow that justice requires making everyone's health as equal as possible.[2] Let us term this view *outcome equality* in health.[3]

Critics often observe the following two problems with outcome equality in health.[4] First, some inequalities in health originate in individuals' freely chosen lifestyle. The ideal of outcome equality in health would mean that society is committed, as a matter of distributive justice, to equalizing the health of the chain-smoker and that of the diligent jogger.[5] Note that equalizing the health of the smoker and the jogger is a far more demanding requirement than simply equalizing their access to health *care*. For, the ideal of outcome equality says that there is something *unjust* about the inequality in health between the jogger and the smoker even when that inequality is a direct result of their voluntary and informed choices. This seems problematic. We may think it is right to grant the jogger and the smoker equal access to health care, and we may even attempt to curb the health inequality between them through some preventive measure (e.g. a ban on smoking in public places, subsidies for gym membership). But it seems implausible to say that there is something 'unjust' in the way that health happens to be

---

[1] In writing this chapter I have benefited from comments and suggestions by Dick Arneson, Greg Bognar, Dan Brock, Eric Cavallero, Norman Daniels, Nir Eyal, Iwao Hirose, Adi Koplovitz, Martin McIvor, David Miller, Ole Norheim, Daniel Schwartz, Neema Sofaer, Zofia Stemplowska, and Dan Wikler.

[2] See, for example, A. J. Culyer and A. Wagstaff, 'Equity and Equality in Health and Health Care', *Journal of Health Economics*, 12 (1993), 431–457.

[3] Of course, it is highly probable that there will exist an inequality of health between a 20-year-old and a 70-year-old. But proponents of outcome equality in health need not characterize this state of affairs as unjust. Rather, outcome equality in health takes a lifetime view of equality, comparing individuals' health throughout their lives, say in the form of healthy life expectancy.

[4] See for example, N. Daniels, B. Kennedy, and I. Kawachi, 'Health and Inequality, or, Why Justice is Good for Our Health' in S. Anand, F. Peter, and A. Sen (eds), *Public Health, Ethics, and Equity* (Oxford: Oxford University Press, 2004), 63–91, at 73.

[5] See S. Marchand, D. Wikler, and B. Landesman, 'Class, Health, and Justice', *The Milbank Quarterly*, 76 (1998), 463–465.

distributed between the two, when that inequality is owed in its entirety (as stipulated) to their respective choices. Call this the *smoker/jogger* objection to outcome equality in health.[6]

Here is the second common objection to outcome equality in health (and to the suggestion that health inequalities are always unjust). In almost any contemporary society men have shorter healthy life expectancy compared to women. But it is often pointed out that inequalities in life expectancy between men and women are not normally considered unjust.[7] If this view is correct (I return to examine this assertion later on, but will accept it for now for the sake of argument), then it cannot be true that health inequalities are *always* unjust. Call this the *inequality between the sexes* objection to outcome equality in health.[8]

My aim here is to help advance the egalitarian discussion of health equity beyond these two familiar objections. To do so, I offer two competing egalitarian principles that may overcome these initial objections. The two principles represent, respectively, a luck egalitarian approach and an approach based on Rawls's Fair Equality of Opportunity Principle. Here are the two principles:

1. *Equality of opportunity for health*: It is unfair for an individual to end up less healthy than another if she invested at least as much effort in looking after her health.

2. Fair *equality of opportunity for health*: It is unfair for an individual to end up less healthy than another if she invested at least as much effort in looking after her health, *provided she has at least as good a genetic disposition as that other person.*

I will argue that the first principle is superior to the second principle, and consequently that the luck egalitarian approach to health equity is superior to the Rawlsian approach. However, both these egalitarian principles (as well as the ideal of outcome

---

[6] The view that health inequalities that are owed to freely chosen lifestyles are not unjust is offered also in J. Le Grand, 'Equity, Health, and Health Care', *Social Justice Research*, 1 (1987), 257–274 and M. Whitehead, 'The Concepts and Principles of Equity and Health', *Health Promotion International*, 6 (1991), 217–228. For a review of health inequalities and responsibility for health see D. Wikler, 'Personal and Social Responsibility for Health' in Anand *et al.* (eds), *Public Health, Ethics, and Equity*, 109–134, especially 113–117. See also F. Peter, 'Health Equity and Social Justice' in that same volume, 93–105, at 94–95.

[7] A. K. Sen, *Inequality Reexamined* (Cambridge, MA: Harvard University Press, 1992), ch. 6; 'Why Health Equity?' in Anand *et al.* (eds), *Public Health, Ethics, and Equity*, 21–33.

[8] Note that I speak of inequalities in health between the 'sexes', whereas some recent literature on health equity refers to '*gender* inequalities', '*gender* differences', and '*gender* discrimination' (S. Anand, 'The Concern for Equity in Health' in Anand *et al.* (eds), *Public Health, Ethics, and Equity*, 15–20, at 19; Sen, 'Why Health Equity?', 30; *Development as Freedom* (Oxford: Oxford University Press, 1999), 20; C. J. L. Murray, 'Rethinking DALYs' in C. J. L. Murray and A. D. Lopez (eds), *The Global Burden of Disease* (Cambridge, MA: Harvard School of Public Health, World Health Organization, World Bank, 1996), 1–98, at 16, 18; M. Powers and R. Faden, *Social Justice: The Moral Foundations of Public Health and Health Policy* (Oxford: Oxford University Press, 2006), 62. Now, 'gender' usually refers to the social construct of sex. The *Oxford English Dictionary* defines it as 'a euphemism for the sex of a human being, often intended to emphasize the social and cultural, as opposed to the biological, distinctions between the sexes'. 'Gender discrimination' or 'gender inequalities' on that understanding, then, appear to be a tautology, for 'gender' *already* implies 'sex-based differences'. It is therefore more accurate, I think, to speak of 'inequalities between the *sexes*'.

equality) are vulnerable to yet a third objection, namely, the 'levelling down' objection. Consequently, I argue that a revised version of the luck egalitarian principle, namely, a luck *prioritarian* principle, avoids all three objections to outcome equality in health, and as such presents the most attractive account of health equity on offer. Here is that principle:

> *Prioritizing the opportunity for health of the worse-off.* Fairness requires giving priority to improving the health of an individual if she has invested more rather than less effort in looking after her health, and of those who have invested equal effort, priority should be given to those who are worse off (health-wise).

The argument unfolds as follows. Section 12.1 presents the two above-mentioned competing egalitarian principles of health equity—the luck egalitarian 'equality of opportunity for health' and the Rawlsian '*fair* equality of opportunity (FEO) for health'—and examines how they cope with the jogger/smoker objection and the inequality between the sexes objection. FEO for health, it will turn out, copes better with the latter objection than does the luck-egalitarian principle. In section 12.2, though, I present two decisive objections to adopting FEO for health. Having rejected the Rawlsian approach, I return in section 12.3 to examine in detail how the luck egalitarian approach copes with the 'inequality between the sexes' objection. I try to argue there that, despite its prominence in the literature, this objection is misplaced. Finally, in order to avoid the levelling objection, I argue, in section 12.4, why *luck prioritarian health equity* is a plausible and attractive account of justice in the distribution of health.

Before moving to present the two competing egalitarian approaches to health equity I should bracket an important question. This chapter is concerned with 'health equity', which is the concern for a just distribution of health *independently* of a just distribution of other goods. In other words, I take it, for the sake of argument, that we can discuss justice in the sphere of health in isolation from a more comprehensive theory of social justice. That is, to be sure, a controversial premise, for it is far from obvious that we ought to treat health as a separate sphere of justice, and be concerned with the just distribution of health independently of a more general theory of justice. Indeed, we may think that anyone who is concerned with justice in health ought to be concerned, at least as a matter of principle, with *overall* inequalities (in whatever the relevant currency is, say welfare).[9] (In fact, luck egalitarians are normally happy to take the all-inclusive 'opportunity for welfare' as their sole equalisandum.) In contrast, and as several philosophers stress, we may think that health is special and, as such, deserving of a separate principle of justice. That special status of health could be attributed to the unique impact that health has on our ability to pursue whatever it is we want to pursue in life. (Some people speak in this respect about health's impact on opportunities for

---

[9] See D. M. Hausman, 'What's Wrong with Health Inequalities', *Journal of Political Philosophy*, 15 (2007), 46–66; Powers and Faden, *Social Justice*.

the pursuit of life plans while others focus on its impact on our basic capabilities.) Consequently, many people think that inequalities in health deserve priority and, as such, a separate principle of justice.[10] I take no stand on that debate in this chapter. Rather, my argument merely takes, as its starting point, the quest for a separate account of justice in health, and thus sets out to examine plausible candidates for that account. Notice also that in discussing health equity in isolation from a general theory of justice the term 'worse off' refers (unless stated otherwise) to 'worse off health-wise', rather than 'worse off all things considered'.

Finally, let me pause, as promised, for a technical remark. 'Healthy life expectancy' is an accepted currency of inequalities in health.[11] It takes into account not only the length but also quality (health-wise) of one's life. Healthy life expectancy can be measured either in 'quality adjusted life years' (QALY) or in 'disability adjusted life years' (DALY).[12] (The difference between these two measurements is irrelevant for the purposes of my discussion.) I should also mention that I use 'health equity', 'just health', and 'justice in health', interchangeably.

12.1 Rawlsian vs. luck egalitarian justice in health

Let me, then, sketch the two competing egalitarian principles of health equity and the different approaches that underpin them. Here is the first principle mentioned:

1. *Equality of opportunity for health*: It is unfair for an individual to end up less healthy than another if she invested at least as much effort[13] in looking after her health.

Now, it is easy to see how this principle avoids the smoker/jogger objection. According to this principle it is *not* unfair for the smoker to end up less healthy than the jogger, for she did not invest as much effort in looking after her health as did the

---

[10] N. Daniels, *Just Health Care* (Cambridge: Cambridge University Press, 1985); *Just Health: Meeting Health Needs Fairly* (Cambridge: Cambridge University Press, 2008), ch. 2; Sen, 'Why Health Equity?'; Anand, 'The Concern for Equity in Health'. Notice, though, that even a separate theory of justice in health cannot be considered in isolation from the way in which inequalities in health interact and overlap with inequalities in other goods and burdens (more on which below). It might also be the case that, effectively, there is little difference between the two approaches. Since it is very plausible that good health underpins much of what constitutes human welfare, it would turn out to be the case that even general theories of justice (ones that take welfare as their sole equalisandum) would end up prioritizing health.

[11] See E. E. Gakidou, C. J. L. Murray, and J. Frenk, 'Defining and Measuring Health Inequality: An Approach based on the Distribution of Health Expectancy', *Bulletin of the World Health Organization*, 78 (2000), 42–54.

[12] See Murray and Lopez (eds), *The Global Burden of Disease*. Note that, since 'an individual life expectancy' is meaningless (see also D. M. Hausman, Y. Asada, and T. Hedemann, 'Health Inequalities and Why They Matter', *Health Care Analysis*, 10 (2002), 177–191, at 186), on the account discussed here 'health inequalities' are inevitably inequalities between groups. What counts as a group for the purposes of health inequalities, however, is left open.

[13] It is often pointed out that the level of effort an individual is able to exert may itself be subject to morally arbitrary constraints. I should stress, then, that 'effort' is here meant as a place-holder for whatever it is the reader considers to be within the individual's control.

jogger.[14] This approach to justice in health is essentially a luck egalitarian one because it seeks to equalize opportunities for health rather than health itself.[15] The idea that people are entitled to an equal opportunity to be healthy has an immediate appeal. It not only avoids the smoker/jogger objection but appears, in general, less paternalistic than equalizing health as such. For society, according to the ideal of equal opportunity for health, only seeks to allow individuals to be as healthy as they themselves choose to be.[16]

Notice, however, that this approach is still vulnerable to the 'inequalities between the sexes' objection. For it is a medical fact that even at birth (and arguably even earlier)[17] men and women do not enjoy an equal opportunity for health. Pursuing equal opportunity to be healthy would require, then, equalizing opportunities for health between men and women. 'Equal opportunity for health' is therefore still vulnerable to the 'inequality between the sexes' objection. I turn now to the alternative approach that, as will emerge, easily avoids *both* objections to outcome equality in health.

The alternative egalitarian principle, FEO for health, is able to avoid the 'inequality between the sexes' objection by switching from the general notion of equal opportunity to the more specific Rawlsian 'fair equality of opportunity' principle (FEOP). According to Rawls's FEOP, equally talented individuals, who exercise an equal level of effort in honing their talents, should have equal access to jobs and careers. In contrast to *formal* equality of opportunity, the FEOP thus seeks to neutralize all social impediments to individuals reaping the fruits of their talent and effort.[18] Here is how, I said, one may formulate FEO *for health*:

2. *Fair equality of opportunity for health*: It is unfair for an individual to end up less healthy than another if she invested at least as much effort in looking after her health, provided she has at least as good a genetic disposition as that other person.

Notice that in adopting the FEOP as the principle of justice regulating inequalities in health we would be treating health in the same way we treat jobs: normally, we do not object to some people having better jobs than others, but we do object when equally

---

[14] Notice also that according to the stated principle it is also *not* unfair for the smoker and the jogger to end up having the exact same health outcome. For, unfairness only obtains when there is *inequality* in health. It is *only* unfair, according to the stated principle, if the person investing as much or more effort (the jogger) ends up being less healthy than the other (the smoker).

[15] See, for example, R. Arneson, 'Equality and Equal Opportunity for Welfare', *Philosophical Studies*, 56 (1989), 77–93, at 85–86.

[16] That is, effectively, the position held by Le Grand, 'Equity, Health, and Health Care'. See also R. M. Veatch, 'Justice and the Right to Health Care: An Egalitarian Account' in T. J. Bole and W. B. Bondeson (eds), *Rights to Health Care* (Dordrecht: Kluwer, 1991), 83–102, especially 83; M. Whitehead, *The Concepts and Principles of Equity and Health* (Copenhagen: World Health Organization, 1990), 9; P. Rosa Dias and A. M. Jones, 'Giving Equality of Opportunity a Fair Innings', *Health Economics*, 16 (2007), 109–112.

[17] Sen cites the interesting finding that female foetuses have higher chances of survival than male ones. See his *Development as Freedom*, 105.

[18] J. Rawls, *A Theory of Justice* (Oxford: Oxford University Press, 1971), §14.

qualified individuals do not have an equal shot at those better jobs. I have mentioned that FEOP in Rawls's scheme holds between individuals of equal talents and skills. That is why, I propose, we could perhaps fit genetic differences between the sexes into the category of 'talents and skills'. Thereby, FEO for health would mandate that society guarantee individuals of equal genetic disposition (as pointed out, men compared to men, and women compared to women, but also many other instances)[19] an equal shot at being healthy,[20] thereby avoiding the 'inequality between the sexes' objection.[21]

FEO for health also easily avoids the jogger/smoker objection. Rawls's FEOP, recall, requires equal access (to jobs and positions) between individuals of equal talent, but also of equal *effort*. Individuals who possess equal natural talent, and who invest an equal measure of effort in honing these natural talents and developing those skills, ought to have an equal chance in the competition for jobs.[22] As mentioned, in the application to health we may say that the extent to which people lead a healthy lifestyle corresponds, in a way, to exerting effort in the Rawlsian sense.[23] Applying the FEOP to health would therefore mean that people of equal genetic disposition, who invest the same effort in looking after their health, ought to have the same health prospects.[24] In this way, we see, the FEOP allows us to escape the counter-intuitive conclusion that the jogger and the smoker are entitled to an identical health outcome.

12.2 Two problems with fair equality of opportunity for health

Although initially attractive, there are nevertheless some undesirable consequences to using the FEOP to regulate justice in health. It seems to me that the two problems I am about to outline ought to lead us to reject FEO for health (and endorse, rather, the luck egalitarian approach).

---

[19] Supposing, for example, it were possible to distinguish different smokers' genetic propensity to contract lung cancer, Rawls's FEOP would warrant equalizing health within, and not between, these groups of smokers.

[20] An approach to measuring health inequalities that in fact assumes something like the FEO for health is presented in A. Bommier and G. Stecklov, 'Defining Health Inequality: Why Rawls Succeeds where Social Welfare Theory Fails', *Journal of Health Economics*, 21 (2002), 497–513.

[21] Notice that the pathway I draw between FEOP and health is of the opposite direction compared to the one drawn by Daniels. I look here at FEO *for* health, whereas Daniels proposes health *for the sake of* FEO (for life plans). Having said that, Daniels would probably endorse also FEO for health. The closest he comes to endorsing that position is in saying that society ought not be committed to 'the futile task of leveling all natural differences between persons'. *Just Health Care*, 46. For further discussion of Daniels's view on the place of responsibility in just health policies see his chapter in this volume.

[22] Rawls, *A Theory of Justice*, 84; *Political Liberalism* (New York: University of Columbia Press, 1993), 184.

[23] See for example, J. E. Roemer, 'A Pragmatic Theory of Responsibility for the Egalitarian Planner', *Philosophy and Public Affairs*, 22 (1993), 146–166.

[24] So according to FEO for health it is *not unfair* for a person of better genetic disposition (say a female smoker compared to a male smoker) to end up having better health. It is also not *unfair* if the female smoker and the male smoker end up having *equal* health. It *is* unfair if the female smoker ends up being *less* healthy than the male smoker.

The first objection to using the FEOP as a principle of health equity is, perhaps, rather straightforward. FEOP, remember, mandates equal opportunity for health between individuals of equal genetic disposition. It is a principle that stresses a societal obligation to remove social obstacles to good health. Removing social obstacles to good health is, admittedly, an attractive feature of the FEOP since, in effect, it mandates that group membership, and social background more generally, should not determine one's prospects of attaining the goods and positions in question (in this case, health). And indeed, health disparities caused by socio-economic and racial background are precisely the type of health disparities that many commentators see as the ones especially warranting our attention.[25] Furthermore, a societal obligation to remove only social obstacles to good health might also seem desirable given that doing so sidesteps the (arguably) counter-intuitive outcome of equalizing life expectancy between men and women. At the same time, note, to pursue equal opportunity for health between individuals of equal 'natural' disposition is to imply that justice requires us to attend *only* to the social causes of ill health. That means that justice, on this reading, does not require treating medical conditions that result from genetic factors. That, however, would be highly implausible as we commonly think that a just health policy is one that attends to bad health also when it has natural (genetic) causes.[26]

To illustrate the point, consider the following case. Andrea and Beatrice have an identical genetic disposition. Clarissa and Dina also have an identical genetic disposition to one another, and one that is weaker compared to Andrea and Beatrice. Suppose, for the sake of simplicity, that all four individuals exert an identical effort in trying to keep a healthy lifestyle. According to FEO for health it is unfair for Andrea to end up with worse health than Beatrice. (The same applies for Clarissa and Dina.) FEO for health also maintains that it is *not* unfair for Andrea and Beatrice to end up having better health than Clarissa and Dina. The following situation is therefore not unfair: A: (75, 55), where the numbers represent the healthy life expectancy of the two pairs. Imagine now that we could invest enough resources, medical and otherwise, in Clarissa and Dina such that they end up having a closer level of health to that enjoyed by Andrea and Beatrice. Note that this redistribution in Clarissa's and Dina's favour may entail that Andrea and Beatrice now enjoy a somewhat lower level of health than they could otherwise have had. Suppose the new situation is (B): (70, 65). Egalitarians would clearly favour policy B over A. That otherwise desirable policy, however, is not recommended by FEO for health (admittedly, neither is it ruled out by it). For, according to that principle, it is not a requirement of justice that we give those of weaker genetic disposition (Clarissa and Dina) an equal (or at least, more equal than

[25] See Anand, 'The Concern for Equity in Health', 19; Sen, 'Why Health Equity?', 23; Hausman *et al.*, 'Health Inequalities and Why They Matter'.

[26] See, on a similar point, S. Marchand, 'Liberal Theories and Health', unpublished manuscript (cited with permission of the author).

previously) opportunity for health compared to that enjoyed by those of better genetic disposition. This, it seems to me, is a distinctive weakness of FEOP in its application to health.

Now, it might be said that I needlessly assume that, on the Rawlsian account, the FEOP is the only principle of justice regulating health inequalities. Instead, one might argue, it is possible to complement FEO for health with other principles, ones that would take care of naturally caused illness. It is possible, for example, to complement FEO for health with a principle that maximizes the health of the worse-off, along the lines of the difference principle. (According to the difference principle (DP), recall, inequalities are justified so long as they are to the benefit the worse-off.)[27] DP would then be taking care of the remainder of health deficits, including, critically, those owed to natural causes. This would seem to bypass the objection I outlined here. There is even some basis for this in the Rawlsian rationale for the two principles. We may think of the FEOP as the principle in charge of removing social obstacles to individuals gaining access to jobs, whereas the DP is a principle ameliorating the disadvantages of being naturally worse off (lack of talent, say). In short, even in the Rawlsian scheme we might view the FEOP as responsible for correcting social inequalities, whereas the DP is in charge of compensating for natural ones. It might be suggested that the same division of labour, as it were, may be applied to health. FEO for health would get rid of social obstacles to good health whereas the DP would be improving the health of those who have a weak genetic disposition. Or, in other words, the FEO would regulate the social determinants of health, whereas the DP would regulate health's natural determinants.

This is an attractive idea. One particular weakness in this moral division of labour between the two principles, however, is that it is a little arbitrary. Namely, when it comes to health it seems arbitrary to think that the neutralization of social inequalities should take lexical priority over the neutralization of natural ones. And it is furthermore arbitrary to require strict equality in social access to health but to nevertheless allow inequalities in natural access to it.[28] But these are not necessarily insurmountable problems for the Rawlsian position. A different thing to note, though, is that the response under consideration here in effect amounts to saying that (the good of) health should be regulated *twice* in a Rawlsian scheme: first by the FEOP, and then again by the DP. Rawls himself, it should be noted, does not allow for anything of this sort. While it is the case, admittedly, that each of his three principles of justice[29] *constrains* the operation of the principles that are lexically inferior to it, it is also the case that liberties, opportunities, and other primary goods are *distributed* only by one of the three principles of justice in Rawls's scheme. There is a good reason for that, and it is the same reason that explains why the response under review ultimately has no force

---

[27] Rawls, *A Theory of Justice*, §11.

[28] I am grateful to an anonymous Oxford University Press referee for helping me clarify this point.

[29] Rawls's three lexically ordered principles are the principle of equal basic liberties, the FEOP, and the DP. See *A Theory of Justice*, 60.

here: it is impossible to distribute the same good, namely health, according to two different patterning principles, one stipulating strict equality and the other stipulating maximin. Consider, for example, what it would be like to distribute access to jobs and careers both by the FEOP and by the DP. The FEOP requires strictly equal access (between individuals of equal talent). The lexically inferior DP tells us to distribute the same good in a way that would most benefit the worse-off. The DP may thus recommend an end-state whereby individuals who have the same talent do not have an equal opportunity for a particular job. This may happen, for example, if unequal opportunity would somehow make everyone, including the worse-off, have better access to jobs than they previously had. (Suppose that in exchange for having a greater opportunity for certain jobs, the well-off promise to create more jobs for other, less well-off individuals (more on this issue shortly).) The two principles may therefore recommend conflicting policies. The same would happen if we tried to regulate health both by the FEOP and by the DP. Either opportunity for health ought to be strictly equal between those of equal natural disposition, or, alternatively, opportunities for health are allowed to be unequal between those of equal natural disposition (provided everyone is made better off). We cannot have both.

Here is my second objection to FEO for health. Rawls, it is worth remembering, stipulated that opportunities for jobs should be equalized even if to do otherwise would somehow generate more jobs for everyone. Allowing for this levelling down effect is perhaps the main difference between the FEOP and the DP, and is also the reason why the FEOP is, in the first place, lexically prior to the DP in the Rawlsian scheme. Rawls thought that the 'waste' involved in levelling down is an appropriate price to pay here. The reason being that when it comes to jobs, he maintained, it is important to guarantee a truly equal (rather than merely a Pareto optimal) access, and for a variety of reasons.[30] Note, then, that FEO for health would demand equalizing people's opportunities for health, even when having unequal opportunities would somehow improve everyone's health. Suppose, for example, that some medical procedure could improve public health, but would make those who are already healthier even more proportionally healthy than others. In other words, suppose the procedure in question could improve everyone's health, *while* aggravating already existing health disparities. Note that as a matter of fact this sort of thing happens quite often. It is generally the case that individuals who are better off (health-wise and otherwise, the two are almost universally correlated) are more likely to benefit more (than those who are already

---

[30] '[I]f some places were not open on a basis fair to all, those kept out would be right in feeling unjustly treated even though they benefited from the greater efforts of those who were allowed to hold them. They would be justified in their complaint not only because they were excluded from certain external rewards of office but because they were debarred from the realization of self which comes from a skilful and devoted exercise of social duties. They would be deprived of one of the main forms of human good.' Rawls, *A Theory of Justice*, 84.

worse off than they are) from any given medical intervention.[31] In fact, it has been observed that only a minority of medical procedures improve population health *without* deepening already existing inequalities in health.[32] To avoid increasing inequalities in health we would have to deny medical treatment to individuals who would otherwise benefit from it, which hardly seems like a desirable policy. Equalizing opportunity for health appears, then, to mandate levelling down potential absolute levels of health.[33] And that seems like a distinctively undesirable consequence of FEO for health.[34]

A proponent of the FEO for health might remind us that it is no accident that Rawls's FEOP allows levelling down in the first place. Rawls's reason for rejecting unequal access to jobs even when that would improve everyone's access (to jobs) is based on considerations of self-respect. His concern was that Pareto-optimal access might undermine the self-respect of those who end up having lesser access.[35] A similar concern might be employed in order to counter my argument here. Namely, it might be said that to give some individuals lesser opportunity for health compared to others, in order to avoid levelling down, is disrespectful. However, it is not obvious that

---

[31] This phenomenon is owed to a whole host of factors, such as the better-off having superior education and a more flexible working day. These factors contribute both to individuals' ability to secure better medical care for themselves, and to their ability to better comply with medical advice.

[32] D. Mechanic, 'Disadvantage, Inequality, and Social Policy', *Health Affairs*, 21 (2002), 48–59. The following example is often mentioned in this context. In the US, black infant mortality rates were 64 per cent higher than infant mortality rates for whites in 1954, and were even higher (130 per cent higher) in 1998, even though white rates dropped by 20.8 per thousand and blacks dropped by 30.1 per thousand in that period. So while everyone's health has improved considerably, health inequalities were at the same time aggravated. (See also A. Deaton, 'Policy Implications of the Gradient of Health and Wealth', *Health Affairs*, 21 (2002), 13–30, at 25). Another example, cited by Daniels, is that stop-smoking campaigns may be more effective for individuals from higher socio-economic groups than for individuals from lower socio-economic groups. (See E. M. Barbeau, N. Krieger, and M.-J. Soobader, 'Working Class Matters: Socio-Economic Disadvantage, Race/Ethnicity, Gender, and Smoking in NIHS', *American Journal of Public Health*, 94 (2004), 269–287). An exception to the rule that public health interventions benefit the rich and healthy more than they do the poor and ill is the fluoridation of water. Many well off people in the US drink only bottled water, and so the fluoridation of water seems to be one type of health intervention that has a distinctly egalitarian effect, benefiting the poor more than it does the rich. I owe that observation to Eric Cavallero.

[33] See also Sen, 'Why Health Equity?', 25. Some may object to the use of the term 'leveling down' in this context, for what is at stake is not levelling down *actual* levels of health (say, stopping to treat healthier patients, or even deliberately harming their health). Rather, my illustration so far only describes a case where the FEOP prevents us from exacerbating inequalities even when doing so would benefit the worse-off. In effect, then, the case before us only concerns levelling down *potential* gains (to health) rather than current gains. While I do not dispute that observation, I cannot see how it affects the undesirability of FEO for health. For though levelling down potential gains to health is perhaps not as repugnant as levelling down current levels of health (for one thing, the latter may involve violating the self-ownership that individuals have over their own bodies whereas the former perhaps does not), but it is undesirable nevertheless.

[34] Rawls, it seems, was aware of the levelling down effect of his FEOP, and his 'second priority rule' (*A Theory of Justice*, 303) tries to address this problem. It says that 'an inequality of opportunity must enhance the opportunities of those with the lesser opportunity'. But of course that priority rule now conflicts with Rawls's earlier rationale for strict equality required by the FEOP (see again *A Theory of Justice*, 84). It is therefore either the case that opportunities are to be treated like any other social primary good (and hence be regulated under a Maximin principle), or maintain their lexical priority over social primary goods and thus be distributed equally.

[35] Rawls, *A Theory of Justice*, 84.

allowing inequalities in health that improve the position of those whose health is worse off would be disrespectful.[36] If due publicity is given to the fact that an equalizing policy would have inevitably resulted in significant loss of health to the worse-off, then it is far from obvious that such a policy would be perceived as disrespectful.

It might still be objected that the consequence of levelling down does not yet demonstrate that FEOP is defective as a principle of *justice* in health. For, there are other ethical considerations besides those of justice that a health policy ought to take into account, such as a concern for maximizing utility (in this case, health). FEO for health might not be desirable *all things considered*, the critic might say, but that does not mean that FEO for health is *unjust*. Notice that my second objection was not that the FEO for health leads to unjust results by virtue of its levelling down, but rather that it leads to *undesirable* results. To escape those consequences, the FEOP needs not only to be traded off with other principles and values, but must actually be overridden. For, the FEOP, recall, does not merely *permit* levelling down; it actually requires doing so. Thus, coupling the FEOP with the DP in order to escape levelling down in fact implies overriding the requirements of justice. A luck egalitarian account of justice in health, I will argue below, may escape the levelling down objection without the recourse to overriding the requirements of justice. In that sense, it proves superior to FEO for health.

Let us take stock of what has been said so far. At the beginning of the chapter I outlined two common objections to outcome equality in health, namely the jogger/ smoker objection and the inequality between the sexes objection. FEO for health, I then said, overcomes both these objections. But, as I have demonstrated in this section, FEO for health has at least two decisive weaknesses, and so, despite its initial attraction, appears not so attractive as an account of justice in health.

12.3 Health inequalities between the sexes revisited

By rejecting FEO for health we now fall back to the luck egalitarian account of health equity. Recall, however, that that principle did not cope so well with the 'inequality between the sexes' objection. (Or in any case, it did not cope with that objection as well as the FEOP did.) Furthermore, on the face of it, the luck egalitarian principle is also likely to be as vulnerable as the FEOP to the levelling down objection. In the rest of this chapter, then, I defend (and in the process also modify) the luck egalitarian approach from these two objections. I begin, in this section, by addressing the 'inequality between the sexes' objection.

The FEOP, recall, avoided the inequality between the sexes objection by advocating equalizing opportunities for health between individuals *of equal genetic disposition*. The luck egalitarian principle does not contain a proviso of that kind. It is therefore

---

[36] To borrow from Arneson's discussion of FEO for jobs. See R. Arneson, 'Against Rawlsian Equality of Opportunity', *Philosophical Studies*, 93 (1999), 77–112, at 104–105.

vulnerable to the 'inequalities between the sexes' objection because pursuing equal opportunity to be healthy would require equalizing the opportunity for health between men and women.[37] Recalling the example we used earlier, equal opportunity for health would not only recommend narrowing the gap in life expectancy between Andrea and Clarissa; it would also recommend doing so between Andrea and Christopher, say. Many people find that suggestion to be counter-intuitive.[38] Indeed, it has been suggested that the view that we ought to attempt and equalize the opportunity for health between men and women is 'absurd'.[39] Any luck egalitarian account of health equity, then, would have to overcome this obstacle. I want to suggest that a luck egalitarian account of health equity in fact bites this bullet and asserts, against a widespread (but ultimately misguided) intuition, that inequalities in health between the sexes *are* a concern for justice. To do so, I examine first some possible arguments that may potentially back the apparently popular view that health inequalities between the sexes are not unjust. (These hypothesized views are italicized.)

1. *Inequalities in life expectancy between men and women are, in effect, inequalities between very old people. And, whether someone lives to be 78 instead of 75 should be very low indeed on our list of priorities given that there is so much life-saving and health-improving to be done for other, younger patients.*

This, however, is a common misconception that overlooks the fact that the term 'life expectancy' represents a statistical average that normally takes into account deaths of both younger and older individuals. In fact, then, we are dealing here with differences in mortality between men and women of *all* ages. Moreover, suppose we do accept the suggestion that inequalities in life expectancy between men and women are not of moral concern since they only amount to negligible differences in life years late in life. On that rationale, note, the frequently invoked disparities between socio-economic classes could turn out to be even *less* worthy of moral concern. For, it is sometimes the case that differences in life expectancy between men and women are *greater* than the

---

[37] Notice that the luck egalitarian equality of opportunity for health does not necessarily condemn outcome inequality in life expectancy between women and men (for that inequality might be the result of individuals' voluntary action). But EOP for health does condemn an inequality *in opportunity* between men and women as such. That is, it rules as unjust the fact that one's sex determines one's health prospects.

[38] The thought that inequalities in life expectancy between the sexes are *not unjust* is the reason why, for example, the Human Development Index, which drew inspiration from Sen's capability approach, sets a different life expectancy target for men and women (82.5 and 87.5 respectively), while setting all other targets as equal between the sexes. (The United Nations Development Program, *Human Development Report: Concept and Measurement of Human Development* (Oxford: Oxford University Press, 1990)). There is also some quantitative evidence for respondents' preference for reducing health inequalities between socio-economic groups and for *resisting* giving preference in medical treatment on the basis of sex. See P. Dolan, R. Shaw, A. Tsuchiya, and A. Williams, 'QALY Maximization and People's Preferences: A Methodological Review of the Literature', *Health Economics*, 14 (2005), 197–208; P. Anand and A. Wailoo, 'Utilities versus Rights to Publicly Provided Goods: Argument and Evidence from Health Care Rationing', *Economica*, 67 (2000), 543–577.

[39] J. Kekes, 'A Question for Egalitarians', *Ethics*, 107 (1997), 658–669, at 662.

much-talked-about differences in life expectancy between social classes (as is the case, in fact, in the UK).[40]

> 2. *There is nothing unjust about health inequalities between the sexes because differences in life expectancy between men and women are due to natural factors alone. Women's genetic make-up simply allows them to live longer, and there is, therefore, no concern for justice here to begin with.*

Setting aside for a moment the controversial normative premise at the base of this view, the factual premise here turns out to be mistaken. For, health disparities between men and women are in fact owed not only to genetic factors but to social ones as well. Concerning genetics, the most influential factor seems to be the effect of oestrogen, which prolongs women's resistance to cardiovascular diseases by approximately a decade. The *social* factors that cause women to live longer seem to be owed to the fact that men 'smoke more, drink more, engage in risky behavior more often and are exposed to more occupational hazards'.[41] In fact, we know that genetic factors contribute to only about half of the difference in life expectancy between men and women,[42] (and according to some studies, even less).[43] The perception that the inequality in life expectancy between the sexes is owed to natural factors alone is therefore mistaken, and cannot be the reason why inequalities in life expectancy between the sexes should be considered just (or not unjust). Returning to the normative premise, the claim about natural inequalities not being unjust is also not convincing. As Tsuchiya and Williams have noted, it is plausible to think that the inequality between the handicapped and the non-handicapped is unjust even when it is owed to natural factors alone.[44] The fact that they are natural does not show the inequalities between the sexes to be unjust.

> 3. *The social factors just mentioned are also not unjust because they are risk factors, things that men assume voluntarily (e.g. smoking, drinking, and occupational hazards).*

---

[40] A. Tsuchiya and A. Williams, 'A "Fair Innings" between the Sexes: Are Men being Treated Inequitably?', *Social Science and Medicine*, 60 (2005), 277–286; A. Williams, 'If We Are Going to Get a Fair Innings, Someone Will Need to Keep the Score!' in M. L. Barer, T. E. Getzen, and G. L. Stoddart (eds), *Health, Health Care, and Health Economics* (New York: Wiley, 1998), 319–330, at 327.

[41] Murray, 'Rethinking DALYs', 18. One could argue, I suppose, that even these ostensibly social factors are also in fact natural, for such reckless behaviour may be attributed to high levels of testosterone. (This is a possibility entertained by Tsuchiya and Williams. See their 'A "Fair Innings" between the Sexes', 281). But it would be difficult to attribute all the aforementioned differences in lifestyle to genetic factors, leaving men no room for free will whatsoever (see argument 3 in the text).

[42] Although that figure varies from developed to developing countries. The less developed a society is, the greater is the difference in life expectancy between men and women (Murray, 'Rethinking DALYs', 18). This indicates, not surprisingly, that social factors have a stronger effect on the disparity in life expectancy between the sexes in developing countries.

[43] *The World Health Report 2004* (Geneva: World Health Organization, 2004), 120–125.

[44] Tsuchiya and Williams, 'A "Fair Innings" between the Sexes', 280.

One problem with this view is that it assumes a measure of voluntariness in the way that men lead their lives that is somewhat implausible. Many of the risk factors that men assume are of the type that would exact a considerable cost to avoid. For instance, few men, especially in developing countries, can afford quitting work in hazardous workplaces.[45] More generally, we may say that some of the risk taking that causes men to have shorter lives is precisely the product of gender. That is to say, these higher risk factors are the consequence of the allocation of risks between male and female family members. (Although here we should probably assume that the inequality in risk factors between men and women decreases as we move from traditional to more modern societies.) Therefore it does not seem fair that a theory of justice in health, especially one that stresses gender,[46] would overlook the gendered origins of men's unhealthy lifestyle. That, again, seems especially to be the case with regard to occupational hazard. And, occupational hazard, it turns out, is a much stronger determinate of disparities in life expectancy between men and women than other risk factors such as smoking or drinking.[47]

Someone might still insist that the inequality in life expectancy between men and women is not unjust because, perhaps, she thinks the following:

4. *Differences in life expectancy happen to work to women's advantage. Women are generally worse off than men in almost all other aspects of well-being. Inequalities in health are therefore like some sort of 'cosmic affirmative action', and are thus an acceptable, and even desirable, incidence of inequality.*

In response, let us suppose, counterfactually, that the inequality in health were to work to men's advantage. We would probably not regard those inequalities in health between the sexes as acceptable. If this is so, then it cannot be the case that current inequalities in health between the sexes are themselves just, but rather are, at best, unjust inequalities that are countervailed by other considerations of justice. Similarly, observe, current health disparities between socio-economic classes *are* commonly perceived to be a concern for justice. And, the fact that, hypothetically, the correlation between socio-economic status and health could have gone the other way does not change that initial judgement. In other words, if it were the case that the richer one was, the less healthy one tended to be, we would probably be less alarmed by health disparities between the classes.[48] But that would hardly be an indication of

---

[45] Sen, *Development as Freedom*, see especially the 'Introduction'; J. Wolff and A. de-Shalit, *Disadvantage* (Oxford: Oxford University Press, 2007), especially ch. 3.

[46] See footnote 8.

[47] Differences between men and women in percentage of deaths that could be attributed to alcohol or smoking (cardiovascular diseases) are not so high (in the WHO sample of 2004 it accounted for 27.2 per cent of all male deaths, as compared to 31.7 percent of all female deaths), compared to the differences in rates of deaths originating in occupational hazard or violence (11.6 per cent of all male deaths compared to 6.3 per cent of all female deaths). *The World Health Report 2004*, 120–125.

[48] Daniels *et al.* entertain that thought experiment in 'Health and Inequality', 83. See also F. Kamm, 'Health and Equity' in C. J. L. Murray, J. A. Solomon, C. D. Mathers, A. D. Lopez (eds), *Summary Measures of*

health disparities between the classes being irrelevant to justice. The concern that a given state of affairs raises is not a conclusive measure for the justice or injustice of that state of affairs since, as we saw, countervailing forces may be at work and explain our intuitions.[49]

Consider, finally:

> 5. *Even if health inequalities between men and women are unjust, there is simply nothing we can do about those inequalities. For men to complain about the 'unfairness' of having a shorter life expectancy would be like them complaining about the 'unfairness' of not having the ability to get pregnant and give birth. There is simply no concern for justice here.*

In reply note, first, that the fact that nothing can be done directly to rectify a state of affairs does not necessarily bear on how just that state of affairs is. We often encounter cases where we can do little for people born with natural handicaps. The fact that we can do little to cure their handicaps does not undermine the injustice of their worse-off position. If nothing else, it is always possible to grant monetary compensation to such a person who is unjustly worse off. If the inability to become pregnant and give birth was truly seen as a disadvantage (the way having a shorter life commonly is), then there may be a case to compensate those who suffer that disadvantage. But even that point aside, it is simply false that nothing can be done to reduce inequalities in life expectancy between men and women. Having shorter life expectancy is different, in that respect, from not having the capability to be pregnant.[50] It is possible, among other things, to invest more resources on the causes of morbidity and mortality in men than on those that afflict women.[51] For example, we could, if we deemed it necessary (and I by no means say we should do so, all things considered), invest more in research for cardiovascular treatment and less on breast, ovarian, and cervical cancer.

It is not so easy, it seems, to find reasons to support the view that inequalities in life expectancy between men and women, at least in an otherwise ideal world, are acceptable.[52]

Population Health: Concepts, Ethics, Measurement and Applications (Geneva: World Health Organization, 2002), 685–706, at 694.

[49] Cf. Hausman *et al.*, 'Health Inequalities and Why They Matter', 182; Hausman, 'What's wrong with Health Inequalities'.

[50] Cf. A. Buchanan, D. W. Brock, N. Daniels, and D. Wikler, *From Chance to Choice: Genetics and Justice* (Cambridge: Cambridge University Press, 2000), 221.

[51] If nothing else, doing so would promote the prospect of more heterosexual couples ending their lives at closer points of time than is currently the case. Pursuing equality in life expectancy between men and women thus appears to reduce the extent of widowhood, which is surely a desirable end.

[52] Let me mention nevertheless one more potential reason why people may generally not be so troubled by differences in life expectancy between men and women. It might be thought that comparing life expectancy between men and women does not capture the entire story. Women, it may be suggested, may live longer, but their health, overall, is poorer. Women, especially in developing countries, disproportionately suffer the various health effects of sexual intercourse (AIDS, rape), pregnancy, and childbirth. Strictly comparing life expectancy, then, skews the picture in favour of men. However, it turns out that even when we compare *healthy* life expectancy (as we actually do here) rather than life expectancy as such, it is still

If health disparities between men and women are a concern for justice then that would seem to put these inequalities on a par with inter-class and inter-racial health disparities. But many people think that this is problematic, since they, very plausibly, think that the latter are much more objectionable than the former. It seems to me that it is correct to think that there is something deeply disturbing about health disparities between classes and between races. And I also do not dispute that these health disparities are more troubling than, say, health disparities between the sexes. The reason being that health disparities between social groups tell us that there is some systematic disadvantage that generates these patterns of health disparities. Health inequalities, in these cases, work as a 'sensitive barometer of the fairness of the underlying social order'.[53] That in itself does not demonstrate, however, that those health inequalities are in themselves unjust. For, on that occasion health disparities point out the injustice of the background conditions that generate those disparities, and not necessarily the injustice of the disparities themselves.[54] Instead, I propose, these health disparities *are unjust* in and of themselves, independently of the unjust social background that exacerbated them, since it is *always* unjust for one person to be less healthy than another for no fault of her own. That, in a nutshell, is the input that luck egalitarianism brings to discussions of health equity.[55] It therefore does not matter, on the luck egalitarian view, whether health inequalities stem from natural or social factors. Accordingly, health disparities between men and women are as unjust as those between social classes, even though they might be less alarming or less repugnant.

Let me mention a qualification in conclusion of this long section. Amartya Sen writes that giving priority in clinical care to men (due to them being worse off in terms of healthy life expectancy) is wrong because to do so would violate the principle of 'nondiscrimination in certain vital fields of life, including the need for medical care for treatable ailments'.[56] Nothing of what I have said so far contradicts that assertion. In particular, my argument thus far is compatible with the suggestion that disregarding inequalities between the sexes in clinical care might be the most desirable policy, *all things considered*. Having said that, it is worth noticing that the kind of reasoning

---

men who end up being worse off than women. See, for example, C. J. L. Murray, *US Patterns of Mortality by County and Race: 1965–1994* (Cambridge, MA: Harvard School of Public Health, 1998); Tsuchiya and Williams, 'A "Fair Innings" between the Sexes'.

[53] Hausman, 'What's Wrong with Health Inequalities', 59.

[54] A. K. Sen, 'Mortality as an Indicator of Economic Success and Failure', *The Economic Journal*, 108 (1998), 1–25 (cited in Peter, 'Health Equity and Social Justice').

[55] An account that comes close to this luck egalitarian position without explicitly saying so is offered in C. J. L. Murray, E. Gakidou, and J. Frenk, 'Health Inequalities and Social Group Differences: What Should We Measure?', *Bulletin of the World Health Organization*, 77 (1999), 537–543; and Gakidou *et al.*, 'Defining and Measuring Health Inequality'. (Cf. A. Wagstaff, P. Pact, and E. Van Doorslaer, 'On the Measurement of Inequalities in Health', *Social Science and Medicine*, 33 (1991), 545–557. They conceive of health inequalities as being of moral concern only when they 'reflect a socio-economic dimension', 556).

[56] Sen, 'Why Health Equity?', 30.

employed by Sen here would apply equally to prioritizing other statistical groups that happen to be worse off in terms of health, such as the poor or African-Americans.[57] There is, therefore, nothing in Sen's objection to differentiate inequalities between the sexes from inequalities between classes or races. Furthermore, it should be obvious that we can bypass that aversion to discrimination in clinical care by giving men priority in non-clinical interventions such as public health measures or, more likely, medical research. In other words, to avoid discrimination we may give the worse-off (men, African-Americans, the poor) priority in the way that health care systems are *set up* rather than in the way that health care is *delivered*.

12.4 Luck prioritarian justice in health

The luck egalitarian account of health equity is not vulnerable to the 'inequalities between the sexes' objection, then, for that objection is misplaced. But how does the luck egalitarian account cope with the other objections that have led us to reject the FEOP for health? In particular, luck egalitarianism, I have already conceded, is as vulnerable to the levelling down objection (the latter of the objections mentioned in section 12.2) as is the FEOP. Luck egalitarian health equity, recall, says that 'it is unfair for an individual to end up less healthy than another if she invested at least as much effort (compared to that other person) in looking after her health'. That principle could potentially be satisfied by making the healthier person as sick as the other person, or indeed by letting both of them die. Both would have equal health, namely none. For that reason, I want to suggest that luck egalitarians can and should sidestep the problem of levelling down by adopting a position that is 'a plausible close cousin of luck egalitarianism',[58] namely luck *prioritarianism*.

My argument depends on the supposition, for which I cannot argue here,[59] that it is permissible to give up on the quest for equality in health, and to focus rather on giving priority to the worse-off. That supposition, recall, is not something FEO for health could endorse, for it is committed to strict equality. I want to argue in this final section that, in contrast, luck egalitarianism can combine with the prioritarian account and provide a coherent guide to health equity. So: What, exactly, does a *luck* prioritarian approach to justice in health look like? To answer that we need, first, a clear view of what luck prioritarianism as such is.

Luck prioritarianism seeks to capture the sentiment 'that one ought as a matter of justice to aid the unfortunate, and the more badly off someone is, the more urgent is

---

[57] As Kekes, in his critique of egalitarianism, rightly points out. Kekes, 'A Question for Egalitarians', 664. See also E. Gakidou, J. Frenk, and C. Murray, 'A Health Agenda' in J. Cohen and J. Rogers (eds), *Is Inequality Bad for our Health?* (Boston: Beacon Press, 2000), 71–78; Deaton, 'Policy Implications of the Gradient of Health and Wealth', 26.

[58] R. Arneson, 'Luck Egalitarianism and Prioritarianism', *Ethics*, 110 (2000), 339–349, at 341.

[59] See my *Health, Luck, and Justice* (Princeton, NJ: Princeton University Press, 2010), ch. 8.

the moral imperative to aid'.[60] The ideal consists, obviously, of two premises: luck egalitarianism (or 'luckism') and prioritarianism. The first premise is that 'it is morally bad if some are badly off through no fault or choice of their own'.[61] The second premise is that 'the moral value of obtaining a benefit for a person is greater . . . the lower the person's life time expectation of well-being prior to receipt of the benefit'.[62] Luck prioritarianism has, therefore, two goals: neutralize brute luck inequalities, and give priority to the worse-off. It thus stipulates: improve the position of those who are badly off through no fault of their own, and of those, give priority to a person the more worse off she is.

Luck prioritarian health equity, in turn, requires aiding those who are not responsible for their disadvantaged level of health, and among those, giving higher priority to individuals the less healthy they are. We could formulate the principle of luck prioritarian health equity as follows:

> *Prioritizing the opportunity for health of the worse-off*: Fairness requires giving priority to improving the health of an individual if she has invested more rather than less effort in looking after her health, and of those who have invested equal effort, priority should be given to those who are worse off (health-wise).

One immediate objection to luck prioritarian health equity so formulated is that its policy implications may appear harsh and counter-intuitive. Contrary to common sense, it does *not* tell us, first, to look out for those who are worse off, and only then compare levels of effort (or, prudence in looking after one's health). Rather, the luck prioritarian ideal tells us to compare levels of prudence first, and use the severity of the medical condition only as a tie-breaker between those who were equally prudent in looking after their health. That appears not only harsh but also impractical. Would it not make more sense, at the very least, to switch the order of the principle's two components?[63] Notice that as an operative principle that suggestion would make far more sense. For, surely it is best to look at the severity of individuals' medical condition before comparing anything else, let alone degrees of prudence. Yet a principle of justice in

---

[60] Arneson, 'Luck Egalitarianism and Prioritarianism', 343. See also his 'Egalitarianism and Responsibility', *The Journal of Ethics*, 3 (1999), 225–247; 'Equality of Opportunity for Welfare Defended and Recanted', *The Journal of Political Philosophy*, 7 (1999), 488–497, at 497; 'Welfare Should be the Currency of Justice', *Canadian Journal of Philosophy*, 30 (2000), 497–524, at 502; 'Perfectionism and Politics', *Ethics*, 111 (2000), 37–63, at 57.

[61] Arneson, 'Luck Egalitarianism and Prioritarianism', 340.

[62] Arneson, 'Luck Egalitarianism and Prioritarianism', 343. See also his 'Desert and Equality' in N. Holtug and K. Lippert-Rasmussen (eds), *Egalitarianism* (Oxford: Oxford University Press, 2007), 262–293, at 263. Cf. Arneson's chapter in this volume.

[63] Note that Arneson sometimes does revert to that differently ordered formulation of the luck prioritarian ideal, saying that we ought to give priority to the worse-off, and of those, to those who are less rather than more responsible for their condition (e.g. 'Luck Egalitarianism and Prioritarianism', 340). Arneson perhaps does not notice that he has two different formulations of luck prioritarianism, and moreover ones that are likely to produce different results. In any case, the formulation adopted here seems to me to better represent the luck prioritarian ideal, which is, first to neutralize luck, and then to give priority to the worse-off. In other words, it is luck first, prioritarianism second.

health, notice, is not a triage principle. It is not intended as a set of guidelines for clinicians. Instead, *prioritizing the opportunity for health of the worse-off* is a principle of justice. It tells us how to evaluate the justice of a distribution, not how to go about delivering medical care in the ER. And, as a principle of justice, luck prioritarianism tells us to neutralize bad brute luck first, which (according to the luck egalitarian reading) is the point of egalitarian justice. Only then luck prioritarianism tells us to distribute benefits in the order of their moral weight, which, given the principle's prioritarian tilt, implies distributing these benefits according to how worse off persons are. Notice also that the principle first tells us to treat all those who are not responsible at all for their ill health, and among those give priority to those whose health is the worst off. So in fact once we have identified the prudent, the principle tells us, even in its pure form, to simply give priority (among prudent patients) to the worse-off. At least in that respect, then, it does seem to conform to common practice.

Let us see, finally, how prioritizing the opportunity for health of the worse-off sidesteps the objections to outcome equality and Rawlsian justice in health. It is easy to see how the principle avoids the smoker/jogger objection. Luck prioritarian health equity gives priority to improving the health of an individual if she has invested more rather than less effort in looking after her health. It thus maintains that the smoker has a weaker claim to full health compared to the jogger. The luck prioritarian approach to health equity also sidesteps the two particular problems observed in the application of Rawls's FEO for health. The first problem with FEO for health was that it justifies treatment of only social but not natural (genetic), causes of ill health. Luck prioritarian health equity avoids that problem. Luck prioritarians (and luck egalitarians more generally) treat *all* involuntary inequalities in health, whether social or natural, as of concern for justice. The second weakness of FEO for health concerned its vulnerability to levelling down potential absolute levels of health. By virtue of its prioritarianism, the approach offered here sidesteps the problem of levelling down. Luck prioritarian health equity allows for unequal levels of health between individuals even when they have invested equal amounts of effort in looking after their health, provided that inequality improves the health of the worse-off (health-wise) person. The luck prioritarian approach to health equity thus avoids the two problems that afflict FEO for health.

12.5 Conclusion

I have sought in this chapter to advance the egalitarian discussion of health equity beyond two familiar objections to outcome equality in health, the smoker/jogger objection and the inequality between the sexes objection. I have presented two alternative principles that can overcome those objections, namely the principle of equal opportunity for health and the principle of fair equality of opportunity (FEO) for health. I then showed how the latter is defective as a principle of justice in health. Finally, I demonstrated how a revised version of the former, namely prioritizing the worse-off's opportunities for health copes well with the different objections to FEO for health. I therefore hope to have demonstrated that a concern for justice in health does not imply directly equalizing health, nor does it imply equalizing 'fair' opportunity for health, nor equalizing opportunity for health. Rather, health equity requires prioritizing the opportunity for health of the worse-off. I therefore conclude that luck prioritarianism is the best guide to health equity.

13

Individual and Social Responsibility for Health

Norman Daniels

13.1 Some recent social experiments promoting responsibility for health

Most of us believe that society has robust obligations to promote and protect population health and to treat those in medical need. But many people also believe that we owe people less if they have contributed to their ill health through imprudent choices.[1] Recent social experiments in health-care delivery, both in the United States and elsewhere, raise in a sharp way deep and difficult questions about how we should view the division between individual and social responsibility for health. My goal in this chapter is to address some of those questions.

Before turning to the questions, however, consider first three of the social experiments that pose them.[2] (I use the term 'social experiments' advisedly.[3])

---

[1] Some evidence supports the idea that people believe that those responsible for their ill health are owed less or given lower priority (P. A. Ubel, C. Jepson, J. Baron, T. Mohr, S. McMorrow, and D. A. Asch, 'The Allocation of Transplantable Organs: Do People Want to Punish Patients for Causing Their Illness?', *Liver Transplantation*, 7 (2001), 600–607; P. Dolan and A. Tsuchiya, 'The Social Welfare Function and Individual Responsibility: Some Theoretical Issues and Empirical Evidence from Health' (Sheffield Health Economics Group, University of Sheffield, Discussion Paper Series, 3 (2003), http://www.shef.ac.uk/~sheg/discussion/discussion.htm). Contrary evidence comes from D. Schwappach ('Does it Matter Who You Are or What You Gain? An Experimental Study of Preferences for Resource Allocation', *Health Economics*, 12 (2003), 255–262) and NICE's Citizen's Council (NICE Citizen's Council, *Report of the NICE Citizen's Council on Determining Clinical Need*, 2002, http://www.nice.org.uk/archivedsite/newsarchive/news2002/report_of_the_first_meeting_of_the_citizens_council.jsp, accessed 25 January 2008), which rejected the idea that self-inflicted injury or illness should affect judgements about clinical need and care with the National Health Service.

[2] See H. Schmidt ('Health Responsibility, the Left, and the Right', *Bioethics Forum/The Hastings Center Report*, 6 July 2007, http://www.bioethicsforum.org/personal-responsibility-health-care-Medicaid-Membership-Agreement.asp, accessed 25 January 2008) for a discussion noting that these examples (plus one from the UK) emphasizing responsibility cut across right—left political boundaries.

[3] See N. Daniels, *Just Health: Meeting Health Needs Fairly* (New York: Cambridge University Press, 2008), ch. 9; N. Daniels 'Toward Ethical Review of Health System Transformations', *American Journal of Public Health*, 96 (2006), 447–451; and J. F. Wharam and N. Daniels, 'Toward Evidence-Based Policy Making and Standardized Assessment of Health Policy Reform', *Journal of the American Medical Association*, 298 (2007),

Experiment 1: *West Virginia*.[4] The Medicaid experiment is aimed at determining if more responsible patient behaviour can be induced by rewarding it with an enhanced benefit package while penalizing its absence with a more restricted one.

Specifically, Medicaid recipients will be offered an enhanced benefit package if they sign (for themselves and their children) an agreement to be responsible for their health in specific ways, including showing up to appointments on time and complying with drug regimens and other healthy behaviours that are recommended by their physicians.[5] The enhanced benefit package includes additional care for diabetes, cardiac problems, vision and dental needs, prescription drugs, smoking cessation and drug abuse programmes, greater mental health benefits, and others. If Medicaid patients fail to comply (or fail to have their children comply), or if they refuse to sign the agreement, they (and their children) will receive a basic benefit package, for example, one that allows only four prescriptions instead of unlimited prescriptions each month in the enhanced package, and is missing such important services as inpatient mental health.[6] The enhanced benefit package for children includes more robust vision, dental, hearing services, skilled nursing care, orthotics and prostheses, diabetes, and mental health services, including drug abuse services, not available to children in

---

676–679. The reforms in these experiments are intended to change utilization patterns for health care; they promise benefits but also may impose risks to patients; their outcomes are not known; and, if they are monitored and evaluated properly, they can increase our knowledge about health and health-care delivery. Unlike clinical experiments with human subjects, however, they are not subject to careful scientific and ethical review. I shall not mention further here what I believe is a failure of social responsibility implied by such experimentation without review.

[4] Full details of the West Virginia plan as approved in 2006 are available at: http://www.wvdhhr.org/bms/oAdministration/bms_admin_WV_SPA06-02_20060503.pdf, accessed 8 January 2008.

[5] The full list of member responsibilities is as follows:

Member Responsibilities:

- I will follow the rules of the West Virginia Medicaid program.
- I will do my best to stay healthy. I will go to special classes as ordered by my medical home.
- I will read the booklets and papers my medical home gives me. If I have questions about them, I will ask for help.
- I will pick a medical home within 30 days or one will be picked for me.
- I will go to my medical home when I am sick.
- I will take my children to their medical home when they are sick.
- I will go to my medical home for check-ups.
- I will take my children to their medical home for check-ups.
- I will take the medicines my health care provider prescribes for me.
- I will show up on time when I have my appointments.
- I will bring my children to their appointments on time.
- I will call the medical home to let them know if I cannot keep my appointments or those for my children.
- I will let my medical home know when there has been a change in my address or phone number for myself or my children.

[6] A comparison of the alternative plans is found in tables at the url noted in footnote 4 above.

the basic plan. The benefit package for children thus varies with their parents' willingness to sign or ability to comply, not with the children's responsibility for health.

Experiment 2: *Florida*. This experiment is aimed at inducing more responsible health behaviours solely by rewarding them with cash credits that can be used to buy health-related over-the-counter products at participating pharmacies.

In contrast to the West Virginia plan, there are no sanctions, only a missed chance to obtain modest benefits equivalent to $150 total for the purchase of various kinds of health-related products. To earn the benefits, Medicaid patients must participate in such healthy behaviours as getting a vision or dental exam, Pap smear, participate in a smoking cessation programme or exercise regimen, or show up for all appointments.[7]

Experiment 3: *Germany*. Can a system of co-pays and other financial incentives hold patients accountable for helping to internalize the externalized costs of their imprudent behaviours and encourage enrollees to engage in more healthy behaviours?

The German experiment departs from the Florida experiment by mixing positive and negative economic incentives. Schmidt notes that the German experiment, in keeping with its social security code that calls for 'co-responsibility' for health, requires different levels of co-pays for dental services, depending on how frequently there are check-ups, and gives different levels of positive financial incentives for participation in exercise regimens or screening programmes or other health promotion services. More controversial among the 'co-responsibility' measures, Schmidt notes, is the decision that people who develop medical complications from 'lifestyle choices' such as cosmetic surgery, tattooing, and body piercing can no longer claim free care. Similarly controversial are the different levels of co-pay required for chronically ill and cancer patients depending on their compliance with medical treatment regimens.[8]

The Florida experiment seems to involve no implication that we owe people less needed care if they act less prudently with regard to their health. Rather, it embodies a social objective of encouraging certain health promoting behaviours with actual incentives. The German experiment is more ambiguous. Like Florida, it's policy need not imply that we owe people less if they contribute to their illness, even while it is committed to the view that people are 'co-responsible' and should contribute more than others who behave prudently to the additional treatment costs that result from imprudent behaviour. If no treatment is ever actually denied or withheld, however, then the German experiment falls short of implying that people are owed less if they contribute to their ill health. If, however, needed treatment is foregone as a result of the increased co-pays that accompany non-compliance in the case of the chronically ill

[7] A complete list can be found at: http://ahca.myflorida.com/Medicaid/Enhanced_Benefits/approved_credit_amounts_090106.pdf, accessed 9 January 2008.
[8] Schmidt, 'Health Responsibility'.

or cancer patients or complications that result from lifestyle choices like cosmetic surgery, then the German experiment does seem to imply that society owes less in those cases.

The West Virginia experiment seems most troubling for three reasons. First, denying needed care of the sort available to more 'responsible' patients does seem to imply that less is owed them. Do we owe them less? Even if providing incentives for more responsible behaviour is a worthwhile public health objective (as it might be in Florida or Germany), should we define what we owe to those who are most dependent on public insurance by this appeal to responsibility for health? Second, unlike the German policy, which applies to the whole population or even to better-off parts of it in some sickness funds, the West Virginia experiment is applied to the most vulnerable parts of its population. Should we hold the most vulnerable parts of our population—its poorest, least educated, most seriously ill and disabled group—to a standard of healthy behaviour that we do not require of the rest of the population? For example, should we reward and sanction compliance and non-compliance by providing or withholding arguably essential care, such as cardiac rehabilitation or diabetes care or skilled nursing for children when such rewards and sanctions are not in place for the non-poor? These kinds of sanctions are not part of the Florida experiment and arguably not part of the German one. Third, should we hold children accountable for the imprudent or irresponsible behaviour of their parents? Should we visit in this way the sins of parents on their children?

My goal in this chapter is to provide a coherent basis for answering these questions. As we shall see, two quite different theoretical approaches to responsibility for health give different answers, even though they may come closer at the level of policy for various reasons I shall note. Overall, my argument shall be as follows: we have social obligations (and social responsibility) to promote and protect population health and to distribute it equitably. This social responsibility requires that we preserve some form of appeal to individual responsibility for health, but just what the appropriate form is for that appeal requires addressing both theoretical and practical issues. I shall argue that one view of the division of social and individual responsibility, associated with Rawls's view of justice as fairness, gives a better account of how we should think about individual responsibility for health than a family of luck egalitarian views. My argument is compatible with Scanlon's view that attributing responsibility relevant to moral praise or blame is different from the substantive responsibility that affects what we owe each other. I shall conclude with some final thoughts about the responsibility experiments.

13.2 The primacy of social responsibility over individual responsibility for health: one view

In this section, I argue that our social responsibility to promote health is primary in a normative sense to our individual responsibility for health, namely, that we can and should specify what we owe by way of promoting and protecting health independently of knowing how responsibly people have made health-affecting choices. Such a view nevertheless leaves room for a robust appeal to individual responsibility for adopting healthy behaviours, and it also leaves room for allowing choices made in particular contexts to affect what we owe each other. It is, we shall see, compatible with Scanlon's account of the difference between attributive and substantive accounts of individual responsibility. In the next section I explore further how my view fits with Rawls's account of the division of social and individual responsibility.

Health, I have argued for over twenty-five years, is of special moral importance because maintaining it makes a significant if limited contribution to protecting the range of exercisable opportunities open to individuals.[9] Since a number of accounts of social justice, including Rawls's, support the claim that we have social obligations to protect opportunity, they provide a basis for claiming that we have social obligations to protect normal functioning—or health—in the population. In effect, by identifying the moral importance of meeting health needs as a special case of meeting the 'needs' of citizens for the protection of their opportunity my view subsumes institutions that promote health under the principles of justice as fairness. This was my route to extending Rawls's theory so that it could address the variations in health from which he had notoriously abstracted in *A Theory of Justice*.[10]

The central intuition is that these social obligations are of primary importance in protecting the exercisable opportunity range (or capabilities) of free and equal citizens, whereas individual responsibility for health is secondary. The primary—secondary distinction here has at least a causal claim underlying it, for arguably a just distribution of the broad determinants of health has more to do with promoting population health and distributing it fairly than individual responsibility for adopting healthy behaviours.[11] But it is not simply a causal claim. We need to distinguish two further senses in which social responsibility for health is primary and individual responsibility secondary. First, the social responsibility is epistemically primary in this specific sense: we can specify the content of our social obligations regarding health—we can determine what health protection we owe free and equal citizens—without first determining what health consequences follow from the lifestyle choices that people make and subtracting that domain from what health protection we owe people. In effect, we can know what society owes people without first determining what they have done to

[9] N. Daniels, 'Health Care Needs and Distributive Justice', *Philosophy and Public Affairs*, 10 (1981), 146–179; *Just Health Care* (Cambridge: Cambridge University Press, 1985); *Just Health*.

[10] A. K. Sen ('Equality of What?' in S. McMurrin (ed.), *The Tanner Lectures on Human Values I* (Salt Lake City: University of Utah Press, 1980), 195–220), concerned about the same simplification in Rawls, suggested that the target of justice was the space of *capabilities*—exercisable options to do or be something. My extension works in the same space, albeit with a different terminology, for the idea is to protect a share of the plans of life it is reasonable for individuals to pursue (N. Daniels, *Just Health*, ch. 2).

[11] M. Marmot, *The Status Syndrome: How Social Standing Affects Our Health and Longevity* (New York: Henry Holt, Times Books, 2004).

harm themselves. Second, the primary—secondary distinction has a normative component: We should let individual choices and the individual responsibility we sometimes recognize as following from those choices overrule social obligations only under specifiable circumstances or conditions. Otherwise, our social responsibility is binding on us and should not be overridden by appeals to individual responsibility. (This normative claim about the primacy of obligations regarding health is a point of agreement with the more general priority assigned meeting the needs of free and equal citizens by Anderson.[12])

The social obligations we have to promote and protect health include the just distribution of the broad social determinants of population health (income; education; opportunity; the bases for self-respect, social cohesion, and political participation; and basic liberties that protect the security of the person). In this way social justice, broadly understood, promotes population health and distributes it fairly.[13] Our social obligations also include traditional public health measures (such as clean water, air, safe workplaces, proper sanitation, and immunization against infectious diseases), including various forms of health promotion. In addition, they include providing access to appropriate medical care.[14] These social obligations are correlative to any claims we have to a right to health or health care.

It is important to see that on this view of justice and health, there is a social obligation to promote population health and to distribute it fairly. The focus on fair distribution might be thought to be all that is implied by the underlying appeal to a fair equality of opportunity principle. But the ultimate objective of providing normal functioning (health) to all is the ultimate objective of both the health egalitarian and the health maximizer. The point follows from the fact that health is taken as a limit concept—unlike income or wealth, where there is no limit to how rich we can be. When we are healthy, however, we are healthy, and if all are fully healthy, then we have both equalized health and maximized it in a population. Of course, health maximizers and egalitarians will pursue different strategies short of their ultimate goal, and my account here requires us to be concerned about equity in health and not just maximization of aggregate health in a population. Still, it remains an obligation of justice, for example, to provide appropriate health promotion campaigns.

More specifically, consider first what the primacy of the social obligations means in the context of medical care. On my view, in order to protect individuals' fair shares of the opportunity range, society has obligations to make available to them a reasonable array of preventive and treatment services, given resource limits. (Jim Sabin and

[12] E. Anderson, 'What is the Point of Equality?', *Ethics*, 109 (1999), 287–337; 'How Should Egalitarians Cope with Market Risks?', *Theoretical Inquiries in Law*, 9 (2008), 239–270.

[13] N. Daniels, B. Kennedy, and I. Kawachi, 'Why Justice is Good for Our Health: The Social Determinants of Health Inequalities', *Daedalus*, 128 (1999), 215–251; *Is Inequality Bad for Our Health?* (Boston: Beacon Press, 2000).

[14] These obligations are characterized more fully elsewhere; Daniels, *Just Health*.

I propose a fair, deliberative process—'accountability for reasonableness'[15]—as a way to resolve disputes about what is reasonable.) Access should be on the basis of need and not ability to pay. Many forms of financing and organization of the health system are compatible with this requirement of justice.

Against the background of what interventions a society is responsible for providing through a health system, the individual remains 'responsible' for utilization decisions in this important sense: a competent, informed individual must still consent to—choose—treatment and can in any case refuse appropriate treatment. In effect, an individual's right to health care is mediated by her own consent. For example, although we ordinarily think health providers owe resuscitation efforts to people whose hearts have stopped, if patients have Do Not Resuscitate (DNR) orders, their choice to forego treatment should be respected. In this context, and under conditions where the choice was properly made (it is informed and the patient is competent to make it), we value the choices of individuals in ways that help to determine what we owe them.

We value choice in this context, as Scanlon has argued, for both instrumental and non-instrumental reasons.[16] We, rather than doctors, generally know what is best for us, all things considered, so choice has predictive value. Choice here may also have representative value: the illness and the dependency it involves might be viewed as so demeaning by someone that living with it does not represent them as they want to be seen in relations with others. Choice has symbolic value here as well, for respecting it here marks our competence to make self-regarding judgements. This is one context where the choice to refuse the benefits of treatment and to face the risks of non-treatment makes the individual fully responsible for the possible harms, including death, that follow. Note, however, that it is a context in which what society owes individuals—contingent claims on reasonable treatments—has already been given them and it is one in which there are (we hope) careful safeguards to make sure the choice is properly made, i.e. that it is informed and that the patient is competent.

Though we give significant weight to choice in this context, allowing it to affect our views about what we owe each other, we should not think that choice is either a necessary or sufficient condition for addressing questions about what we owe each other. To see the point, it will be helpful to revisit Scanlon's argument and, specifically, to consider briefly his example of the clean-up of the hazardous material that spilled in a neighbourhood.[17] He imagines that if city officials do not clean it up, significant harms will result, e.g. to the water supply, but that, even if all reasonable steps are taken

---

[15] N. Daniels and J. Sabin, 'Limits to Health Care: Fair Procedures, Democratic Deliberation, and the Legitimacy Problem for Insurers', *Philosophy and Public Affairs*, 26 (1997), 303–350; *Setting Limits Fairly: Can We Learn to Share Medical Resources?* (New York: Oxford University Press, 2002); *Setting Limits Fairly: Learning to Share Resources for Health*, second edition (New York: Oxford University Press, 2008).

[16] T. M. Scanlon, 'The Significance of Choice' in Sterling McMurrin (ed.), *The Tanner Lectures on Human Values VIII* (Cambridge: Cambridge University Press, 1988), 151–216; *What We Owe to Each Other* (Cambridge, MA: Harvard University Press, 1998).

[17] Scanlon, *What We Owe.*

to protect against the risks of the clean-up and transport of the hazardous material itself, people will still be at risk. Thus, in addition to different forms of warning, city officials must build fences around the site and secure the material as best they can during transport. He stipulates that the city officials do all that can reasonably be expected to protect people against the risks of the clean-up. Without these efforts, anyone could reasonably complain about the clean-up. With them, however, the clean-up programme cannot reasonably be rejected by those who are adversely affected by it.

Consider now what some people, Curious, Determined, Oblivious, and Forgetful, do despite the steps taken by the city. Curious climbs the fence to see the site anyway and is harmed. Determined is aware of the risk but decides she has limited time in which to do something that exposes her but that she deems worth doing anyway. Oblivious never heard the warnings and chooses to take his customary walk, encountering the risk. Forgetful had been warned but forgets and exercises outdoors with his Walkman on high.

Curious and Determined not only have no reasonable complaint against the clean-up, but also they have only themselves to blame for what happens to them. It is not the mere fact of their choice to expose themselves to a risk, whether foolish in the case of Curious, or not in the case of Determined, that tells us that they have no basis for complaint. That fact matters only because the city officials did all that could be reasonably expected. Had they not done so, the choice to face the risk would not eliminate a basis for their complaint about the outcome. Consequently, their choice alone is not sufficient to determine what we owe them. The fact that 'they broke it' is not sufficient to determine that 'they own it' unless the further fact about the city's efforts is true. Not only is choice not sufficient, but also it is not necessary to determine what is owed. Oblivious, who did not knowingly choose to face the risk, still has no reasonable complaint and is not owed anything because (by stipulation) the city officials did all that they reasonably could have done to warn and protect him.[18] Forgetful also did not knowingly choose to face the risk; he (perhaps) has even less claim than Oblivious on further assistance from the city.

This argument provides an alternative account to what Scanlon calls the Forfeiture View, the view that a person who knowingly passes up an alternative that would have avoided a certain outcome (exposure to the spilled chemical during its clean-up) cannot complain about the outcome. On the Forfeiture View, Curious and Determined cannot complain simply because they chose to expose themselves, but Oblivious and Forgetful did not knowingly so choose and so may be owed something. Scanlon's Value of Choice account shows that we place a value on choice for certain generic reasons—both instrumental and non-instrumental. These reasons help to clarify the conditions or opportunities under which we want choice to play an

---

[18] An alternative take on Oblivious might be that he is owed something because the city should be prepared to help those it fails to reach, given all reasonable efforts; this is really a quibble about what follows from Scanlon's stipulation.

important role in determining what we are owed. The Value of Choice account thus better explains our reactions to the case of the clean-up than the Forfeiture View.

In other contexts, including many public health contexts, we do not give individual choice much control over what we think we owe to people in the way of health protection. For example, a worker cannot 'choose' not to accept the protection of a workplace health hazard standard in the way in which we would accept his informed refusal of a medical treatment. If we clean up a workplace so that exposure to lead or benzene falls below some limit judged technologically feasible, then individual workers cannot reject that protection in the way they may forego a medical intervention to which they are entitled. Indeed, if they attempt to forego workplace protections, such as masks or safety procedures, they (and/or their employers) may be sanctioned for failing to act responsibly. An attributive notion of responsibility is thus embraced[19] without it influencing our substantive views about what society is responsible for (what it owes) by way of health protection. In setting workplace exposure standards, we depart from 'consent to risk' as the method of distributing the benefits and burdens of risk taking, for we believe we have social obligations to reduce exposure to certain risks, especially when they fall unequally on people, as in many workplace contexts.[20] Many public health measures thus provide protection in a way not mediated by individual consent, as in medical contexts.[21]

In other contexts, however, public health promotion strongly appeals to individual responsibility since health promotion campaigns clearly aim to make people more responsible for adopting healthy behaviours. Health promotion informs people about which behaviours are healthy and about the consequences of not engaging in them. Health promotion sometimes provides people with opportunities, including the means, to engage in those behaviours. For example, a 'safe sex' or 'clean needles' campaign not only provides people with information about various practices and their risks, but also it may distribute condoms or clean needles (or needle cleaning kits) that enable people to protect themselves against some of the risks of unsafe sex or drug use. A premise of such efforts is the view that properly informed and equipped individuals can act more responsibly to avoid some risky behaviours.

Although public health advocates must embrace efforts to engage people in healthy practices, including appealing to their responsibility to so behave, the appeal to responsibility has a specific function and clear limits. Unfortunately, we have only limited knowledge about how to modify the behaviour of people in general, and especially people in vulnerable groups. Informing adolescents about the risks of smoking, drug abuse, and unsafe sex fails to produce full and general compliance with healthy practices. Complex factors, including peer pressures and other cultural and psychosocial factors provide counter-influences. In the case of smoking and more

[19] Scanlon, *What We Owe.*
[20] Daniels, *Just Health,* ch. 7.
[21] See Daniels, *Just Health,* ch. 5.

recently obesity, we see that the agents whose 'responsibility' is at issue are often just children. Behaviours and risks incurred in childhood and early adolescence, including addictions and hard-to-modify habits surrounding diet and exercise, do not seem to be clear cases where we want 'imprudence' to determine what we owe people even if we very much want to encourage and develop 'responsibility' as a public health tool.[22]

An account that emphasizes social obligations to promote and protect health cannot, then, ignore appealing to individual responsibility for adopting health behaviours. But attributing responsibility to people—including children or adolescents—in this way is not to be confused with specifying what we owe them.[23] Billy is 'responsible' for eating the fries rather than the salad when he chooses the former over the latter in the school cafeteria. Indeed, the school nurse or his parents may criticize him for his failure to eat in a healthy way. But attributing responsibility to him that is relevant to praise or blame does not tell us what we owe him by way of weight reduction programmes or diabetes treatment later in life, even if there are warning signs in the cafeteria and an 'eat healthy' educational campaign in the school. Determining what we owe Billy is another, different task the answer to which does not follow from the mere attribution of responsibility—indeed, it is independent of that attribution. Much as we might want Billy to make healthy eating choices, the conditions are not present for assigning his choices the weight of determining what health protection we owe him. The fact that he 'broke it' does not imply that he 'owns it'.

13.3 Social hijacking, risky choices, and fair terms of cooperation

One familiar objection to separating the attribution of responsibility for healthy choices from the task of determining what we owe by way of health protection is that it encourages a form of social hijacking by 'risky' and therefore medically expensive lifestyle choices. After all, irresponsible, risky behaviour will impose burdens on society, namely, to meet health needs that would otherwise be avoidable.[24] There is substantial evidence that individuals can do much to avoid incurring risks to their health—by avoiding smoking, excessive alcohol, unsafe sex, and certain foods, and by getting adequate exercise and rest.[25] Indeed, that is one of the motivations for the health promotion efforts I earlier argued we owe people. Why should

---

[22] Cf. Susan Hurley's chapter in this volume.

[23] Scanlon, *What We Owe*.

[24] The objection presupposes that we should count as externalities the costs of the medical expenses that the unhealthy choices cause; it often ignores the 'savings' that result when society does not have to pay the medical costs of expensive diseases late in life (Alzheimer's) because of an increase in early mortality.

[25] There is considerable social epidemiological evidence that risky behaviour differences among groups of different socio-economic status (SES) explains only a modest portion of the health inequalities across those groups; in addition there is evidence that health promotion campaigns have a bigger impact on higher SES groups. Health promotion should avoid 'blaming' people whose behaviour is risky even while it attempts to make them more responsible in their choices.

others—especially those who may take great care to engage in healthy behaviours—be obliged to pay for meeting health needs that are the result of the imprudent, irresponsible choices of some? It is one thing to respect the self-regarding choices of individuals in order to avoid intrusive forms of paternalism, but it is another to ignore choices that impose externalities on others. As I noted earlier, the co-pays in the German experiment can be thought of as a way of making imprudent people accountable for these externalities of their choices; at the same time, they constitute incentives for people to behave more responsibly.

This objection takes us back to the original motivation for Rawls invoking a distinction or division between social and individual responsibility. In the early 1980s, a different version of the social hijacking worry played a prominent role in work on distributive justice. Dworkin, for example, argued that if egalitarians were concerned to make people equal with regard to their welfare, then people with expensive tastes that they could not satisfy would be owed something by people with more moderate tastes.[26] For him this became one reason for focusing on a different space or target of justice, one concerned with resources, not welfare. Rawls, also a non-welfarist, responded to the problem of social hijacking by expensive tastes by saying that society was responsible for the just distribution of the primary social goods—for meeting the needs of free and equal citizens, as he later came to see their role—but individuals were responsible for pursuing their plans for a good life within the limits imposed by justice.[27] It was simply too bad for them if they ended up worse off than others as a result of cultivating expensive tastes. They are not owed more than the fair shares determined by the principles of justice as fairness. Rather, they are responsible for adapting their tastes in this division of responsibility—on the assumption that society delivers what it owes as a matter of justice.[28]

Notice that on Rawls's 'ideal' account of the division of social and individual responsibility, individuals are responsible for adjusting to fair terms of cooperation provided society responsibly meets their needs as free and equal citizens. The division arises as an issue within an 'ideal' theory of justice, that is, when the principles of justice are generally conformed to. Accordingly, we may hold individuals responsible for their risky lifestyle choices, viewed as 'expensive tastes' (not always an apt analogy, as I note later), against a background in which society is meeting its obligations to protect and promote health. Thus, had we just distributions of what Rawls calls the primary social goods (basic liberties, opportunities, power, income, wealth, and the social bases of

---

[26] R. Dworkin, 'What is Equality? Part 1: Equality of Welfare', *Philosophy and Public Affairs*, 10 (1981), 185–246.

[27] J. Rawls, 'Social Unity and the Primary Goods' in A. K. Sen and B. Williams (eds), *Utilitarianism and Beyond* (Cambridge: Cambridge University Press, 1982), 159–185.

[28] G. A. Cohen ('On the Currency of Egalitarian Justice', *Ethics*, 99 (1989), 906–944) objected that unchosen tastes were not the responsibility of individuals and that compensation is owed people who are disadvantaged by such tastes. John Rawls (*Political Liberalism* (New York: Columbia University Press, 1993)), however, holds people responsible for their tastes, cultivated or not, unless there is evidence of some pathology that makes revising them a problem. Then treatment for the pathology is owed (see above).

self-respect), and were health inequalities only those that resulted from otherwise just social inequalities, and had we highly effective programmes aimed at altering risky behaviours, and had we competent, informed adults deciding not to accept the benefits of these programmes, then we might think this analogous to informed, competent patients refusing a curative medical intervention under well-controlled conditions. We might then give some force to the 'choice' exercised in that setting, for example by making people accountable for the externalized costs of their avoidable medical conditions. (I return to the disanalogy between expensive tastes and lifestyle choices that bear on health shortly.)

Society has not, however, in general discharged its obligations regarding measures to reduce risky lifestyle practices. Smoking is a good example. Only recently have some developed countries used various combinations of education, taxation, and regulation to produce significant drops in smoking prevalence, at least among some SES groups. These efforts take place against a social history in which governments subsidized tobacco production, did not regulate cigarette advertising by corporations, with the result that cigarette smoking became an icon of what it was to be cool and sexy, and did not adequately counter the construction of 'controversy' about scientific results by corporations when indeed a scientific consensus had emerged.[29] As a result of these societal failures, many young people became addicted to smoking. Obesity is an even more complex epidemic for which we have even less successful measures at health protection, in part because we know less not only about the causes of the epidemic, but about effective measures to alter it. If individuals are to be held responsible for the externalities of their lifestyle choices, viewed as analogous to 'expensive tastes', then we depart from Rawls's account of a division of responsibility. We fail to meet social responsibilities but we (erroneously) insist on individual ones.[30]

For the sake of argument, let us set aside the 'ideal theory' constraint in Rawls's appeal to the division of social and individual responsibility. Suppose also that the lifestyle choices people make should be viewed as analogous to expensive tastes and that they should be held responsible for them even in non-ideal contexts. What exactly does that imply? Does it imply that we should carry out the most careful accounting possible of the externalities they impose in the form of avoidable medical costs and hold them responsible for contributing all or part of those costs? Call this the Strict Accounting View.

Consider an argument against the Strict Accounting View. It is adapted from a different argument Charles Fried introduced more than forty years ago.[31] He was interested in the risks we impose on others without their consent by our everyday

---

[29] A. Brandt, *Cigarette Century: The Rise, Fall, and Deadly Persistence of the Product That Defined America* (New York: Basic Books, 2007).

[30] This is true even if we set aside differences between the philosophical examples of expensive tastes that are clearly cultivated, like preferences for expensive wines or plover eggs, and the 'choice' an adolescent makes to smoke when she is under peer pressure to be cool and 'liberated'.

[31] C. Fried, *An Anatomy of Values* (Cambridge, MA: Harvard University Press, 1969).

actions. When we drive instead of walk to get the newspaper at the corner store, we risk hitting a child at play who would be safer had we walked. How can we justify imposing such risks that no one has consented to? His suggestion is that there is a pool of such imposed risks that we should accept because we all benefit by letting people impose them as long as the risk-imposition is (roughly) fairly distributed. Similarly, the risky behaviours that people engage in through different 'choices'—some in sport, some in diet, some in sex—can all be thought of as a living space in which we all benefit from the liberty we allow people by not sanctioning them for their choices and by caring for them even when they make bad ones. People may see some of their choices as expressing their sense of who they are or want to be. (We might also look in the same way at the second chance we give people through bankruptcy—to reorganize their businesses and to become productive again—despite the bad option luck they encountered.[32]) We should, given the primary (social) obligation to protect normal functioning, try to educate people to make more prudent choices. We may punish those who exceed their budget of risk-imposition, say by driving under the influence or by speeding when getting the newspaper, but a more careful audit of risk imposition is not in our collective interest. Adapting Fried's idea in this way may remind us of the importance of not being too intrusive as a result of worries about imposed risks (or externalities), even if we want to take some collective measures to reduce them (driver education, stop signs, education of children about safe play, and specific sanctions for especially risky behaviour). We have important reasons to tolerate the burden of some of those externalities.[33] Indeed, we might think of this argument as pointing to the way in which a public good (individual liberty or its effect—diversity) is generated through this form of risk sharing.

I noted earlier that Rawls is willing to hold people responsible for adjusting even unchosen expensive tastes or preferences and not just explicitly cultivated expensive ones. This might lead us to thinking that in his view people should also be responsible for less than fully informed lifestyle choices. I believe this conclusion places too much weight on the (poor) analogy between lifestyle choices and expensive tastes. Rawls was clearly thinking of isolated tastes or preferences, perhaps the result of some early childhood experience.[34] For such cases, the idea that one could be held responsible for modifying the tastes or preferences to fit better within the limits set by justice is not implausible. On Rawls's view we are all capable of forming and revising our conceptions of the good, and that capability should let us work our way around specific preferences, whether we happened to cultivate them or simply acquired them. If, however, one is unable to modify them because of some pathological condition, say

---

[32] Cf. Avner de-Shalit and Jonathan Wolff, this volume.

[33] My adaptation of Fried's argument suggests that allowing people some liberty in choosing even unhealthy or risky behaviours has some redeeming social value, for it facilitates a sense of reciprocity in risk-sharing, perhaps even toleration or solidarity. Whether this is a 'value of choice' that can be subsumed under the three values Scanlon cites (representational?) or an additional one I leave unanswered.

[34] Rawls, *Political Liberalism*.

some compulsive disorder or phobic condition, then that condition warrants treatment, thus restoring the capability to modify the preference or taste and be held accountable for it.

Many lifestyle choices, however, are clearly different in their nature and consequences from isolated preferences and tastes. As noted earlier, adolescent choices to start smoking or using drugs may end up in addictions, and tobacco companies deliberately modified nicotine levels to create addiction. Many dietary habits are established as the result of cultural influences or the influence of family dietary patterns that are strongly influenced by education and income levels. These habits are difficult for many to modify, and though we have good public health reasons for encouraging people to be responsible for them, we are much less successful at changing them than individuals are at modifying isolated preferences or finding ways to avoid acting on them. (A recent study by Dixon *et al.* focuses on the ineffectiveness of behaviour interventions, such as counselling and other attempts to modify the diet and exercise patterns of obese people with diabetes, whereas surgical restrictions on the stomach have much greater success in producing both weight loss and remission from the diabetes. The issue warrants more discussion than can be given it here, and I only note its relevance to my claim that we should not confuse the difficulty of modifying deeply rooted behaviours regarding diet and some other lifestyle choices as compared to avoiding the effect of isolated tastes and preferences.[35])

To summarize the argument so far: in the previous section, I argued that our social responsibilities to promote and protect health have priority over our individual responsibilities regarding our health. We can and should specify what we owe each other regarding health promotion and protection independently of assessing the consequences of individual choices that affect our health. Still, our social responsibilities regarding health include encouraging, even through incentives, individually responsible choices of health lifestyles. Attributing responsibility to individuals for such choices must be distinguished from deciding what we owe them by way of prevention and treatment. Nevertheless, as I claim in this section, the individuals are responsible for adapting their preferences and choices so that their plans of life respect the fair terms of cooperation embodied in principles of justice. If we think of risky or unhealthy lifestyle choices as 'expensive tastes', then in some sense individuals are responsible for them. Leaving aside worries about whether such choices are generally informed and people are competent to make them, it would seem acceptable to hold people responsible or accountable for internalizing some of the externalized costs of their lifestyle choices. Though this is plausible in principle, given the division of responsibility between society and the individual, we should be wary of ignoring the value of letting people make a range of choices about lifestyles since we enjoy a collective benefit from doing so.

---

[35] J. B. Dixon, P. E. O'Brien, J. Playfair, L. Chapman, L. M. Schachter, S. Skinner, J. Proietto, M. Bailey, and M. Anderson, 'Adjustable Gastric Banding and Conventional Therapy for Type 2 Diabetes: A Randomized Controlled Trial', *Journal of the American Medical Association*, 299 (2008), 316–323.

13.4 What we owe each other and what policies we should follow: responsibility-sensitive egalitarian and prioritarian views

Rawls's response to the 'hijacking by expensive tastes' argument, we have seen, was to hold individuals responsible for modifying their tastes to fit within a prior, independent account of what we owe each other. Other theorists focused on individual responsibility in a far more general way and responded to the same argument by concluding that we could not specify what we owe each other until we were clear about what individuals brought on themselves with their own choices. Arneson and Cohen thus rejected the plausibility of egalitarians pursuing equality of welfare by saying (initially) that what matters to egalitarians is equal opportunity for welfare (Arneson) or advantage (Cohen; there is a welfarist component in Cohen's concept of advantage).[36] (Both theorists later abandon egalitarian concerns in favour or prioritarian ones.) This 'foregrounding of choice'[37] eliminates the possibility of determining what we owe each other independently of knowing what deficits in welfare or advantage derive from the choices people make. We owe people assistance whenever they lack, as a result of bad 'brute' luck, equal opportunity for welfare, but if they bring deficits on themselves through their own choices ('option luck'), then they lose their claim on us for assistance. (This formulation of the 'but' clause about choices is close to what Scanlon refers to as the Forfeiture View;[38] the initial clause about compensation for bad brute luck led Anderson to label this family of views 'luck egalitarianism'.[39]) So before we can tell what we owe each other (our social responsibilities), we must be clear about what people brought on themselves. Obviously, this is a rejection of the view that our social responsibilities are primary and individual responsibilities secondary in the specific sense I gave to the primary—secondary distinction earlier.[40]

---

[36] R. J. Arneson, 'Equality and Equal Opportunity for Welfare', *Philosophical Studies*, 56 (1989), 77–93; Cohen, 'On the Currency'. In contrast, Dworkin rejected equality of welfare in favour of equality of resources. Dworkin, 'What is Equality?'.

[37] Cohen, 'On the Currency'.

[38] Scanlon, *What We Owe*.

[39] E. Anderson, 'What is the Point of Equality?', *Ethics*, 109 (1999), 287–337. More recently Anderson qualifies the label so that the family still includes Arneson's 'responsibility-catering prioritarianism'. E. Anderson, 'How Should Egalitarians Cope with Market Risks?', *Theoretical Inquiries in Law*, 9 (2008), 239–270; see also R. J. Arneson, 'Equality of Opportunity for Welfare Defended and Recanted', *Journal of Political Philosophy*, 7 (1999), 488–497 and Arneson's chapter in this volume.

[40] The Rawlsian account of a division between social and individual responsibility is a deep feature of his view, one I do not do justice to when I portray it as a response to the worry about expensive tastes. Blake and Risse (M. Blake and M. Risse, 'Two Models of Equality and Responsibility', *Canadian Journal of Philosophy*, (2008), 165–199) divide theories of justice into 'direct' accounts of how equality follows from respect for ons or similar notions and 'indirect' theories, like Rawls's, where other facts about the relations among ·, such as that they seek fair terms of cooperation among free and equal citizens, play an important role ving concerns about equality. Individual responsibility then plays very different roles in these types of It is used to define the space of what we owe each other—corrections for bad luck—in direct uch as those of the luck egalitarians. In Rawls, as soon as we aim for fair terms of cooperation,

cooperation that govern the design of the basic structure of society must integrate concerns about various dimensions of justice, including liberty and efficiency. The result is that Rawls's principles of justice as fairness integrate constraints on ranges of distribution of different goods (basic liberties must remain equal, there must be fair worth of political participation, fair equality of opportunity, and inequalities must work to the maximal benefit of the worst off), but the whole structure is one in which the outcome of fair terms of cooperation counts as fair. Markets will produce inequalities, and we encourage risk taking in them to gain the efficiency they involve, but we constrain those outcomes as well.[47] To Cohen[48] and other luck egalitarians (or prioritarians), mixing in these other facts about human motivations, the importance of incentives, and other considerations makes Rawls's focus on the design of the institutions in the basic structure a matter of policy. But Rawls (and I) take justice to be a property of institutions primarily; if they are fairly designed so they embody fair terms of cooperation, then specific distributions in them may include some inequalities that we ought to view as fair distributions, even though some come about in ways that involve luck.

This deep difference in beliefs about the subject (and content) of justice is not likely to be resolved by implications for health and health care, but my argument in this chapter is intended to show that my (Rawlsian) account of justice and health does a better job of matching our views about what health promotion and protection we owe each other than the luck egalitarian family of views. I try to make this contrast clearer in the concluding section.

13.5 The social experiments: further thoughts

I conclude by summarizing the implications of these contrasting approaches to responsibility for the social experiments noted earlier. My preferred account says that social (societal) responsibilities to protect and promote health are primary and that individual responsibility is secondary in the sense that what we owe each other can be specified independently of individual choices that influence health. On this view, some features of the social experiment in West Virginia seem objectionable, especially the attempt to limit what we owe the most vulnerable groups in society when they do not act responsibly with regard to their health or their children's.[49]

---

[47] In a deep discussion of distributive justice and the regulation of risk-taking, Anderson ('How Should Egalitarians Cope') argues that two versions of luck egalitarianism, one focusing on desert the other on responsibility, both fail to regulate market risks appropriately, whereas a theory like Rawls's arguably does.

[48] Cohen, 'On the Currency'.

[49] Carl Knight (personal communication) has suggested that, in the unlikely eventuality that the incentive effects proved to be very strong and made the health of the most vulnerable groups much better, the West Virginia experiment might be acceptable on the view proposed above. I am not persuaded my objection is empirically contingent in this way; not everything we might do that produced better health is acceptable or is something we owe people. Even if forcing poor young children into religious orders that promoted safe sex and avoided drugs improved their health, we do not owe them that and should not do it.

The family of luck egalitarian or responsibility-sensitive views takes an opposite view. We cannot specify what health protection and promotion we owe each other independently of knowing what health conditions individuals are (at least partly) responsible for bringing on themselves through their lifestyle choices. In this view, in theory at least, where real choices are involved, the West Virginia measures that limit care are justifiable—though there may be policy qualifications.[50] We may face unmanageable administrative difficulties in identifying the degree of responsibility people have and may conclude that our policy should be to ignore attempts to limit care. So whereas the institutional design of the West Virginia plan is unjust on the social responsibility view, it might be thought to be bad policy on a luck egalitarian view, since it ignores an administrative difficulty in precisely assigning responsibility. Though it may be judged bad policy, it is not in theory unjust: in fact, ideal theory in this view fails to tell us what practice to put in place.

Consider now some implications for the Florida experiment. I have argued that our social responsibilities include encouraging people, with incentives where useful, to adopt healthier choices about their behaviours—this is part of our social obligation to promote population health. These social obligations also include requirements to distribute the broader determinants of health, including education, opportunities, income and wealth, the social bases of self-respect, and measures to support political participation and social cohesion, in accord with the principles of justice as fairness. A consequence of such a distribution of the determinants of health would be the flattening of socio-economic gradients of health and a reduction in the inequalities of risky behaviours across SES and ethnic groups. In such a climate, we may be more successful than now in promoting individual responsibility for health.

Luck egalitarian (responsibility-sensitive) views emphasize that they are capturing something central in our thinking about justice, namely that prominence ought to be given to individual choice or responsibility for what happens to us. It might seem these views should then encourage individual responsibility for healthy lifestyle choices, at least as emphatically as the social responsibility view. But why should there be such an effort at health promotion, given the limits individual responsibility sets to what we owe each other? If people behave irresponsibly, we do not owe them assistance for the problems they create. Whether they act responsibly or not, we do not owe them assistance for what results—we owe them assistance only for what they are not responsible for producing. A peculiar consequence of the theory, then, seems to be that it is hard to see why a proponent would want to make people act more responsibly with regard to their health. Rather than there being more support for health promotion

---

[50] Real choices are not always involved. A luck egalitarian, of course, is not committed to thinking that a Medicare recipient in West Virginia who has not been adequately informed about a drug regimen she is supposed to follow, and who then concludes she should not follow it, is 'choosing' to act imprudently; nor is the luck egalitarian committed to thinking someone is 'choosing' to act imprudently if he fails to keep a Medicare appointment because the transportation system fails regularly to deliver such patients to appointments.

because of the emphasis put at the core of the theory on individual responsibility, there is no reason for promoting it as a matter of justice.[51]

This contrast has implications for the Florida experiment. Measures like those in Florida's Medicaid plan are untested incentives that could contribute to more responsible behaviour, though there is also the possibility they are inadequate, given other inequalities in society, to have a significant impact on such practices as weight loss or compliance with medical regimens. A risk is that they increase stigmatization of less compliant parts of the population, and that imposes unknown levels of risk on them. A further risk is that it is the most vulnerable groups among the eligible poor that are most likely to fail to benefit from these incentives, while better-off groups will take advantage of them, but not because they have modified their behaviours. Nevertheless, promoting healthy behaviours is a requirement of justice, and the social responsibility view would support evidence-based efforts at doing that in Florida. In principle, if the risks noted here do not materialize, there is nothing wrong with the Florida effort and it may be justifiable. But on the luck egalitarian family of views, especially those tracking responsibility closely, if I am right, there is no justice-based rationale for promoting healthy behaviours (but see footnote 51). As a matter of justice we do not owe people assistance for what they bring on themselves as a result of their choices of imprudent behaviour, so we do not owe them any effort at making them act more prudently. I find no support for Florida's experiment in the luck egalitarian framework, and this is a problem for the framework.

The view that social responsibility is primary, I earlier argued, may provide some basis for asking people to be accountable for the externalized costs of their unhealthy behaviours. Though there are problems with the analogy between expensive tastes and lifestyle choices, if we accept the analogy, Rawls seems committed to the idea that people are responsible for living with the fair terms of cooperation. So if they need more health care than others with more prudent behaviours, then they may have to contribute some fair portion of the additional costs. This view makes it primary that we promote and protect the health of all free and equal citizens, and that means we cannot deny needed care, but the view is open to internalizing some of the costs of that care. The health policy literature has examples of trying to do that: high taxes on cigarettes that are then directed to cover health-care costs makes the contribution proportional to the risk if there is a monotonically increasing dose—response curve for smoking. Other unhealthy behaviours might be harder to address in this way (including aspects of diet,

---

[51] A more precise statement of my case would acknowledge that some health promotion that aims at making people act more responsibly is simply removing the unlucky factors that interfere with people making responsible choices, such as lack of access to information or other things that interfere with the voluntariness of their choices. The luck egalitarian can also say, as some do about the possibility of avoiding medical abandonment, that health promotion campaigns are not matters of distributive fairness but are the result of other values coming into play. My claim is that health promotion is a matter of justice, and these two views of justice differ in a way that casts some doubt on the luck egalitarian account. I thank Nir Eyal for pointing out these qualifications.

exercise, and unsafe sex). Certain risky sports could be regulated so that special insurance plans or taxes on their equipment might internalize some of the medical costs. In principle, then, the social responsibility view might endorse some of the features of the German system, though some important qualifications might be in order.[52]

From a luck egalitarian perspective, however, we have a problem related to the one noted for health promotion. We have reason to internalize the externalized costs of unhealthy behaviours when we are obliged to treat people regardless, as we are on the social responsibility view. Where the extra costs are not things we are obliged to pay for, since on the luck egalitarian view we may not owe treatment for those conditions, then we have less reason to adopt practices that involve internalizing those costs. We would, however, have good reason to impose cost-sharing on those with imprudent behaviours if we knew precisely how to quantify what proportion of the outcome they are responsible for. There is no obligation of justice for others to contribute to the costs the individual is responsible for. Since, however, we rarely know what share to assign individuals and it would be administratively impossible to figure that out,[53] we might have to adopt a policy of cost-sharing. If we did this, we would have to admit the institution is not strictly speaking just, because our approximation is only an approximation, but policy is, on this view, always like that.

I have spent little time on two of the questions noted in the opening section, namely the questions raised by the West Virginia study because of its focus on a vulnerable population and its holding children accountable for the compliance of their parents. Whether my view or a luck egalitarian view is correct, both would agree that it would be unfair to hold a vulnerable group accountable for their behaviour, perhaps by reducing their benefit package, when the same standard is not applied to the whole population. Both views would also agree there is no justification for making the benefit package available to children depend on facts about the compliance of their parents. I have focused my discussion on what I took to be controversial in the approach, not where egalitarians of various stripes, and many others, would agree something is clearly wrong with the West Virginia focus on vulnerable groups and children.

---

[52] Some possible limitations, suggested to me by Ole Norheim might be these:

    (i) the illness is completely or partly a result of individual behaviour and choice;
    (ii) the illness is not life-threatening;
    (iii) the illness does not limit the use of political rights or the exercise of fundamental capabilities;
    (iv) the cost of treatment, and so the co-pay, is low relative to the income of the patients.

Diseases that meet all these conditions may be rare.

[53] Unless we adopt a solution such as Roemer's. See J. E. Roemer, 'Equality of Opportunity', *Boston Review*, April/May 1995, http://bostonreview.net/BR20.2/Roemer.html.

Bibliography

Allais, M. and O. Hagen, *Expected Utility Hypotheses and the Allais Paradox* (Dordrecht: Reidel, 1979).

Anand, P. and A. Wailoo, 'Utilities versus Rights to Publicly Provided Goods: Argument and Evidence from Health Care Rationing', *Economica*, 67 (2000), 543–577.

Anand, S., 'The Concern for Equity in Health' in S. Anand, F. Peter and A. K. Sen (eds), *Public Health, Ethics, and Equity* (Oxford: Oxford University Press, 2004), 15–20.

Anderson, E. S., 'What is the Point of Equality?', *Ethics*, 109 (1999), 287–337.

Anderson, E. S., 'Rethinking Equality of Opportunity: Comment on Adam Swift's *How Not to Be a Hypocrite*', *Theory and Research in Education*, 2 (2004), 99–110.

Anderson, E. S., 'Fair Opportunity in Education: A Democratic Equality Perspective', *Ethics*, 117 (2007), 595–622.

Anderson, E. S., 'How Should Egalitarians Cope with Market Risks?', *Theoretical Inquiries in Law*, 9 (2008), 239–270.

Arneson, R. J., 'Equality and Equal Opportunity for Welfare', *Philosophical Studies*, 56 (1989), 77–93.

Arneson, R. J., 'Liberalism, Distributive Subjectivism, and Equal Opportunity for Welfare', *Philosophy and Public Affairs*, 19 (1990), 158–194.

Arneson, R. J., 'Egalitarianism and the Undeserving Poor', *Journal of Political Philosophy*, 5 (1997), 327–350.

Arneson, R. J., 'Against Rawlsian Equality of Opportunity', *Philosophical Studies*, 93 (1999), 77–112.

Arneson, R. J., 'Egalitarianism and Responsibility', *The Journal of Ethics*, 3 (1999), 225–247.

Arneson, R. J., 'Equal Opportunity for Welfare Defended and Recanted', *Journal of Political Philosophy*, 7 (1999), 488–497.

Arneson, R. J., 'Human Flourishing versus Desire Satisfaction', *Social Philosophy and Policy*, 16 (1999), 113–142.

Arneson R. J., 'Luck Egalitarianism and Prioritarianism', *Ethics*, 110 (2000), 339–349.

Arneson, R. J., 'Perfectionism and Politics', *Ethics*, 111 (2000), 37–63.

Arneson, R. J., 'Egalitarian Justice versus the Right to Privacy', *Social Philosophy and Policy*, 17 (2000), 91–119.

Arneson, R. J., 'Welfare Should be the Currency of Justice', *Canadian Journal of Philosophy*, 30 (2000), 497–524.

Arneson, R. J., 'Luck and Equality', *Proceedings of the Aristotelian Society*, Supplementary Volume, 75 (2001), 73–90.

Arneson, R. J., 'Why Justice Demands Transfers to Offset Income and Wealth Inequalities', *Social Philosophy and Policy*, 19 (2002), 172–200.

Arneson, R. J., 'The Smart Theory of Responsibility and Desert' in Serena Olsaretti (ed.), *Desert and Justice* (Oxford: Oxford University Press, 2003), 233–258.

Arneson, R. J., 'Luck Egalitarianism Interpreted and Defended', *Philosophical Topics* (Spring and Fall, 2004) [actually published in fall, 2006], 1–20.

Arneson, R. J., 'Desert and Equality' in K. Lippert-Rasmussen and N. Holtug (eds), *Egalitarianism: New Essays on the Nature and Value of Equality* (Oxford: Oxford University Press, 2007), 262–293.

Ashcroft v. Free Speech Coalition 122 S.Ct. 1389 (2002).

Barbeau, E. M., N. Krieger, and M.-J. Soobader, 'Working Class Matters: Socio-Economic Disadvantage, Race/Ethnicity, Gender, and Smoking in NIHS', *American Journal of Public Health*, 94 (2004), 269–287.

Bargh, J. A., 'Bypassing the Will: Towards Demystifying the Nonconscious Control of Social Behavior' in R. R. Hassin, J. S. Uleman, and J. A. Bargh (eds), *The New Unconscious* (New York: Oxford University Press, 2005), 37–58.

Bargh, J. A. and T. L. Chartrand, 'The Unbearable Automaticity of Being', *American Psychologist*, 54 (1999), 462–479.

Bargh, J. A., M. Chen, and L. Burrows, 'Automaticity of Social Behavior: Direct Effects of Trait Construct and Stereotype Activation on Action', *Journal of Personality and Social Psychology*, 71 (1996), 230–244.

Barry, B., *Political Argument* (London: Routledge & Kegan Paul, 1965).

Barry, B., *Liberty and Justice: Essays in Political Theory*, volume 2 (Oxford: Oxford University Press, 1991).

Barry, N., 'Defending Luck Egalitarianism', *Journal of Applied Philosophy*, 23 (2006), 89–107.

Bedau, H., 'Radical Egalitarianism' in R. Pennock and J. Chapman (eds), *Nomos IX: Equality* (New York: Atherton Press, 1967), 3–27.

Beitz, C., *Political Theory and International Relations* (Princeton: Princeton University Press, 1979).

Blake, M., 'Distributive Justice, State Coercion, and Autonomy', *Philosophy and Public Affairs*, 30 (2001), 257–296.

Blake M. and M. Risse, 'Two Models of Equality and Responsibility', *Canadian Journal of Philosophy*, 38 (2008), 165–199.

Bommier, A. and G. Stecklov, 'Defining Health Inequality: Why Rawls Succeeds where Social Welfare Theory Fails', *Journal of Health Economics*, 21 (2002), 497–513.

Bossert W., M. Fleurbaey, and D. Van de gaer, 'Responsibility, Talent, and Compensation: A Second-Best Analysis', *Review of Economic Design*, 4 (1999), 35–56.

Brandt, A., *Cigarette Century: The Rise, Fall, and Deadly Persistence of the Product That Defined America* (New York: Basic Books, 2007).

Bratman, M., 'Shared Cooperative Activity' in M. Bratman, *Faces of Intention* (Cambridge: Cambridge University Press, 1999), 93–108.

Broome, J., *Weighing Goods* (Oxford: Basil Blackwell, 1991).

Buchanan, A., 'Justice and Charity', *Ethics*, 97 (1987), 558–575.

Buchanan, A., D. W. Brock, N. Daniels, and D. Wikler, 'Genes, Justice, and Human Nature' in their *From Chance to Choice: Genetics and Justice* (Cambridge: Cambridge University Press, 2000), 61–103.

Buchanan, A., D. W. Brock, N. Daniels, and D. Wikler, *From Chance to Choice: Genetics and Justice* (Cambridge: Cambridge University Press, 2000).

Byrne, R. and A. Whiten, *Machiavellian Intelligence* (Oxford: Oxford University Press, 1988).

Caney, S., 'Cosmopolitan Justice, Rights and Global Climate Change', *Canadian Journal of Law and Jurisprudence*, 19 (2006), 255–278.

Cappelen, A. W. and O. F. Norheim, 'Responsibility in Health Care: A Liberal Egalitarian Approach', *Journal of Medical Ethics*, 31 (2005), 476–480.

Cappelen, A. W. and B. Tungodden, 'Responsibility and Reward', *FinanzArchiv*, 59 (2002), 120–140.

Cappelen, A. W. and B. Tungodden, 'Reward and Responsibility: How Should We be Affected When Others Change Their Effort?', *Politics, Philosophy and Economics*, 2 (2003), 191–211.

Cappelen, A. W. and B. Tungodden, 'A Liberal Egalitarian Paradox', *Economics and Philosophy*, 22 (2006), 393–408.

Cappelen, A. W. and B. Tungodden, 'Rewarding Effort', *Economic Theory*, 39 (2009), 425–441.

Carter, I., 'Is There a Freedom-based Justification for the Safety-net?', unpublished paper, 2009.

Carver, C., R. Ganellen, W. Froming, and W. Chambers, 'Modelling: An Analysis in Terms of Category Accessibility', *Journal of Experimental Social Psychology*, 19 (1983), 403–421.

Chartrand, T. L. and J. A. Bargh, 'Automatic Activation of Impression Formation and Memorization Goals: Nonconscious Goal Priming Reproduces Effects of Explicit Task Instructions', *Journal of Personality and Social Psychology*, 71 (1996), 464–478.

Chartrand, T. L. and J. A. Bargh, 'The Chameleon Effect', *Journal of Personality and Social Psychology*, 76 (1999), 893–910.

Chater, N. and M. Oaksford, 'Human Rationality and the Psychology of Reasoning: Where Do We Go From Here?', *British Journal of Psychology*, 92 (2001), 193–216.

Clark, A., 'Reason, Robots, and the Extended Mind', *Mind and Language*, 16 (2001), 121–145.

Coase, R., 'The Problem of Social Cost', *The Journal of Law and Economics*, 3 (1960), 1–44.

Cohen, G. A., *History, Labour and Freedom* (Oxford: Oxford University Press, 1988).

Cohen, G. A., 'On the Currency of Egalitarian Justice', *Ethics*, 99 (1989), 906–944.

Cohen, G. A., 'Equality of What? On Welfare, Goods and Capabilities', *Recherches Economiques de Louvain*, 56 (1990), 357–382 [reprinted in M. Nussbaum and A. Sen (eds), *The Quality of Life* (Oxford: Oxford University Press, 1993), 9–29].

Cohen, G. A., 'Incentives, Inequality, and Community' in G. B. Petersen (ed.), *The Tanner Lectures on Human Values*, volume 13 (Salt Lake City: University of Utah Press, 1992), 263–329.

Cohen, G. A., *Self-Ownership, Freedom, and Equality* (Cambridge: Cambridge University Press, 1995).

Cohen, G. A., 'Where the Action Is: On the Site of Distributive Justice', *Philosophy and Public Affairs*, 26 (1997), 3–30.

Cohen, G. A., 'Joint Session 2001: Reply to Hurley and Arneson', unpublished manuscript, 2001.

Cohen, G. A., 'Facts and Principles', *Philosophy and Public Affairs*, 31 (2003), 211–245.

Cohen, G. A., 'Expensive Taste Rides Again' in J. Burley (ed.), *Dworkin and His Critics* (Oxford: Blackwell, 2004), 3–29.

Cohen, G. A., *Rescuing Justice and Equality* (Cambridge, MA: Harvard University Press, 2008).

Cohen J. and C. Sabel, 'Extra Rempublicam Nulla Justitia?', *Philosophy and Public Affairs*, 34 (2006), 147–175.

Cohen, L. J., 'Who is Starving Whom?', *Theoria*, 47 (1981), 65–81.

Cosmides, L. and J. Tooby, 'Cognitive Adaptations for Social Exchange' in J. H. Barkow, L. Cosmides, and J. Tooby (eds), *The Adapted Mind: Evolutionary Psychology and the Generation of Culture* (New York: Oxford University Press, 1992), 163–228.

Cullity, G., *The Moral Demands of Affluence* (Oxford: Clarendon Press, 2004).

Culyer, J. and A. Wagstaff, 'Equity and Equality in Health and Health Care', *Journal of Health Economics*, 12 (1993), 431–457.

Daniels, N., 'Health Care Needs and Distributive Justice', *Philosophy and Public Affairs*, 10 (1981), 146–179.

Daniels, N., *Just Health Care* (Cambridge: Cambridge University Press, 1985).

Daniels, N., *Justice and Justification: Reflective Equilibrium in Theory and Practice* (Cambridge: Cambridge University Press, 1996).

Daniels, N., *Is Inequality Bad for Our Health?* (Boston: Beacon Press, 2000).

Daniels, N., 'Toward Ethical Review of Health System Transformations', *American Journal of Public Health*, 96 (2006), 447–451.

Daniels, N., *Just Health: Meeting Health Needs Fairly* (New York: Cambridge University Press, 2008).

Daniels, N., B. Kennedy, and I. Kawachi, 'Why Justice is Good for Our Health: The Social Determinants of Health Inequalities', *Daedalus*, 128 (1999), 215–251.

Daniels N., B. Kennedy, and I. Kawachi, 'Health and Inequality, or, Why Justice is Good for Our Health' in S. Anand, F. Peter, and A. K. Sen (eds), *Public Health, Ethics, and Equity* (Oxford: Oxford University Press, 2004), 63–91.

Daniels, N. and J. Sabin, 'Limits to Health Care: Fair Procedures, Democratic Deliberation, and the Legitimacy Problem for Insurers', *Philosophy and Public Affairs*, 26 (1997), 303–350.

Daniels, N. and J. Sabin, *Setting Limits Fairly: Can We Learn to Share Medical Resources?* (New York: Oxford University Press, 2002).

Daniels, N. and J. Sabin, *Setting Limits Fairly: Learning to Share Resources for Health*, second edition (New York: Oxford University Press, 2008).

Darwall, S., *The Second-Person Standpoint: Morality, Respect, and Accountability* (Cambridge, MA: Harvard University Press, 2006).

Davidson, D., *Essays on Actions and Events* (Oxford: Oxford University Press, 1982).

Deaton, A., 'Policy Implications of the Gradient of Health and Wealth', *Health Affairs*, 21 (2002), 13–30.

Dennett, D. C., *Elbow Room: The Varieties of Free Will Worth Wanting* (Oxford: Clarendon Press, 1984).

Dijksterhuis, A., 'Why We Are Social Animals: The High Road to Imitation as Social Glue' in S. Hurley and N. Chater (eds), *Perspectives on Imitation: From Neuroscience to Social Science* 2 (Cambridge, MA: MIT Press, 2005), 207–220.

Dijksterhuis, A., H. Aarts, and P. K. Smith, 'The Power of the Subliminal: On Subliminal Persuasion and Other Potential Applications' in R. R. Hassin, J. S. Uleman, and J. A. Bargh (eds), *The New Unconscious* (New York: Oxford University Press, 2005), 77–106.

Dijksterhuis, A., T. L. Chartrand, and H. Aarts, 'Effects of Priming and Perception on Social Behavior and Goal Pursuit' in John A. Bargh (ed.), *Social Psychology and the Unconscious: The Automaticity of Higher Mental Processes* (New York: Psychology Press, 2007), 51–131.

Dixon, J. B., P. E. O'Brien, J. Playfair, L. Chapman, L. M. Schachter, S. Skinner, J. Proietto, M. Bailey, and M. Anderson, 'Adjustable Gastric Banding and Conventional Therapy for Type 2 Diabetes: A Randomized Controlled Trial', *Journal of the American Medical Association*, 299 (2008), 316–323.

Dolan, P., R. Shaw, A. Tsuchiya, and A. Williams, 'QALY Maximization and People's Preferences: A Methodological Review of the Literature', *Health Economics*, 14 (2005), 197–208.

Dolan, P. and A. Tsuchiya, 'The Social Welfare Function and Individual Responsibility: Some Theoretical Issues and Empirical Evidence from Health', Sheffield Health Economics Group, University of Sheffield, *Discussion Paper Series*, 3 (2003), http://www.shef.ac.uk/~sheg/discussion/discussion.htm.

Dworkin, R., *Taking Rights Seriously* (London: Duckworth, 1977).

Dworkin, R., 'What Is Equality? Part 1: Equality of Welfare', *Philosophy and Public Affairs*, 10 (1981), 185–246.

Dworkin, R., 'What Is Equality? Part 2: Equality of Resources', *Philosophy and Public Affairs*, 10 (1981), 283–345.

Dworkin, R., *Sovereign Virtue* (Cambridge, MA: Harvard University Press, 2000).

Dworkin, R., '*Sovereign Virtue* Revisited', *Ethics*, 113 (2002), 106–143.

Dworkin, R., 'Equality, Luck and Hierarchy', *Philosophy and Public Affairs*, 31 (2003), 190–198.

Dworkin, R., 'Replies', in Justine Burley (ed.), *Dworkin and His Critics* (Oxford: Blackwell, 2004), 339–396.

Ellsberg, D., 'Risk, Ambiguity, and the Savage Axioms', *Quarterly Journal of Economics*, 75 (1961), 643–669.

Ellsberg, D., '[Risk, Ambiguity, and the Savage Axioms]: Reply', *Quarterly Journal of Economics*, 77 (1963), 336–342.

Epstein, R., *Simple Rules for a Complex World* (Cambridge, MA: Harvard University Press, 1995).

Evans, J., *Bias in Human Reasoning* (Hove: Erlbaum, 1989).

Evans, J. and D. Over, *Rationality and Reasoning* (Hove: Psychology Press, 1996).

Eyal, N., 'Egalitarian Justice and Innocent Choice', *Journal of Ethics and Social Philosophy*, 2 (2007), 1–18.

Feinberg, J., 'Action and Responsibility' in M. Black (ed.), *Philosophy in America*, (London: George Allen & Unwin, 1965), 134–160 [reprinted in J. Feinberg, *Doing and Deserving: Essays in the Theory of Responsibility* (Princeton: Princeton University Press, 1970), 119–151].

Feinberg, J., *Doing and Deserving: Essays in the Theory of Responsibility* (Princeton: Princeton University Press, 1970).

Feldman, F., 'Desert: Reconsideration of Some Received Wisdom', *Mind*, 104 (1996), 63–77.

Ferguson, M. J. and J. A. Bargh, 'How Social Perception Can Automatically Influence Judgment', *Trends in Cognitive Science*, 8 (2004), 33–39.

Fischer, J. M. and M. Ravizza, *Responsibility and Control: A Theory of Moral Responsibility* (Cambridge: Cambridge University Press, 1998).

Fishkin, J., *The Limits of Obligation* (New Haven: Yale University Press, 1982).

Fiss, O., *The Irony of Free Speech* (Cambridge, MA: Harvard University Press, 1998).

Fleurbaey, M., 'Equal Opportunity or Equal Social Outcome?', *Economics and Philosophy*, 11 (1995), 22–55.

Fleurbaey, M., 'Egalitarian Opportunities', *Law and Philosophy*, 20 (2001), 499–530.

Fleurbaey, M., 'Equality of Resources Revisited', *Ethics*, 113 (2002): 82–105.

Fleurbaey, M., 'Freedom with Forgiveness', *Politics, Philosophy and Economics*, 4 (2005), 29–67.

Fleurbaey, M., *Fairness, Responsibility, and Welfare* (Oxford: Oxford University Press, 2008).

Frankfurt, H., 'Alternate Possibilities and Moral Responsibility', *Journal of Philosophy*, 66 (1969), 829–839.

Frankfurt, H., 'Equality as a Moral Ideal', *Ethics*, 98 (1987), 21–43.

Frankfurt, H., *The Importance of What We Care About* (Cambridge: Cambridge University Press, 1988).

Freeman, S., *Justice and the Social Contract* (Oxford: Oxford University Press, 2006).

Fried, C., *An Anatomy of Values* (Cambridge, MA: Harvard University Press, 1969).

Gakidou, E. E., J. Frenk, and C. J. L. Murray, 'A Health Agenda' in J. Cohen and J. Rogers (eds), *Is Inequality Bad for our Health?* (Boston: Beacon Press, 2000), 71–78.

Gakidou, E. E., C. J. L. Murray, and J. Frenk, 'Defining and Measuring Health Inequality: An Approach Based on the Distribution of Health Expectancy', *Bulletin of the World Health Organization*, 78 (2000), 42–54.

Gallie, D., *Resisting Marginalization: Unemployment Experience and Social Policy in the European Union* (Oxford: Oxford University Press, 2004).

Gauthier, D., *Morals by Agreement* (Oxford: Oxford University Press, 1986).

Gigerenzer, G., *Adaptive Thinking: Rationality in the Real World* (Oxford: Oxford University Press, 2000).

Gigerenzer, G., P. M. Tood, and the ABC Group (eds), *Simple Heuristics that Make Us Smart* (New York: Oxford University Press, 1999).

Gilbert, D. T., 'How Mental Systems Believe', *American Psychologist*, 46 (1991), 107–119.

Gilbert, D. T., 'The Assent of Man: Mental Representation and the Control of Belief' in D. M. Wegner and J. W. Pennebaker (eds), *Handbook of Mental Control* (Englewood Cliffs, New Jersey: Prentice Hall, 1993), 57–87.

Gilbert, D. T., R. W. Tafarodi, and P. S. Malone, 'You Can't Not Believe Everything You Read', *Journal of Personality and Social Psychology*, 65 (1993), 221–233.

Gilbert, M., *On Social Facts* (London: Routledge, 1989).

Ginet, C., 'The Epistemic Requirements for Moral Responsibility', *Philosophical Perspectives*, 14 (2000), 267–277.

Glover, J., *Responsibility* (London: Routledge and Kegan Paul, 1970).

Gollwitzer, P. M., U. C. Bayer, and K. C. McCulloch, 'The Control of the Unwanted' in R. R. Hassin, J. S. Uleman, and J. A. Bargh (eds), *The New Unconscious* (New York: Oxford University Press, 2005), 485–515.

Greene, J. and J. Cohen, 'For the Law, Neuroscience Changes Nothing and Everything', *Philosophical Transactions of the Royal Society B*, Biological Sciences, Special Issue on Law and the Brain, 359 (2004), 1775–1785.

Haji, I., *Moral Appraisability: Puzzles, Proposals, and Perplexities* (Oxford: Oxford University Press, 1998).

Halpern, D. and C. Bates, *Personal Responsibility and Changing Behaviour: The State of Knowledge and its Implications for Public Policy* (London: Prime Minister's Strategy Unit, 2004).

Hart, H. L. A., *Punishment and Responsibility* (Oxford: Oxford University Press, 1968).

Hassin, R. R., J. S. Uleman, and J. A. Bargh (eds), *The New Unconscious* (New York: Oxford University Press, 2005).

Hausman, D. M., 'What's Wrong with Health Inequalities', *Journal of Political Philosophy*, 15 (2007), 46–66.

Hausman, D. M., Y. Asada, and T. Hedemann, 'Health Inequalities and Why They Matter', *Health Care Analysis*, 10 (2002), 177–191.

Henrich, J., R. Boyd, S. Bowles, C. Camerer, E. Fehr, and H. Gintis (eds), *Foundations of Human Sociality* (Oxford: Oxford University Press, 2004).

Hild, M. and A. Voorhoeve, 'Equality of Opportunity and Opportunity Dominance', *Economics and Philosophy*, 20 (2004), 117–146.

Hinton, T., 'Must Egalitarians Choose Between Fairness and Respect?', *Philosophy and Public Affairs*, 30 (2001), 72–87.

Hitchens, C., *The Missionary Position: Mother Teresa in Theory and Practice* (London and New York: Verso, 1995).

Honoré, T., 'Responsibility and Luck: The Moral Basis of Strict Liability' in his *Responsibility and Fault* (Oxford: Hart, 1999), 14–40.

Hurka, T., 'The Justification of National Partiality' in R. McKim and J. McMahan (eds), *The Morality of Nationalism* (New York: Oxford University Press, 1997), 139–157.

Hurley, S., *Natural Reasons* (New York: Oxford University Press, 1989).

Hurley, S., 'Luck and Equality,' *Proceedings of the Aristotelian Society*, Supplementary Volume, 75 (2001), 51–72.

Hurley, S., *Justice, Luck, and Knowledge* (Cambridge, MA: Harvard University Press, 2003).

Hurley, S., 'Bypassing Conscious Control: Media Violence, Imitation, and Freedom of Speech' in S. Pockett, W. Banks, and S. Gallagher (eds), *Does Consciousness Cause Behavior?* (Cambridge, MA: MIT Press, 2006), 301–337.

Hurley, S., 'Choice and Incentive Inequality' in C. Sypnowich (ed.), *The Egalitarian Conscience* (Oxford: Oxford University Press, 2006), 130–153.

Hurley, S. and M. Nudds, 'The Questions of Animal Rationality: Theory and Evidence' in S. Hurley and M. Nudds (eds), *Rational Animals?* (Oxford: Oxford University Press, 2006), 1–83.

Husak, D., 'Is Drunk Driving a Serious Offense?', *Philosophy and Public Affairs*, 23 (1994), 52–73.

Jackson, F., 'Group Morality' in P. Pettit, R. Sylvan, and J. Norman (eds), *Metaphysics and Morality* (Oxford: Basil Blackwell, 1987), 91–110.

Jacoby, L. L., 'A Process Dissociation Framework: Separating Automatic from Intentional Uses of Memory', *Journal of Memory and Language*, 30 (1991), 513–541.

James, A., 'Constructing Justice for Existing Practice: Rawls and the Status Quo', *Philosophy and Public Affairs*, 33 (2005), 281–316.

Jencks, C., *Rethinking Social Policy: Race, Poverty, and the Underclass* (Cambridge, MA: Harvard University Press, 1992).

John, A. H., 'The London Assurance Company and the Marine Insurance Market of the Eighteenth Century', *Economica*, 98 (1958), 126–141.

Julius, A. J., 'Basic Structure and the Value of Equality', *Philosophy and Public Affairs*, 31 (2003), 321–355.

Julius, A. J., 'Nagel's Atlas', *Philosophy and Public Affairs*, 34 (2006), 176–192.

Kacelnik, A., 'Meanings of Rationality' in S. Hurley and M. Nudds (eds), *Rational Animals?* (Oxford: Oxford University Press), 87–106.

Kagan, S., *The Limits of Morality* (Oxford: Oxford University Press, 1989).

Kagan, S., 'Equality and Desert' in O. McLeod and L. P. Pojman (eds), *What Do We Deserve?: A Reader on Justice and Desert* (Oxford: Oxford University Press, 1998), 283–297.

Kahneman, D., 'Maps of Bounded Rationality: Psychology for Behavioural Economics', *American Economic Review*, 93 (2003), 1449–1475.

Kahneman, D., P. Slovic, and A. Tversky, *Judgements under Uncertainty: Heuristics and Biases* (Cambridge: Cambridge University Press, 1982).

Kahneman, D. and A. Tversky, 'Choices, Values, and Frames' in D. Kahneman and A. Tversky (eds), *Choices, Values, and Frames* (Cambridge: Cambridge University Press, 2000), 1–16.

Kamm, F., *Morality, Mortality: Volume 2* (New York: Oxford University Press, 1996).

Kamm, F., 'Health and Equity' in C. J. L. Murray, J. A. Solomon, C. D. Mathers, and A. D. Lopez (eds), *Summary Measures of Population Health: Concepts, Ethics, Measurement and Applications*, (Geneva: World Health Organization, 2002), 685–706.

Kekes, J., 'A Question for Egalitarians', *Ethics*, 107 (1997), 658–669.

King, D., *In the Name of Liberalism: Illiberal Social Policy in Britain and the United States* (Oxford: Oxford University Press, 1999).

Knight, C., 'In Defence of Luck Egalitarianism', *Res Publica*, 11 (2005), 55–73.

Knight, C., 'The Metaphysical Case for Luck Egalitarianism', *Social Theory and Practice*, 32 (2006), 173–189.

Knight, C., 'The Method of Reflective Equilibrium: Wide, Radical, Fallible, Plausible', *Philosophical Papers*, 35 (2006), 205–229.

Knight, C., 'A Pluralistic Approach to Global Poverty', *Review of International Studies*, 34 (2008), 713–733.

Knight, C., *Luck Egalitarianism: Equality, Responsibility, and Justice* (Edinburgh: Edinburgh University Press, 2009).

Kymlicka, W., *Contemporary Political Philosophy*, second edition (Oxford: Oxford University Press, 2002).

Lamont, J., 'The Concept of Desert in Distributive Justice', *Philosophical Quarterly*, 44 (1994), 45–64.

Laslett, P., 'Introduction' in P. Laslett (ed.), *Philosophy, Politics and Society* (Oxford: Blackwell, 1956), vii–xv.

Le Grand, J., 'Equity, Health, and Health Care', *Social Justice Research*, 1 (1987), 257–274.

Le Grand, J., *Equity and Choice* (London: Routledge, 1991).

Lessig, L., 'The Regulation of Social Meaning', *University of Chicago Law Review*, 62 (1995), 943–1045.

Lippert-Rasmussen, K., 'Equality, Option Luck, and Responsibility', *Ethics*, 111 (2001), 548–579.

Lippert-Rasmussen, K., 'Hurley on Egalitarianism and the Luck-Neutralizing Aim', *Politics, Philosophy, and Economics*, 4 (2005), 249–265.

Lippert-Rasmussen, K., 'Publicity and Egalitarian Justice', *Journal of Moral Philosophy*, 5 (2008), 30–49.

Lord, C. G., M. R. Lepper, and E. Preston, 'Considering the Opposite: A Corrective Strategy for Social Judgment', *Journal of Personality and Social Psychology*, 47 (1984), 1231–1243.

McFadden, D., 'Rationality for Economists?', *Journal of Risk and Uncertainty*, 19 (1999), 73–105.

McKerlie, D., 'Equality and Time', *Ethics*, 99 (1989), 475–491.

McKerlie, D., 'Justice Between the Young and the Old', *Philosophy and Public Affairs*, 30 (2002), 152–177.

Macleod, C. M., *Liberalism, Justice and Markets: A Critique of Liberal Equality* (Oxford: Oxford University Press, 1998).

Marchand, S., D. Wikler, and B. Landesman, 'Class, Health, and Justice', *The Milbank Quarterly*, 76 (1998), 463–465.

Markovits, D., 'Luck Egalitarianism and Political Solidarity', *Theoretical Inquiries in Law*, 9 (2008), 271–308.

Marmot, M., *The Status Syndrome: How Social Standing Affects Our Health and Longevity* (New York: Henry Holt, Times Books, 2004).

Martin, L. L., J. J. Seta, and R. A. Crelia, 'Assimilation and Contrast as a Function of People's Willingness and Ability to Expend Effort in Forming an Impression', *Journal of Personality and Social Psychology*, 59 (1990), 27–37.

Marx, K. and F. Engels, 'Manifesto of the Communist Party' in Robert Tucker (ed.), *The Marx—Engels Reader*, second edition (New York: W. W. Norton and Co., 1978), 469–500.

Mason, A., *Levelling the Playing Field: The Idea of Equal Opportunity and Its Place in Egalitarian Thought* (Oxford: Oxford University Press, 2006).

Matravers, M., *Justice and Punishment* (Oxford: Oxford University Press, 2000).

Matravers, M., *Responsibility and Justice* (Cambridge: Polity Press, 2007).

Mechanic, D., 'Disadvantage, Inequality, and Social Policy', *Health Affairs*, 21 (2002), 48–59.

Mill, J. S., *On Liberty and Other Essays*, J. Dunn (ed.) (Oxford: Oxford University Press, 1991).

Miller, D., *Market, State, and Community: Theoretical Foundations of Market Socialism* (Oxford: Clarendon Press, 1989).

Miller, D., *Principles of Social Justice* (Cambridge, MA: Harvard University Press, 1999).

Miller, D., '"Are They My Poor?": The Problem of Altruism in a World of Strangers', *Critical Review of International Social Philosophy and Policy*, 5 (2002), 106–127 [reprinted in J. Seglow (ed.), *The Ethics of Altruism* (London: Frank Cass, 2004), 107–127].

Miller, D., 'Comparative and Non-Comparative Desert' in S. Olsaretti (ed.), *Desert and Justice* (Oxford: Clarendon Press, 2003), 25–44.

Miller, D., *National Responsibility and Global Justice* (Oxford: Oxford University Press, 2007).

Miller, D., 'The Responsibility to Protect Human Rights' in L. Meyer (ed.), *Legitimacy, Justice and Public International Law* (Cambridge: Cambridge University Press, 2009), 232–251.

Miller, R., 'Cosmopolitan Respect and Patriotic Concern', *Philosophy and Public Affairs*, 27 (1998), 202–224.

Moller Okin, S., *Justice, Gender, and the Family* (New York: Basic Books, 1989).

Moors, A. and De Houwer, J., 'What is Automaticity? An Analysis of Its Component Features and Their Interrelations', in J. A. Bargh (ed.), *Social Psychology and the Unconscious: The Automaticity of Higher Mental Processes* (New York: Psychology Press, 2007), 11–50.

Mulgan, T., *The Demands of Consequentialism* (Oxford: Clarendon Press, 2001).

Murphy, L., *Moral Demands in Nonideal Theory* (Oxford: Oxford University Press, 2000).

Murray, C., *Losing Ground: American Social Policy 1950–1980* (New York: Basic Books, 1984).

Murray, C. J. L., 'Rethinking DALYs' in C. J. L. Murray and A. D. Lopez (eds), *The Global Burden of Disease* (Cambridge, MA: Harvard School of Public Health, World Health Organization, World Bank, 1996), 1–98.

Murray, C. J. L., *US Patterns of Mortality by County and Race: 1965–1994* (Cambridge, MA: Harvard School of Public Health, 1998).

Murray, C. J. L., E. E. Gakidou, and J. Frenk, 'Health Inequalities and Social Group Differences: What Should We Measure?', *Bulletin of the World Health Organization*, 77 (1999), 537–543.

Murray, C. J. L. and A. D. Lopez (eds), *The Global Burden of Disease* (Cambridge, MA: Harvard School of Public Health, World Health Organization, World Bank, 1996).

Nagel, T., 'Equal Treatment and Compensatory Discrimination', *Philosophy and Public Affairs*, 2 (1973), 348–363.

Nagel, T., 'Moral Luck', *Proceedings of the Aristotelian Society*, supplementary volume, 50 (1976), 137–151 [reprinted in T. Nagel, *Mortal Questions* (Cambridge: Cambridge University Press, 1979), 24–38].

Nagel, T., *Equality and Partiality* (Oxford and New York: Oxford University Press, 1991).

Nagel, T., 'Justice and Nature', *Oxford Journal of Legal Studies*, 17 (1997), 303–321.

Nagel, T., 'The Problem of Global Justice', *Philosophy and Public Affairs*, 33 (2005), 113–147.

Narveson, J., 'Is World Poverty a Moral Problem for the Wealthy', *The Journal of Ethics*, 8 (2004), 397–408.

Narveson, J., 'Welfare and Wealth, Poverty and Justice in Today's World', *The Journal of Ethics*, 8 (2004), 305–348.

NICE Citizens Council, *Report of the NICE Citizen's Council on Determining Clinical Need*, 2002, http://www.nice.org.uk/archivedsite/newsarchive/news2002/report_of_the_first_meeting_of_the_citizens_council.jsp.

Nisbett, R. and L. Ross, *Human Inference: Strategies and Shortcomings of Social Judgement* (Englewood Cliffs: Prentice Hall, 1980).

Nosek, B. A., A. G. Greenwald, and M. R. Banaji, 'The Implicit Association Test at Age 7: A Methodological and Conceptual Review' in J. A. Bargh (ed.), *Social Psychology and the Unconscious: The Automaticity of Higher Mental Processes* (New York: Psychology Press, 2007), 265–292.

Nozick, R., *Anarchy, State, and Utopia* (New York: Basic Books, 1974).

Nussbaum, M., 'Aristotelian Social Democracy' in R. Douglas, G. Mara, and H. Richardson (eds), *Liberalism and the Good* (New York: Routledge, 1990), 203–252.

Nussbaum, M., 'Human Functioning and Social Justice: In Defense of Aristotelian Essentialism', *Political Theory*, 20 (1992), 202–246.

Nussbaum, M., *Frontiers of Justice: Disability, Nationality, and Species Membership* (Cambridge, MA: Harvard University Press, 2006).

Olsaretti, S. (ed.), *Desert and Justice* (Oxford: Oxford University Press, 2003).

Olsaretti, S., 'Responsibility and the Consequences of Choice', *Proceedings of the Aristotelian Society*, 109 (2009), 165–188.

Otsuka, M., 'Luck, Insurance, and Equality', *Ethics*, 113 (2002), 40–54.

Otsuka, M., 'Liberty, Equality, Envy, and Abstraction' in J. Burley (ed.), *Ronald Dworkin and His Critics* (Oxford: Basil Blackwell, 2004), 70–79.

Otsuka, M., *Libertarianism without Inequality* (Oxford: Oxford University Press, 2006).

Parfit, D., *Reasons and Persons* (Oxford: Oxford University Press, 1984).

Parfit, D., 'Equality and Priority?' in A. Mason (ed.), *Ideals of Equality* (Oxford: Blackwell Publishers, 1998), 1–20.

Pateman, C., *The Sexual Contract* (Cambridge: Polity Press, 1988).

Payne, B. K. and B. D. Stewart, 'Automatic and Controlled Components of Social Cognition: A Process Dissociation Approach' in J. A. Bargh (ed.), *Social Psychology and the Unconscious: The Automaticity of Higher Mental Processes* (New York: Psychology Press, 2007), 293–315.

Peter, F., 'Health Equity and Social Justice', in S. Anand, F. Peter, and A. K. Sen (eds), *Public Health, Ethics, and Equity* (Oxford: Oxford University Press, 2004), 93–105.

Pojman, L. P. and R. Westmoreland (eds), *Equality: Selected Readings* (New York: Oxford University Press, 1997).

Pojman, L. P., 'Does Equality Trump Desert?' in O. McLeod and L. P. Pojman (eds), *What Do We Deserve?: A Reader on Justice and Desert* (Oxford: Oxford University Press, 1998), 298–314.

Powers, M. and R. Faden, *Social Justice: The Moral Foundations of Public Health and Health Policy* (Oxford: Oxford University Press, 2006).

Rakowski, E., *Equal Justice* (Oxford: Oxford University Press, 1991).

Rawls, J., 'Justice as Fairness', *Philosophical Review*, 67 (1958), 164–194.

Rawls, J., *A Theory of Justice* (Cambridge, MA: Harvard University Press, 1971).

Rawls, J., 'The Independence of Moral Theory', *Proceedings and Addresses of the American Philosophical Association*, 47 (1975), 5–22.

Rawls, J., 'Social Unity and the Primary Goods', in A. K. Sen and B. Williams (eds), *Utilitarianism and Beyond* (Cambridge: Cambridge University Press, 1982), 159–185.

Rawls, J., 'Justice as Fairness: Political not Metaphysical', *Philosophy and Public Affairs*, 14 (1985), 223–252.

Rawls, J., 'The Priority of Right and Ideas of the Good', *Philosophy and Public Affairs*, 17 (1988), 251–276.

Rawls, J., *Political Liberalism* (New York: University of Columbia Press, 1993).

Rawls, J., *A Theory of Justice*, revised edition (Cambridge, MA: Harvard University Press, 1999).

Rawls, J., 'Social Unity and Primary Goods' in J. Rawls, *Collected Essays*, S. Freeman (ed.), (Cambridge: Harvard University Press, 1999), 359–387.

Rawls, J., *The Law of Peoples* (Cambridge, MA: Harvard University Press, 1999).

Rawls, J., *Justice as Fairness: A Restatement*, E. Kelly (ed.), (Cambridge, MA: Harvard University Press, 2001).

Ripstein, A., *Equality, Responsibility, and the Law* (Cambridge: Cambridge University Press, 1999).

Roemer, J. E., 'Equality of Talent', *Economics and Philosophy*, 1 (1985), 151–188.

Roemer, J. E., 'A Pragmatic Theory of Responsibility for the Egalitarian Planner', *Philosophy and Public Affairs*, 22 (1993), 146–166.

Roemer, J. E., 'Equality of Opportunity', *Boston Review*, April/May 1995, http://bostonreview.net/BR20.2/Roemer.html.

Roemer, J. E., *Theories of Distributive Justice* (Cambridge, MA: Harvard University Press, 1996).

Roemer, J. E., *Equality of Opportunity* (Cambridge, MA: Harvard University Press, 1998).

Roemer, J. E., 'Egalitarianism Against the Veil of Ignorance', *Journal of Philosophy*, 99 (2002), 167–184.

Roemer, J. E., 'Equality of Opportunity: A Progress Report', *Social Choice and Welfare*, 19 (2002), 455–471.

Rosa Dias, P. and A. M. Jones, 'Giving Equality of Opportunity a Fair Innings', *Health Economics*, 16 (2007), 109–112.

Rosen, G., 'Culpability and Ignorance', *Proceedings of the Aristotelian Society*, 103 (2003), 61–84.

Rosen, G., 'Skepticism about Moral Responsibility', *Philosophical Perspectives*, 18 (2004), 295–313.

Ross, W. D., *The Right and the Good* (Oxford: Oxford University Press, 1930).

Sa, W. C. and K. E. Stanovich, 'The Domain Specificity and Generality of Mental Contamination: Accuracy and Projection in Judgments of Mental Content', *British Journal of Psychology*, 92 (2001), 281–302.

Sadurski, W., *Giving Desert Its Due* (Dordrecht: Reidel, 1985).

Sandel, M., *Liberalism and the Limits of Justice* (Cambridge, MA: Cambridge University Press, 1982).

Sapolsky, R. M., 'The Frontal Cortex and the Criminal Justice System', *Philosophical Transactions of the Royal Society B*, Biological Sciences, Special Issue on Law and the Brain, 359 (2004), 1787–1796.

Satz, D., 'Equality, Adequacy, and Education for Citizenship', *Ethics*, 117 (2007), 623–648.

Scanlon, T. M., 'Freedom of Expression and Categories of Expression', *University of Pittsburgh Law Review*, 40 (1979), 519–550.

Scanlon, T. M., 'The Significance of Choice' in S. McMurrin (ed.), *The Tanner Lectures on Human Values*, volume 8 (Cambridge: Cambridge University Press, 1988), 151–216.

Scanlon, T. M., *What We Owe to Each Other* (Cambridge, MA: Harvard University Press, 1998).

Scheffler, S., *The Rejection of Consequentialism* (Oxford: Clarendon Press, 1982).

Scheffler, S., *Boundaries and Allegiances: Problems of Justice and Responsibility in Liberal Thought* (Oxford: Oxford University Press, 2001).

Scheffler, S., 'Equality as the Virtue of Sovereigns: A Reply to Ronald Dworkin', *Philosophy and Public Affairs* 31 (2003), 199–206.

Scheffler, S., 'What is Egalitarianism?', *Philosophy and Public Affairs*, 31 (2003), 5–39.

Scheffler, S., 'Choice, Circumstance, and the Value of Equality', *Politics, Philosophy, and Economics*, 4 (2005), 5–28.

Schmidt, H.,'Health Responsibility, the Left, and the Right', *Bioethics Forum/The Hastings Center Report*, 6 July 2007, http://www.bioethicsforum.org/personal-responsibility-health-care-Medicaid-Membership-Agreement.asp.

Schmidt, H., 'Patients' Charters and Health Responsibilities', *British Medical Journal*, 335 (2007), 1187–1189.

Schmidt, H., 'Personal Responsibility for Health', *European Journal of Health Law*, 14 (2007), 241–250.

Schmidtz, D., 'Taking Responsibility' in R. E. Goodin and D. Schmidtz, *Social Welfare and Individual Responsibility* (Cambridge: Cambridge University Press, 1998), 1–96.

Schmidtz, D., *The Elements of Justice* (Cambridge: Cambridge University Press, 2006).

Schokkaert, E., D. Van de gaer, F. Vandenbroucke, and R. Luttens, 'Responsibility-Sensitive Egalitarianism and Optimal Linear Income Taxation', *Mathematical Social Sciences*, 48 (2004), 151–182.

Schwappach, D., 'Does it Matter Who You Are or What You Gain? An Experimental Study of Preferences for Resource Allocation', *Health Economics*, 12 (2003), 255–262.

Searle, J. R., 'Collective Intentions and Actions' in P. R. Cohen, J. Morgan, and M. E. Pollack (eds), *Intentions in Communication* (Cambridge, MA: MIT Press, 1990), 401–416.

Segall, S., 'In Solidarity with the Imprudent: A Defence of Luck-Egalitarianism', *Social Theory and Practice*, 33 (2007), 177–198.

Segall, S., *Health, Luck, and Justice* (Princeton: Princeton University Press, 2010).

Selgelid, M. J., 'Ethics and Infectious Disease', *Bioethics*, 19 (2005), 272–289.

Selgelid, M. J., 'Ethics and Drug Resistance', *Bioethics*, 21 (2007), 1–12.

Seligman, M., 'Luck, Leverage, and Equality: A Bargaining Problem for Luck Egalitarians', *Philosophy and Public Affairs*, 35 (2007), 267–292.

Sen, A. K., *On Economic Inequality* (Oxford: Oxford University Press, 1973).

Sen, A. K., 'Equality of What?' in S. McMurrin (ed.), *The Tanner Lectures on Human Values*, volume 1 (Salt Lake City: University of Utah Press, 1980), 195–220.

Sen, A. K., *Choice, Welfare, and Measurement* (Oxford: Blackwell, 1982).

Sen, A. K., 'Well-being, Agency, and Freedom: The Dewey Lectures 1984', *Journal of Philosophy*, 82 (1985), 169–220.

Sen, A. K., 'Justice: Means versus Freedoms', *Philosophy and Public Affairs*, 19 (1990), 111–121.

Sen, A. K., *Inequality Reexamined* (Cambridge MA: Harvard University Press, 1992).

Sen, A. K., 'Capability and Well-being' in M. Nussbaum and A. K. Sen (eds), *The Quality of Life*, (Oxford: Oxford University Press, 1993), 30–53.

Sen, A. K., *Development as Freedom* (Oxford: Oxford University Press, 1999).

Sen, A. K., 'Why Health Equity?' in S. Anand, F. Peter, and A. Sen (eds), *Public Health, Ethics, and Equity* (Oxford: Oxford University Press, 2004), 21–33.

Sen, A. K. and B. Williams (eds), *Utilitarianism and Beyond* (Cambridge: Cambridge University Press, 1982).

Sgard, J., 'On Legal Origins and Bankruptcy Laws: the European Experience (1808–1914)', *CEPII Working Paper*, 26 (2006), http://www.cepii.fr/anglaisgraph/workpap/summaries/2006/wp06-26.htm.

Shiffrin, S. V., 'Egalitarianism, Choice-Sensitivity, and Accommodation' in P. Pettit, S. Scheffler, M. Smith, and R. J. Wallace (eds), *Reason and Values: Themes from the Moral Philosophy of Joseph Raz* (Oxford: Oxford University Press, 2004), 270–302.

Simonson, I. and A. Tversky, 'Choice in Context: Tradeoff Contrast and Extremeness Aversion', *Journal of Marketing Research*, 29 (1992), 281–295.

Smart, J. J. C., 'Free-will, Praise, and Blame', *Mind*, 70 (1960), 291–306.

Smilansky, S., 'Responsibility and Desert: Defending the Connection', *Mind*, 105 (1996), 157–163.

Sperber, D., 'Metarepresentations in an Evolutionary Perspective' in D. Sperber (ed.), *Metarepresentations: A Multidisciplinary Perspective* (Oxford: Oxford University Press, 2000), 117–137.

Sperber, D., 'Modularity and Relevance: How Can a Massively Modular Mind be Flexible and Context-Sensitive?' in Peter Carruthers, Stephen Laurence, and Stephen Stich (eds), *The Innate Mind: Structure and Content* (New York: Oxford University Press, 2005), 53–68.

Steinbock, B., 'Drunk Driving', *Philosophy and Public Affairs*, 14 (1985), 278–295.

Steiner, H., 'Choice and Circumstance', *Ratio*, 10 (1997), 296–312.

Stemplowska, Z., 'Holding People Responsible For What They Do Not Control', *Politics, Philosophy and Economics*, 7 (2008), 355–377.

Stemplowska, Z., 'Making Justice Sensitive to Responsibility', *Political Studies*, 57 (2009), 237–259.

Sterelny, K., *Thought in a Hostile World* (Oxford: Blackwell, 2003).

Sterelny, K., 'Folk Logic and Animal Rationality' in S. Hurley and M. Nudds (eds), *Rational Animals?* (Oxford: Oxford University Press, 2006), 293–312.

Stewart, N., N. Chater, and G. D. A. Brown, 'Decision by Sampling', *Cognitive Psychology*, 53 (2006), 1–26.

Strawson, P. F., 'Freedom and Resentment,' *Proceedings of the British Academy*, 48 (1962), 187–211.

Sverdlik, S., 'Punishment', *Law and Philosophy*, 7 (1988), 179–201.

Tan, K-C., 'A Defense of Luck Egalitarianism', *Journal of Philosophy*, 105 (2008), 665–690.

Tawney, R. H., *Equality* (London: Allen and Unwin, 1931).

Taylor, C., *Philosophy and the Human Sciences* (Cambridge: Cambridge University Press, 1985).

Tännsjö, T., 'The Morality of Collective Actions', *Philosophical Quarterly*, 39 (1989), 221–228.

Temkin, L., 'Harmful Goods, Harmless Bads' in R. G. Frey and C. W. Morris (eds), *Value, Welfare, and Morality* (Cambridge: Cambridge University Press, 1993), 290–324.

Temkin, L., *Inequality* (Oxford: Oxford University Press, 1993).

Temkin, L., 'Weighing Goods: Some Questions and Comments', *Philosophy and Public Affairs*, 23 (1994), 350–380.

Temkin, L., 'Equality, Priority, and the Levelling Down Objection' in M. Clayton and A. Williams (eds), *The Ideal of Equality* (Basingstoke: MacMillan, 2000), 126–161.

Temkin, L., 'Egalitarianism: A Complex, Individualistic, and Comparative Notion' in Ernest Sosa and Enrique Villanueva (eds), *Philosophical Issues 11, Social, Political, and Legal Philosophy* (Oxford: Blackwell Publishers, 2001), 327–352.

Temkin, L., 'Egalitarianism Defended', *Ethics*, 113 (2003), 764–782.

Temkin, L., 'Exploring the Roots of Egalitarian Concern', *Theoria*, 69 (2003), 125–151.

Temkin, L., 'Thinking about the Needy, Justice, and International Organizations', *The Journal of Ethics*, 8 (2004), 349–395.

Temkin, L., 'A "New" Principle of Aggregation' in Ernest Sosa and Enrique Villanueva (eds), *Philosophical Issues 15, Normativity* (Oxford: Wiley-Blackwell, 2005), 218–234.

Temkin, L., 'Answers to Questions', in M. E. J. Nielsen (ed.), *Political Questions: 5 Questions on Political Theory* (New York: Automatic Press/VIP, 2006), 147–167.

Temkin, L., 'Illuminating Egalitarianism' in Thomas Christiano and John Christman (eds), *Contemporary Debates in Philosophy* (Oxford: Blackwell, Publishing 2009), 155–178.

Thomson, J. J., 'Morality and Bad Luck', *Metaphilosophy*, 20 (1989), 203–221 [reprinted in Daniel Statman (ed.), *Moral Luck* (Albany: State University of New York, 1993), 195–216].

Tsuchiya, A. and A. Williams, 'A "Fair Innings" between the Sexes: Are Men being Treated Inequitably?', *Social Science and Medicine*, 60 (2005), 277–286.

Tungodden, B., 'Responsibility and Redistribution: The Case of First Best Taxation', *Social Choice and Welfare*, 24 (2005), 33–44.

Ubel P. A., C. Jepson, J. Baron, T. Mohr, S. McMorrow, and D. A. Asch, 'The Allocation of Transplantable Organs: Do People Want to Punish Patients for Causing Their Illness?', *Liver Transplantation*, 7 (2001), 600–607.

United Nations Development Programme, *Human Development Report: Concept and Measurement of Human Development* (Oxford: Oxford University Press, 1990).

Vallentyne, P., 'Brute Luck, Option Luck, and Equality of Initial Opportunities', *Ethics*, 112 (2002), 529–557.

Vallentyne, P., 'Brute Luck Equality and Desert' in S. Olsaretti (ed.), *Desert and Justice* (Oxford: Oxford University Press, 2003), 169–185.

Van de gaer, D., *Equality of Opportunity and Investment in Human Capital*, PhD thesis (Katholieke Universiteit Leuven, 1993).

Van Parijs, P., *Real Freedom for All* (Oxford: Oxford University Press, 1995).

Van Parijs, P., 'Difference Principles' in S. Freeman (ed.), *The Cambridge Companion to Rawls* (Cambridge: Cambridge University Press, 2003), 200–240.

Vargas, M., 'The Revisionist's Guide to Responsibility', *Philosophical Studies*, 125 (2005), 399–429.

Vargas, M., 'Revisionism' in J. Fischer, J. Kane, D. Pereboom, and M. Vargas, *Four Views on Free Will* (Oxford: Basil Blackwell, 2007), 126–165.

Veatch, R. M., 'Justice and the Right to Health Care: An Egalitarian Account' in T. J. Bole and W. B. Bondeson (eds), *Rights to Health Care* (Dordrecht: Kluwer, 1991), 83–102.

Voigt, K., 'The Harshness Objection: Is Luck Egalitarianism Too Harsh on the Victims of Option Luck?', *Ethical Theory and Moral Practice*, 10 (2007), 389–407.

Vonnegut, K., 'Harrison Bergeron' in *Welcome to the Monkey House* (New York: Dell Publishing, 1998), 7–14.

Wagstaff, A., P. Pact, and E. Van Doorslaer, 'On the Measurement of Inequalities in Health', *Social Science and Medicine*, 33 (1991), 545–557.

Wallace, R. J., *Responsibility and the Moral Sentiments* (Cambridge, MA: Harvard University Press, 1994).

Wason, P. C., 'Reasoning' in B. M. Foss (ed.), *New Horizons in Psychology I* (Harmondsworth: Penguin, 1966), 135–151.

Watson, G., 'Two Faces of Responsibility' in *Agency and Answerability* (Oxford: Oxford University Press, 2004), 260–288.

Wegner, D. M., *The Illusion of Conscious Will* (Cambridge, MA: MIT Press, 2002).

Wexler, D. B. and B. J. Winick, *Law in Therapeutic Key: Developments in Therapeutic Jurisprudence* (Durham, NC: Carolina Academic Press, 1996).

Wharam, J. F. and N. Daniels, 'Toward Evidence-Based Policy Making and Standardized Assessment of Health Policy Reform', *Journal of the American Medical Association*, 298 (2007), 676–679.

White, S., *The Civic Minimum* (Oxford: Oxford University Press, 2003).

Whitehead, M., *The Concepts and Principles of Equity and Health* (Copenhagen: World Health Organization, 1990).

Whitehead, M., 'The Concepts and Principles of Equity and Health', *Health Promotion International*, 6 (1991), 217–228.

Wikler, D., 'Personal and Social Responsibility for Health' in S. Anand, F. Peter, and A. K. Sen (eds), *Public Health, Ethics and Equality* (Oxford: Oxford University Press, 2004), 109–134.

Williams, A. [Alan], 'If We Are Going to Get a Fair Innings, Someone Will Need to Keep the Score!' in M. L. Barer, T. E. Getzen, and G. L. Stoddart (eds), *Health, Health Care, and Health Economics* (New York: Wiley, 1998), 319–330.

Williams, A. [Andrew], 'Equality for the Ambitious', *Philosophical Quarterly* 52 (2002), 377–389.

Williams, A., 'Living as Equals: Right or Responsibility?', paper presented to Political Theory Research Seminar, Department of Politics, Oxford University, 8 June 2005.

Williams, A., 'Liberty, Equality, and Property', in John S. Dryzek, Bonnie Honig, and Anne Phillips (eds), *The Oxford Handbook of Political Theory* (Oxford: Oxford University Press, 2006), 488–506.

Williams, A. and P. Casal, 'Equality of Resources and Distributive Justice' in J. Burley (ed.), *Ronald Dworkin and His Critics* (Oxford: Basil Blackwell, 2004), 150–169.

Williams, B., 'The Idea of Equality' in P. Laslett and W. G. Runciman (eds), *Philosophy, Politics, and Society*, Second Series (Oxford: Basil Blackwell, 1962), 110–131.

Wilson, R. A., *Boundaries of the Mind* (Cambridge: Cambridge University Press, 2004).

Wilson, T. D. and N. Brekke, 'Mental Contamination and Mental Correction: Unwanted Influences on Judgements and Evaluations', *Psychological Bulletin*, 116 (1994), 117–142.

Wolff, J., 'Fairness, Respect, and the Egalitarian Ethos', *Philosophy and Public Affairs*, 27 (1998), 97–122.

Wolff, J. and A. de-Shalit, *Disadvantage* (Oxford: Oxford University Press, 2007).

Wood, A., 'The Marxian Critique of Justice', *Philosophy and Public Affairs*, 1 (1972), 244–282.

Wootton, B., *Crime and the Criminal Law: Reflections of a Magistrate and Social Scientist* (London: Stevens & Sons, 1963).

World Health Report 2004 (Geneva: World Health Organization, 2004).

Young, M., *The Rise of Meritocracy* (London: Penguin, 1958).

Zaitchik, A., 'On Deserving To Deserve', *Philosophy and Public Affairs*, 6 (1977), 370–388.

Zimmerman, M. J., 'Luck and Responsibility', *Ethics*, 97 (1987), 374–386.

Zimmerman, M. J., *An Essay on Moral Responsibility* (Totowa, NJ: Rowman & Littlefield, 1988).

Zimmerman, M. J., 'Moral Responsibility and Ignorance', *Ethics*, 107 (1997), 410–426.

Zimmerman, M. J., 'Taking Luck Seriously', *Journal of Philosophy*, 99 (2002), 553–576.

Index

Note: page numbers followed by 'n' denote mentions in the footnote of the given page.

abandonment of negligent victims 9, 168–71, 263, 281–2
absolute justice and proportional justice 55–6
acting justly vs. acting for reasons of justice 58–61
affluence and health-care 32–3
agency, classical conceptions of individual rational 193
agent brute luck 165–6
agent-neutral vs. agent-relative justice-based reasons 59–61
agent responsibility 11–13, 14, 15–16
  definitions of 11, 174–5
  and desert 16–17
alienability of rights 53
altruistic prisoners dilemmas 231–2
ambition-sensitivity 4
Anderson, Elizabeth 9, 132, 271, 280, 283n
antibiotics use by well-off people 32–3
anti-manipulation principle 212–13
anti-paternalist principle 188–9, 209–10, 211–12
appraisal 154–7
  for non-acts 164–6
  responsibility vs. desert 158–62
Arneson, Richard 7, 10, 18, 225–6, 263n, 280
Ashworth v. Free Speech Coalition case 210–11
assimilation of behaviour 198–9
asymmetry thesis 224–8
attractiveness and social justice 43–4
attributive responsibility *see* agent responsibility
authorship and agent responsibility 12–13
avoidable disadvantage
  compensation for 122–4, 125–8
  and cost of action 129

bankruptcy laws, capping in 218, 223–4
basal desert 158, 162
basal responsibility 154–7, 162
  and non-acts 164–5
  see also agent responsibility
Basic Needs Premise 168–71
behavioural anomalies 195–6
  in social contexts 197–9
behavioural outcomes 193–4
beliefs
  and behaviour 194

and comprehension 200
  see also false beliefs
believed value baseline 182–4
bequests, equalizing 79–81, 88
blame and imaginary outcomes 179
blameworthiness 12, 13
  and alcohol 33
broad responsibility 176–8, 185
  and false beliefs 178–9
  causal condition of 177–8
Broome, John 54–5
brute luck
  agent 165–6
  compensation for 165–7
  and desert 166
  and equality of opportunity 19
  and insurance 6
  vs. option luck 4–5, 16, 34–6
  and social justice 43

capability and real freedom 39–40
capitalism, criticism of 24–5
capitalist economy 223–4
capping, asymmetry of 218, 223–4
causal responsibility 12, 174, 176, 240
Chater, N. and M. Oaksford 202
childcare, preferences about 8
choice
  asymmetry in 217–18
  behavioural anomalies in 195–6
  and broad responsibility 177–8
  vs. circumstances 4–5
  definition of 121
  and degrees of luck 34–6
  vs. desert 35–6
  and fairness 228
  full costs of 217
  and individual responsibility for health 272–5
  and morality 163
  prudent vs. imprudent 122–4, 125–8
circumstance characteristics 86
  vs. responsibility characteristics 78–9, 83
Clark, A. 202, 206
  vs. heuristics 202
coercion and social interactionism 48

cognitive anomalies 196–7
  in social contexts 199–201
cognitive processes, influences on 208
cognitive science and priority of private
    responsibility 190
Cohen, G. A. 2n, 7–8, 10, 63n, 98n, 107n,
    113, 280, 283
Cohen, L. J. 243n
coherent resolution of conflicts among
    goals 192
collective responsibility 20, 104–5
  and partial compliance 235–7, 238–45
  attribution of 20
collective targets 231
collectivistic views of group responsibility 103–5
comparative fairness 17–18, 62–6
  vs. comparative justice 66–9
  and equality 74–5
comparative justice and proportional
    justice 54–5, 56–8
compatibilism 145–6, 156, 157n, 172
compensation
  for avoidable disadvantage 122–4, 125–8
  for brute luck 165–7
  for disadvantageous choices 106, 112
  as egalitarian-equivalent criterion 86, 92
  for expensive tastes 6–7, 8–9
  vs. neutrality 87–9, 92, 95
compulsory insurance 127
conditional-equality criterion 87, 90,
    94–5, 96
conditionality of social equality 132
conscientiousness and desert 32
consequential responsibility 13–14
  and desert 17
consequentialist vs. non-consequentialist
    frameworks of luck egalitarianism 41–2
constitutions
  and desert 144–5
  faulty 137–9
control
  of behaviour 145
  and thin vs. thick luck 15–16
cosmetic surgery 43–4
criminals as faulty units 137

Daniels, Norman 23, 249n, 251n, 255n
Darwall, Stephen 45–6n
Dawkins, Richard 137
decision theory and behavioural anomalies 195–6
democratic interpretation of equality of
    opportunity 3
democratic public scaffolding principle
    213–15
desert
  and agent responsibility 16–17
  as appraisal responsibility 156

and brute luck 166
vs. choice 35–6
and comparative justice 67–9
and constitutions 144–5
and good deeds 35–6
and luck egalitarianism 29–33, 109–110
and morality 153, 158–61
as necessarily moral 158–164
and proportional justice 53–8
and retributive justice 141–4
interpersonal 155n
moral 54–6, 60, 66n, 67–9
desert bases 158–64
desert-sensitive justice 152–3, 162
  and brute bad luck 166–7
  and responsibility-sensitive justice 152, 162,
    171–3
deserving acts 157–64
  see also desert
de-Shalit, Avner 18, 22
desirability challenge 218–19
determinism and free will 10, 55–6, 190–1
difference principle 3, 28, 253–6
  and luck 4
disability and welfare 36
disadvantage, avoidable see avoidable
    disadvantage
disadvantageous choices 106, 112
distribution of welfare 3–4
distributive justice
  holism 141–2, 143, 146–7
  vs. retributive justice 141–4, 149–50
Dixon, J. B. et al. 279
drunk driving 33, 278
  responsibility and justice 65–6
Dworkin, Ronald 4, 5–7, 8, 10, 34, 37, 276

ecological liberalism 212–15
education vouchers, distribution of 88
efficiency argument 220–3
effort and talent 80, 85, 87
egalitarian-equivalent criterion 86, 87,
    90–3, 96
egalitarian reasons of comparative fairness 64
egalitarianism
  and collective responsibility 20, 99–104
  different views of 36
  luck see luck egalitarianism
  maximizing function of 36–40
  responsibility-sensitive see responsibility-
    sensitive egalitarianism
environments and rationality 204–6
equality
  conceptions of 61
  of extended circumstances 79–81
  and fairness 62–6
  forms of 69–71

in maximizing function 37–8
social 131–3
for welfare 7–8, 36, 117n, 248, 280
equality of opportunity 121–4, 126–7, 226
for equal interests model 128–31
fair (FEO) 247–8, 250–6, 264
for health 249–50, 256–7, 261–2
interpretations of 2–3
for maximum advantage model 124–8
for welfare 7–8, 36, 117n, 248, 280
and responsibility-sensitive
egalitarianism 18–19, 121–4, 126–7
ex ante equality 71–6
ex post equality 71–2, 74–6
exoneration view 226–7
expensive tastes
and equality of welfare 6–7, 8–9
and health 277
and judgmental tastes 10–11
exposure avoidance 201
extended circumstances, equalizing 79–81
Eyal, Nir 285n

Fair Equality of Opportunity Principle
(FEOP) 247–8, 250–6, 264
fairness
and ability to rectify 260
and asymmetry thesis 225–6, 228
and collective goals 231
comparative see comparative fairness
and equality 62–6
and partial compliance 238–45
and social responsibility for health 271
false beliefs and broad responsibility 178–9
see also imaginary outcomes
false consensus effects 199–200
faulty constitutions 137–9
feasibility challenge 218–19
Feldman, Fred 164
Fischer, J. M. and M. Ravizza 145
Fleurbaey, Marc 9, 19
Florida Medicaid program 268–9, 284–5
foreseen value baseline 182–4
Forfeiture View 273–4, 280
framing
and cognitive processes 200
of outcomes 196
free speech 210–11
free will
and cognitive science 190–1
existence of 10
and proportional justice 55–7
in responsible acts 154
freedom
maximizing 127
sacrificing to avoid disadvantage 129
Fried, Charles 277–8

friendships and social interactionism 48–9
full costs of choices 217

gambling
and fairness 227–8
and feasibility 220
and option luck 6
Gauthier, David 44
gender inequality see sex inequality in life
expectancy
German health care experiment 268–9, 286
Gigerenzer, G. 202
global justice 46–7
global responsibility vs. local responsibility 66
goods, relational vs. non-relational 116–17
government
and asymmetry thesis 222
and ecological liberalism 212–15
policies see policies
'grouching' in the face of others' non-
compliance 234, 238
grounds of appraisal 154–7
for non-acts 164–6
responsibility vs. desert 158–62
groups
collective responsibility of 20, 104–5
and individual responsibility 105–10
inequality between 99–104

handicaps, natural distribution of 139–40, 146, 149
Hart, H. L. A. 11
health
equality of opportunity 249–50, 256–7,
261–2
fair equality of opportunity (FEO) for 247–8,
250–6, 264
vs. health care 246–7
individual responsibility for 272–5, 281–3
luck prioritarianism 262–4
outcome equality 246–7
promotions 274–5
social obligations towards 270–2
social vs. individual responsibility for 276–9,
283–6
health care
cosmetic surgery 43–4
experiments 267–9, 284–6
vs. health 246–7
policies 32–3, 256
schemes and responsibility 22–3
healthy life expectancy, definition of 249
'help yourself' context 80
heuristics 205
vs. classical rationality 202
holism
of consequential responsibility 14
vs. desert 141–2, 173

holism (*cont.*)
  of distributive justice 141–2, 143, 146–7
  of retributive justice 147–9
Honoré, Tony 13n
Human Development Index 257n
humanitarian reasons vs. egalitarian reasons 64
humanitarian obligations vs. obligations
    of justice 242–3
Hurley, Susan 10, 14, 76n, 156
hypothetical impact requirement 181–2

ideal theory 133, 219
imaginary outcomes 178–9, 185–6
  and prudential value 181–4
  and responsibility 179–81
implicit association tests (IATs) 201
imprudent vs. prudent choices 122–4, 125–8
incompatibilism 142
individual responsibility 14, 105–10
  for health 272–5, 281–3
  vs. social responsibility 276–9, 283–6
  see also responsibility
individualism
  of punishment 148–9
  of retributive justice 143–4
individualistic views of group
    responsibility 105–10
inequality
  badness of 98–104, 111
  and the choices/circumstances distinction 4–5
  in life expectancy 247, 250, 256–62
influences
  on behaviour 198–9
  on cognitive processes 199–201
informed preference satisfaction and personal
    good 40
instrumental sensitivity 191
insurance
  against brute luck 6
  for avoidable disadvantage 122–4, 127–9
  compulsory 127
  and economic growth 221–2
interests and moral desert 159
internalism in classical rationality 194–5
intervention and circumstance characteristics 83
Irresponsibility Premise 168–9
irresponsible acts 154
isolation and moral rights 44–5

jobs
  equality of opportunities for 254
  quality and responsibility 93–4
jogger/smoker objection 247–51
judgements, cognitive anomalies in 197
justice
  conceptions of 52–3
  and different types of action 58–61

as fairness 5, 57
  and partial compliance 230–45
  proportional 53–8, 161
  and rights 53
justice consequentialism 243n

Kahneman, D. and A. Tversky 196, 212
Kamm, Frances 243–4n
Kant 65
Kekes, J. 262n
Knight, Carl 17, 283n
Kymlicka, Will 4

Lagerlof, Selma 218n
levelling down objection to outcome equality in
    health 248, 254–6, 262
liberal interpretation of equality of
    opportunity 3
liberalism 187–9
  naturalistic challenge to 189–90
libertarian interpretation of responsibility 81–3,
    84–5
life expectancy unequal between the sex 247,
    250, 256–62
Lippert-Rasmussen, Kasper 20
local responsibility vs. global responsibility 66
losses
  capping 218, 223–4
  and NDR 221
luck
  and agent responsibility 15–16
  brute vs. option 4–5, 16
  and comparative fairness 63
  and individual responsibility for health 281
  and rights 53
luck egalitarianism 25, 62, 152
  ambiguities in 98–104
  as an asocial theory 42–5, 47–9
  brute vs. option luck 34–6
  consequentialism 41–2
  criticisms of 9–11
  and equality of opportunity 226
  harshness objection to *see* abandonment
    of negligent victims
  and health equality 247–8, 250, 256–7,
    261–3
  ideals of 133–4
  and luckism 45
  maximizing function of 18, 36–40
  morality-based interpretation of luck
    egalitarianism 102
  and NDR 221
  and personal responsibility 28–33
  and responsibility for health 281–3, 284–6
  see also responsibility-sensitive egalitarianism
luck prioritarianism and health 262–4
luckism 45

manipulation and government policy 209, 212–13
Marx, Karl 24–5
Matravers, Matt 14
maximizing function of luck egalitarianism 18, 36–40
mean-of-mins criterion 79–81, 85, 89–90, 95
Mechanic, D. 255n
Medicaid program 267–9, 284–6
medical treatment
    equality of 254–5
    see also health; health care
mental contamination 200–1
metaphysical libertarianism 10
Mill, J. S. 152, 155n, 209
Miller, David 20, 158, 160–1
min-of-means criterion 89, 95
moral accountability 174–5, 177
moral arbitrariness 5, 136, 143, 145–6, 150
moral blame and imaginary outcomes 179
moral character, reasons for 55
moral equality 133
moral grounds of appraisal 154–6
moral responsibility 12, 145–6
moral wrongdoing 110–11
morality
    and asymmetry thesis 224–8
    and desert 153, 158–61
    vs. prudence 175–6
Mulgan, T. 242n
Murphy, Liam 233
Murray, C. J. L. 258n

narrow responsibility 176
Narveson, Jan 52, 60–1
natural access to health vs. social access to
    health 253–4, 258
natural injustice 60–1
natural liberty 2–3
natural policy of transfers 79, 80–1, 83, 85
natural talents, distribution 139–40, 146
naturalistic challenge to traditional
    liberalism 189–90
negative demand for responsibility (NDR) 220,
    221–3
negative desert bases 158, 159–61
negative responsibility bases 154–6, 166
negligent victims, abandonment of 9, 23, 118,
    126, 168–71, 263, 281–2
neutralist liberalism 187
neutrality
    and circumstance characteristics 83, 86
    vs. compensation 87–9, 92, 95
    of intent vs. effect 82
non-acts 164–6
non-coercive governmental influences 188
non-ideal theory 219, 220
non-relational goods vs. relational goods 116–17

non-responsibility bases 154
Norheim, Ole 286n
Nozick, Robert 44–5, 52, 60–1

Objective List 38
obligation to take up the slack of
    non-compliance 242–3
    see also responsibility
opportunity
    and asymmetry thesis 226–7
    fairness of 70–1
    vs. outcomes 117
opportunity sets 122
option luck
    vs. brute luck 4–5, 16, 63–4
    and comparative fairness 65
    and gambling 6
    and luck egalitarianism 34–6
outcome equality in health 246–7
outcomes 78
    and agent responsibility 174–6
    imaginary 178–9, 185–6
    vs. opportunity 117
    unforeseen 178–9

Pareto-optimal access to health 254–5
partial compliance 230–3
    and collective responsibility 235–7, 238–45
    'grouching' 234, 238
    options for compliant agents 233–7
personal responsibility
    and luck egalitarianism 28–33
    see also responsibility
policies
    on drunk driving 33
    for equality in bequests 79–81, 88
    on health-care 32–3
    experimental health-care 267–9, 284–6
    on health equality 256
    health promotion 274–5
    and liberalism 187–90
    and luck egalitarianism 31–2
    and manipulation 209, 212–13
    on poverty levels 37
    responsibility-sensitive 21–3
    on risky behaviour 282
    for wage rates 91–6
politics and public ecology 208–9
positive demand for responsibility 220–1
positive desert bases 158, 160–1
positive responsibility bases 154–6
possibility vs. imaginary outcomes 178–9
practical reasoning 194
praiseworthiness 12, 13, 31
preferences in work and responsibility 93–4
primary responsibility 190, 244
priming behaviour 198–9

priming cognitive processes 199–201
principle of proximal agency 188–9, 210–12
principle of redress 5
priority
    in maximizing function 38, 64, 173, 262–4
    of private responsibility 189
probabilities and foreseen/believed value
        outcomes 183–4
procedural fairness 72–6
    vs. substantive fairness 71–2
proletarians, fair treatment 24–5
proportional justice 53–8, 161
proximal agency principle 210–12
    of liberalism 188–9
prudence
    vs. morality 158–9, 163, 175–6
prudent choices
    and asymmetry of scope 218
    vs. imprudent choices 122–4, 125–8
prudential grounds of appraisal 154–6
prudential value and imaginary outcomes 181–4
public ecology
    and politics 208–9
    and responsibility 207
publicly intelligible goals 191
punishment
    vs. education 137
    nature of 147–9

Quong, Jonathan 130n

rational agency 191–2
    and situated rationality 207
rational processes 194
    levels 203–4
rationality, classical 194–5
    decoupling of 194–205
    domain generality of 194–5
    skepticism about 195
rationality, situated conceptions of 202–4
    in social environments 204–6
Rawls, John 2–5, 28–31, 39, 57–8, 136–42,
        146, 247, 250–6, 264, 276–8, 282–3
reactive attitudes 171, 175
    and narrow responsibility 176
real freedom approach 39–40
reason-responsiveness 15, 145, 190–1, 207–8
reasons, justice-based 59–61
reasons for helping others, non-egalitarian 64
redress, principle of 5
reference-dependence and choices 196
reflective equilibrium 172
relational goods vs. non-relational goods 116–17
resources, maximizing 38–9
respect-standing vs. luck egalitarianism 9
responsibility
    broad 176–9, 185

concepts of 11
and control of behaviour 145
for crimes 138
definitions of 11–14, 27, 121
vs. desert appraisal grounds 158–64
for health 270–5, 281
and imaginary outcomes 179–81
and justice 65–6
and liberalism 188–90
moral 12, 145–6
narrow 176
and partial compliance see partial compliance
and preferences in work 93–4
primary vs. secondary 190, 244
and public ecology 207
and rights 53
significance of 26
social vs. individual 276–9, 283–6
utilitarian interpretation of 82, 83–4, 89–90,
        96
weak asymmetry thesis 22, 217, 228–9
see also agent responsibility, collective
        responsibility, consequential responsibility,
        individual responsibility
responsibility bases 154–7, 162
    and non-acts 164–5
responsibility characteristics vs. circumstance
        characteristics 78–9, 83
responsibility-sensitive egalitarianism
        (RSE) 115–16
    criticisms of 168–71
    equality of opportunity for equal interests
        model of 128–31
    equality of opportunity for maximum
        advantage model of 124–8
    equality of opportunity model of 18–19,
        121–4, 126–7
    vs. social egalitarianism (SE) 118–20, 131–4
    and types of goods 117
    see also luck egalitarianism
responsibility-sensitive justice
    for brute bad luck 166–7
    and desert-sensitive justice 152, 162, 171–3
    for non-acts 165–6
responsibility-sensitive policies 21–3
responsible acts 153–7
retributive justice 14
    and criminals as faulty units 137
    vs. distributive justice 141–4, 149–50
    holism 147–9
reversibility of non-compliance 237
rights
    different notions of 52–3
    and luck 53
    and responsibilities 53
risk-taking
    and asymmetry thesis 220, 222–3

and individual responsibility for health 273–4, 275–6, 277–8, 281–3, 285–6
and life expectancy 258–9
and option luck 6, 65
Roemer, J. E. 79, 156

Sabin, Jim 271–2
sacrifice of self 102
scale, asymmetry of 217–18
Scandinavian social democracy and global justice 46
Scanlon, Thomas 154n, 157n, 211, 270, 272–3, 280
Scheffler, Samuel 4–5, 104, 131n, 132, 141–9, 281
Schmidt, H. 268
scope, asymmetries of 218
secondary responsibility 190, 244
Segall, Shlomi 23
Sen, Amartya 70, 209, 250n, 255n, 257n, 261–2
sex inequality in life expectancy 247, 250, 256–62
situated conceptions of rationality 202–4
and rational agency 207
in social environments 204–6
Smart, J. J. C. 156
Smilansky, Saul 167
smoking
jogger/smoker objection 247–51
regulation of 188
responsibility for health 277
social access to health vs. natural access to health 253–4, 258
social egalitarianism (SE) vs. responsibility-sensitive egalitarianism (RSE) 118–20, 131–4
social environments and situated conceptions of rationality 204–6
social equality 131–3
social hijacking 276
social interactionism and luck egalitarianism 47–9
social justice 57–8
vs. health equity 248–9
social responsibility for health 270–2
vs. individual responsibility 276–9, 283–6
social status 131–4
Sperber, D. 203, 205
Steiner, Hillel 122n, 128n
Stemplowska, Zofia 19, 221n
Sterelny, K. 205
stereotypes
exposure and influence on cognitive processes 199, 201
influence on 214
and unconscious rational processing 203–4
Strict Accounting View 277–8

substantive fairness 74–6
vs. procedural fairness 71–2
sufficiency in maximizing function 37
Sverdlik, Steven 14n
system of natural liberty 2–3

talent
see natural talent
talent and effort 80, 85, 87
'talent spoils' case 80
Tan, Kok-Chor 42n
tastes, voluntariness of 8–9
tax rates 41
teams, collective responsibility of 240–1
Temkin, Larry 17–18, 239n
theoretical reasoning 194
therapeutic jurisprudence 137
thick luck vs. thin luck 15–16
threshold for social equality 120
traditional liberalism 188–90
transferable circumstances 79–81, 88
transferable outcome case 85
transfers and personal effort 80, 87–8
Tsuchiya, A. and A. Williams 258

ultimatum games, behavioural anomalies in 197–8
Undeservingness Premise 169–70
unforeseen outcomes 178–9
utilitarian interpretation of responsibility 82, 83–4, 89–90, 96

Vallentyne, Peter 13, 83n
Value of Choice account 273–4
Van de gaer, D. 89–90
Vonnegut Jr., Kurt 73

wage rates
and the conditional-equality criterion 94–5, 96
and the egalitarian-equivalent criterion 91–3, 96
and the mean-of-mins and min-of-means criteria 95, 96
Wason, P. C. 202
weak asymmetry thesis of responsibility 22, 217, 228–9
weak-willed actions 191–2
welfare
and disability 36
fair distribution of 3–4, 70
maximizing 38
well-being, responsibility for 180–1
West Virginia Medicaid program 267–9, 284, 286
Williams, Andrew 134n
Wolff, Jonathan 9, 18, 22
Wootton, Barbara 137–8

Lightning Source UK Ltd.
Milton Keynes UK
UKHW021533090220
358411UK00017B/450